TRUMP MUST GO

BILL PRESS

TRUMP MUST GO

THE TOP 100 REASONS TO DUMP TRUMP (AND ONE TO KEEP HIM)

THOMAS DUNNE BOOKS
ST. MARTIN'S PRESS ≈ NEW YORK

THOMAS DUNNE BOOKS.
An imprint of St. Martin's Press.

www.thomasdunnebooks.com
www.stmartins.com

The Library of Congress Cataloging-in-Publication Data is available upon request.

ISBN 978-1-250-30647-0 (hardcover)
ISBN 978-1-250-30648-7 (ebook)

Our books may be purchased in bulk for promotional, educational, or business use. Please contact your local bookseller or the Macmillan Corporate and Premium Sales Department at 1-800-221-7945, extension 5442, or by email at MacmillanSpecialMarkets@macmillan.com.

First Edition: September 2018

10 9 8 7 6 5 4 3 2 1

To the Resistance, which is already making a difference—in making America America again

CONTENTS

I would give myself A+
       —Donald Trump

INTRODUCTION: ENOUGH IS ENOUGH

Enough is enough.

We can't take it any longer.

The country can't absorb any more.

Chaos and corruption have become our new normal.

Trump must go.

Somehow, we've managed to endure almost two years of Donald Trump's disastrous presidency. The fact that we've survived at all is no credit to him. It's a testimony to the stability, solidity, and strength of the American people that we can still maintain a steady course, despite having a total buffoon in the White House.

But this madness cannot continue. Trump has already done so much damage, at home and abroad, that it will take us decades to recover. Every day he's in office brings another tear in the fabric that makes up the American republic. We cannot risk another two years. We cannot risk another year. We cannot risk another six months.

His poll numbers reflect that. Trump started out with a low approval rating of 45 percent, and it hasn't fluctuated much since. He ended 2017 with only 35 percent of Americans approving his performance in office, the lowest level recorded since the dawn of modern polling. At the end of their first year in office, George W. Bush enjoyed an 86 percent approval rating; John F. Kennedy, 77 percent; Dwight Eisenhower, 69 percent. Not only did his overall approval ratings scrape bottom, but according to a September 2017 ABC News / *Washington Post* poll, 66 percent of Americans say Donald Trump is doing more to divide the country than unite it.[1]

The majority of Americans agree: Trump must go. And he must go now.

How that happens is yet to be determined. There are several ways to get him out of office. Each of them is plausible and, to some degree, already under way.

For one, he might well be found guilty of criminal conduct by special counsel Robert Mueller. The special counsel's investigation has been under way for almost two years and has clearly penetrated all the way to the Oval Office, despite the relentless efforts by Donald Trump and congressional Republicans to undermine and discredit Mueller, the FBI, and the Justice Department.

Alternatively, he could, and should, be impeached. By the end of 2017, seven Democratic members of Congress—Al Green (TX), Brad Sherman (CA), Steve Cohen (TN), Luis Gutiérrez (IL), Marcia Fudge (OH), John Yarmuth (KY), and Adriano Espaillat (NY)—had independently introduced articles of impeachment in the House of Representatives, which ended up being supported by roughly sixty House Democrats. And by the end of May 2018, California billionaire Democratic activist Tom Steyer had collected over 5.4 million signatures on an online petition to impeach the president.[2]

Impeachment, in fact, may be easier than it appears. Because, while Article I, Section 3 of the Constitution says that "the President, Vice President and all civil Officers of the United States shall be removed from Office on Impeachment for, and Conviction of, Treason, Bribery, or other high Crimes and Misdemeanors," it never actually lays out what constitutes an "impeachable offense." As we learned from the Monica Lewinsky imbroglio in 1998, that's up to Congress to decide.

In other words, to be impeached, Donald Trump doesn't have to be accused by special counsel Robert Mueller of having actually committed a crime. He could be impeached for whatever Congress decides is worth impeaching him for—from actual crimes to dereliction of duty to offensive words and behavior. The definition of *impeachable offense* is wide open. It's ultimately up to Congress to decide what's an impeachable offense and what's not, which is not good news for Donald Trump, especially as his allies abandon the sinking ship.

If history is any judge, Congress would certainly consider obstruction of justice an impeachable offense. That was, in fact, the first article of impeachment directed against President Richard Nixon—that he had "prevented, obstructed, and impeded the administration of justice"—and one of two articles set forth by the House of Representatives against President Bill Clinton, using that identical phrase. And as we'll discuss later on, Trump has already admitted to obstruction of justice several times over.

Before resigning, Nixon faced the near certainty of impeachment for what Congress deemed having "made false or misleading public statements for the purpose of deceiving the people of the United States." It would be hard to find any rational American who could not find Donald Trump guilty of the same offense. Indeed, he does it daily.

Evidence of how wide open the definition of *impeachable offense* really is came from none other than former special counsel Ken Starr, a hero to most Republicans for his aggressive leadership of the investigation that resulted in the impeachment of President Bill Clinton two decades ago. Appearing on ABC's *This Week* on January 28, 2018, Starr noted the gravity of reports that Trump had actually ordered White House counsel Don McGahn to fire special counsel Robert Mueller, even though he'd denied doing so on several occasions. "You're now talking about something called lying to the American people," warned Starr, "and I think that is something that Bob Mueller should look at."[3]

If not indicted or impeached, Trump could instead be, and he well deserves the dubious honor, the first president removed from office by procedures laid out in the Twenty-Fifth Amendment. That amendment, added to the Constitution in 1967 to clear up the presidential succession after the Kennedy assassination, declares that the president can be removed and replaced with the vice president if the veep and a majority of the cabinet believe the president is "unable to discharge the power and duties of his office."[4]

On August 15, 2017, after Trump made his outrageous comments defending white supremacists who marched in Charlottesville, Virginia, and killed thirty-two-year-old Heather Heyer, California congresswoman Jackie Speier tweeted: "POTUS is showing signs of erratic behavior and mental instability that place the country in grave danger. Time to invoke the 25th Amendment."[5]

Or Trump could be forced or shamed into resigning, especially if his top aides or family members are convicted of crimes as a result of the FBI investigation. Offering to resign in exchange for a lighter prison sentence for sons Donald Jr. and Eric, daughter Ivanka, or son-in-law, Jared Kushner, could strike Trump as a fair deal, especially if he himself is miserable in the job. And some of the above are clearly targets of Mueller's investigation.

Or Trump could be removed from office by any combination of the above.

If how he goes is not yet resolved, *why* Trump must go is woefully clear. There are thousands of reasons for ending the Trump presidency as soon as legally possible, of which only the top one hundred are documented here.

Donald Trump is no student of American history. He doesn't know much of anything other than that he is the greatest businessman, greatest politician, greatest candidate, and greatest president this country has ever known. Too bad. Because with even the slimmest knowledge of history, Trump might realize that the American people do not take kindly to leaders who abuse their power as brazenly and willfully as he has.

In fact, in many ways, we now face the same challenge our Founding Fathers and Mothers faced over 240 years ago: a despotic leader who knew nothing of world affairs, ignored the advice of his closest advisors, created political instability, despised the people, often shocked the world with his bizarre personal behavior, and in his early seventies was widely believed to be clinically insane.

The only difference is that colonial leaders then were dealing with a mad king; we are dealing with a mad president. Nonetheless, our responsibility is the same: to rise up, cast off the yoke, and free ourselves from a corrupt and tyrannical autocrat, as expressed in Thomas Jefferson's powerful preamble to the Declaration of Independence:

We hold these truths to be self-evident, that all men are created equal, that they are endowed by their Creator with certain unalienable Rights, that among these are Life, Liberty and the pursuit of Happiness. That to secure these rights, Governments are instituted among Men, deriving their just powers from the consent of the governed, That whenever any Form of Government becomes destructive of these ends, it is the Right of the People to alter or to abolish it, and to institute new Government, laying its foundation on such principles and organizing its powers in such form, as to them shall seem most likely to effect their Safety and Happiness.[6]

Yes, but how do we do that? The first step is by doing exactly what Jefferson laid out in 1776: Tell the American people the truth. As the Declaration of Independence continues:

The history of the present [and this president!] is a history of repeated injuries and usurpations, all having in direct object the establishment of an absolute Tyranny over these States. To prove this, let Facts be submitted to a candid world.[7]

And such is the purpose of this book. As Jefferson dictated, so we comply; before we move forward to restore our nation, let's lay out the reasons for dumping Donald Trump.

These reasons cover many aspects of the Trump presidency, starting with his own bizarre personal behavior (anything but presidential) and moving on to disastrous acts committed as president, both at home and abroad: brazenly defying the law, fanning the flames of racism, declaring war on the environment, playing footsie with Russia, turning the government over to special interests, alienating our allies, and sowing discord, not unity.

Taken together, the one hundred reasons outlined in this book paint the picture of a man unequipped for the job of president, who should never have been elected in the first place, who's disgraced the presidency ever since, who's wreaked havoc at home and abroad, and who must be removed from the office of president as our laws allow before he does any more lasting damage.

Let facts be submitted to a candid world.

Enough is enough.

Trump must go.

Now.

1

TRUMP'S UNFIT FOR THE JOB

In judging any president, it's his policies that count the most. And that's the way it should be. When all is said and done, what has the president done to make America an even greater and stronger country and to improve the everyday lives of average Americans? What has he done to address new problems, take advantage of new opportunities, and lead the nation in responding to unforeseen crises?

That's the measure by which we weigh the presidencies of every national leader from George Washington to Barack Obama. But there's something different about Donald Trump, something you must deal with first before you get to his policies and programs, good or bad.

Before you consider Donald Trump the president, you have to deal with Donald Trump the person. Because his bizarre personality "trumps" all. We have never had a more loathsome, disreputable, obnoxious person in the Oval Office, nor anyone so manifestly unfit for the job of president.

Conservative voices agree.

After a phone conversation about immigration, media mogul Rupert Murdoch, a friend of Trump's, allegedly exclaimed, "What a fucking idiot."[1]

Eliot Cohen, counselor to Secretary of State Condoleezza Rice, summed up Trump's presidency: "This fundamentally boils down to character, and his character is rotten. He's a narcissist who happens to have taken control of the Republican party."[2]

In response to a presidential tweet attacking him, Republican senator Bob Corker famously observed, "It's a shame the White House has become an adult day care center. Someone obviously missed their shift this morning."[3]

National security experts agree.

In August 2016, fifty national security and foreign policy experts who had served in Republican administrations from Richard Nixon to George W. Bush issued a public letter opposing the candidacy of Donald Trump. "We know the personal qualities required of a President of the United States," they wrote. "Mr. Trump lacks the character, values, and experience to be President. Indeed, we are convinced that he would be a very dangerous President and would put at risk our country's national security and well-being . . . None of us will vote for Donald Trump."[4]

Even members of his cabinet agree.

Following a Pentagon meeting on nuclear weapons, where Trump proposed increasing our nuclear arsenal tenfold, then secretary of state Rex Tillerson called him "a fucking moron."[5]

According to BuzzFeed, at a private dinner party in July 2017, national security advisor H. R. McMaster reportedly unloaded about Trump, referring to him as an "idiot," a "dope," and a man with the intelligence of a "kindergartner."[6]

And the American people agree.

According to a Quinnipiac University poll conducted in January 2018, at the end of his first year in office, Americans said 69–28 percent that Donald Trump was not levelheaded, and a stunning 57–40 percent agreed he was not fit to serve as president.[7]

In that same poll, 69 percent of voters described his first year in office as a "disaster," followed by 62 percent who say "chaotic." Asked to grade his performance in office, 39 percent gave Trump an F, while 17 percent gave him a D.[8]

"It is on a supposition that our American governors shall be honest, that all the good qualities of this Government are founded," Patrick Henry, of "Give Me Liberty or Give Me Death!" fame, warned us in 1788 during the debates over the Constitution. "But its defective, and imperfect construction, puts it in their power to perpetrate the worst of mischiefs, should they be bad men."[9]

My fellow Americans, we have ourselves a bad man.

There are many aspects of Donald Trump's personality that are offensive, starting with what's arguably his core defect: He is psychologically incapable of telling the truth.

1. HE'S A PATHOLOGICAL LIAR

If there's one trait that defines Donald Trump more than any other, it's that he's an inveterate, pathological liar. He lies about what he's said. He lies about what he's done. He lied about the weather at his inauguration. He probably lies about what he's had for breakfast.

Usually, these are not little lies or slight exaggerations that have an element of truth in them and could be taken either way. No, these are big, bold lies that are often manifestly ridiculous and easily disprovable.

To take one of innumerable examples: After his first State of the Union speech on January 30, 2018, Trump issued several tweets claiming that he'd pulled in the biggest TV audience ever to watch a presidential State of the Union, including this one on Thursday morning, February 1:

Thank you for all of the nice compliments and reviews on the State of the Union speech. 45.6 million people watched, the highest number in history.[10]

Except it wasn't. According to Nielsen, which has been tracking State of the Union viewers, there have been four TV audiences since 1994 bigger than Trump's. The largest were actually for George W. Bush: 51.8 million in 2002, and a whopping 62 million in 2003, after the start of the wars in Afghanistan and Iraq. Barack Obama also outdrew Trump, scoring 48 million viewers in 2010, his first State of the Union.[11]

Ironically, Donald Trump's State of the Union audience was also beaten by—Donald Trump! His first address to a joint session of Congress, on February 28, 2017, was watched by 47.7 million. But that's Trump for you. He lies instinctively, without purpose or thought. Whatever demonstrable falsehood bubbles up to the surface of his brain is always, for him, the right thing to say at that moment. And if he said it, then it must be true.[12]

Of course, it's no surprise that Trump ended his first year with a big lie about the size of his TV audience. He began his first year with a big lie about the size of his inaugural crowd—"the audience was the biggest ever." He soon followed by claiming:

- That rain clouds disappeared and the sun broke out once he began his inaugural address
- That he had the largest electoral college win since Ronald Reagan
- That (as he claimed after the election) he also won the popular vote; because
- Millions of people voted for Hillary Clinton illegally.[13]

Lies, lies, lies.

He can't help himself. Like the scorpion crossing the river, it is his nature. At a March 2018 fund-raiser, in what alcoholics sometimes refer to as a moment of clarity, Trump confessed he was basically bullshitting his way through a recent meeting with Canadian prime minister Justin Trudeau. When Trudeau said the United States has a trade surplus with Canada, Trump insisted the opposite. "I didn't even know," he later admitted. "I had no idea. I just said, 'You're wrong.'" As if getting away with an outright presidential lie were a sign of leadership. Another surprising moment of honesty occurred in June 2018, just after Trump's summit with North Korea. When asked what would happen if the deal had gone wrong in six months, Trump confessed: "I don't know that I'll ever admit that, but I'll find some kind of an excuse."[14]

Charting new grounds for White House reporting, both *The New York Times* and *The Washington Post* kept a running total of Trump's lies. In fact, for the first time, both papers shunned the normal euphemisms like *exaggerations*, *embellishments*, or *misstatements*, and called Donald Trump's untruths exactly what they were: knowingly, deliberately, not telling the truth.

As BuzzFeed reminded its readers: "A lie isn't just a false statement. It's a false statement whose speaker knows it's false."[15]

Even on the front page, *The Times* and *The Post* called the president's statements lies. They accused Donald Trump of lying to the American people over and over again.[16]

According to *The Post*'s official Trump Fact Checker, Trump told a total of 2,140 lies in his first 365 days in office, or an average of 5.8 lies a day—several of them repeated many times. In one two-week period in June 2018, he told 71 outright lies. The week after that, he went for 103. And remember, those are just the lies we know about. God knows how many lies a day he privately tells to his staff, his friends, or his wife.[17]

His supporters occasionally try to defend him by arguing that all presidents lie, that Trump's no different. Which is simply not true. Sure, all presidents, for whatever reason, may occasionally not tell the truth or not tell the whole truth. The difference is, they usually know when they're fudging. Donald Trump doesn't know and doesn't care. Facts simply don't matter to him. He lives in his own fact-free universe. He doesn't bother to find out what the truth is. He believes that the truth is whatever he says it is. Yes, he actually believes that shit.

Not only that. When they realized, or were caught not telling the truth, other presidents stopped doing it. Obama didn't continue claiming you could keep your existing health insurance under Obamacare. George W. Bush softened his claims about Saddam Hussein's nuclear arsenal. Not Donald Trump. He has not once backed down from a lie or apologized. He just doubles down and attacks anybody who challenges his "truthiness."[18]

It would be foolhardy here to list all the known Donald Trump lies. After he's gone, maybe somebody will publish *The Collected Lies of Donald Trump* in twelve volumes! But to make the point, here are some of his greatest hits: twelve whoppers great and small, about every subject imaginable, that stand out from 2017 and 2018.

1. On *Time* magazine, he still claims, "I have been on their cover fourteen or fifteen times. I think we have the all-time record in the history of *Time* magazine."

    Fact: Trump was on the cover eleven times. Richard Nixon—fifty-five times.[19]

2. On Florida 2016, "The Cuban Americans, I got 84 percent of that vote."

    Fact: He actually received 54 percent of the Cuban American vote.[20]

3. On health care, some sixty times he claimed that Obamacare is "dying" or "essentially dead."

    Fact: Despite all of Trump's attempts to gut it, Obamacare is still very much alive for now, covering over twenty-two million people.[21]

4. On tax cuts, at least forty times, he bragged about delivering the biggest tax cut in history, and he fifty times claimed the United States pays the highest corporate taxes or is one of the highest-taxed nations.

    Fact: According to Trump's own Treasury Department, the GOP tax cut of 2017 is only the eighth largest, and corporations, in fact, after deductions and benefits, pay a far lower rate than many other countries.[22]

5. More on tax cuts: "No, I don't benefit. I don't benefit. In fact, very, very strongly, as you see, I think there's very little benefit for people of wealth."

    Fact: Since he won't release his tax returns, we don't know how much Donald Trump actually benefits. But according to Vox, 82.8 percent of the Trump tax cuts go to the top 1 percent.[23]

6. On 2016 results, "We got 306 because people came out and voted like they've never seen before, so that's the way it goes. I guess it was the biggest electoral college win since Ronald Reagan."

    Fact: As noted above, George H. W. Bush, Bill Clinton, and Barack Obama all won bigger margins in the electoral college.[24]

7. On voter fraud, Trump claimed "thousands" of people were "brought in on buses" from Massachusetts to vote in the New Hampshire Republican primary.

    Fact: The New Hampshire secretary of state, the Massachusetts attorney general, and the U.S. Attorney's office from Boston found zero evidence to support Trump's claim. He keeps repeating it anyway.[25]

8. On Obama: "Terrible! Just found out that Obama had my 'wires tapped' in Trump Tower just before the victory. Nothing found. This is McCarthyism!"

    Fact: Even though he repeated this charge several times in March 2017, he has produced zero evidence of a wiretap. The Justice Department told Congress that no wiretap on Trump Tower had been sought or authorized.[26]

9. On gun safety: "When you look at the city with the strongest gun laws in our nation, it's Chicago."

    Fact: Several other cities, notably New York and Los Angeles, have tougher gun laws. At one time, so did Washington, D.C.[27]

10. On crime: Shortly after taking office, Trump told a group of sheriffs that the murder rate in the United States is the highest it's been in "forty-five to forty-seven years."

    Fact: Just the opposite. The murder rate today is roughly half of what it was twenty years ago. According to FBI records, in 1980, the murder rate was 10.2 per 100,000 people—compared to 5.3 per 100,000 in 2016.[28]

11. On the Muslim ban: Donald Trump blamed the huge crowds of protestors that showed up at airports the day after his Muslim ban on computer problems by Delta Airlines. "Only 109 people out of 325,000 were detained and held for questioning. Big problems at airports were caused by Delta computer outage."

    Fact: At least 746 people were detained. And Delta's computer crash happened two days later.[29]

12. On the Mueller investigation: As part of his never-ending efforts to discredit special counsel Robert Mueller, Trump often claims, "The story that there was collusion between the Russians and Trump campaign was fabricated by Dems as an excuse for losing the election."

    Fact: The FBI investigation began months before the election, when Trump aide George Papadopoulos was discovered bragging about his secret meetings with Russians.[30]

We're just getting started. As we will see, there are many more reasons why Trump must go. But this may be the most important of all. Because once you realize that Donald Trump lies with every breath he takes, and once you know you can't believe a word the president of the United States or anybody else at the White House says, then you've already hit a brick wall.

For the basic building block of our political system, and the key to getting anything done, is trust. Nobody can trust Donald Trump, the Liar in Chief.

2. HE'S WOEFULLY IGNORANT

Donald Trump is the smartest man ever to occupy the Oval Office. Just ask him. He'll tell you he's not just smart. He's a genius.

When Michael Wolff, in his book *Fire and Fury*, quoted anonymous White House sources questioning Trump's mental acuity (and sanity), Trump lashed back. On Twitter, of course.

"Actually, throughout my life, my two greatest assets have been mental stability and being, like, really smart," he asserted.[31]

Rule #1: When somebody feels compelled to tell you they are mentally stable and really smart, that's a pretty good sign they're neither.

Trump continued making his case. "I went from VERY successful businessman, to top T.V. Star to President of the United States (on my first try). I think that would qualify as not smart, but genius . . . and a very stable genius at that!"[32]

Naturally, to qualify as a genius, Donald Trump must have a very high IQ—which he will gladly tell you, and often has, is the case. In countless tweets, he includes some version of "my I.Q. is one of the highest." And early in his administration, when Secretary of State Rex Tillerson reportedly called him a "moron," Trump challenged him to a duel. "I think it's fake news, but if he did that, I guess we'll have to compare IQ tests. And I can tell you who is going to win."[33]

Genius? Remarkably high IQ? That's not how White House aides, off the record, describe him.

Frustrated with trying to brief Trump on basic facts about the economy, chief economic advisor Gary Cohn described him as "dumb as shit." After threatening to resign over Trump's racist comments on the Charlottesville protests, Cohn finally threw in the towel and resigned his post in March 2018 over a disagreement on tariffs.[34]

In his interviews for *Fire and Fury,* author Michael Wolff heard several top Trump staffers identify a central difficulty in dealing with their boss: "He didn't read. He didn't really even skim. Some believed that for all practical purposes he was no more than semi-literate."[35]

Indeed, because Donald Trump doesn't read, doesn't listen, and doesn't think, how to brief him on national security issues became one of the first challenges of the Trump White House, especially after he told Fox News during the transition he was going to cancel the presidential daily brief (PDB) used by seven previous presidents because he didn't need it. "I'm like a smart person," he told Chris Wallace.[36]

White House aides soon learned it was impossible to schedule the PDB first thing in the morning, as with George W. Bush and Barack Obama, because Trump didn't like to roll into the office until around 11:00 a.m. When they discovered he wouldn't read an entire intelligence file, they boiled the PDB down to just three issues, one page each, preferably with charts. When he wouldn't even read that, they resorted to a short video or a quick, oral brief, which Trump often skips.[37]

Upon leaving office, President Obama warned it would be a mistake to ignore daily updates from intelligence officials. "If you're not getting their perspective—their detailed perspective—then you are flying blind." On national security, and almost everything else, Donald Trump is flying blind.[38]

You can't say Donald Trump is completely stupid. Even born with Daddy's money, he wouldn't be where he is, in business or politics, were he stupid. But there's no doubt that he's woefully ignorant of policies and issues he's forced to deal with as president.

Trump has displayed this ignorance on a wide range of matters: hailing Frederick Douglass as one of today's great civil rights leaders, "somebody who has done an amazing job and is being recognized more and more, I notice"; professing no idea what the "nuclear triad" is; praising the "invisible" F-35 fighter jet; insisting "nobody knew that health care could be so complicated." But it's most apparent when it comes to the major issues before the White House and Congress: health care, tax cuts, infrastructure, or immigration.[39]

Just listen to Donald Trump. It's obvious he has no clear understanding of these or any other issues. That was most painfully obvious when Trump invited TV cameras to record fifty-five minutes of a meeting with congressional leaders on immigration on January 9, 2018. He bounced back and forth like a Ping-Pong ball, changing his mind on every issue after every speaker. Republicans in the room freaked out when Trump appeared to agree with Democratic senator Dianne Feinstein on how to proceed on immigration, and then had to persuade him back to their side of the issue. By the end, a clearly clueless Trump shrugged. "I think my positions are going to be what the people in this room come up with."[40]

Which is how White House aides have learned to operate: On any issue, wait until everybody else has spoken to the president and then weigh in, since the "very stable genius" will likely parrot the last thing he heard. They know that Trump has no mind of his own. More often than not, he'll agree with the last person he spoke to on any subject.

Many members of Congress, meanwhile, have learned to take whatever the president says with a grain of salt. In February 2018, in the middle of serious negotiations on a two-year budget deal, Trump demanded that Congress shut the government down if the deal did not include money to build his wall. Mitch McConnell and Chuck Schumer simply ignored him. They didn't shut down the government. They passed a two-year budget bill. With zero funding for the wall. And Trump signed it.[41]

3. HE'S AN OVERGROWN TODDLER

When General John Kelly was brought in to replace Reince Priebus as chief of staff, he was not only praised as the man who would bring discipline and order to a White House out of control. Among the White House press corps, he soon became known as the "Adult in the Room."[42]

The implication was clear. If Kelly was the adult in the room, Donald Trump was the Toddler in Chief. And, in fact, he so acted like one that White House staffers soon felt that their primary function was to serve as high-paid babysitters.

In April 2017, Tufts University professor and *Washington Post* contributor Daniel Drezner, citing a story about 45's penchant for watching TV all day, tweeted, "I'll believe that Trump is growing into the presidency when his staff stops talking about him like a toddler." Soon thereafter, he began collecting all the instances when "senior aides" described the leader of the free world with the same phrasing one might use for a bratty child in a restaurant. By the end of the year, he had found, and shared, more than two hundred examples.[43]

To author Michael Wolff, many of the White House aides he spoke to painted Trump as a surly, spoiled brat who abuses his staff, screams at the TV, and demands constant positive reinforcement. "Here was a man singularly focused on his own needs for instant gratification," Wolff writes, "be that a hamburger, a segment on *Fox & Friends,* or an Oval Office photo op. 'I want a win. I want a win. Where's my win?' he would regularly declaim. He was, in words used by almost every member of the senior staff on repeated occasions, 'like a child.'"[44]

Like a child, Trump is also known for his short attention span. After meeting the president in the Oval Office, NATO secretary general Jens Stoltenberg reportedly observed, "The president of the United States has a 12-second attention span." Preparing for Trump's first visit to Europe, NATO advised foreign leaders to limit their prepared remarks to two to four minutes, leading one EU official to complain, "It's like they're preparing to deal with a child—someone with a short attention span and mood who has no knowledge of NATO, no interest in in-depth policy issues, nothing."[45]

Also like a child, Trump is never happier than when planted in front of a TV set. The only difference is that while they're watching cartoons, he's watching the cartoonish Fox News, where he can bask in the glow of positive coverage, revel in his own version of reality, and glean the material for an endless string of boastful, adolescent, meaningless, and embarrassing tweets. More on this coming up.

Sadly, there's only so much of Trump's cable TV bingeing Kelly and staff can prevent. No matter how much they fill up his day with phony meetings and photo ops to keep him away from the TV set in the small room just off the Oval Office, they have no control over his so-called executive time—mornings and evenings in the residence—where, by his own admission, he spends as many as four hours a day, and sometimes eight hours (!), watching TV—and fuming, and tweeting.[46]

Like all good babysitters everywhere, White House staffers also reward their toddler with a special treat whenever he behaves. For Trump, that means a steady supply of Diet Coke at the press of a specially installed button, extra ketchup for his well-done steak, both at home and instead of foreign food while traveling overseas, and two scoops of vanilla ice cream, where his guests only get one. It pays to be the Toddler in Chief.[47]

4. HE'S A RACIST

Invariably, whenever anyone on TV or Twitter calls Donald Trump a racist, some defender of civility will declare that *racist* is a loaded term that should not be thrown around carelessly. Rather, it should only be used on those rare occasions when we encounter someone who clearly believes that people of color are not worth as much as white people—and speaks and acts accordingly.

Well, by that test, there's no doubt about it: Donald Trump is a dyed-in-the-wool racist and has been from day one. He invariably talks about and treats people differently based on their race. Always has and still does.

Let's look at the ledger. Trump first came to public notice in the 1970s when he and his father, Fred—who, by the way, was arrested at a KKK rally in 1927—were sued by the U.S. Justice Department for refusing to rent apartments to African Americans.[48]

He generated more notoriety in 1989 by spending $85,000 on full-page ads in New York newspapers demanding the death penalty for five black and Latino teenagers accused of raping a white woman in Central Park. "Send a message loud and clear to those who would murder our citizens and terrorize New York," he screamed. "BRING BACK THE DEATH PENALTY!"[49]

Thank God they didn't. All five were eventually exonerated by DNA evidence and, after a serial rapist already in prison (whose DNA matched the crime scene) confessed, their sentences were vacated in 2002—after all five had served the time. Nonetheless, in October 2016, Trump still insisted despite all this that they were guilty—prompting Senator John McCain to rebuke the "outrageous statements about the innocent men in the Central Park Five case."[50]

Along the way, Trump has uttered a number of outright racist things.

One of his Atlantic City hotel executives quoted his complaining about an African American accountant: "Black guys counting my money! I hate it . . . I think that the guy is lazy. And it's probably not his fault, because laziness is a trait in blacks." And, of course, every time Trump repeats his claim that he has "better" genes, he is inferring that everybody else, especially people of color, had "bad" genes.[51]

In 1989, appearing on NBC, he said, "I think sometimes a black may think they don't have an advantage or this and that. I've said on one occasion, even about myself, if I were starting off today, I would love to be a well-educated black, because I really believe they do have an actual advantage."[52]

Flash forward to the Obama era. As we'll discuss in more detail later on, Donald Trump first made his mark on national politics by leading the birther movement for five years, denying the legitimacy of America's first African American president because, he charged, with absolutely zero evidence, that Barack Obama was born in Kenya, not the United States.[53]

Even though he insists he is "the least racist person" you'll ever meet, Trump's presidential campaign and first couple of years in office were rocked by one racist statement after another, many of which we'll also talk about further on.[54]

- In fact, Trump explicitly ran as a racist from the start. In June 2015, he kicked off his 2016 campaign by calling Mexican immigrants criminals and rapists. "They're bringing drugs. They're bringing crime. They're rapists. And some, I assume, are good people."[55]

- In June 2016, he denounced federal judge Gonzalo Curiel, hearing a case against Trump University, because he was of Mexican heritage. Even Speaker Paul Ryan said this was "sort of like the textbook definition of a racist comment."[56]

- In December 2015, Trump called for "a total and complete shutdown of Muslims entering the United States." And, sure enough, his first major act as president was to order a ban against all

Muslims entering this country—a ban that was blocked multiple times by judges because of its clearly racist intent.[57]

- During the summer of 2017, he defended white supremacists marching—just like his father, Fred, had done ninety years before—in Charlottesville, Virginia. Even after the murder of thirty-two-year-old Heather Heyer by a white supremacist in a car, Trump continued to insist there were "very fine people" marching on both sides. (After this fiasco, one of his aides groaned, "Cleanup on aisle Trump.") He also refused to repudiate KKK leader David Duke's praise of his remarks.[58]

- He endorsed Alabama Senate candidate Roy Moore, who praised the slavery era and said a Muslim should not be seated in Congress because of his religion.[59]

- He also pardoned Sheriff Joe Arpaio, who ran a self-proclaimed "concentration camp" where inmates died, and he was sued by the Justice Department for the worst case of racial profiling in U.S. history. Trump called him an "eighty-five-year-old American patriot who kept Arizona safe."[60]

- He ended temporary protected status (TPS) for hundreds of thousands of immigrants from Sudan, El Salvador, Haiti, Nicaragua, Nepal, and Honduras, making them subject to immediate deportation.[61]

- In January 2018, he told members of Congress that instead of more immigrants from "shithole" countries like Haiti, El Salvador, Nicaragua, and certain African countries, we needed more white immigrants from Norway. "Why are we having all of these people from shithole countries come here?" he declared. "Why do we need more Haitians? Take them out."[62]

- In February 2018, *USA Today* reported that, of Donald Trump's first eighty-seven judicial nominees, 92 percent were white: only one was African American and one was Latino. (Five were Asian American.)[63]

- The last president to appoint so many white judges was Ronald Reagan. And even back then, Jefferson Beauregard Sessions of Alabama was considered too racist to be a federal judge. Trump appointed Sessions, more recently an Alabama senator, to be attorney general of the United States.[64]

- He named only one African American, HUD secretary Ben Carson, to his cabinet—presumably, wags surmised, because the department has *Urban* in its title. Trump's cabinet is whiter and more male than any presidential cabinet since Ronald Reagan's.[65]

- He named only one African American, former *Apprentice* star Omarosa Manigault, to his senior staff. Later fired, Omarosa said she would never vote for Trump again, "not in a million years." "It's not going to be okay, it's not," she said of Trump's White House. "It's so bad." "I feel like I just got freed off of a plantation," she said in a later interview. "I haven't even told people some of the horrors I experienced."[66]

- In July 2018, he rolled back the clock on affirmative action. On his orders, the Justice and Education Departments abandoned seven Obama administration policies that provided guidance to universities on how they could voluntarily use race in the interest of promoting diversity on campus. In the age of Trump, diversity is no longer a goal to be achieved, even voluntarily.[67]

No wonder some people believe Trump's slogan "Make America Great Again" really stands for "Make America White Again." In fact, on Independence Day 2018, Quinnipiac University released a poll showing that 49 percent of all American voters believe Donald Trump is a racist. And 44 percent believe his immigration policies are driven, not by national security concerns, as he pretends, but by "racist beliefs."[68]

Add it all up. There's no doubt that Donald Trump has a serious problem with people of color. He doesn't like them, he doesn't trust them, he doesn't respect them. He's a racist.

5. HE'S SEXIST

African Americans, Muslims, and Latinos aren't the only people Donald Trump has no respect for. To their numbers, you can add all women, regardless of race.

During his first year as president, that lack of regard for women was perhaps no more apparent than in his response in February 2018 to the resignation of White House staff secretary Rob Porter after details of domestic violence against Porter's two ex-wives, including the photo of one of them with a black eye, were published by *The Daily Mail*.[69]

Even after Porter was gone, Trump continued to defend him, pointing out that Porter, like Trump, had denied the charges. (In Trump's world, if you deny it happened, it never happened.) "We wish him well," he said before a group of stunned reporters. "He worked very hard."[70]

> We found out about it recently, and I was surprised by it, but we certainly wish him well, and it's a tough time for him. He did a very good job when he was in the White House, and we hope he has a wonderful career, and he will have a great career ahead of him. But it was very sad when we heard about it, and certainly he's also very sad now. He also, as you probably know, says he's innocent, and I think you have to remember that. He said very strongly yesterday that he's innocent, so you have to talk to him about that, but we absolutely wish him well. He did a very good job when he was at the White House.[71]

The next day, in a tweet that sums up his entire approach to women, Trump lamented the fate of men charged with sexual assault or domestic violence and implied that many female victims who had come forward were lying.

"Peoples' lives are being shattered and destroyed by a mere allegation," he tweeted. "Some are true and some are false. Some are old and some are new. There is no recovery for someone falsely accused—life and career are gone. Is there no such thing any longer as Due Process?"[72]

In any event, CNN's Jake Tapper pointed out the obvious: "In point of fact, two ex-wives talking on the record to journalists and to the FBI and one ex-girlfriend on background, with a photo of a black eye and a police report is not a 'mere allegation.'"[73]

But for Trump, this was hardly anything new. Like his attitude toward racial minorities, his lack of respect for women was on full public display long before he got close to the White House.

As a brash, publicity-hungry New York businessman, Trump became a frequent guest on Howard Stern's radio show—perhaps because he was the only one who could match, or even surpass, Stern in insulting women. Unfortunately for Trump, all the tapes are out there.

He gleefully calls women fat pigs, dogs, slobs, and disgusting animals. He bragged about probably being able to get Princess Diana into bed. He claims women throw themselves at him. "They'll walk up, and they'll flip their top, and they'll flip their panties." After calling his daughter "voluptuous," he followed up with an incest joke: "If Ivanka weren't my daughter, perhaps I'd be dating her."[74]

As owner of the Miss Teen USA, Miss USA, and Miss Universe pageants, he became known for requiring contestants to parade in front of him and even walking unannounced into dressing rooms full of naked young women. After Alicia Machado won the Miss Universe contest in 1996, Trump called her "Miss Piggy." Meanwhile, on the set of *The Apprentice*, Trump would ask the male contestants which of the women they wanted to fuck, and he offered his own unsolicited commentary on the subject.[75]

As presidential candidate, Trump proved to be the same male sexist pig—starting in the very first GOP debate when then Fox News anchor Megyn Kelly challenged him about his misogynistic and sexist comments. After the debate, Trump called her a "bimbo," and later suggested she asked the question because she was menstruating. "You could see there was blood coming out of her eyes. Blood coming out of her wherever."[76]

He was equally cruel to fellow Republican candidate Carly Fiorina, alleging her looks disqualified her from being president. As *Rolling Stone* reported, Trump crowed to his campaign aides, "Look at that face. Would anyone vote for that?" Then, as always, he doubled down. "Can you imagine that, the face of our next president? I mean, she's a woman, and I'm not supposed to say bad things, but really, folks, come on. Are we serious?"[77]

But Trump saved some of his cruelest and most sexist remarks for his Democratic opponent. He not only accused Hillary Clinton of being an "unbelievably nasty, mean enabler" of her husband's affairs, he suggested it was all her fault. "If Hillary can't satisfy her husband, what makes her think she can satisfy America?" In their first debate, he interrupted Hillary twenty-five times in the first twenty-six minutes and asserted she did not have the stamina for the job. And in their last debate, he stalked her around the stage like a big male bully.[78]

Then came the lowest of many low points of his campaign, so low it's getting its own number—it's still hard to believe this didn't knock him out of the race—the release of the *Access Hollywood* tape. More about that coming up.

Was Trump chagrined by the release of the tape? (At the time, he said, "I pledge to be a better man tomorrow and will never, ever let you down.") Did he change his ways toward women once in the White House? Of course not.[79]

He continued to call Senator Elizabeth Warren "Pocahontas." He smeared MSNBC's Mika Brzezinski as showing up to visit him at Mar-a-Lago "bleeding badly from a face-lift." He embarrassed us all yet again when he went to Paris in July 2017. While saying good-bye to President Emmanuel Macron, Trump turned to his wife, Brigitte Trogneux, gestured at her body, and told her, "You know, you're in such good shape. Beautiful." To Trump, the First Lady of France was nothing more than another sex toy.[80]

And when, in December 2017, Senator Kirsten Gillibrand of New York suggested that the president not get a free pass on allegations of sexual harassment, Trump crudely accused her of selling her body for campaign contributions. On Twitter, he lashed out at "Lightweight Senator Kirsten Gillibrand, a total flunky for Charles E. Schumer and someone who would come to my office 'begging' for campaign contributions not so long ago (and would do anything for them.)"[81]

We could go on and on. Our forty-fifth president is an unabashed, inveterate sexist. And, as he himself admitted on a tape released a month before the 2016 election, worse.

6. HE'S A SEXUAL PREDATOR

In the fall of 2017, a long-overdue reckoning began. Spurred initially by a slew of rape and sexual assault allegations against Hollywood mogul Harvey

Weinstein, the #MeToo movement swept the country. Weinstein's career demise was quickly followed by the fall from power of Matt Lauer, Mark Halperin, Garrison Keillor, Charlie Rose, Kevin Spacey, Senator Al Franken, and countless other prominent figures in Hollywood, Wall Street, politics, and the media.

Meanwhile, America's number one sexual predator remained safely ensconced in the White House, seemingly above the law.

What's unusual about Donald Trump's sexual predation on women is that, at first, he didn't even deny it. He admitted it. He laughed about it. He bragged about it. On a bus with anchor Billy Bush to an *Access Hollywood* taping, Trump said he was looking forward to meeting the show's publicist because he'd treat her like he treats all women.

"I better use some Tic Tacs just in case I start kissing her," he told Bush and producers. "You know, I'm automatically attracted to beautiful—I just start kissing them. It's like a magnet. Just kiss. I don't even wait."

You think that's bad? It gets worse. "And when you're a star, they let you do it. You can do anything."

BUSH: "Whatever you want."

TRUMP: "Grab 'em by the pussy. You can do anything."[82]

Trump tried to dismiss his remarks as mere "locker-room talk," also insisting "I've never said I'm a perfect person," but the truth remains—by any definition, that is sexual assault, and Donald Trump, president or not, should be held responsible.[83]

And we all know that, with Donald Trump, it's not just talk. By December 2017, *HuffPost* could list twenty women over three decades, from the 1980s through 2013, who have accused Trump of sexual misconduct: from forced kissing to grabbing their breasts, buttocks, or genitals to pressuring them for sex. Even rape.[84]

Trump has denied every one of the accusations, while the White House continues to defend him as women's champion. Says former communications director Hope Hicks, "Nobody has more respect for women than Donald Trump." If so, he has a strange way of showing it.[85]

For now, through denials and expensive lawyers, Trump has managed to avoid serious legal consequences of those sexual assault charges. But that might change. One suit against Donald Trump, brought by former *Apprentice* contestant Summer Zervos, remains active in New York Superior Court, where the state supreme court refused a request by Trump's lawyers to dismiss the case because the president's schedule was too busy. If Paula Jones's case against President Bill Clinton could proceed in 1997, ruled the Supreme Court, then Summer Zervos's case against Donald Trump could proceed. In June 2018—shades of Paula Jones again—a Manhattan judge ordered that Trump sit for seven hours of deposition by January 2019.[86]

Still, Donald Trump continues to feign innocence. In February 2018, *The Washington Post* ran a story about Rachel Crooks, one of Trump's accusers, running for a seat in Ohio's statehouse. Crooks said that, as a twenty-two-year-old receptionist working in Trump Tower, she was cornered and groped by fifty-nine-year-old Trump in the hallway—which, given everything we know about Donald Trump from his own words, definitely has the ring of truth.[87]

Not me! cries Trump. "A woman I don't know and, to the best of my knowledge, never met, is on the FRONT PAGE of the Fake News Washington Post saying I kissed her (for two minutes yet) in the lobby of Trump Tower 12 years ago," he tweeted. "Never happened! Who would do this in a public space with live security . . ." (Who would do it at all is the better question—of course, that one never seemed to have occurred to Trump.)

Crooks calmly replied, "Please, by all means, share the footage from the hallway outside the 24th floor residential elevator bank on the morning of January 11, 2006. Let's clear this up for everyone. It's liars like you in politics that have prompted me to run for office myself."[88]

At least one woman who's accused Donald Trump of sexual assault may get her day in court yet. Another may be able to help defend Ohio from his terrible agenda. And the #MeToo movement may finally make it all the way to the Oval Office. Sooner or later, the reckoning will come.

7. HE'S ADDICTED TO TWITTER AND FOX NEWS

Yet another lie that candidate Trump told America: He would put his phone down once he got to the White House. "Don't worry, I'll give it up after I'm president," he promised at a Rhode Island rally in April 2016. "We won't tweet anymore. I don't know. Not presidential." Obviously, that didn't happen. In fact, it got worse. Because, believe it or not, he suddenly had more time on his hands.[89]

The reality—and I'll talk more about this in a bit—is that the most powerful man on the planet spends less time on the job every day than the average office employee. White House aides confirm: He arrives at the office around 11:00 a.m. and leaves around 5:00 p.m.[90]

The rest of the time—they call it his "executive time"—he's either lying in bed or stretched out on the sofa in the White House residence, watching TV with a Diet Coke in one hand and his iPhone in the other. Note: He got an iPhone a few months into his presidency because his earlier phone represented a national security risk—someone could hack into it, tweet like Trump, and start World War III. Unfortunately, as we all discovered in May 2018, Trump has, for months at a time, been refusing to let security keep his iPhone secure and hacker-free because it's "too inconvenient."[91]

He's not just watching, of course; he's live-tweeting what he's watching, especially in the morning when he hangs on every word of *Fox & Friends*—and relays their slanted fix on the news of the day to his fifty-three million Twitter followers (a good number of which are no doubt Russian bots and hate followers, like me!).

It's frightening to think that Steve Doocy, Ainsley Earhardt, and Brian Kilmeade are setting American policy, but a study by Media Matters for America, the progressive media watchdog, proved that is, indeed, the case. Investigative reporter Matt Gertz spent three months watching *Fox & Friends* and tracking Donald Trump's tweets. There's no doubt when the president is getting all his news, Gertz concluded: "The president was live-tweeting the network's coverage."[92]

He often used the same headlines Fox was showing on-screen. Sometimes he even admitted his source of information. Early on February 12, 2018, for example, he tweeted: "Thank you to Sue Kruczek, who lost her wonderful and talented son Nick to the Opioid scourge, for your kind words while on @foxandfriends."[93]

Which raises the question: What would happen if Fox News took a position that didn't agree with the official Trump White House policy? No problem. Trump would side with Fox News, not his own administration. Which is exactly what he did in early 2018 on the Foreign Intelligence Surveillance Act, or FISA.

The Trump White House had previously endorsed legislation to extend the operations of FISA, including the FISA court, scheduled for a vote in Congress on January 11, 2018. Yet early that morning, Trump stunned his own staff by sending out a tweet opposing the legislation. "This is the act that may have been used . . . to so badly surveil and abuse the Trump Campaign by the previous administration and others?"[94]

Republican leaders in Congress and White House aides scrambled to find out what the hell was going on, only to discover that Trump was, again, only echoing an argument he had heard legal analyst Andrew Napolitano make on *Fox & Friends,* apparently unaware that he was opposing his own White House. Later that day, press secretary Sarah Huckabee Sanders said, in effect, that both were true: the White House was both supporting and opposing the FISA legislation, but insisted that was no contradiction.[95]

Trump also undercut his own team on his very first executive order, blocking all Muslims from entering the country. While White House lawyers were in court, arguing that this was strictly a necessary executive policy to solve a serious immigration problem, and not a "travel ban," Trump tweeted out just the opposite: "The lawyers and the courts can call it whatever they want, but I am calling it what we need and what it is, a TRAVEL BAN!" It was fun watching then press secretary Sean Spicer trying unsuccessfully to unravel that one.[96]

Trump's Twitter addiction is so real that no White House staffer can limit or control it, and chief of staff John Kelly admitted on day one that he wasn't even going to try. Smart move. You can't stop an adolescent from being an adolescent. You can't stop Trump from being Trump.[97]

Still, his tweets cause no small amount of consternation for his aides and especially his lawyers, who are afraid Trump will ruin the prospects for legislation or destroy his legal defense against the Mueller investigation with another barrage of ill-advised tweets. On the day former FBI director James Comey appeared before Congress to discuss the circumstances of his dismissal by Trump, one senior White House official pleaded, "Keep him away from Twitter, dear God, keep him away from Twitter." Aides even thought about vetting all of Trump's tweets with lawyers first, to no avail. The beast cannot be contained.[98]

According to Mashable, Trump tweeted a staggering 2,444 times between Election Day, November 7, 2017, and November 7, 2018 (and passed no major legislation). That's an average of 6.6 tweets a day, with the exception of occasional tweetstorms, where he tweeted as many as 25 or 30 times. By day five hundred of his presidency, he was up to 3,496 tweets—7 times a day.[99]

Trump is generally at his Twitter worst, as one aide pointed out, "when he's bored and alone and the TV is on"—which is why his team tried to fill up his schedule with events whenever there's bad news on the television. But if the president gets free for a day, look out.[100]

Take, for example, President's Day Weekend 2018, when Trump was down at Mar-a-Lago but promised he wouldn't play golf as usual out of respect for the seventeen victims of the recent mass shooting at nearby Marjory Stoneman Douglas High School, forty miles away. (He ended up golfing anyway.)[101]

So, instead, Trump took to Twitter and embarrassed himself and everyone else many times over. He railed against the FBI, saying they could have prevented the shooting if they weren't investigating his potential collusion with Russia. (CNN's Anderson Cooper called this a "pivot away from the murder of seventeen people to himself.") He complained about Obama and "Liddle Adam Schiff," the Democratic ranking member of the House Intelligence Committee. He applauded Ken Starr and NASCAR and railed against "very insecure Oprah Winfrey," whom he was then watching on *60 Minutes*. He rambled on and on, with no sense at all of the gravity of the moment.[102]

Aside from their content—mainly ugly name-calling, personal insults, bragging, and taking credit for stuff he had nothing to do with—what can you say about a man who tweets so much? He has too much time on his hands, and he's not doing the job he was elected to do. But as his aide Omarosa told everyone after she left the White House, "He's never getting off Twitter."[103]

8. HE'S A NARCISSIST

Hey, he got elected president, although with fewer votes than his opponent. So a lot of Americans must still love him. But nobody loves Donald Trump more than Donald Trump loves himself. And he makes no bones about it.

This is not your run-of-the-mill "Hey, I guess I did pretty well yesterday" or "Thanks, I had a good day" kind of self-praise. No, this is out-and-out "I'm serious. There is nobody better, smarter, more successful, better looking than me on the entire planet" self-praise. Donald Trump is Al Franken's Stuart Smalley gone to seed and on steroids.

Remember, this is the man who told the Republican National Convention in July 2016: "I alone can fix it."[104]

His incessant boasting is so far over the top, and Trump is so dependent on self-praise or adulation of others, that thousands of mental health professionals believe Trump, in fact, manifests a narcissistic personality disorder. Leading psychologist John Gartner told *The Atlantic:* "This is the worst case of malignant narcissism I've ever seen."[105]

In October 2017, twenty-seven psychiatrists and mental health experts published their concerns about Donald Trump's mental acuity in a powerful book, *The Dangerous Case of Donald Trump.* In it, they list sixteen symptoms of a clinically ill narcissistic personality.

- Believing that you're better than others.
- Fantasizing about power, success, and attractiveness.
- Exaggerating your achievements or talents.
- Expecting constant praise and admiration.
- Believing that you're special and acting accordingly.
- Failing to recognize other people's emotions and feelings.
- Expecting others to go along with your ideas and plans.
- Taking advantage of others.
- Expressing disdain for those whom you feel to be inferior.
- Being jealous of others.
- Believing that others are jealous of you.
- Having trouble keeping healthy relationships.
- Setting unrealistic goals.
- Being easily hurt and rejected.
- Having a fragile self-esteem.
- Appearing tough-minded or unemotional.[106]

Read that list over again carefully. Together, they are the very definition of Donald J. Trump.

"I will say that never has there been a president, with few exceptions—in the case of F.D.R. he had a major Depression to handle—who's passed more legislation, who's done more things than what we've done," Trump said in June 2017, when he hadn't yet passed one single piece of major legislation.[107]

The scary part is, he actually seems to believe he's accomplished more than any president since FDR. He actually believes what he claims Senator Orrin

Hatch of Utah told him—that "he's the best in the history of the country," better than Washington or Lincoln. He actually believes he won the popular vote. He actually believes he's the most popular president ever. He actually believes his oft-repeated lie that the Trump Tower has sixty-eight stories when, in fact, it has only fifty-eight. He's getting high off his own supply.[108]

Another example: How much does Donald Trump love to see his name on things? As of September 2010, he owned 222 different companies, all named for him, many emblazoned with the giant, golden letters TRUMP at the top of their buildings. (Thank God, the name TRUMP does not yet appear on the White House.) And let's not forget Trump Wine, Trump Airlines, *Trump* magazine, Trump Vodka, Trump Steaks, Trump University, Trump Water, and so on.[109]

And whenever Donald Trump has had enough self-praise, he will demand and bask in the praise of others. Never more nakedly than in a June 2017 cabinet meeting, his very first, where he asked each person in turn to tell him how great he was. Tossing any self-respect out the window, they almost all complied, led by Vice President Mike Pence—"The greatest privilege of my life is to serve as vice president to the president who's keeping his word to the American people"—and chief of staff Reince Priebus—"We thank you for the opportunity and the blessing to serve your agenda."[110]

To his credit, Secretary of Defense James Mattis, who said it was an "honor to represent the men and women of the Department of Defense," demurred from praising the boss.[111]

The ritual repeated itself six months later at a December 2017 cabinet meeting, with Mike Pence again leading the adoring choir. As Aaron Blake of *The Washington Post* pointed out, Pence praised Trump once every twelve seconds for three full minutes.[112]

In a memorable May 2017 interview in the Oval Office, John Dickerson of CBS News queried Trump on how he made sure that he heard from dissenting voices in his job. "How do you know that people aren't always just telling you what you want to hear?" Trump acted like Dickerson was from Mars. So the host of *Face the Nation* tried again: "Who tells you no?" Trump again seemed to have no inkling of what Dickerson was talking about. Soon thereafter, when the interview got even mildly critical, Trump put an end to it.[113]

This obsessive need for adulation is not lost on foreign leaders either, and it makes him an extremely easy mark. All over the world, from China to Saudi Arabia and Israel to Japan, diplomats and world leaders have learned the secret to dealing with Donald Trump: Just tell him how great he is, and Trump will give them anything they want. "Trump risks mistaking personal flattery for geopolitical realities," one diplomatic expert put it. In other words, Trump's all-consuming vanity could one day bring us all to tears—or war.[114]

9. HE LOVES TO PICK FIGHTS

It'd be one thing if, for all his many other faults, Donald Trump was at least a relatively congenial sort who could be trusted with keeping the peace. But, no. Presumably because of his many deep and festering insecurities, Trump is always looking to pick a fight. No fight is too dumb or too petty not to wade into.

Like evidence of his racism and sexism, evidence of Donald Trump's excessive appetite for picking fights goes way back. He seems to have been born with a chip on his shoulder.

If not at birth, it started in high school. Buried in a chapter called "Revenge" in his 2007 book, *Think Big and Kick Ass: In Business and in Life,* is Trump's unusual, yet now familiar, take on how to win friends and influence people: "I learned it in high school, you've got to hit a bully really hard, really strongly, right between the eyes."[115]

You can't let any insult go unpunished, Trump insists. Otherwise, you're a weakling. "Get even! If you don't get even, you are just a schmuck."[116]

So that was Donald Trump in high school. And Donald Trump in 2007. And, of course, that's the Donald Trump we saw on the campaign trail in 2016 and in the White House thereafter.

Candidate Trump could not outwit his primary opponents, nor keep up with them in a debate on policy, so he just belittled them instead. Who could ever forget "Lyin' Ted Cruz"? Or "Low-Energy Jeb" Bush? "Crooked Hillary" Clinton? Or "Little Marco" Rubio? In fact, as we will see, for a man obsessed with size—of his body, hands, and other body parts—*little* is one of his favorite pejoratives.[117]

Once he won the presidency, you'd think a sane, well-adjusted person would no longer feel compelled to engage in sophomoric insults. Not Donald Trump. He just went into overdrive.

On January 3, 2018, *The New York Times* published a two-page spread of the 426 people, places, and things that Trump had insulted on Twitter over the past few years, including his first year in office. It was a wide range. He spared no one. He insulted everyone.[118]

He picked fights with members of Congress: "Liddle Bob Corker," "Sneaky Dianne Feinstein," "Fake Tears" and "Cryin' Chuck Schumer," "Dicky Durbin," "Jeff Flakey," and "Little Adam Schiff," among many others.[119]

He picked fights with members of the media, calling CNN's White House reporter Jim Acosta "crazy"; Anderson Cooper's *AC-360* show "a waste of time"; accusing the Associated Press of "dishonest reporting"; and repeatedly referring to the "failing" *New York Times*, even though their subscriptions under Donald Trump have reached an all-time high.[120]

He especially enjoyed picking fights with celebrities, renewing attacks on old favorite targets like Rosie O'Donnell and Michael Moore—and adding new ones to the list, like Madonna ("disgusting"), Mark Cuban ("not smart enough to run for president"), and Meryl Streep ("over-rated").[121]

Even worse, he picked fights with foreign leaders, including our closest allies. On her first visit to the White House, Trump refused to shake hands with German chancellor Angela Merkel during their Oval Office photo op. (He did shake hands with her earlier in the day.) His relationship to UK prime minister Theresa May has been dysfunctional at best. He accused her of not doing enough to combat terrorism in the UK—naturally, Trump being Trump, he first yelled at the wrong Theresa May on Twitter—and canceled a visit to England because she did not promise a warm enough welcome.[122]

And, of course, for the first year of his tenure, he unleashed nonstop verbal attacks on Kim Jong-un, the leader of North Korea, whom he has branded "Little Rocket Man" and of whom he bragged, "I too have a Nuclear Button, but it is a much bigger and more powerful one than his." Who said penis envy is dead? It may even get us all killed. Unless Trump's sudden decision to thaw his relationship with Kim Jong-un pays unexpected dividends.[123]

Trump even picked fights with ordinary citizens who dared disagree with him. He accused Indianapolis labor leader Chuck Jones, head of United Steelworkers Local 1999, whose members work at the Carrier plant Trump promised to save, but didn't, of "doing a terrible job representing workers." He got into a Twitter spat with LaVar Ball, father of Lakers star Lonzo Ball, calling him "a poor man's version of Don King, but without the hair."[124]

Meanwhile, forced to defend their bully in the Oval Office, all timid White House aides could do was shake their heads and warn—if you hit him, he's going to hit you back. Which is the same lame excuse taken up by First Lady Melania Trump, the self-proclaimed opponent of cyberbullying, who wouldn't dare criticize the Bully in Chief. When Trump attacked MSNBC host Mika Brzezinski, calling her "Crazy Mika" and describing her as "bleeding badly from a face-lift," Melania instructed staffer Stephanie Grisham to tweet out the lame excuse: "As the First Lady has stated publicly in the past, when her husband gets attacked, he will punch back 10 times harder." Except she's not talking about an unruly teenager, she's talking about the president of the United States.[125]

As if that's not embarrassing enough, Melania also gave her husband a free pass, even when he attacked men and women who have fought, been captured, and died in our nation's service.

10. HE EVEN ATTACKS MILITARY HEROES

Okay, so if Donald Trump just spent his days insulting Hollywood celebrities, TV anchors, and politicians, that'd be distasteful enough—especially when his schoolyard insults might provoke World War III.

But Trump didn't stop there. He's even brutally attacked military heroes. And gotten away with it. So far.

The first incident arose shortly after Trump declared his candidacy for president, when asked to respond to critical comments made by "American war hero" Senator John McCain. Speaking to a Family Leadership Summit (!) in Ames, Iowa, in July 2015, Trump grumbled, "He's not a war hero, because he was captured. I like people who weren't captured."[126]

In the firestorm of outrage that followed his remarks, Trump, in typical Trumpian fashion, refused to back down. Instead, he "punched back ten times harder," alleging, "I think John's done very little for veterans." In fact, whatever his many faults in other arenas, McCain—who spent five and a half years in the Hanoi Hilton, two of them in solitary confinement, and was routinely tortured—has spent his entire political career working to help veterans obtain jobs and adequate VA health care.[127]

Many pointed out, correctly, that McCain's sacrifice presented a stark contrast to a man who got four college deferments to avoid going to Vietnam, plus one more deferment for what he claimed were "bone spurs." Although, later, Trump could not tell reporters which foot actually had the bone spurs. Left or right foot, it doesn't seem to have interfered with his golf game.[128]

As disgusting as Trump's attack on John McCain, equally disgusting was the cowardly reaction of fellow Republicans, almost all of whom eventually fell into line behind Trump despite these disqualifying attacks.

Texas governor Rick Perry called his comments "disgraceful"—but then endorsed Trump for president and became his energy secretary.[129]

RNC spokesperson Sean Spicer put out a statement declaring, "There is no place in our country for comments that disparage those that serve honorably"—and then accepted the job of White House press secretary.[130]

At first, McCain's friend Lindsey Graham seemed to break ties with Trump. "If there were ever any doubt that @realDonaldTrump should not be our Commander-in-Chief," he tweeted, "this stupid statement should end all doubt." Then Graham went on to vote for everything Trump wanted from Congress and became one of his regular golf buddies. If there's one thing missing in Washington, it's backbone.[131]

But that wasn't the end of it for Trump. He was just getting started. Next up: a Gold Star family.

On the last night of the Democratic National Convention, July 28, 2017, Khizr Khan and his wife, Ghazala, took the podium to denounce Trump's proposed ban on Muslims. Mr. Khan pointed out that their son, army captain Humayun Khan, a Muslim, had been killed in a suicide bombing in 2004 while serving in Iraq. Pulling a pocket-size copy of the Constitution from his jacket, Mr. Khan addressed Trump directly, urging him to look at those who paid the ultimate sacrifice to serve in the military: "You will see all faiths, genders, and ethnicities. You have sacrificed nothing and no one."[132]

For Trump—even though his shifting bone spurs gave him no leg to stand on—this was another occasion to strike back. The very next day, he denounced the Khan family and Islam in general, suggesting that, in accordance with Muslim tradition, Mrs. Khan herself had been forbidden from speaking. "If you look at his wife, she was standing there," Trump harrumphed. "She had nothing to say. She probably, maybe she wasn't allowed to have anything to say." Meanwhile, Trump supporters began spreading rumors that Khan was actually an Islamic terrorist and a member of the Muslim Brotherhood.[133]

Again, in response to the inevitable firestorm of protest that erupted, Trump refused to back down. He insisted that he himself had, in fact, made "a lot of sacrifices." He told ABC's George Stephanopoulos he'd "created thousands and thousands of jobs" and "built great structures." Stephanopoulos didn't have to point out there's a big difference between building a high-rise and laying down your life on the battlefield.[134]

Meanwhile—remember his high school pledge—he defended his attacks on the Khan family, no matter how cruel: "I was viciously attacked by Mr. Khan at the Democratic Convention. Am I not allowed to respond?"[135]

Surely, even for Donald Trump, attacking a Gold Star family was a bridge too far? Not for Republican leaders. Mitch McConnell and Paul Ryan both condemned Trump's remarks but refused to rescind their endorsement. Even John McCain didn't withdraw his support until several months later, in October, when the *Access Hollywood* tape was released.[136]

Lesson learned for Donald Trump? Yes, but the wrong one. As long as his base supporters would accept attacking war heroes as legitimate, why stop? Even widows of the fallen were fair game.

On October 4, 2017, four American soldiers were killed in a Special Forces operation in Niger. Trump said nothing about it for almost two weeks. It was only twelve days later, at a press event in the Rose Garden, in a response to a reporter's question, that he spoke out. And then, of course, it was by going into attack mode.[137]

How dare you ask for my response to the death of an American in combat, Trump essentially fired back. I've done more than most. In fact, he said, "If you look at President Obama and other presidents, most of them didn't make calls, a lot of them didn't make calls." For example, Trump said— suddenly invoking his chief of staff's deceased son—Obama never called General John Kelly when his son was killed in Afghanistan in 2011.[138]

Not for the first time, Trump had his facts wrong. Spokespersons for Presidents Bill Clinton and George W. Bush countered that they had, in fact, made many such calls, and it was the toughest thing they ever did. Obama staffers pointed out that he held a special lunch at the White House for Gold Star families—where General John Kelly and his wife sat at the First Lady's table.[139]

That was bad enough, then Trump made it even worse. As if to prove his point, Trump called Myeshia Johnson, the widow of Sergeant La David Johnson, one of those killed in Niger. Reaching her in a car with an army officer on the way to receive her husband's body, Trump—who never even mentioned her husband's name—coldly told her, "He knew what he signed up for, but I guess it still hurt."[140]

Mrs. Johnson broke down in tears. Trump denied making that statement, but two other people in the car, Sergeant Johnson's mother and Congresswoman Frederica Wilson, heard the conservation on speakerphone and confirmed every word.[141]

That was not the only call that went wrong. The father of another soldier lost in battle told reporters of receiving a call from the president promising to send him a check for $25,000—except the check never arrived. Only when the story broke did the White House quickly follow up with a check.[142]

Attacking a genuine war hero, a Gold Star family, and the widow of a slain Special Forces soldier? After the tempest of protest had blown over, a White House official told *The Daily Beast* the president had no regrets. "He considers the issue won."[143]

Of course Donald Trump had no regrets, because he has no sense of decency at all.

Nor did he ever get any better at sympathy calls. In February 2018, Samantha Fuentes, a senior who was shot in the Parkland, Florida, school shooting, received a phone call from Trump from her hospital bed. He "didn't make me feel better in the slightest," she told reporters afterward. "Talking to the president, I've never been so unimpressed by a person in my life."[144]

11. HE'S STILL OBSESSED WITH HILLARY CLINTON

We know White House staffers are busy babysitting the leader of the free world these days, but surely one of them could take a minute to do Donald Trump and the entire country a huge favor. Simply whisper in his ear,

"Psst. The election's over. You won. You don't have to attack Hillary Clinton anymore."

Good idea, but most likely, it wouldn't do any good. Trump loved beating up on Hillary so much during the election that he just can't stop. He even surprised the prime minister of Norway, over a year after the election, by bringing up Hillary in a joint news conference with her.

Asked whether he'd be willing to testify under oath to special counsel Robert Mueller, Trump out of the blue suddenly complained that Clinton had not been placed under oath when the FBI interviewed her about her emails—on a Fourth of July weekend, no less. As Amy Davidson Sorkin wrote of this strange episode in *The New Yorker,* "as has become increasingly clear over the first year of Trump's Presidency, he cannot stop himself from turning almost any occasion—almost any critical note—into a cue for a complaint about Clinton."[145]

Indeed, rarely a week goes by when Trump does not mention Hillary Clinton, or more often than not "Crooked Hillary," on Twitter. By the five hundredth day of his presidency, he had tweeted about Clinton 118 times.[146] Who knows why? Perhaps Joe Scarborough, host of MSNBC's *Morning Joe,* has the best theory: Trump just can't accept the fact that Hillary beat him in the popular vote.

The morning after Trump's joint appearance with the Norwegian prime minister, Scarborough explained, "She crushed him by over 3 million votes. He lost by 3 million votes and every day it's in his way. When he goes to bed at night, he feels inadequate because Hillary Clinton, the worst presidential major candidate of our lifetime, crushed Donald Trump by 3 million, just crushed him."[147]

For whatever reason, now almost two years later, Trump still can't get Hillary Clinton out of his head or stop talking about her, more so than anyone can really measure. In November 2017, Vox calculated that Trump had tweeted about Hillary 75 times since Election Day 2016. According to Factbase, in that same twelve months, he'd talked about her 229 times. And in its January 3, 2018, rundown of 426 people, places, and things Trump had insulted on Twitter in 2017, 51 of them were about "Crooked Hillary."[148]

Whatever the count, the fact is Donald Trump appears to be completely obsessed with Hillary Clinton, even when he should now be focused on the job of running the country. Judging from his own words, he's consumed with her for at least four different reasons.

1. Because he thinks she was a bad candidate.

   September 13, 2017: "Crooked Hillary Clinton blames everybody (and everything) but herself for her election loss. She lost the debates and lost her direction."[149]

2. Because he believes she cheated in the election.

   November 3, 2017: "Bernie Sanders supporters have every right to be apoplectic of the complete theft of the Democratic primary by Crooked Hillary."[150]

3. Because he wants to suggest that she, not Trump, played footsie with the Russians.

   January 11, 2018: "Did Dems or Clinton also pay Russians? Where are smashed and hidden DNC servers? Where are Crooked Hillary emails? What a mess!"[151]

4. Because she and President Clinton had their own (real or perceived) scandals.

   March 27, 2017: "Why isn't the House Intelligence Committee looking into the Bill and Hillary deal that allowed big Uranium to go to Russia? . . . money to Bill, the Hillary Russian 'reset,' praise of Russia by Hillary, or Podesta Russian Company. Trump Russia story is a hoax."[152]

A funny footnote to the Hillary obsession (and a sure sign of how clueless senior staffers of this White House are): In November 2017, senior counselor Kellyanne Conway assured CNN's Chris Cuomo: "We don't care about her. Nobody here talks about her."[153]

No, nobody talks about Hillary except the big boss, and he can't stop. He can't quit her.

12. HE'S AGAINST EVERYTHING OBAMA WAS FOR

Of course, Hillary isn't the only prominent figure haunting Trump's mental landscape: 45 is also obsessed with his more talented and more popular predecessor, Barack Obama.

Even before they start campaigning for the job, most presidential candidates spend a lot of time talking to experts, figuring out what they want to accomplish if successful so they can arrive in the White House with their own positive agenda.

Not Donald Trump. He didn't need experts. Instead, he showed up in the Oval Office animated by a guiding principle: "If Obama was for it, I'm against it." And so he immediately set himself to reversing everything Obama had accomplished.

Whether you agree with them or not—for example, I'm no fan of the Trans-Pacific Partnership (TPP) with Asian nations—when Barack Obama left the White House, he could feel justifiably proud of several major achievements: Obamacare; the Paris climate accord; the Iran nuclear deal; the groundwork for the TPP; some protection for DREAMers; and restoration of relations with Cuba. Within a year, brick by brick, Donald Trump had worked to destroy or reverse them all. Yes, Obamacare remains alive, but Trump is still clearly hoping to pull the plug if Republicans hold Congress after November 2018.

Those were the big things. But Trump also went after the little things: overturning Obama's ban on the Keystone Pipeline; scrapping a rule requiring airlines to disclose baggage fees to passengers; ending rules against the killing of migratory birds by oil companies and wind developers. Again, the sole guiding principle was: If Obama's for it, Trump's against it. As one wag commented on Twitter: "Can somebody please tell Trump that the Obama administration passed a regulation banning the president from destroying his own balls with a hammer?"[154]

Why the compulsion to destroy anything that had Obama's fingerprints on it? Probably because Trump didn't have any ideas of his own, other than building a wall and having Mexico pay for it. Or because Trump, a lifelong racist, wanted to roll back all record of achievement by America's first black president. Or Trump is enormously insecure about the much more competent and beloved president who came before him. Whatever is driving this weird compulsion, of course Trump always paints it as necessary to clean up the disasters Obama left behind.

Soon after taking office, he painted a bleaker picture of the country than most Americans saw: "To be honest, I inherited a mess. It's a mess. At home and abroad, a mess. Jobs are pouring out of the country. You see what's going on with all of the companies leaving our country, going to Mexico and other places, low pay, low wages, mass instability overseas no matter where you look. The Middle East is a disaster. North Korea. We'll take care of it, folks." Not to mention the "American carnage" he lamented in his inaugural address.[155]

Trump has even reversed Obama's legacy in ways that theoretically agree with his own positions. After the mass shooting in Parkland, Florida, in February 2018, Donald Trump declared on Twitter that the killer should have been stopped beforehand because he was clearly mentally disturbed. One problem: A year earlier, Trump had signed a Republican law repealing Obama-era regulations that made it harder for people with mental illness to acquire guns. (When CBS subsequently asked the administration for a picture of Trump signing the legislation, they were refused.)[156]

Presidential scholars agree that it's not unusual, indeed it's expected, for one president to take a different direction from his predecessor's. The difference is, they do so with a forward-looking direction of their own. Not Mr. Trump. As Shirley Anne Warshaw, director of the Fielding Center for Presidential Leadership Study at Gettysburg College, told *The New York Times,* "I have not seen any constructive bills in this vein that Trump has put forth. As far as I can tell, he has no independent legislative agenda other than tearing down."[157]

It's still early, but with nothing to call his own except giant tax cuts for the rich and a bloated federal deficit, it looks like Donald Trump's already well on his way to becoming what even conservative columnist George Will has already dubbed him: our "worst-ever president."[158]

With no positive ideas of his own, Trump can only tear down, not build, thus destroying his own chances of building any lasting legacy.

New York Times columnist Charles Blow summed it up best: "Trump can't hold a candle to Obama, so he's taking a tiki torch to Obama's legacy . . . The example Obama set makes the big man with the big mouth look smaller by the day."[159]

13. HE'S LAZY

As we'll discuss, President Donald Trump has broken so many of his campaign promises it's hard to keep track of them all, but just as with his promise to stop tweeting, one broken promise in particular stands out because of its sheer absurdity: his pledge to work hard.

"If I win I may never see my property, I may never see these places again," he told a campaign rally in August 2016. "I'm going to be working for you. I'm not going to have time to go golfing, believe me. Believe me. Believe me, folks."[160]

Ha! That was then, this is now. Since he's been in the White House, Trump has put in less time and accomplished less than any president in modern history. For him, if anything, the presidency is little more than a part-time job. His real job is tweeting like a madman.

We already talked about his so-called executive time. He saunters into the Oval Office around 11:00 a.m.—unlike even George W. Bush, who showed up ready for work at 6:45. Trump sits through a couple of meetings, followed by a second chunk of executive time watching TV in the small study off the Oval Office. By 6:00 p.m., he's back in the residence for more executive time, on the couch or in bed in front of three big-screen TVs, especially installed so he can watch Fox, CNN, and MSNBC at the same time. You can almost hear him brag to Melania: "Honey, I shrunk the presidency."[161]

And believe it or not, it could be even worse. According to *Morning Joe* host Mika Brzezinski, who told the story on *MSNBC Live with Stephanie Ruhle,* Trump apparently has been telling people his biggest complaint about living in the White House is that he's not allowed to watch porn.[162]

It's actually on weekends that Trump may work the hardest. On both Saturday and Sunday, Trump hardly misses an opportunity to work hard—on his golf game. And always at one of three Trump National Golf Club courses: in Bedminster, New Jersey; Sterling, Virginia; or West Palm Beach, Florida.[163]

Trump's obsession with golf is especially ironic, given his relentless criticism of Barack Obama for his golf outings. "Can you believe that with all of the problems and difficulties facing the U.S., President Obama spent the day playing golf. Worse than Carter," Trump tweeted on October 13, 2014.[164]

Again, that was then, this is now. At today's rate, Trump will far surpass Obama's golf record. By day five hundred of his presidency, Trump had spent more than 20 percent of his time in office at one of his golf clubs and made 102 visits to his golf clubs—at a projected cost to taxpayers of roughly $68 million. That's the equivalent of nearly three regular-season PGA tours. By comparison, Obama had played thirty-seven rounds by day five hundred, only around a third of Trump's total.[165]

Trump is so addicted to the game that he even spent Martin Luther King Day 2018 on the golf course: a day that both President George W. Bush and President Barack Obama spent doing some form of public service with the First Lady. Then, as noted earlier, he played again on President's Day Weekend, as families mourned and buried the seventeen murdered at Marjory Stoneman Douglas High School, forty miles away.[166]

Now, admittedly, golf can sometimes be politics by other means. In my 2016 book, *Buyer's Remorse,* I was critical of President Obama for so rarely golfing with members of Congress, and especially Republicans, to help get his agenda through. And Trump agreed! "Obama should play golf with Republicans & opponents rather than his small group of friends," the future president tweeted in September 2012. "That way maybe the terrible gridlock would end." Flash forward to now and, by the end of his first year in office, Trump had not golfed with a single Democratic legislator.[167]

So far as we know, of course; as with other presidents, Trump's golf game is shrouded in secrecy. Typically, the White House won't reveal how many holes he plays, whom he's playing with, what his score is, or even if he's playing golf at all. But we got some insights from an interview by Norwegian golf pro Suzann Pettersen, who's played golf with Trump several times.

"He cheats like hell," she told the Norwegian newspaper *Verdens Gang.* She said she'd never seen him break 80. "But what's strange is that every time I talk to him, he says he golfed a 69, or that he set a new course record, or won a club championship some place."[168]

Pettersen also said Trump must pay his caddies well, since drives that are headed for the woods somehow always end up back in the fairway. "So

I don't quite know how he is in business," she observed. "They say that if you cheat at golf, you cheat at business." Clearly, Trump cheats at both.[169]

14. HE MAY HAVE DEMENTIA

When the history of the Trump presidency is written, one of the names that should figure prominently is Harold Bornstein. He's the hirsute Upper Manhattan gastroenterologist, allegedly Trump's doctor, who, in December 2015, without examining him, proclaimed that Donald Trump would be "the healthiest individual ever elected to the presidency."[170]

Never mind that that rose-colored diagnosis doesn't pass the basic eye test: Who in their right mind would argue Donald Trump is in better physical shape than Barack Obama? To no one's surprise, and as Bornstein admitted later after he, too, became estranged from the president, Donald Trump had dictated to him that dubious medical bill of health.[171]

In fact, there were questions about Donald Trump's mental capacity as candidate. Those questions have become more serious since he was elected. They increased dramatically with the publication of Michael Wolff's *Fire and Fury,* in which White House staffers expressed their worry on record about signs that Trump was starting to lose it mentally, or "sundowning," starting with frequent repetitions.

"It used to be inside of 30 minutes he'd repeat, word-for-word and expression-for-expression, the same three stories," Wolff wrote. "Now it was within 10 minutes."[172]

Many people took that and other aberrations as unmistakable signs of early dementia and started openly questioning the president's mental health.

Headline in *Esquire,* December 2017: A PORTRAIT OF A MAN IN COGNITIVE DECLINE.[173]

Headline in *The Atlantic,* January 3, 2018: IS SOMETHING NEUROLOGICALLY WRONG WITH DONALD TRUMP?[174]

Possible signs of dementia also appeared more often in Trump's interviews, including notably a December 2017 sit-down with Michael Schmidt of *The New York Times*—in which he repeated the phrase *no collusion* sixteen times. For the entire interview, he meandered meaninglessly, displaying both his sense of grandiosity and lack of connection with reality as if he didn't fully understand the complexity of certain issues.[175]

"But, Michael, I know the details of taxes better than anybody. Better than the greatest CPA. I know the details of health care better than most, better than most. And if I didn't, I couldn't have talked all these people into doing ultimately only to be rejected."[176]

He didn't do much better when Schmidt asked him to explain his plan for immigration reform:

I'm always moving. I'm moving in both directions. We have to get rid of chainlike immigration, we have to get rid of the chain. The chain is the last guy that killed . . . The last guy that killed the eight people . . . So badly wounded people . . . Twenty-two people came in through chain migration. Chain migration and the lottery system. They have a lottery in these countries. They take the worst people in the country, they put 'em into the lottery, then they have a handful of bad, worse ones, and they put them out. 'Oh, these are the people the United States . . .' We're gonna get rid of the lottery, and by the way, the Democrats agree with me on that. On chain migration, they pretty much agree with me.[177]

Or try to follow the all-over-the-place response he gave to the Associated Press on immigration in August 2017:

People want the border wall. My base definitely wants the border wall, my base really wants it—you've been to many of the rallies. Okay, the thing they want more than anything is the wall. My base, which is a big base; I think my base is 45 percent. You know, it's funny. The Democrats, they have a big advantage in the electoral college. Big, big, big advantage. . . . The electoral college is very difficult for a Republican to win, and I will tell you, the people want to see it. They want to see the wall.[178]

Most troubling, perhaps, several journalists have reported on the differences between coherent interviews Trump gave ten or twenty years ago and his staccato, repetitive outbursts today. He once seemed able to speak in complete sentences and actually make a point. Today, he seemingly finds it hard to connect two thoughts together. Over the years, his fluency has regressed and his vocabulary has contracted.[179]

Scientists tell us that, after forty, the brain decreases in volume by about 5 percent every decade, especially in the frontal lobes, which control speech. After analyzing Trump's speech patterns over the years, psychologist Ben Michaelis told journalist Sharon Begley of *STAT* that Trump has exhibited a "clear reduction in linguistic sophistication over time" with "simpler word choices and sentence structure."[180]

After reading Trump's incoherent interview with *The Times*'s Schmidt, columnist Charles Pierce, whose father died from Alzheimer's, concluded, "In my view, the interview is a clinical study of a man in severe cognitive decline, if not the early stages of dementia."[181]

Or according to one group of mental health professionals, as we'll see in a moment, it could be worse.

Those of us of a certain age, like Pierce and myself, remember going through this with Ronald Reagan. Once again, the signs are all there.

In December 2017, Trump was giving a speech on Israel when he began strangely slurring his words. (The White House said the culprit was dry mouth; others thought it might be a denture slip.) A week later, for the second time in as many months, Trump paused in the middle of a speech to hold and drink water with both hands—another strange potential sign of encroaching dementia.[182]

A month later, at the 2018 College Football Championship, Trump mumbled his way through the national anthem as if he'd somehow forgotten the words. The month after that, not half a minute after introducing Senator John Cornyn of Texas at the Republican Congressional Retreat, he turned to Cornyn and asked, "Did they forget your name? What's going on here? John Cornyn, but everybody knows. They didn't put his name up, but that's okay." A few months after that, when Justice Anthony Kennedy retired from the Supreme Court, Trump couldn't even remember his name. "Justice . . . Anthony . . . You know who I'm talking about."[183]

According to Joe Scarborough, a former Republican congressman with a lot of sources on that side of the aisle, Trump's dementia is "getting worse, and not a single person who works for him doesn't know it . . . He repeats the same stories over and over again. His father had it." (Trump's father, Fred, suffered from Alzheimer's in the final years of his life.)[184]

In January 2018, as part of his presidential exam, Trump did take a ten-minute cognitive screening test for dementia—which involves tasks like drawing a clock face, counting backward from one hundred by seven, and recognizing a rhino—and got a perfect score. Trump himself determined from this that he is a one-of-a-kind very stable genius. Speaking of North Korea afterward, he told a reporter that his predecessors in office "guess they all realized they were going to have to leave it to a president that scored the highest on tests." But many doctors aren't so sure—this ten-minute assessment, they say, is only a blunt instrument. It cannot measure deterioration over time and is too easy to catch deterioration anyway in many patients: more tests are needed.[185]

In any event, Trump—the same guy who, in 2003, introduced his son Donald Jr. to his future and now ex-wife Vanessa Trump twice in the space of twenty minutes—once boasted about having "one of the great memories of all time." At the very least, that no longer seems to be an operative statement.[186]

15. HE MAY BE CERTIFIABLY MENTALLY ILL

The problem with Trump could be narcissism. It could be dementia. Or, according to one group of mental health professionals, it could be something even worse.

For the last few months of 2017, a very frightening book remained on *The New York Times* bestseller list: *The Dangerous Case of Donald Trump*. In their book, twenty-seven of the nation's leading health professionals, led by Yale University's Dr. Bandy Lee, give their professional opinion that Donald Trump is seriously mentally ill and unfit to hold the job of president of the United States.

Rejecting the argument that they were bound by the so-called Goldwater rule of the American Psychological Association—created after Barry Goldwater's disastrous presidential bid in 1964—not to give professional opinions about the mental state of someone they have not personally evaluated, the authors countered that they were actually bound by a higher rule: their duty to intervene whenever there is a real danger to an individual or the public. And they argue persuasively that signs of mental illness exhibited by Trump have risen to that level of danger—especially given that he has his fingers so close to the nuclear button.[187]

As one contributor, Dr. James Gilligan, argues, "The issue that we are raising is not whether Trump is mentally ill. It is whether he is dangerous." Gilligan cites what he calls "an endless stream of threats of violence, boasts of violence, and incitements to violence"—many of which we have just discussed—as specific examples of Trump's dangerous behavior.[188]

Dr. Lee concludes, "As he is unraveling he seems to be losing his grip upon reality and reverting to conspiracy theories. There are signs that he is going into attack mode when he is under stress. That means he has the potential to become impulsive and very volatile."[189]

Even before publication of *The Dangerous Case,* another prominent psychiatrist had raised the warning flag. John Gartner, a former professor of psychiatry at Johns Hopkins University, founded an organization of mental health professionals called Duty to Warn and circulated a petition warning about Trump's mental instability. It states:

> We, the undersigned mental health professionals, believe in our professional judgment that Donald Trump manifests a serious mental illness that renders him psychologically incapable of competently discharging the duties of President of the United States. And we respectfully request he be removed from office, according to article 4 of the 25th amendment to the Constitution, which states that the president will be replaced if he is "unable to discharge the powers and duties of his office."[190]

By September 2017, more than sixty thousand mental health professionals had signed the petition.

Heeding their warnings, Maryland Democratic congressman Jamie Raskin has introduced legislation to create an independent commission of physicians and psychiatrists to interview the president and determine his ability to continue as president—as a first step toward implementation of the Twenty-Fifth Amendment, enacted in 1967 to deal with presidential succession when a president is still alive but no longer physically or mentally able to serve.[191]

Citing a "sustained pattern of behavior" and nonstop "errant and seemingly deranged tweets," Raskin says it's clear that "something is seriously wrong" with Trump.[192]

When tens of thousands of mental health experts warn that Donald Trump is already certifiably mentally unstable, if not insane, it's not something that should be taken lightly. It's time to move from expressing concern to taking action.

In a *Columbia Journalism Review* article entitled "Avoiding Questions About Donald Trump's Mental Health Is a Betrayal to Public Trust," author Lee Siegel concludes, "When someone is compulsively lying, continuously contradicting himself, imploring the approval of people even as he is attacking them, exalting people one day and abusing and vilifying them the next, then the question of his mental state is moot. The safe thing to do is not just to stay away from him, but to keep him away from situations where he can do harm."[193]

It's safe to say that nobody in the world has more capacity to do more harm to others than the president of the United States. We can't afford to have a cruel, racist, sexist, abusive, intolerant, dim-witted, narcissistic, and potentially senile sociopath in our nation's highest office.

For all of these reasons and many more to come, Trump must go.

2

TRUMP'S DISASTROUS ACTS AS PRESIDENT

Donald Trump, as we've seen, is an inexperienced, uninformed, indolent, and possibly clinically dangerous man who had no business getting anywhere near the White House. Unfortunately for us all, that's where he currently resides. In this chapter, let's look at the incredible damage he's done to the country since he's been there.

One of the most often-heard takes on Trump's first two years in office is that he has been largely ineffective, all bark and no bite. After all, in his first year, despite bragging about accomplishing more than any president since FDR, he only succeeded in signing one major piece of legislation, his giant tax cuts for the wealthy and big corporations—and that only in the last week of December 2017. By that point, despite his claims that he had "signed more bills—and I'm talking through the legislature—than any president ever," Trump had signed fewer laws than any president in the last sixty years. Legislatively speaking, the first six months of 2018 were no better for him.[1]

Still, that take is dead wrong. It ignores all the destruction Trump has done from the White House alone by example, rhetoric, or executive order. Even if he has been a legislative do-nothing, he has already undone or rolled back decades of progress in civil rights, women's rights, LGBTQ rights, immigration reform, criminal justice reform, environmental protection, and many other areas. Let's roll the tape.

16. HE IMPOSED A BAN ON MUSLIM IMMIGRANTS

Right out of the box, Trump proved to be just as callous, prejudiced, and ignorant as president as he had been as a candidate.

Why should we be surprised? This is the same man, we all remember, who launched his candidacy with racist slurs about Mexican immigrants.

Along the way, he also called for reinstating police spying on Muslim communities; announced he would "strongly consider" shutting down all mosques; falsely claimed he saw "thousands and thousands" of Muslims dancing in New Jersey streets as World Trade towers fell on September 11; suggested all "young, strong" Muslim men were ISIS-affiliated and part of an immigration "Trojan horse"; and attacked the Gold Star family of army captain Humayun Khan.[2]

Not only that, "Donald Trump," the candidate proclaimed in December 2015, "is calling for a total and complete shutdown of Muslims entering the United States until our country's representatives can figure out what the hell is going on." And that's exactly what he did, or tried to do, with his first executive order on January 27, 2017, exactly one week after taking the oath of office.[3]

Executive Order 13769 slammed the door on all immigrants, and even travelers, from seven predominately Muslim countries—Iraq, Iran, Libya, Somalia, Sudan, Syria, and Yemen—for ninety days, with further restrictions to follow—only because of their religion.[4]

On the face of it, the ban seemed discriminatory, racist, and unconstitutional—and the courts soon agreed. Just one week later, on February 3, a federal judge in Seattle blocked the ban. Six days later, his order was upheld by the U.S. Ninth Circuit Court of Appeals.[5]

For a while, Trump's ban had a rough going. In March 2017, he issued a second, revised ban—only six countries this time, dropping Iraq—which was also shot down by the lower courts, but revived in a limited fashion by the Supreme Court.[6]

Trump then followed in September with yet a third version of his ban, dropping Sudan this time, and adding a non-Muslim nation, North Korea, for cover (plus government officials from Venezuela). But third time was not the charm. The ban was yet again invalidated nationwide by federal courts in Hawaii and Maryland.[7]

This set up a final showdown in the Supreme Court, where Trump's stolen pick, Neil Gorsuch, proved decisive. "We express no view on the soundness of the policy," Chief Justice Roberts wrote in a 5-4 opinion on June 26, 2018, but, nonetheless—thanks to Gorsuch—the ban was upheld. In her blistering dissent, Justice Sotomayor wrote that the rabid conservatives on the Court had reached this decision by "ignoring the facts, misconstruing our legal precedent, and turning a blind eye to the pain and suffering the Proclamation inflicts upon countless families and individuals, many of whom are United States citizens."[8]

Even though Trump got his way in the end, ironically, one of the biggest legal obstacles the ban faced was Trump himself, who, as always, was his own worst enemy.

For one, Trump kept repeating the word *ban*. White House lawyers bent over backward to assure the courts that this executive order does *not* constitute a "ban," which is probably unconstitutional, but instead a necessary "adjustment to" or "change in" immigration rules for national security reasons. Problem is, nobody told Trump. He undercut his attorneys multiple times with tweets advocating his Muslim "ban."[9]

For example, June 3, 2017: "We need to be smart, vigilant and tough. We need the courts to give us back our rights. We need the Travel Ban as an extra level of safety."[10]

Or, two days later, June 5, 2017: "That's right, we need a TRAVEL BAN for certain DANGEROUS countries, not some politically correct term that won't help us protect our people!"[11]

Or again, in September 2017: "The travel ban into the United States should be far larger, tougher and more specific-but stupidly, that would not be politically correct!"[12]

Nor did Trump help his case by approvingly suggesting that WWI general John J. Pershing killed Muslim terrorists in the Philippines with bullets dipped in pig's blood (he didn't). It didn't help either when, in November 2017, Trump retweeted virulently anti-Muslim videos by the far right-wing outfit Britain First. (Neal Katyal, a lawyer for the other side, tweeted back at Trump: "Thanks! See you in court next week.")[13]

The cries of "ban" and consistent racism of these tweets were not lost on presiding judges. "What do we do," a Virginia judge asked, about "multiple instances" of anti-Muslim tweets, "before the election, during the election, and just a week or so ago? Do we just ignore reality?"

"The 'initial' announcement of the Muslim ban," another Maryland judge wrote while striking it down, "offered repeatedly and explicitly through President Trump's own statements, forcefully and persuasively expressed his purpose in unequivocal terms."[14]

Trump also created another problem with the majority of Muslim countries included in his travel ban, and those not covered. Fifteen of the nineteen terrorists on September 11 were from Saudi Arabia. So why wasn't Saudi Arabia on the list? Or why was Sudan, repeatedly named as one of the world's worst human rights violators, dropped from the list on Trump's third version of the ban?

Answer: Follow the money!

As first reported by *Daily News,* the Trump Organization doesn't hold any business interests in any of the countries on the list but holds major stakes in several of those excluded from it.[15]

Take the first Muslim ban on Iran, Iraq, Libya, Somalia, Sudan, Syria, and Yemen. Not a single American was killed on U.S. soil by citizens from any of those countries between 1975 and 2015, according to the Cato Institute. Yet nearly three thousand Americans were killed by citizens from Saudi Arabia, the United Arab Emirates, and Egypt in the same time period, and people from those three countries are still welcome to apply for U.S. visas.[16]

And wouldn't you know? The Trump business empire holds multimillion-dollar licensing and development deals in all three countries—in addition to Turkey and Indonesia, also hotbeds for terrorist activity and also excluded from the list.[17]

As for the Sudan switcheroo, *The Intercept*'s Ryan Grim and Alex Emmons reported in September 2017 that Trump and company were the beneficiaries of a lobbying campaign organized by the United Arab Emirates, who, as with Saudi Arabia, have been relying on Sudan's boots on the ground to wage war in Yemen. Since "Sudan is doing the UAE's dirty work," as one anonymous source put it in the story, UAE ambassador Yousef Al Otaiba lobbied the administration hard on behalf of Sudan. ("Otaiba," the story notes, "is particularly close with White House advisor Jared Kushner," who, as we will discuss later on, has overseen a number of seeming quid pro quo arrangements during his tenure.)[18]

Clearly, the driving force behind Trump's Muslim ban is not our national security. It's his bottom line.

17. HE CANCELED PROTECTED STATUS FOR DREAMERS

Years from now, presidential historians will have a field day debating which was the most egregious of Donald Trump's lies. But all of them will agree that this was one of the worst. "I have a great heart for the folks we are talking about, a great love for them," Donald Trump told reporters on September 5, 2017, just hours after he had summarily canceled the DREAMers program and challenged Congress to vote to extend it in six months or else.[19]

The Deferred Action for Childhood Arrivals program, or DACA, was established by President Obama by executive order in June 2012. As established, young people who had been brought to the United States illegally could apply for protected status, enabling them to stay in the country without fear of deportation, for two years.[20]

Rules were tough: No one with a criminal record was accepted. DREAMers had to renew their status, at their own expense, every two years. And they were never eligible for U.S. citizenship. By 2017, 800,000 young people had applied for protected DACA status, out of an estimated total 1.8 million who fit the DREAMers definition.[21]

Obama created the DREAMers program after Congress rejected several attempts to pass the DREAM Act. If Congress refused to protect the DREAMers, the least controversial players in the whole immigration debate, Obama decided, then he would do so by executive order.

We call them *DREAMers* because they occupy a special place among immigrants who came here in pursuit of the American dream. These are young people who were brought by their parents, through no choice of their own, before they were sixteen years old, and have lived here continuously since 2007. Most of them come from Mexico, El Salvador, Guatemala, and Honduras, but they have lived in no other country. They're in school or have graduated, have jobs, pay taxes, and have families. Nine hundred of them have served in the military. They're American citizens in every sense but one, lacking a certain piece of paper.[22]

And they have broad public support. According to ABC News, in September 2017, when Trump canceled the program, 86 percent of Americans believed they should be allowed to remain in the country. A separate CBS News poll in January 2018 found 87 percent of Americans still agreed.[23]

When Donald Trump took office, the DREAMers program was actually a dream itself. Everything was running smoothly. Eight hundred thousand young people had signed up. An estimated one million more were considered eligible, and more of them were signing up every year. Most importantly, the program gave DREAMers the opportunity to get an education, get a job, or start a family without facing the constant fear of deportation.

And where did Donald Trump stand on the DREAMers program? Was he for it? Against it? Or uncertain? Yes. All of the above.

Among other promises made on June 16, 2015, when he announced he was running for president, was a pledge to terminate the DREAMers program immediately—a pledge he repeated often during the campaign.[24]

Yet, shortly after his election, Trump told *Time* magazine he sympathized with the DREAMers. Indeed, nobody described their plight more accurately: "They got brought here at a very young age, they've worked here, they've gone to school here. Some were good students. Some have wonderful jobs. And they're in never-never land because they don't know what's going to happen."[25]

At other times he acknowledged that DACA was "a very, very difficult subject" for him because "I love these kids" and he promised to work "with a big heart" to help craft a "bill of love."[26]

But, in the end, for Donald Trump, there was one big problem with the DREAMers program: It had been started by Barack Obama. Therefore, it must be bad. Therefore, he had to end it. Which he proceeded to do.

In September 2017, Trump effectively killed DACA by shutting it down, and—under the pretext that Obama did not have the power as president to take any unilateral action on immigration, even though Trump was at the same time arguing that he had the power to order a unilateral Muslim ban—gave Congress six months, until March 5, 2018, to pass a law making the program permanent or it would cease to exist and DREAMers would be immediate targets for deportation.[27]

Then, in typical fashion, Congress did nothing—which Trump should have expected. Neither Senate majority leader Mitch McConnell nor House Speaker Paul Ryan made any effort to pass an immigration bill containing protection for DREAMers. In the one week slotted for debate on the issue, four different bills failed to pass the Senate.[28]

President Trump didn't do anything, either. In fact, he made it impossible for both sides to come together by insisting that any bill extending the DREAMers program also include $30 billion for the wall he wants to build along our southern border with Mexico. You know, the same wall Mexico was supposed to pay for. No wall, no deal.[29]

All the while, Trump continued to lie shamelessly about what he and his party were up to. "The Republicans are with you; they want to get your situation taken care of," he told DREAMers at the White House in March. "The Democrats fought us, they just fought every single inch of the way. They did not want DACA in this bill."[30]

A month later, *USA Today* reported that twenty-three-year-old Juan Manuel Montes, who'd lived in the United States since he was nine, was asked for his papers while out getting dinner in Calexico, California. Three hours later, he was in Mexico, and the first DREAMer we know of deported by Trump.[31]

Meanwhile, Democrats in Congress—and even many moderate Republicans—continued to work to save DACA, despite Trump's constant, blatant lies to the contrary. In fact, when a discharge petition that would force a vote on DACA was circulated in the House by Carlos Curbelo, a Florida Republican in an immigrant-heavy district, in May 2018, Paul Ryan and the House GOP leadership worked frantically behind closed doors to block it.[32]

And so, as of this writing, the DREAMers still remain in limbo. Disgusted with the nonstop political games being played with DACA, several DREAMers remarked, "We feel like bargaining chips." That's because, to Donald Trump, that's all they are.[33]

18. HE ENDED PROTECTED STATUS FOR MANY IMMIGRANTS

Give me your tired, your poor,
Your huddled masses yearning to breathe free,
The wretched refuse of your teeming shore.
Send these, the homeless, tempest-tossed, to me:
I lift my lamp beside the golden door.[34]

For much of our history, give or take a few periods of nativist reaction, those inspiring words of Emma Lazarus summed up the gist of America's immigration policy. People from all over the world came here to pursue the American dream, and we welcomed them with open arms.

With open arms, yes, but not necessarily with open borders. We have crafted limits on how many total new residents we could accept and how many from each country. But in keeping with the circumstances of our founding, we have tried to make a special exception for people fleeing violence, danger, or oppression in their home country.

As such, the Temporary Protected Status program, or TPS, was begun in 1990 by President George H. W. Bush in order to grant emergency assistance to immigrants fleeing danger in their home countries caused by armed conflict, natural disasters, or other strife. It's been invoked by every president since to welcome immigrants from dozens of countries. It's the welcome mat we Americans rolled out when someone's house was burning down.[35]

But no longer. Not under Donald Trump.

Trump has turned American immigration policy upside down, not only trying to limit both legal and illegal immigration, not only ending special recognition for 1.8 million DREAMers, but also ending TPS for immigrants from six countries and, in effect, shutting down the program. By executive order, with no input from Congress, he slammed the door on some 425,000 refugees from Sudan, Nicaragua, Haiti, El Salvador, Nepal, and Honduras and subjected them to immediate expulsion.[36]

Refugees from Sudan were the first target. In September 2017, Trump announced that more than one thousand refugees who had been displaced by war, pestilence, and famine would be sent back. Cruel? Yes, and Trump was just getting warmed up.[37]

Then Nicaragua. In the wake of devastation caused by Hurricane Mitch in 1999, President Bill Clinton allowed five thousand Nicaraguans to come to the United States under the emergency TPS program. They've lived here for nineteen years. They have jobs, homes, and families. They pay taxes. On November 6, 2017, the Trump administration summarily told all five thousand they'd been here long enough. They were given one year to pack all their belongings and return to Nicaragua. No exceptions.[38]

Next: Haiti. Already the poorest country in the Western Hemisphere, Haiti suffered even more devastation from Hurricane Matthew in October 2010 and a 7.0 earthquake that struck near Port-au-Prince in January 2011, killing over three hundred thousand people. Again, invoking TPS, President Obama, with broad bipartisan support, opened America's doors to sixty thousand refugees from Haiti. But again, revoking TPS, President Trump rolled up the welcome mat in November 2017, giving Haitian immigrants eighteen months to get out of the country on their own or be expelled.[39]

Then the country with the biggest number of protected immigrants: El Salvador. It was not just devastation caused by two major earthquakes that drove Salvadorans to flee their native land but danger resulting from a long civil war in which the United States, by funding and arming El Salvador's ruthless dictator, was a major player. Starting in 2001, under President George W. Bush, Salvadorans were welcomed under the auspices of TPS.[40]

By 2017, some 200,000 Salvadorans had taken advantage of the opportunity to live and work legally in the United States. According to the Center for Migration Studies of New York, 88 percent of them were part of the labor force, owned homes, and paid taxes. And almost 193,000 of them had American-born children who were, of course, American citizens.[41]

Too bad. Donald Trump didn't care. On January 18, 2018, he took away protected status for immigrants from El Salvador and ordered them to make plans to return, after sixteen years or so in the United States, to what is known as one of the most dangerous countries in the Western Hemisphere.[42]

He wasn't done. In late April 2018, Trump canceled TPS for nine thousand Nepalis who had been given refuge here after a catastrophic 2015 earthquake. Then eighty-six thousand Hondurans, many of whom had also been living here for two decades since Hurricane Mitch, were also given the boot by Trump.[43]

And in June 2018, looking for ever more ways to close the golden door to people in need, Jeff Sessions overturned an immigration court ruling granting asylum to an El Salvadoran woman battered by her husband, and declared he was ending the rule that had allowed thousands of victims of domestic violence to find refuge in the United States and escape their abusers.[44]

Was all this legal? Yes. Was it cruel and unnecessary? Also yes. Isn't it telling that this is almost entirely happening to immigrants from non-white countries? Yes, again. And, as if adding insult to injury, Donald Trump called Haiti, El Salvador, and certain African nations "shithole" countries. More on that fiasco later on.

19. HE HAS UNLEASHED ICE AS A BRUTAL POLICE FORCE

What do you think of when you hear the term *fascism*? A secret, unaccountable police force trampling on basic constitutional rights? People being asked for their papers and arrested without warrant or charges? Activists being jailed for their political views, and families forced to live every day in fear of being rounded up, broken up, and locked up or deported?

Welcome to Donald Trump's America. For him, that secret, unaccountable police force is U.S. Immigration and Customs Enforcement, or ICE.

True, Barack Obama wasn't exactly known for being soft on those in this country illegally. He oversaw the deportation of so many more people than George W. Bush that he became known as the Deporter in Chief. But, at the same time, he was pushing Congress to provide a path to citizenship for undocumented immigrants. When Congress refused, Obama limited ICE enforcement actions to those people with serious criminal violations. Just being in the United States illegally did not count.[45]

All that's changed under Trump. All restrictions are off. And, of course, the net effect of lowering the standards for roundup and arrest is that ICE cops go after the easiest targets. As one agent put it, the goal is no longer to catch the bad guys but simply to "fill the beds." Perhaps unwittingly, ICE deputy director Thomas D. Homan confirmed their new priority: "ICE will enforce the law, and if you are found to be breaking the law, you will be held accountable."[46]

And the obvious results soon followed. In Trump's first year, arrests by ICE went up 40 percent, especially among those with no criminal record. In 2017 alone, ICE made 37,734 "noncriminal arrests," more than twice the number in 2016.[47]

As Brian Tashman of the ACLU noted in February 2018, "In the past year, ICE has gone after parents dropping off their children at school; primary caregivers to family members with disabilities; domestic abuse survivors seeking legal protections; religious minorities who fear persecution; political activists; community leaders; and people who work everywhere from convenience stores to dairy farms."[48]

The results are thousands of modern-day gestapo arrests that are unworthy of a free society and amount to nothing less than clear and dangerous suppression at the hands of the federal government. News accounts give countless examples. Among them are the following, as listed by immigration activist Tania Unzueta Carrasco in *USA Today*.

- In February 2017, Daniela Vargas, a young immigrant in Jackson, Miss., was detained following a press conference where she spoke out about the recent raid in her home and her family's detention.

- In March, Enrique Balcazar and Zully Palacios, two members of Migrant Justice leading the organization's campaign for fair wages in Vermont's milk industry, were followed by Border Patrol agents as they left their local community meeting. Both now face deportation.

- In May, a California student, Claudia Rueda, was detained by Border Patrol agents outside her home. She had been trying to win enough public support to get her mother out of immigration detention.

- In December, Maru Mora-Villalpando, an activist defending the rights of those detained by Immigration and Customs Enforcement was issued a deportation notice, without any prior contact with the police or ICE.

- [In February 2018] Scott Warren of the humanitarian organization No More Deaths in Tucson, Ariz. was arrested for giving food, water, and a bed to two suspected undocumented immigrants who'd crossed the desert. He was charged with a felony and could get five years in prison.[49]

Yes, in the Gospel According to Donald Trump, giving water to a thirsty person is a felony.

And Carrasco is just revealing the tip of the iceberg. Whether it's cruelly breaking up families or stalking family courts, every week seems to bring news of another egregious injustice committed by ICE under Trump's authority.

In February 2017, ICE agents swooped down upon a Texas courthouse where a Mexican El Paso resident was filing a protective order against her abusive boyfriend. Very likely tipped off by this woman's abuser, ICE placed the woman under arrest. "This is really unprecedented . . . It really was a stunning event," said El Paso attorney Jo Anne Bernal. "It has an incredible chilling effect for all undocumented victims of any crime in our community."[50]

In October 2017, ICE agents entered a Portland, Oregon, home—without a warrant—and arrested Carlos Bolanos. Thankfully for Bolanos, a friend caught the whole incident on tape. "You've got officers that are violating the most sacred laws of the country," said one immigration attorney of the warrantless arrest. "There are only so many of these that are caught on tape."[51]

In December 2017, ninety-two Somalis were shackled and abused by ICE for forty hours straight on a deportation flight. "As the plane sat on the runway," read the legal complaint they later filed, "the ninety-two detainees remained bound, their handcuffs secured to their waists, and their feet shackled together . . . When the plane's toilets overfilled with human waste, some of the detainees were left to urinate into bottles or onto themselves. ICE agents wrapped some who protested, or just stood up to ask a question, in full-body restraints." All the while, ICE taunted their captives with racist jabs. "They called them 'niggers,'" one of the Somalis' lawyers revealed. "They called them 'boy.' They've said things like 'We're sending you boys back to the jungle.'"[52]

Then, in February 2018, reports surfaced that ICE detainee Laura Monterrosa was held in solitary confinement for sixty hours at the T. Don Hutto Residential Center in Texas (a private prison) and told she could not leave until she recanted allegations of sexual abuse there. How often this sort of thing happens at ICE facilities is an open question, especially since, in 2017, the agency requested license to more quickly destroy the internal documents related to deaths, sexual assaults, and solitary confinement.[53]

In addition to accelerated arrests for noncriminal causes, activists correctly cite two additional problems with ICE. First are the shocking conditions in ICE detention facilities, where advocacy groups have documented numerous cases of sexual assault, substandard medical care, poor food service, overuse of solitary confinement, and physical assault by custody staff. From 2016 to December 2017, twenty-three persons died in ICE detention facilities.[54]

The second problem is the pressure on sanctuary cities. In order for ICE to ramp up its number of arrests and deportations, Attorney General Jeff Sessions demands that cities and states allow ICE agents unlimited access to jails and delay releasing immigrants from custody until ICE agents can detain them. Which is something sanctuary cities rightfully refuse to do, leading Sessions to threaten to withhold funding from cities and states—a move that, so far, courts have found to be unconstitutional.[55]

Sessions has also been trying to bully mayors and city officials to let ICE act unrestrained in these cities. When Oakland mayor Libby Schaaf issued a public warning that ICE was operating in the area, Sessions fumed that "800 wanted criminals that ICE will now have to pursue by other means" had escaped thanks to her. That was the last straw for one whistleblower. In March 2018, ICE spokesman James Schwab resigned because of Sessions's comments. "I quit because I didn't want to perpetuate misleading facts," Schwab said. "I told them that the information was wrong, they asked me to deflect, and I didn't agree with that . . . I didn't feel like fabricating the truth to defend ourselves against [Mayor Schaaf's] actions was the way to go about it."[56]

President Trump, meanwhile, not only defended ICE. He accused any critics of ICE—including Senators Dick Durbin, Kamala Harris, and Elizabeth Warren—as being in favor of open borders, violent crime, and MS-13 gangs. "The Liberal Left, also known as the Democrats," he tweeted on July 1, 2018, "want to get rid of ICE, who do a fantastic job." Without ICE, Trump warned, playing the ultimate fear card, "you're going to have a country that you're going to be afraid to walk out of your house."

And then there's the frightening and disgusting matter of Trump and Sessions's detention camps for migrant children.

"Between October 2017 and May 2018," Vox reported in June 2018, "at least 2,700 children have been split from their parents. 1,995 of them were separated over the last six weeks of that window—April 18 to

May 31—indicating that at present, an average of 45 children are being taken from their parents each day." The devious tricks being used to separate families by ICE and CBP—for example, taking kids away just so they can "have a bath"—will chill anyone who's ever read anything about Nazi Germany in the 1930s. Already, one Honduran father committed suicide in detention after having his three-year-old son ripped from him.[57]

"I hate the children being taken away," Trump bemoaned on Twitter. And yet, he declared he must commit these "horrible" deeds because of the "Democrats' law"—"that's what the Democrats gave us." As always, Trump is egregiously lying. Of course no such law exists. Separating kids from their parents began in April 2018 with the announcement of a new, "zero tolerance" policy by Attorney General Jeff Sessions. In fact, when a shocked Congress put forward a bill explicitly *preventing* the separation of families at the border, Trump announced he would not sign it.[58] Why? Because he was holding these migrant children "hostage" until Congress agreed to give him $25 million to build his stupid wall.

Democrats weren't the only ones to raise hell about Trump's detention camps for kids. In *The Washington Post*, former first lady Laura Bush called Trump's "zero tolerance" policy "cruel" and "immoral." Reacting to video of kids crowded into cages, she wrote: "These images are eerily reminiscent of the Japanese American internment camps of World War II, now considered to have been one of the most shameful episodes in U.S. history."[59]

So where did these children go? In June 2018, a few journalists were allowed to tour a former Walmart now serving as the abhorrently-named "Casa Padre" in Brownsville, Texas, where more than 1,400 boys separated from their parents were being held. In the jail-like environment, where the kids are only allowed outside for two hours a day, the reporters were initially greeted with a giant mural of Donald Trump, the White House, and the flag, with the inscription—from Trump's *Art of the Deal*— "Sometimes by losing a battle you find a new way to win the war." The following day, the administration borrowed a page from Sheriff Joe Arpaio and announced they were going to build a "tent city" in Tornillo, Texas, to house 450 more children, the first such federal "tent city" setup to hold immigrants.[60]

Outrage at these child internment camps eventually grew so strong that Trump was forced to backtrack and sign an executive order that pledged to stop separating kids from their parents. (Instead, families would be detained together . . . indefinitely.) But, in terms of indefensible and unconstitutional policies at the border, Trump was just getting warmed up. "We cannot allow these people to invade our Country," he tweeted on June 24, 2018. "When somebody comes in, we must immediately, with no Judges or Court Cases, bring them back from where they came." Here was the president of the United States declaring due process null and void. Just as alarming was his declaration a few days earlier that "illegal immigrants" wanted "to pour into and infest our Country"—the word "infest" eerily reminiscent of Nazi propaganda against Jews in the 1930s and '40s.[61]

One sadly ironic historical footnote: ICE's zeal to round up and deport as many immigrants as possible today stands in sharp contrast to our shameful immigration policy post–World War II, when thousands of Nazi collaborators and accomplices were allowed into the United States. From 1945 to 1979, what was then called the U.S. Immigration and Naturalization Service repeatedly failed to investigate and deport for prosecution Nazi war criminals, including Holocaust perpetrators.[62]

We treated Nazis better at that time than we treat a poor refugee from El Salvador today. That's all because of ICE, which was only created as part of the Department of Homeland Security bill in 2003. We did fine without them before then; it's time for this flagrantly unaccountable and un-American police force to go.

20. HE WANTS TO BUILD A STUPID WALL

We know three things about Donald Trump's wall:

- It's never going to get built.
- Mexico's never going to pay for it.
- But Donald Trump will never stop talking about it.

On January 18, 2018, Trump tweeted: "The Wall is the Wall, it has never changed or evolved from the first day I conceived of it." That is not true. In fact, almost every time he talks about it, his description of the wall changes. At various times, about this same wall he has said all of the following:

- It will be a concrete wall—or transparent
- Or it will actually be a fence

- Or it will be part wall and part fence
- It will have solar panels on top of it, or not
- It will have a "big, beautiful door right in the middle of the wall" to allow access for those who come in to pick grapes
- It will have a few "openings" in the wall, through which people "will come in and they're going to come in legally"
- It'll be 1,000 miles long, or 650 miles long
- It will be 35 feet, or 40 feet, or 50 feet high
- It will cost $6 billion, or $10 billion, or $12 billion, or $25 billion
- Mexico will pay for it; if not, U.S. taxpayers will[63]

There are, of course, several practical problems with Trump's proposal. Geography, for starters. The southern border is not a two thousand–mile stretch of solid land. For one thousand miles, the border is a mix of wetlands, rivers, and mountain ranges where no wall is possible.

Another problem: This is not government property. In fact, two-thirds of the land, especially in Texas, is privately or state-owned. So the government would either have to invoke eminent domain to seize the land—which would be tied up in courts for years—or purchase it outright, which would be hugely expensive. Trump's estimated cost of $25 billion does not include the cost of land acquisition.[64]

And finally, the wall is a solution to a problem that no longer exists. At one time, immigrants were flooding across our southern border illegally, but that is no longer the case. According to the Pew Research Center, between 2009 and 2014, more Mexicans actually escaped south across the border than fled north. Since then, the overall flow of immigrants crossing the border illegally has remained historically low.[65]

Not only that, 40 percent of today's undocumented immigrants originally came here legally, with a visa, by plane. They did not walk across the border illegally; they simply overstayed their visas. No wall will ever stop them.[66]

Nor is Trump's wall, as he claims, a national security measure. Since September 11, 80 percent of individuals arrested for terrorist activities in this country were U.S. citizens or permanent residents. And of 154 foreign-born people who committed or plotted terrorist attacks on U.S. soil from 1975 through 2015, only 1 was Mexican.[67]

For many reasons, Trump's stupid wall is nothing but a joke. If it didn't cost $25 billion and wasn't so obviously fueled by racism, it'd be funny.

21. HE'S PACKING COURTS WITH UNQUALIFIED JUDGES

Even though they normally fly under the radar, the most lasting legacy of any president is usually the judges he appoints to the federal bench. By that test, the negative impact of Donald Trump's presidency will already be felt for decades. For, very quietly, he has managed to pack the courts with more judges, and more unqualified judges, than any modern president. And these are lifetime appointments.

The most prominent example, of course, is the nomination of Neil Gorsuch to the Supreme Court, although Senate majority leader Mitch McConnell deserves more credit for Gorsuch than Trump. For over a year, McConnell refused to schedule a hearing on Merrick Garland, President Obama's nominee to fill the vacancy created by the death of Justice Antonin Scalia. It was a ridiculously partisan gambit, but it worked, thereby leaving the seat open for Trump to fill.

And, of course, Trump and McConnell got a second bite at the Supreme Court apple when Justice Anthony Kennedy announced his retirement at the end of June 2018, giving these two partisan hucksters the chance to reshape the highest court in the land for a generation.

But it's at the appellate court level where Trump and Republicans have been really busy. In Trump's first year in office, working in close cooperation with Senate judiciary chairman Charles Grassley, the Trump White House won confirmation of twelve appeals court judges, a modern record. In his first year, President Obama secured only four appellate judges.[68]

Though little known to the public, the influence of appeals court judges cannot be overstated. In 2015, the U.S. Supreme Court decided 82 cases. In 2016, only 69. Compare that to 52,000 cases decided by U.S. courts of appeal in 2015, and 58,000 in 2016. Then add 353,000 cases decided at the district court level in 2015, and 355,000 in 2016. You can see how important are appointments to the lower courts. They decided 99.9 percent of all cases each year.[69]

Two things stand out about Trump's judicial picks. They are overwhelmingly white men. And they are underwhelmingly qualified.

According to *The Hill*, and as noted earlier, 80 out of 87 were white. There was one African American, one Latino, and five Asian Americans, and 81 percent of his nominees are men. And among them all there is not one openly LGBT American.[70]

In only his first year, four of Donald Trump's nominees received a "not qualified" rating from the American Bar Association—which is in itself some kind of record. It took George W. Bush eight years to rack up eight "not qualified" nominees. In his eight years, Barack Obama had none—mainly because, like every other president except Bush 43 and Trump, he didn't nominate anyone that couldn't pass ABA's muster.[71]

Perhaps the most well-known embarrassment of Trump's wannabe judges was FEC commissioner Matthew S. Petersen. He was actually rated as qualified by the ABA but couldn't even answer the most basic questions about legal procedure in his confirmation hearing. He also admitted he had never tried a case, argued a motion, or taken a deposition by himself. Both Republicans and Democrats pressured the White House to withdraw his name.[72]

Of Trump's first four ABA-rated not-qualified judicial picks, one, Steven Grasz, was nevertheless confirmed by the Senate. Another, Brett Talley, withdrew his name after it was revealed he had written a blog post defending the KKK.[73]

The 2017 clock ran out for the two remaining unqualified nominees. But that didn't stop Donald Trump. On January 8, 2018, he renominated both of them: Charles Goodwin, deemed unqualified to handle the job of a federal judge because of his "work habits, including his frequent absence from the courthouse until midafternoon"; and Holly Teeter, rejected by the ABA for her lack of trial judge experience.[74]

However, if some of Trump's nominees don't qualify for the federal bench, all of them qualify for the right-wing extremist Hall of Fame. One nominee, Mark Norris, suggested that being a Muslim is the same as being a terrorist. Jeff Mateer, nominated to the federal court in Texas, was forced to withdraw after declaring that transgender children were evidence of "Satan's plan." Another reject, Brett Talley, of KKK notoriety above, also blasted calls for gun safety legislation in the aftermath of the Sandy Hook

Elementary School shooting as "the greatest attack on our constitutional freedoms in our lifetime."[75]

Three more representative examples: Gordon Giampietro, nominated for the U.S. District Court for the Eastern District of Wisconsin, has called marriage equality "an assault on nature," considers calls for diversity "code for relaxed standards (moral and intellectual)," and claimed Justice Anthony Kennedy "went off the rails years ago" with his 2003 majority opinion in *Lawrence v. Texas,* which struck down Texas's sodomy law. People should simply "ignore Justice Anthony Kennedy's opinion," he wrote, "because it's not really legal reasoning."[76]

And Thomas Farr, Trump's pick for the United States District Court for the Eastern District of North Carolina, has a long history of promoting laws making it more difficult for African Americans to vote. He served as attorney for Jesse Helms's 1990 reelection campaign, which sent over one hundred thousand postcards to black voters in North Carolina with misleading information about voter qualifications. A letter signed by the Congressional Black Caucus argued that Trump couldn't have found an "attorney in North Carolina with a more hostile record on African American voting rights and workers' rights" if he tried.[77]

Then there's Michael Brennan, a white lawyer from Wisconsin who spent a large portion of his confirmation hearing avoiding answering the obvious question of whether racial bias exists in our justice system. Senator Cory Booker, among others, was livid. "To be nominating a federal judge who does not even acknowledge the persistent impact of race within our justice system," he said, "and doesn't even have a plan or thoughts on it, to me, is stunning and absolutely unacceptable, if not offensive." Brennan also never received a "blue slip" from Wisconsin senator Tammy Baldwin, in keeping with the long tradition of senators having a say over judges from their home state.[78]

In their mad rush to appoint more of Trump's unqualified nominees to lifetime seats on the judiciary, Senate Republicans simply threw that tradition out the window. Brennan was confirmed by the Senate in May 2018, and the others are on the way to becoming Trump judges, too. And there's many more rabid conservative ideologues waiting in the wings, since Trump, lazy as ever, has effectively outsourced his judicial picks to right-wing organizations like the Federalist Society and the Heritage Foundation. God save the courts![79]

22. HE'S BLOATED THE NATIONAL DEBT

Hey, friends, we must be getting old. Because we all remember the days when Democrats were big spenders and Republicans were deficit hawks. Or to be more precise, we remember the days when Republicans bragged about being deficit hawks while Democrats were in power but threw all spending constraints out the window once they took over.

So it was with Ronald Reagan and George W. Bush, and so it is with Donald Trump. There's a method in the madness, of course. It's a diabolical ploy unmasked by David Stockman, Reagan's budget director, as "starving the beast." First, rack up the biggest budget deficits you can. Then, use those deficits you've created as an excuse to cut social programs. In other words, spend as much as you can, leaving the government with less cash, then use the specter of huge deficits as a rationale to take away the benefits millions of Americans depend on.[80]

And nobody's been better at playing that game today than House Speaker Paul Ryan, who masquerades as a fiscal conservative. Shortly after he guided the GOP's budget-busting tax cuts through the House at the end of 2017, he let the cat out of the bag. "We're going to have to get back next year at entitlement reform," he said on talk radio, "which is how you tackle the debt and deficit." He should have added, "Which we just created more of."[81]

As it happened, they didn't get to entitlement reform, or anything else, in the first half of 2018. And Paul Ryan, seeing a blue wave rising in November, decided to call it quits and not run again. But he's still announced the basic GOP blueprint for his successor in the House.[82]

Under Donald Trump, Paul Ryan, and Mitch McConnell, it's so déjà vu, so all over again. But our kids and grandkids are the ones who will have to pay for it.

After building the wall, balancing the budget was something candidate Donald Trump—who bankrupted six companies and never balanced a budget in his life—promised in every speech and interview. "When you start cutting, you're gonna balance the budget—believe me, you're gonna balance the budget. So we have that," he told a campaign rally on October 3, 2015.[83]

"It can be done . . . It will take place, and it will go relatively quickly . . . If you have the right people, like, in the agencies and the various people that do the balancing . . . you can cut the numbers by two pennies and three pennies and balance a budget quickly and have a stronger and better country," he assured talk show host Sean Hannity on February 22, 2016.[84]

Trump actually promised not only to get rid of the deficit but to eliminate the country's then $20 trillion national debt over a period of eight years. If not, he told radio conspiracy nut Alex Jones, "we're not going to have a nation anymore."[85]

Once in the White House, Trump led the Republican Party over the fiscal cliff. It started with the GOP tax cut bill, which Trump called "the biggest tax cut in the history of our country." It wasn't. And which the White House argued would not add to the deficit. "The president is not going to sign something that he believes is going to increase the deficit," said Treasury secretary Steve Mnuchin. Except he did. And it did.[86]

According to the Congressional Budget Office, the tax cut bill will add $1.4 trillion to the deficit over the next ten years, which the administration insists will be more than paid for by greater economic growth resulting from tax cuts. The same promise George W. Bush made for his tax cuts, with no results.[87]

That was step one. In February 2018, step two was the bipartisan agreement to keep the government running for the next two years—which added another $300 billion in both defense and nonmilitary spending to the deficit. Trump readily embraced the plan.[88]

Step three was Trump's own 2019 budget, which adds a staggering $7.1 trillion to the national debt over the next decade. In their feeble attempts to defend their out-of-control spending, White House aides insisted the budget would reduce the debt by $3 trillion—but that's only if they are actually able to cut Medicare, Medicaid, and Social Security and only if they're able to achieve 3 percent annual economic growth. If not, the cost will be $10 trillion, not $7 trillion.[89]

On Wall Street, flamboyant real estate developer Donald Trump was so strung out on bank loans and IOUs he was known as the King of Debt. That title fits him in the White House, too. Burying American taxpayers in a mountain of debt, that's what he'll be remembered for.[90]

23. HE'S MADE INCOME INEQUALITY WORSE

President Obama called it "the defining challenge of our time." Pope Francis called it "the root of social evil." Canadian prime minister Justin Trudeau calls it "the staggering gap between the rich and the poor." Two-thirds of Americans believe it's a serious problem that should be addressed immediately and is only getting worse.[91]

Donald Trump probably doesn't even know what *income inequality* is, but he's already made it worse.

And, yes, this is the same man who campaigned as a billionaire who would fight hard for working-class Americans and raise taxes on the rich. The truth is, he doesn't give a rat's ass about anyone except his fellow millionaires and billionaires. They're the only people he knows, hangs out with, understands, and cares about.

It's a given that top-earning Americans have always cornered the lion's share of income, but in the last half century, their share has grown disproportionately. According to Vox, from 1979 to 2013, the share of after-tax income held by the top fifth of earners has grown by 6.5 percentage points, while the share held by the bottom fifth has dropped by 1.2 percentage points. Most of that growth, in fact, has been gobbled up by the top 1 percent.[92]

And that's the small, inordinately wealthy slice of Americans who benefits most from Donald Trump's tax cuts—which shrink taxes on corporations they own, cut taxes on "pass-through" businesses they control—Trump has a stake in over five hundred of them—and rolls back estate taxes lucky heirs and heiresses might have to pay on fortunes they did nothing to earn. Or, as they say, the rich get richer, and the poor get poorer.[93]

While it's true that, under Trump's plan, even middle-class Americans also get a (modest) tax cut, their break expires in 2025, while tax breaks for the wealthy continue. Economists predict that by 2027, a full 83 percent of tax cuts would go to the top 1 percent. Again, just further widening the already-wide income gap.[94]

Echoing arguments made since Ronald Reagan was president, Republicans claim that cutting taxes on corporations and the rich will boost everybody's income, because the results will "trickle down." But that has never happened with massive tax cuts before and won't happen now.

Almost every leading economist disputes that lame theory. Take, for example, UC–Berkeley economists Emmanuel Saez and Gabriel Zucman, who tracked growth and inequality over the last three decades. They conclude:

> Since 1980, taxes paid by the wealthy have fallen dramatically and income at the top of the distribution has boomed, but gains for the rest of the population have been paltry. Average national income per adult has grown by only 1.4 percent per year—a poor performance by both historical and international standards.
>
> As a result, the share of national income going to the top 1 percent has doubled from 10 percent to more than 20 percent, while income accrued by the bottom 50 percent has been almost halved, from 20 percent to 12.5 percent. There has been no growth at all in the average pretax income of the bottom half of the population over the past 40 years—during which trickle-down enthusiasts promised just the opposite.[95]

In other words, this is pure "voodoo economics," as George Herbert Walker Bush correctly called it before joining the Reagan ticket in 1980. Yet now Republicans are doing it all over again. They never learn. And we don't, either.

Ironically, the Trump tax cut bill passed within days of publication of the annual World Inequality Report, prepared by an international panel of economists, including Saez and Thomas Piketty, renowned author of *Capital in the Twenty-First Century*. Their report shows that "income inequality has increased in nearly all world regions in recent decades."[96]

But what it finds about the United States is most striking: The United States is a good deal more unequal than Europe and China; less so, but still more unequal than sub-Saharan Africa, the Middle East, India, and Brazil; and about even with Russia. In other words, more than almost any other nation on the planet, the wealthiest country allows its wealthiest to hoard most of its wealth.[97]

The adverse impact on the American economy is clear. Even though, on a per capita basis, the U.S. economy is more than twice as large as it was in 1973, the average working person, who works full-time, year-round, earns less today than in 1973, after adjusting for inflation. As long as the 1 percent reap most of the benefits, without the 99 percent earning their fair share, the economy will never perform 100 percent.[98]

In the last century, conservatives used to accuse liberals, a.k.a. "socialists," of wanting to "redistribute the wealth"—meaning to take money from the rich and give it to the poor.

Funny, they don't talk about that anymore. Maybe because they realize that the share of income going to the most affluent of American households has skyrocketed from about 9 percent in the 1970s to more than 20 percent in recent years. That's more than $1 trillion a year.[99]

We now have "redistribution of wealth," all right—from the poor to the rich.

24. HE'S DESTROYING HEALTH CARE

As noted previously (#12), Donald Trump is obsessed with overturning everything accomplished by Barack Obama. And, from the beginning, his number one obsession has been killing the Affordable Care Act, which everybody calls Obamacare.

Channeling Herman Melville, Obamacare is Trump's white whale. The irony is that, since he hasn't yet been able to do so, Obamacare is also Trump's bête noire.

Even as a candidate, Trump expressed a special disdain for Obamacare. True, he promised to build the wall and balance the budget. But Obamacare? He promised to end Obamacare—on day one! While he hasn't succeeded so far, it's not because he and congressional Republicans haven't tried. And tried. And tried.[100]

For all their reputation as being masters of the legislative process, when it came down to repealing Obamacare, House Speaker Paul Ryan and Senate majority leader Mitch McConnell looked more like the Keystone Cops. Even President Trump publicly expressed his frustration at their incompetence in delivering what Republicans had been promising for seven years, if only they could retake the House and Senate. But their efforts to do so were a series of fumbles.[101]

First up was Ryan's baby, a so-called repeal-and-replace bill in the House. But unable to round up enough votes for his own plan, the Speaker was forced to admit defeat and pull the bill on March 24, 2017.[102]

House Republicans went back to the drawing board, made major concessions to the Freedom Caucus, and narrowly approved a repeal-and-replace bill, 217–213, on May 4. But everybody predicted it would be DOA in the Senate, which turned out to be the case.[103]

After struggling unsuccessfully for nearly two months to line up enough votes for their own repeal-and-replace bill, Senate Republicans decided to go for "repeal only." When that vote failed on July 26, McConnell scrambled to put together an emergency, "skinny repeal" bill—but that, too, went down in flames. Late on July 27, John McCain's dramatic thumbs-down meant three Republican senators (along with Susan Collins and Lisa Murkowski) opposed the bill, giving Democrats enough votes to save Obamacare once again.[104]

In a concession speech on the Senate floor, McConnell said, "It is time to move on." Yet some still weren't willing to give up. Senators Lindsey Graham and Bill Cassidy came up with yet a third repeal bill. When it became clear in September that it would also fail to get sixty votes, Senate Republicans threw in the towel. Congressional efforts to repeal Obamacare—again, which Republicans for seven long years had declared over and over again was their top priority—were dead. When some die-hard congressional Republicans contemplated reviving Obamacare repeal in the summer of 2018, a Trump senior official told *The Daily Beast* it was a "suicide mission."[105]

But as the legislative circus dragged on, Trump was doing everything he could by executive action to undermine the Affordable Care Act and discourage people from enrolling. As *Politico* reported on "Trump's War of Attrition on Obamacare" in July 2017, "the administration slashed the advertising budget for new sign-ups by 90 percent, halved the 2018 enrollment period, and churned out anti-Obamacare propaganda to share on social media."[106]

At the same time, Trump also signed an executive order expanding so-called association health plans, short-term plans offered by, say, the U.S. Chamber of Commerce or a consortium of small businesses that can avoid normal state regulations—and exempting them from Obamacare's rules. And he ended billions of dollars in subsidy payments to insurance companies made available under the Affordable Care Act in order to lower deductibles and out-of-pocket costs for lower-income Americans. Without those subsidies, insurers will be forced to charge higher premiums.[107]

Trump still wasn't finished. He insisted that the GOP tax cut bill include repeal of Obamacare's individual mandate, allowing him to crow at its signing, "In this bill, not only do we have massive tax cuts and tax reform, we have essentially repealed Obamacare, and we'll come up with something that will be much better. Obamacare has been repealed in this bill."[108]

Big surprise: Trump was lying yet again. It wasn't repealed, but by canceling the individual mandate, Trump will have caused as many as thirteen million Americans to lose the health protection they had secured for their families, many for the first time, under Obamacare.[109]

The Republicans' "death by a thousand cuts" strategy made another slash a few months later. As part of the bipartisan plan adopted in January 2018 to keep the government running, Congress further weakened Obamacare by suspending three taxes it depended on for funding: the so-called Cadillac tax on high-value health plans, a 2.3 percent levy on medical devices, and the health insurance tax—three cuts the Joint Committee on Taxation projected would add $31.3 billion to the federal deficit over the next several years.[110]

Then Trump tried another tack. In June 2018, Department of Justice lawyers argued before a federal court that, because the Republican tax cuts had repealed the individual mandate, now other critical elements of the Affordable Care Act were unconstitutional—including the provision protecting Americans with preexisting conditions. As of this writing, the case is not settled, but Trump and Sessions are still going out of their way to see reforms that benefit roughly half the country be destroyed.[111]

And yet, despite all that, Obamacare is not dead. Nor is it, as Trump so often claims, in a "death spiral." Obamacare is drastically weakened but still very much alive. A surprisingly large number of people signed up for coverage for 2018. Enrollment was only about 5 percent below last year's total; 8.8 million signed up in market exchanges, and an additional 7 million Americans are now covered by Medicaid under the Affordable Care Act. There's life in the old dog yet. And the funny thing is, as polls have shown, even Republicans like the provisions of Obamacare . . . when it's called the *Affordable Care Act* (or, as in Kentucky before Republicans killed the state exchange, *Kynect*). This conservatives well know—which is why they've taken to constantly calling it Obamacare in the first place.[112]

Meanwhile, in their zeal to deny Americans health care, Donald Trump and congressional Republicans didn't stop at Obamacare. They also played hostage games with the Children's Health Insurance Program, or CHIP.

CHIP should be celebrated as the ideal government program. It's bipartisan, created by Senators Ted Kennedy and Orrin Hatch. It's been around since 1997. And it's successful. Working with states, it provides health insurance to nine million children, giving the United States health coverage for 95 percent of our kids.[113]

What's not to like about it? You'd think it would get universal bipartisan support when its funding ran out in October 2017. But such was not the case. Instead, Republicans decided to play politics with it as part of the debate over Obamacare.

At first, they tied any extension of CHIP to massive cuts in Obamacare and Medicare. When that failed, they used CHIP as a bargaining chip in immigration reform. Democrats had to choose, they said, between CHIP or protection for the DREAMers (see #17). They couldn't have both. Mitch McConnell even posted a ransom note on Twitter pitting the nine million kids receiving CHIP against the seven hundred thousand DREAMers. "Senate Democrats have a choice to make," he sniveled like a Bond villain. "This should be a no brainer . . ."[114]

In the end, Congress opted for CHIP. While the DREAMers remain in limbo, Congress agreed to extend CHIP for six years. But there's no doubt Donald Trump would have let it die if that was the price for killing Obamacare. After all, taking health care away from kids is old hat for Donald Trump. This is the same man who, to spite the family of his dead brother, once sued to cut off health care for his grandnephew with cerebral palsy.[115]

25. HE'S AFTER MEDICARE, MEDICAID, AND SOCIAL SECURITY

Building a wall . . . repealing Obamacare . . . balancing the budget . . . We've seen a string of broken campaign promises from Donald Trump so far.

To which, add another one from May 2015: "I was the first and only potential GOP candidate to state there will be no cuts to Social Security, Medicare & Medicaid. Huckabee copied me."[116]

Again, promise made, promise broken. The 2018 budget proposal Trump sent to Congress would cut all three programs, the backbone of our American social safety net, by billions of dollars.[117]

In a sense, this is the other shoe dropping. As we saw with #22, Trump's first move was to rack up ever higher deficits by giving massive tax cuts to the rich. Now he cuts programs that benefit working- and middle-class families to pay for those tax cuts. Taken together, these cuts would only create more poverty and hardship and swell the ranks of the uninsured.

First, Medicare. As ThinkProgress explained in February 2018, the Trump budget proposes "reforming" Medicare by "changing the way patients are reimbursed for post-acute care, making it harder for physicians to refer patients to other providers, and limiting hospital payments associated with early discharge to hospices." Bottom line: existing Medicare benefits cut $554 billion.[118]

Note: Trump would still not enable Medicare to negotiate directly with pharmaceutical companies for lower prescription drug prices, breaking still another oft-repeated campaign promise.

As for Medicaid: Again under guise of "reform," Trump rewards states for pulling out of the Medicaid expansion encouraged under Obamacare, in part by imposing a Medicaid per capita cap and shifting to block grants to states. Bottom line: $1.1 trillion in cuts, fewer services, in ten years.[119]

And Social Security. The Trump budget would not only cut Social Security, it would cut programs for the most vulnerable of Social Security recipients—the disabled—to the tune of $72 billion in cuts over the next decade.[120]

And, by the way, to prove that he never gives up his number one obsession, the Trump budget also includes the full repeal of Obamacare.

In addition, the Republicans' tax plan officially embraces the concept of "chained CPI," a narrower way of calculating inflation that, if applied to Social Security in the future, could mean billions of dollars in cuts out of the pockets of America's elderly. Policy writer David Dayen called chained CPI a "Trojan horse" that is "intentionally confusing and obscure" and "puts Social Security under threat."

"If it goes through unchecked," he warns, "the slippery slope to impoverishing seniors will get coated in grease."[121]

Of course, while the tax plan is now law, the Trump budget as presented to Congress may not ever be approved. No president's budget is. But there are other ways in which Trump is already gutting Medicaid by executive action.

First, contrary to the policies of previous Republican and Democratic presidents, the Trump administration is encouraging states to impose some kind of work requirement on Medicaid recipients. In other words, it's not enough to be living in or near poverty, the current test. You must also have a job or prove you've been trying to get one.[122]

Which, health care experts point out, is both unnecessary and cruel. Unnecessary, because the vast majority of Medicaid recipients who can work already have jobs. Cruel, because those who don't are either elderly, disabled, retired, sick, or caring for a loved one.

In its December 2017 study of Michigan's Medicaid program, for example, *The Journal of the American Medical Association,* or *JAMA,* found that nearly half of Medicaid enrollees were already working. One-quarter were unable to work or were retired, in school, or acting as homemaker. And many of the 27.6 percent who were "out of work" had obstacles to finding a job: a chronic physical illness, mental illness, or some serious mental or physical condition. They weren't just "lazy bums who refuse to get a job," as Republicans assert.[123]

Nevertheless, Medicaid work requirement plans submitted by Arkansas, Kentucky, and Indiana were quickly approved by the Trump HHS, and several others are pending.

Worse, wherever they can, statehouse Republicans have been trying out additional cruel and demented variations on this terrible idea. In their version, Michigan Republicans exempted people who live in counties with more than 8.5 percent unemployment from the onerous work requirements—which sounds great, until you realize that, in effect and by design, it protects rural white counties, where rates are higher, and punishes urban black ones.[124]

In several other states, meanwhile, Republicans tried to put a lifetime limit on Medicaid—which means millions of America's poor will lose their health care protection. In the past, no state has ever put a limit on how long a person can receive Medicaid benefits. But Arizona and Utah want to adopt a lifetime limit of five years. Wisconsin, four years. Kansas, three years. Maine wants to limit its coverage to three months in any thirty-six-month period.[125]

Thankfully, this, for now, has been deemed a bridge too far; Trump's Centers for Medicare and Medicaid Services administrator Seema Verma rejected the Kansas plan in May 2018. When you're too cruel for Trump-world, that's saying something.[126]

Nonetheless, between budget cuts, chained CPI, and work requirements, Trump has already smashed yet another of his key campaign planks. "Save Medicare, Medicaid, and Social Security without cuts. Have to do it," candidate Donald Trump said on June 16, 2015. Too bad President Trump doesn't remember a word of what candidate Trump promised.[127]

26. HE'S SHREDDING THE SOCIAL SAFETY NET

To take another example, Donald Trump campaigned for president as a populist. But nothing unmasks him more as a fake populist than his attempts to destroy the social safety net, starting with the food stamp program.

Food stamps—now known as the Supplemental Nutrition Assistance Program, or SNAP—is one of the government's most successful, efficient, and cost-effective programs. It prevents about forty-six million low-income Americans, almost a sixth of the population, from falling into hunger. It's not a steady drain on the federal budget; it expands or shrinks, depending on the demand. People sign up when they need it, drop it when they need it no longer. It's available everywhere. It's cheap: The average food stamp benefit works out to be about $1.40 per meal. And 93 percent of every dollar actually goes to providing food to beneficiaries, which makes it one of the least wasteful federal bureaucracies.[128]

In fact, as Sasha Abramsky put it in *The New Yorker,* "SNAP is the single biggest reason why malnutrition has largely vanished from the United States."[129]

But Donald Trump looked at SNAP and said to himself, *This program looks too good to be true. There must be something wrong with it.* (In fact, his 2011 book made up a "food stamp crime wave" that had no basis in reality.) *So, let's get rid of it.* Which he's trying very hard to do, in two ways.[130]

First, in his 2019 budget, Trump proposed cutting the food stamp budget by $213 billion over ten years and imposing more stringent work requirements on recipients, even though most of them already have jobs.[131]

Then, in one of his craziest ideas yet, Trump decided he would make up for the cuts in food stamp money by giving everybody a monthly "America's Harvest Box," consisting of "100 percent U.S.-grown and produced food." In other words, instead of giving people the equivalent of cash so they can buy what they need, the government will tell them what to eat: whatever's in that week's box—mainly processed food in cans, tins, and jars.[132]

There's one other problem, of course. The whole box project rests on the unlikely premise that the federal government, which never managed to successfully deliver premade meals to Puerto Ricans after Hurricane Maria, will somehow deliver boxes of fresh foods to millions of American households each week. Who are they kidding?

Even though Trump's absurd subscription box fig leaf for deep SNAP cuts received the most media attention, it was only one aspect of Donald Trump's assault on the social safety net, which tens of millions of low-income Americans depend on for survival.

By way of the Center on Budget Policy and Priorities, other programs targeted by Trump for deep cuts or elimination include:

- Section 8 Housing—successfully providing subsidies for affordable housing for low-income families since 1937. Trump raises rents on existing stock and cuts funding for repairs by 47 percent.

- Temporary Assistance for Needy Families (TANF)—provides short-term income assistance, work programs, and other support for poor families with children. Trump cuts it by $21 billion over the next decade.

- Workforce Innovation and Opportunity Act (WIOA)—provides employment and training services for dislocated adult and youth workers. Trump cuts the budget from $2.7 billion to $1.6 billion.

- Supplemental Educational Opportunity Grant (SEOG)— supplements Pell Grants for some 1.5 million needy students. Trump eliminates the program. Who needs college anyway?

- Low Income Home Energy Assistance Program (LIHEAP)— helps over six million low-income households pay their home energy bill. Trump eliminates the program. In other words, the rich get tax breaks while the poor freeze in winter.

- Senior Community Service Employment Program (SCSEP)— gives low-income, unemployed people over age fifty-five work experience in community service activities. Trump eliminates the program (even though he wants everyone to work for their Medicaid coverage and Harvest Boxes).[133]

Collectively, cuts to these essential programs hurt those who need help the most. They are all targeted at the very people candidate Donald Trump said would be his priority: those left behind by today's economy or living in distressed urban or rural communities. Of course, Trump forgot them once he arrived in the White House, because he never cared about them in the first place.

In the 2000 presidential primary, candidate George W. Bush, campaigning as a "compassionate conservative," criticized his fellow Republicans for trying to "balance their budget on the backs of the poor."[134]

That message was completely lost on Donald Trump.

27. HE'S UNDERMINED PROTECTIONS FOR LGBTQ AMERICANS

Along with pretending to care about the needs of the most vulnerable, there was another issue Donald Trump occasionally ran on as if he weren't a textbook conservative: LGBTQ rights.

While he began his campaign declaring he was "very much a traditional man" on same-sex marriage—some journalists pointed out he must love traditional marriage, because he's had three of them—he soon seemed to loosen up on the trail. After all, he came from New York City. He had many gay friends. He had even attended a "beautiful" same-sex wedding.[135]

When controversy broke about North Carolina's so-called bathroom law, prohibiting transgender women from using the women's bathroom, Trump tried to have it both ways. At first, he said the law was unnecessary but insisted North Carolina had the right to enact it—no profile in courage but still more tolerant than what we heard from Mike Pence.[136]

So, it was presumed Trump would offer a relatively gay-friendly administration, but once again, he fooled everybody. Having sworn his allegiance to evangelicals, and they to him, he proceeded to turn back the clock on gay rights.

Despite his remarks on the bathroom law as a candidate, he took essentially the same action at the federal level, rescinding protections put into place by President Obama that allowed transgender students to use bathrooms matching their gender identity.[137]

In May 2017, Trump signed a "religious liberty" executive order that many read as allowing faith-based organizations to use their faith as an excuse to discriminate against LGBTQ Americans.[138]

Under Trump, Pride Month lost any official recognition. Under Obama, June was National Pride Month, and the White House, in a stirring civil rights moment, was lit up like a rainbow. In 2017 and 2018, it wasn't. Trump refused to recognize it and never mentioned gay rights, or pride, the entire month and did not, unlike Obama, issue a Pride Month proclamation.

Then, in July—hard to believe in the twenty-first century until you remember Jefferson Beauregard Sessions—the Trump Justice Department ruled that today's civil rights laws do not protect employees from discrimination based on sexual orientation, only on the color of their skin. In other words, according to Trump, you can now legally get fired from any job just because you're gay or lesbian. A giant step backward.

All of which led up to Trump's most anti-LGBTQ move: a tweet out of the blue on July 26, 2017—a tweet not even the secretary of defense knew was coming—announcing a ban on transgender people serving in the military. He ordered the Pentagon to stop accepting any new transgender recruits while figuring out what to do with the fifteen thousand transgender troops now serving in the military. (For their part, the Pentagon said they weren't going to do anything based on a tweet and wanted to see an actual policy memo first.)[139]

Why would he do such a hateful thing, without even consulting the Pentagon? For one, and as we'll discuss more later, Trump always likes to stir the culture wars pot when he's worried about his poll numbers. For another, he's Donald J. Trump. He has never missed a chance to be an asshole. As one White House official put it, summing up Trump's opinion, "It'll be fun to watch [Democrats] defend this."[140]

But, in the end, it wasn't just Democrats. After three different federal judges ruled Trump's executive ban unconstitutional, the military continues to accept transgender recruits and transgender troops remain still on duty.

So Trump lost that round, but not for lack of trying. And just as with the Muslim ban, he decided to try again. Urged on by Vice President Mike Pence, who reportedly coopted Secretary of Defense Jim Mattis's report on the subject calling for inclusiveness, and other "Christian" (read: homophobic) allies at the Heritage Foundation and Family Research Council, Trump announced a revised ban on transgender individuals in the military, with some minor qualifications this time, in March 2018.[141]

The courts were not fooled. The following month, a U.S. district judge upheld the earlier injunction against this revised ban, while another district judge denied the Trump administration's attempt to block a legal challenge to it. As of this writing, round two continues.[142]

Meanwhile, true to form, on December 29, 2017, Trump ended his first year in office by first firing all members of the Presidential Advisory Council on HIV/AIDS (PACHA), created by President Bill Clinton in 1995 and continued by Presidents Bush and Obama—and then disbanding the entire council. Earlier, six members had resigned from the council because, as they told *Newsweek*, "Trump doesn't care about HIV. We're outta here."[143]

By that time, the Log Cabin Republicans felt vindicated. Since its founding in California in the late 1970s, the Log Cabin group has been the leading gay rights advocacy organization in the Republican Party. They exist to endorse and elect gay-friendly Republicans at every level. But in 2016, even after Donald Trump won the Republican nomination, they refused to endorse him—the first time in twelve years they failed to endorse the GOP nominee.[144]

He made vague promises about protecting gay rights, they acknowledged, but in the end, following President Reagan's favorite Russian maxim "trust, but verify," they just didn't trust Donald Trump to do the right thing. And they were right.[145]

28. HE HASN'T FILLED KEY JOB SLOTS

When somebody runs for president, you assume they want to do the job, if elected. Apparently not Donald Trump.

One of any president's first jobs is to fill the thousands of key positions necessary to keep the government running smoothly. Not Donald Trump.

We will talk about the disaster he's made of the State Department in particular later. But even aside from State, Trump has not only put some monumentally unqualified people in important posts, he has failed to nominate anyone for hundreds of positions—leaving many agencies woefully understaffed.

The numbers tell the story. There are some 1,100 top government jobs that require Senate confirmation. Yet, as tracked by *The Washington Post,* seven months into his administration, President Trump had only nominated 277 people to those posts, and only 124 had been confirmed by the Senate. That's compared to 433 nominated and 310 confirmed for President Obama.[146]

NPR took another look at progress in late November 2017 and found there were still 256 key posts for which the president hadn't nominated anyone.[147]

Indeed, the White House Transition Project found that Trump's pace in staffing the government was the slowest in forty years.[148]

Again, it was the State Department that was hardest hit. As of October 2017, over half of State Department positions requiring Senate confirmation still didn't have a nominee. There was no nominee for ambassador to Egypt, Jordan, Saudi Arabia, Qatar, or Turkey. There was no assistant secretary for arms control or assistant secretary for international security and nonproliferation. And, at a time when Trump himself was threatening war on the Korean Peninsula, we had no ambassador to South Korea and no assistant secretary for East Asian and Pacific affairs.[149]

The pace never picked up. At the five hundred–day mark of Trump's administration in June 2018, the nonpartisan Partnership for Public Service reported that 204 positions requiring Senate confirmation remained unfilled, the slowest pace in at least six administrations. Among the empty spots were thirteen inspectors general, who could theoretically oversee any malfeasance occurring in Trump's federal departments.[150]

For Donald Trump, this is no problem. He insists he's not filling these positions on purpose. It's part of his goal of "draining the swamp."

"I'm generally not going to make a lot of the appointments that would normally be—because you don't need them," he told *Forbes* magazine. "I mean, you look at some of these agencies, how massive they are, and it's totally unnecessary. They have hundreds of thousands of people."[151]

The issue is, absent presidential nominees, those positions are usually filled temporarily by long-term federal bureaucrats who are only interested in business as usual. If Trump really wanted to "drain the swamp," you'd think he'd appoint his own people to shake things up.

There's one other problem. By law, posts requiring Senate confirmation can only be held temporarily for three hundred days. That deadline has long passed. Which means that any decision made by Trump's fill-in employees in any agency could be challenged as illegal.[152]

One thing for sure. In this case, Trump can't blame the Senate for not acting. Republicans control the Senate. As evidenced by his shoddy choice of judges, they're ready to rubber-stamp almost anybody Trump sends up. But they can't confirm until he nominates.

What Trump doesn't seem to understand is that sorely understaffed federal agencies not only hurt the American people who are not receiving service they need from the government; in the end, it hurts Trump most of all, because it makes it harder to get things done and accomplish his goals. But apparently, he just doesn't care.

29. HE'S WAGING A WAR ON WEED

In January 2018, Vermont became the ninth state, plus the District of Columbia, to legalize the recreational use of marijuana and the first state to do so legislatively. After legalizing recreational use in 2014, Colorado had reaped more than $500 million in tax revenue from marijuana by mid-July 2017. By the end of 2017, six in ten Americans favored legalization. At this rate, it won't be long before pot is legal nationwide. When that happens, according to one recent study, it could mean $132 billion in federal tax revenue and more than a million new American jobs by 2025.[153]

But not if Donald Trump and Jeff Sessions have anything to do with it. They're determined to reverse the trend. So much for conservatives supporting "states' rights." They've declared war on weed.

It's a classic case of federal versus state law. At the federal level, cannabis is still classified as a Schedule 1 drug, with criminal penalties, even though several states have legalized its use. So what's the federal government's response?[154]

Under President Obama, the Justice Department took a states' rights position: As long as states followed some basic rules, like keeping pot out of the hands of teenagers and preventing export to other states, the feds would keep their distance.[155]

Jeff Sessions has reversed that policy, angering legislators from both parties. No matter what states decide, DOJ will continue to enforce federal laws against pot use in every state and expects states to cooperate. Which means federal agents could raid pot outlets in Colorado, Washington, California, Oregon, Vermont, and four other states and shut them down, even though the operation was perfectly legal under state law.[156]

Republican senator Cory Gardner of Colorado was so livid at Sessions's move that he placed a hold on all Department of Justice nominations. At the very least, the new Sessions policy will cause confusion and uncertainty in the expanding marijuana industry. Is it safe to begin a pot business? Is it too risky an investment? Can you get a bank loan?[157]

This war on pot should not come as a surprise from Sessions, who has long opposed the use of marijuana even for medicinal purposes. But it will probably force Congress to act in one of two ways—either to make pot legal nationwide (which is unlikely), or to prevent federal agents from interfering in states that have approved the recreational use of pot, just as Congress has already restricted DOJ from interfering in states that have approved its medicinal use.[158]

If there's any surprise, it's that Donald Trump would let Jeff Sessions lead him down this no-win path. There is no turning back the clock on marijuana. In Gallup's most recent poll, 64 percent of American adults, including a majority of Republicans, back legalization. And as the plaintiffs in a lawsuit to compel the government to legalize weed recently pointed out, they're not the first enthusiasts. Many of our Founding Fathers, including Washington, Jefferson, and Madison, farmed hemp for various (non-smoking) uses.[159]

But, at least for now, when it comes to pot, Donald Trump is on the wrong side of popular opinion and history.

30. HE'S BRANDED THE MEDIA AS THE ENEMY

Funny thing about Donald Trump: He is 100 percent a creation of the media. He could never have run for president were he not a TV B-list celebrity, hosting NBC's *The Apprentice* for fourteen years. He would never have been elected if cable television hadn't given him far more TV exposure and far more favorable treatment than any other Republican in the 2016 primary and Hillary Clinton in the general election.

No doubt, Donald Trump would not be where he is today without the media. And yet, both during his campaign and since he's been in the White House, he's done nothing but brutally attack them in ways that are unbecoming of America's president and even dangerous.

Unfortunately, Trump is not just some loudmouth in a bar. He's the president of the United States. His negative comments about the media have had serious consequences on press freedoms worldwide and been condemned by the Committee to Protect Journalists, one of the world's most prestigious journalistic organizations.[160]

What a contrast. In his first year in office, Barack Obama was awarded the Nobel Peace Prize. In his first year, Donald Trump was named "the world's most oppressive leader toward press freedom" by the committee. Trump actually edged out Turkey's Recep Tayyip Erdoğan and Russia's Vladimir Putin as "winner" of the organization's top prize for "overall achievement in undermining global press freedom."[161]

It's one honor Donald Trump richly deserves.

Attacking the media, of course, was the hallmark of the Trump campaign for president and the highlight of every campaign rally. He not only banned certain reporters from covering events, he pointed out others he considered unfriendly by name. Journalists in attendance were confined to roped-in pens where Trump would point them out and urge the crowd to express their displeasure. Hostility grew to the point where many news organizations hired security to accompany their reporters to campaign rallies—a new first, and a new low, for American politics.[162]

Trump took his hatred of the media with him into the White House, undermining both the First Amendment and our nation's highest office with his adoption of two favorite phrases, both with scary historical precedents.

It's probably impossible to keep track of all of Trump's crazy anti-media tweets, and there is no room to list them all here. But according to the Trump Twitter Archive (yes, someone's actually archiving all his nonsense), by October 31, 2017, Trump had tweeted about the media being nothing but "fake news" 141 times. And he hasn't stopped since.[163]

In his world, of course, "fake news" is not just "news" as reported that is simply not true. That rarely, rarely happens—and, when it does, it is immediately retracted and corrected by any reputable news organizations. No, to Donald Trump "fake news" is any news story that is in any way critical of his administration or does not portray him in glowing terms.

It's his deliberate way of sowing distrust in the media writ large, which is the same tactic and similar language to that used by Hitler to undermine the media. Where Hitler said "*Lügenpresse*" (lying press), Trump says "fake news."[164]

But it wasn't long before Trump made it even uglier. On February 17, 2017, he tweeted: "The FAKE NEWS media (failing @nytimes, @NBCNews, @ABC, @CBS, @CNN) is not my enemy. It is the enemy of the American people!"[165]

Whoa! Members of the Fourth Estate are committing treason? Those practicing a sacred right enshrined in the First Amendment to the Constitution were the "enemy of the American people"? That statement—from the president of the United States—sent chills through anybody who believed in a democratic society. And again, it carried ominous historical meaning. As Republican senator Jeff Flake of Arizona felt compelled to note on the Senate floor, "enemy of the people" is the same phrase used by Joseph Stalin against the media during his murderous purge of the Russian people.[166]

But, of course, Trump didn't stop with his tweets and hate rallies. He repeatedly attacked journalists by name, calling, for example, Chuck Todd of *Meet the Press* a "sleeping son of a bitch" in March 2018.[167]

He demanded that certain reporters and anchors be fired, like Dave Weigel of *The Washington Post,* Andy Lack of NBC, and Jemele Hill of ESPN.[168]

He threatened to revoke the FCC licenses of news outlets whose reporting he didn't like.[169]

He called for tougher libel laws to intimidate journalists.[170]

And in January 2018, he handed out his own "Fake News Awards," which, no surprise, went to CNN, *The New York Times,* ABC, *The Washington Post, Time,* and *Newsweek*—who just happen to provide the most substantive coverage of the Trump administration.[171]

Trump, in fact, considers everything in the media "fake news" except for *Fox & Friends,* which he watches and tweets about religiously every morning. But not everybody at Fox is a fan of Trump's war on the media. Chris Wallace, host of *Fox News Sunday,* said in a speech that "President Trump is engaged in the most direct, sustained assault on the free press in our history."[172]

And there's no doubt that Trump's sustained assault on the media has had its impact. First, here in the United States, by eroding public confidence in the media. A fall 2017 *Politico* poll found that 46 percent of voters believe major news organizations simply make up stories about Donald Trump.[173]

But it's also had serious consequences around the world. As Senator John McCain pointed out, several hard-line, dictatorial leaders "are already using his words as cover as they silence and shutter one of the key pillars of democracy." After all, if Donald Trump can get away with dismissing any media criticism as "fake news," so can they.[174]

Even after his own many battles with an unfavorable press, Thomas Jefferson famously affirmed, "Were it left to me to decide whether we should have a government without newspapers or newspapers without a government, I should not hesitate a moment to prefer the latter."[175]

Too bad nobody told Donald Trump.

31. HE'S CREATED A STATE-RUN MEDIA

But here's the ultimate irony about Donald Trump: The man who's always complaining about television news can't turn it off. While he said it was a "false story" in the "failing NY Times," reports indicate he watches more television in one day than most people watch in a week.[176]

And there's no secret what channel he's watching. You don't have to guess. He'll proudly tell you. He tweets about it. His TV fix is a steady diet of Fox News. It's his "Home on the Range"—where "seldom is heard a discouraging word, and the skies are not cloudy all day."

Indeed, if you're not watching Fox News yourself, as Matt Gertz of Media Matters for America pointed out in his six-month study of Trump's Twitter habits, you have a hard time understanding Trump's tweets. Which, again, he made no bones about.

We already discussed the momentary panic early one morning in December 2017 when Trump, based on something he saw on *Fox & Friends*, abruptly announced his opposition to legislation extending the timeline of the FISA court—a GOP-sponsored bill scheduled for a vote in Congress later that day and which the White House had told House Speaker Paul Ryan just the evening before that the president fully supported.[177]

Another bizarre firestorm erupted at 4:50 a.m. on Friday morning, March 2, when, apparently and completely out of the blue, POTUS tweeted out a blast at "Alex [*sic*]" Baldwin and his "dieing [*sic*]" career, snidely observing that if it was painful for Baldwin to play DJT on *Saturday Night Live,* it was even more painful to watch.[178]

Yes, Alec (!) Baldwin had, indeed, created a sensation with his *SNL* portrayal of Trump, but he's been playing him since 2016. Where did that tweet come from?

Where else? *Fox & Friends* had just run a story about a recent comment of Baldwin's about how tough it was to play Trump but how willing he was to continue as long as it got under Trump's skin. And their "audience of one" couldn't resist resurrecting the feud.[179]

It was about this time that *Fox & Friends* put out word that they were looking for a new producer. What an incredible opportunity. As several pointed out—given the show's ability to set the daily agenda and priorities for the president of the United States—that was probably the most powerful position in the world! Not for nothing did Israeli prime minister Bibi Netanyahu go on *Fox & Friends* in May 2018 to push an end to the Iran nuclear deal. He knew exactly who was always watching—the one man he wanted to reach.[180]

Trump's echo chamber exists with other Fox shows, too—notably Sean Hannity. When Trump fired James Comey, for example, Hannity said the real story was that now the Justice Department was free to forget about Russia and reopen the investigation into Hillary Clinton's emails and put her behind bars at last—the same argument Trump made over and over again on Twitter.[181]

No kidding. You sometimes wonder: Who's really running the country? Donald Trump? The morning trio of Steve Doocy, Brian Kilmeade, and Ainsley Earhardt? Or Sean Hannity? Usually when somebody says the TV is talking directly to them, you'd think they're off their rocker. But Donald Trump kinda has a point.

Indeed, Fox News today is as close as we've ever come to something Donald Trump would like to see: total state-run media. Fox is nothing more than an extension of the Trump White House—which, in turn, is nothing more than the Washington headquarters of Fox. That's why, even as he calls all the other networks "fake news," Trump has praised Fox's "amazing reporting" and called it "MUCH more important in the United States than CNN."[182]

Whatever you think of *Fox & Friends,* in the end, it's a lousy way to govern.

32. HE'S LIMITING ACCESS TO THE INTERNET

If there's one idea that has almost universal, bipartisan support today, it's net neutrality: the idea that everything on the internet should be equally accessible to all adults. A nonpartisan December 2017 poll found net neutrality was supported by 89 percent of Democrats, 86 percent of independents, and 75 percent of Republicans.[183]

It's a concept as all-American as the highway. We decide where we want to go. We don't want anybody else deciding that for us or telling us that some of us have to poke along in the slow lane while others breeze by us in the fast lane.

Keep your hands off our highways, and keep your hands off our internet. That's what most Americans believe and want—universal access to all sites; no restrictions on what you could download or when; no speed limits on getting to certain sites and not others. And that's what federal rules, adopted in 2015, required.

But, no matter how popular, there was only one problem with those net neutrality rules: They were adopted under President Barack Obama. Therefore, in Donald Trump's rubric, they had to go.

On December 14, 2017, the newly constituted Trump FCC voted 3–2 to abandon net neutrality and transfer control of the internet from public users to the three big internet service providers, or ISPs: Verizon, Comcast, and AT&T. Trump himself had sealed the deal by naming as the new FCC chairman Ajit Pai, a former Verizon corporate lawyer and longtime opponent of net neutrality.[184]

Trump's new rules are not only anticonsumer; they will inevitably saddle internet users with higher fees. As FCC commissioner Mignon Clyburn lamented, "What saddens me is that the agency that is supposed to protect you is abandoning you."[185]

More significantly, the Trump rules are also antidemocratic. In fact, John Nichols of *The Nation* denounced them as "the most brutal blow to Democracy yet." Why? Because the internet today is the key to political activism and organizing—by people on all sides of every issue.[186]

Without the internet, there would have been no Occupy Wall Street movement, no Black Lives Matter, no #MeToo campaign, no March for Our Lives. The corporate ISPs could have shut them all down or certainly made them much more difficult or impossible to organize by throttling internet access. Democratic congressman Ro Khanna, who represents Silicon Valley, warned that without a free and open internet, American innovation will suffer, too.[187]

Is that the end of it? Does abandonment of net neutrality by Trump's FCC mean the end of the internet as we know it? Not yet. The new rules met immediate opposition on several fronts.

By January 16, 2018, twenty-one states and the District of Columbia had filed a lawsuit to block imposition of anti–net neutrality rules. They accused the FCC of ignoring 99 percent of public comments in opposition to their proposed reversal of net neutrality. And, without waiting for the courts, several states already took action on their own.[188]

The new FCC order bans states and cities from adopting rules on broadband providers that contradict its plan. Thankfully, that's being ignored. In March 2018, Washington became the first state to pass its own net neutrality rules. Governors in several other states, including New York, Hawaii, New Jersey, Montana, and Vermont, signed executive orders upholding net neutrality as well. Other states are considering laws banning ISPs from applying new FCC rules in their jurisdiction or allowing only ISPs that still adhere to net neutrality to do business in their state.[189]

Meanwhile, Democratic members of Congress vowed to use the Congressional Review Act—the same law used by Republicans to scuttle dozens of Obama-approved regulations—to overturn the FCC's initiative and return to net neutrality. With three Republican senators crossing over to join Democrats, the Senate voted 52–47 to override the FCC and restore net neutrality in May 2018—but, for now, that resolution is going nowhere in the Republican-controlled House.[190]

Nonetheless, the fight for a free internet is not over.

33. HE LEFT PUERTO RICO FOR DEAD

"This is an island surrounded by water. Big water. Ocean water."[191]

That was Donald Trump's defense of his administration's dismally inadequate response to Puerto Rico in the wake of Hurricane Maria, a response that left thousands of Americans dead and the island in a permanent state of catastrophe. He seemed as surprised to discover that Puerto Rico was an island—and thus impossible to drive relief trucks to—as he was to discover that Puerto Ricans were also American citizens.

Whatever the reason, while FEMA did a relatively good job aiding residents of Texas and Gulf states after Hurricane Harvey and Florida after Hurricane Irma, it totally failed to anticipate or respond adequately to the devastation caused by Hurricane Maria in Puerto Rico.

Trump's comments and behavior following Maria made things even worse. Before traveling there, he blamed the people of Puerto Rico for their own misfortune, tweeting that a "financial crisis looms largely of their own making," as a result of which "all infrastructure was disaster before hurricanes." He also warned residents of Puerto Rico not to expect too much assistance: "We cannot keep FEMA, the Military & the First Responders . . . in P.R. forever!"[192]

In another Twitter snit, Trump also suggested the real problem wasn't the "big ocean water"—it was because he thought Puerto Ricans were lazy. "Such poor leadership by the Mayor of San Juan, and others in Puerto Rico, who are not able to get their workers to help" he tweeted on September 30.

"They want everything to be done for them when it should be a community effort."[193]

Then, once he arrived on the island, Trump proved equally insensitive by vastly underestimating the number of fatalities, compared to deaths from Hurricane Katrina. "Sixteen versus literally thousands of people," he told the governor of Puerto Rico. "You can be very proud." By his measure, what happened in Puerto Rico was not a "real catastrophe." Actually, the death toll from Maria, while still disputed, is much, *much* higher, ranging from the government's "official" count of 64 to CNN's tally of 499 to a Penn State study total of 1,085 to a shocking estimate by Harvard School of Public Health researchers of more than 4,600, which would be more than seventy times Trump's official number.[194]

Before leaving the island, and after hurling rolls of paper towels ("beautiful, soft towels, very good towels") at hurricane survivors like it was a timeout at a basketball game, Trump awarded himself a score of 10 out of 10 for the federal government's response. Which, of course, was news to most residents of the island, because they had no home, no food, no drinking water—and no power to watch the news. But some did have paper towels, I suppose.[195]

In several ways, what happened in Puerto Rico reflected problems with the Trump administration overall: no experience, no expertise, and no idea on how to govern, all tinged with racism. This was nowhere more evident than in contracts awarded by the government to help with Puerto Rico's recovery.

To provide meals, the Trump administration awarded a $150 million contract to an Atlanta firm with no previous government experience to deliver thirty million meals. At a time when, according to their contract, eighteen and a half million meals should have been delivered, the company could account for only fifty thousand. At the same time, in one month, relying mainly on volunteers, chef José Andrés had fed two million people.[196]

To provide emergency supplies, the Trump administration paid Bronze Star, a brand-new Florida firm, $30 million to deliver much-needed tarps and plastic sheeting. This was also Bronze Star's first government contract. Months later, when they'd failed to deliver any materials, the contract was terminated.[197]

And, in the contract that received the most negative publicity, to rebuild Puerto Rico's destroyed electrical grid, FEMA awarded a $300 million no-bid contract to Whitefish Energy Holdings, a small firm from Interior Secretary Ryan Zinke's hometown of Whitefish, Montana—which, at the time, only had two full-time employees. Zinke's son had previously worked for them for a summer.[198]

Whitefish's contract was also canceled, but the results of getting off to such a disastrous start at recovery remain. Five months after Hurricane Maria, 25 percent of Puerto Rico homes were still without power—and Donald Trump had long ago forgotten about them.[199]

34. HE'S IGNORED THE OPIOID CRISIS

The United States is in the middle of a serious public health crisis: the opioid epidemic.

In 2016, more than 42,000 Americans died of a drug overdose involving illicit or prescription opioids. Through the first ten months of 2017, 46,000 had died the same way. At this rate, medical experts predict, in the next decade drug overdoses will take 650,000 lives—equivalent to the entire population of the city of Baltimore.[200]

In terms of public policy, this is a layup. It impacts all fifty states and every single congressional district. Any move to combat the opioid crisis would get overwhelming bipartisan support in Congress.

Yet what has President Trump done about it? For eighteen months, just about nothing. Yes, he made nice promises. He declared it a "public health emergency," appointed a task force headed by "Miss Alternative Facts," White House advisor Kellyanne Conway (who has zero public health credentials), and held a couple of White House meetings, after which he made even more nice promises.

But what did he actually do in his first year in office? Again, nothing. As Vox's German Lopez summed it up in January 2018, "No new funding, nor a push for more funding, no big new strategy." One expert described Trump's approach as "A lot of talk, but little action."

"He's done nothing," said another. "It's remarkable how little we've seen," said yet another.[201]

Instead, Trump has actually taken several steps that make it harder to deal with the opioid epidemic. As of this writing, he's named no one to head either the Drug Enforcement Administration (DEA) or the Office of

National Drug Control Policy (ONDCP), the two principal players in treating drug addiction. Both posts remain empty. His first budget proposed cutting funding for the ONDCP by 95 percent, cutting Medicare by $237 billion, and Medicaid by over $300 billion. And he tried to repeal Obamacare, which greatly expanded access to addiction treatment.[202]

Meanwhile, Attorney General Jeff Sessions, under Trump's direction, has revived the tired, old War on Drugs by cracking down with maximum sentences on nonviolent drug offenses—shades of Nancy Reagan's "Just Say No." In its thirty-plus-year history, the War on Drugs has succeeded only in filling our prisons to the brim, robbing young people of their future, disproportionately locking up people of color, and earning the United States a reputation as the country with the highest incarceration rate on the planet. It has done nothing to stop drug misuse or block the flow of illegal drugs into the country. Yet it's cost over a trillion dollars.[203]

Trump likes to berate his attorney general, but on this bad idea, he's on the same page. When Trump finally announced a comprehensive opioid plan in March 2018, its big idea was the notion of a mandatory death penalty for drug dealers, an idea he admits to cribbing from China and Singapore. "The only way to solve the drug problem is through toughness," he told a Pennsylvania rally. Otherwise, his plan included a crackdown on painkiller prescriptions and some vague, couldn't-be-bothered language—with no serious funding details—about expanding treatment. Trump, in short, is mainly substituting one failed war on drugs with another one.[204]

But in Trump's mind, this apparently did the trick almost immediately, because less than three months later, he declared victory in the war on opioids. "We got $6 billion for opioid and getting rid of that scourge that's taking over our country," he told a Nashville crowd in May 2018. "And the numbers are way down. We're getting the word out—bad . . . It's way down. We're doing a good job with it."[205]

Meanwhile, in the real world, numbers are not "way down"—opioid deaths are up. When Trump allies said he was in fact talking about opioid prescriptions, they pointed to numbers from 2016—before Trump took office—and 2017, before the new funding, which is for two years, kicked in.[206]

Leave it to Donald Trump. When it comes to dealing with the opioid epidemic, the only thing worse than inaction is action in the wrong direction. And that's just what he's doing.

35. HE'S RIGGING THE CENSUS

In politics, there's nothing more boring than reapportionment. Yet in politics, there's nothing more important than reapportionment. The district lines drawn through reapportionment represent the very foundation of our democracy. They determine whether it's a level playing field or a tilted deck. And ever since 2010, it's been a deck tilted far to the right.

That didn't happen by accident. It's the result of a brilliant strategy developed in advance of the 2010 census by RNC chair Ed Gillespie and White House senior advisor Karl Rove. Under their plan, dubbed REDMAP (short for "Redistricting Majority Project"), Rove and Gillespie identified fifteen states where the legislature would be redrawing district lines (some states delegate the job to a panel of experts), which included several blue states with the potential of turning red. They raised $30 million to support candidates for state legislature in the target states—and succeeded in "flipping" ten out of fifteen states from blue to red.[207]

Why was that so important? Because those newly elected state representatives would have the power to draw new legislative and congressional district lines. Which they did, creating districts that do not reflect any geographic, economic, or social commonality but merely make it possible to elect more Republicans.

It's called gerrymandering, and it dates back to 1812 and Massachusetts governor Elbridge Gerry, who created a state senate seat that looked on paper like a salamander. Some of today's districts look even worse, have no contiguity at all, yet they serve their purpose of favoring one party over the other.

By creating districts where it's almost impossible for Democrats to win, gerrymandering, or reapportionment, is directly responsible for Republican control of Congress and state congressional delegations that are way out of proportion to a state's political makeup. In North Carolina, for example, a 50–50 state in voter registration, Republicans control ten out of thirteen seats in Congress. Overall, in the congressional elections of 2012, Democrats won 1.4 million more votes than Republicans, yet—because of the way new districts were drawn in their favor—Republicans won back control of the House of Representatives by a margin of 234–201.[208]

For Republican legislators, not all new lines proved permanent, however. Courts have since struck down district lines drawn in Pennsylvania and North Carolina, which judges called "among the largest racial gerrymanders ever encountered by a federal court." While Wisconsin's GOP-drawn lines were temporarily left in place by the U.S. Supreme Court, the court also referred a legal challenge to the Republican plan back to the trial court for possible retrial.[209]

Now, with the 2020 census looming, the Trump administration is trying to tilt the deck even further right by doing everything it can to prevent an honest count. Trump has still not yet appointed a director of the Census Bureau, even though, for a while, he named anti–voting rights advocate Thomas Brunell as deputy director. Brunell, who argued for more gerrymandering, not less, soon resigned. Trump has also cut the Census Bureau's budget, forcing them to cancel several critical field tests.[210]

Most perniciously, the Trump administration announced in March 2018 that it would be adding a citizenship question to the 2020 census, which is intended to scare immigrants away and produce an inaccurate count, especially in border states. As a result, blue states would not only wind up cheated out of their fair share of congressional seats but also cheated out of billions of dollars in federal funds based on census data. Twelve states and the ACLU have filed suit to remove this noxious question.[211]

Already, evidence indicates that the Trump administration is trying to produce an inaccurate census precisely in order to increase Republican representation in Congress and decrease the number of Democrats. If they succeed, we will be stuck with Trumpism for another decade.

36. HE'S LEFT OUR INFRASTRUCTURE FOR DEAD

Candidate Donald Trump promised to "Make America Great Again." How? Two big promises, repeated over and over again at every campaign rally: build a wall, and rebuild America's crumbling infrastructure. You remember: "a $1 trillion plan," which Trump insisted would deliver "the best, fastest, and most reliable infrastructure in the world."[212]

As someone who was ostensibly a builder for most of his career, you'd think Trump would at least be able to get this one right. But no. Forget the actual infrastructure—his bumbling administration can't even hold an

"Infrastructure Week." This White House has tried to hold an Infrastructure Week no less than three times, and each time it ended up being pushed aside by the latest Trump crisis.[213]

So there our infrastructure sits and rots, in more need of rebuilding than ever before, in many cases a serious public hazard, with no plan to fix it.

Ironically, this was the one issue on which Donald Trump could have achieved immediate, bipartisan success. Had he started off in 2017 with infrastructure, he would have scored a big victory with overwhelming Republican and Democratic support—and proved he was the consummate deal-maker he'd bragged about being. Instead, he started out with the Muslim ban and repeal of Obamacare, accomplishing nothing and only further dividing Congress.

In February 2018, when Trump finally did get around to addressing infrastructure in his third Infrastructure Week—soon overshadowed by the Rob Porter domestic abuse scandal, the horrible school shooting in Parkland, Florida, and the revelation that Trump had an affair with porn star Stormy Daniels—his plan turned out to be a total bust. Instead of $1 trillion, Trump put up only $200 billion over ten years, and half of that is earmarked for block grants, not actual construction funding. But, he insisted, that $200 billion would somehow, magically, spark $1.5–$1.8 trillion in infrastructure spending.[214]

Of course, Trump never indicated where those supplemental trillions would come from. From the states? They don't have the money. If they did, they wouldn't need federal help in the first place. From private developers? They won't make public needs a priority. They'll only build what they want to build, where they want to build it, and where they can make the most money out of it. Like more toll roads, which are not necessarily the projects cities and states need. As *HuffPost* noted, "If you like paying tolls, you're going to love Donald Trump's infrastructure plan."[215]

In other words, the whole scheme is a shell game. The *Los Angeles Times* derided Trump's infrastructure proposal as "all gleam, no grit." What's most striking is what's not included in Trump's sketchy proposal of $200 billion: no meaningful investment in housing, transportation, clean water, or quality schools—which are the kind of infrastructure investments most badly needed and which would most help working families.[216]

Bottom line: As candidates, both Bernie Sanders and Donald Trump promised a $1 trillion infrastructure program. Sanders would have delivered. Trump has not. Don the Builder can't even get infrastructure right.

3

TRUMP'S WAR ON THE ENVIRONMENT

Let's be honest. Nobody expected Donald Trump to be a champion of the environment once he got to the White House. After all, he was nothing but a big-time New York developer. His only exposure to the great outdoors was weekends spent on one of his golf courses. He kept calling climate change a hoax.

But nobody expected him to be this bad from day one.

Any doubts about whether Trump might even be open-minded toward protecting the environment quickly evaporated with the two men he chose as his "environmental" advisors. He could not have picked two more anti-environmental zealots, nor two men more loyal to the oil and gas industry.

Trump nominated Scott Pruitt as administrator of the Environmental Protection Agency—EPA's Public Enemy #1. In his former post as attorney general of Oklahoma, Pruitt would simply reprint oil company missives on state letterhead and was so deep in the pockets of the fracking industry that his state went from having one or two earthquakes a year to one or two earthquakes *a day*. He also made a career of trying to destroy the EPA. He filed lawsuits against the agency fourteen times. Like Trump himself, Pruitt's a climate change denier. He doesn't believe there's any need for a federal environmental agency. His goal is to shut the EPA down. Unable to do so from outside the agency, Trump gave him a green light to do so from within.[1]

For Interior secretary, Trump named former Montana congressman Ryan Zinke, long known as a front man for the coal industry and opponent of environmental legislation. In Congress, he scored only a 4 percent lifetime voting record from the League of Conservation Voters—his one good vote being disaster funding for the water crisis in Flint, Michigan. Environmentalists' fears of how bad he would be came true on his first day in office. After striding in on horseback to the Interior Department, his first official act as secretary was to overturn an Obama administration ban on the use of lead bullets in national wildlife refuges.[2]

With Pruitt at the EPA and Zinke at Interior, Trump had the leaders of his environmental wrecking crew in place. And very shortly thereafter, the three of them began working to destroy all the progress made on environmental protection in the last fifty years. If Barack Obama was our strongest environmental president since Teddy Roosevelt, Donald Trump is by far the worst—only Reagan, thanks to the execrable James Watt, comes close. It will take decades to recover from the damage they've done in just two years—decades that, because the impacts of climate change are accelerating, we simply do not have.

37. HE'S KILLED EVERY ENVIRONMENTAL REGULATION HE COULD

In January 2014, entering his sixth year in office and with Republicans still in control of the House since 2010, President Obama conceded that getting anything passed by Congress would be difficult. But, he insisted, he wasn't going to give up. He'd use every other tool in his toolbox to get things done.

"We're not just going to be waiting for legislation in order to make sure that we're providing Americans the kind of help they need," he told his cabinet on January 14. "I've got a pen, and I've got a phone."[3]

And Obama did indeed proceed to use his pen—among other things, to sign some of the strongest and most sweeping environmental protections ever. The problem is, it didn't take Donald Trump long to figure out that what was done by the pen can quickly be undone by it, too. On the environment, he's used his pen to wipe out almost everything President Obama had accomplished.

As *The New York Times* put it in October 2017, with their usual penchant for understatement: "Since taking office last year, President Trump has made eliminating federal regulations a priority." Boy, did he ever! By that point, according to an analysis by *The Times* using research from Harvard and Columbia's law schools, in nine short months, the Trump administration had already overturned, or had begun the reversal, of more than sixty environmental rules adopted under President Obama—and many more have been targeted since.[4]

Trump, Pruitt, and Zinke are clearly on a search-and-destroy mission to identify any steps taken by the Obama administration to protect the environment or deal with climate change and overturn them as quickly as possible—in many cases, before they'd even kicked in.

There's neither time nor space here to analyze in depth all the harm done, but a listing of some of the more damaging actions taken by the Trump administration reveals a deliberate, carefully calculated crusade to wipe out any environmental protection progress across the board. The breadth and depth of their destructive campaign are simply staggering. They've left no stone unturned. They've left no pro-environment regulation in place.

Here, thanks to *The Times*, is a list of some of the worst. The headlines alone tell the story. Among outrageous actions taken by the Trump wrecking crew:

1. Revoking Obama-era flood standards for federal infrastructure projects.
2. Rejecting a ban on harmful pesticide chlorpyrifos.
3. Lifting a freeze on new coal leases on public lands.
4. Allowing coal companies to dump mining debris in local streams.

5. Overturning ban on hunting of predators in Alaskan wildlife refuges.

6. Rolling back policy protecting migratory birds.

7. Relaxing rules on new braking systems for trains carrying oil and ethanol.

8. Approving Keystone XL pipeline and Dakota Access pipeline.

9. Opening up Arctic National Wildlife Refuge to new exploratory drilling.

10. Relaxing regulations against oil and gas drilling in national parks.

11. Ending rule that coal companies prove they can pay for cleanup at mining sites.

12. Canceling policy discouraging sale of plastic water bottles in national parks.[5]

And that was just for starters. At the EPA, Pruitt abruptly trashed the new Clean Power Plan rules—arguably the most effective measures ever taken to reduce greenhouse gas emissions from existing and new coal-fired power plants.[6]

Then, in April 2018, Pruitt announced the EPA was abandoning the Obama administration's stricter fuel-efficiency standards for cars and trucks, thereby both threatening the nation's ability to grapple with carbon reduction in the face of climate change and setting up a legal battle with California and twelve other states over their stricter emissions caps.[7]

Meanwhile, at Interior, Zinke—as we will discuss more in a moment—opened up the entire Pacific and Atlantic coasts (except Florida!) to new offshore drilling and proposed shrinking several national monuments, including Bears Ears National Monument by 85 percent and Grand Staircase–Escalante almost in half.[8]

In a particularly heartless move, the Interior Department threatened, removed, or denied endangered species protection for a number of animals in danger of going extinct, including bears and lynxes, walruses and woodpeckers, owls and manatees. To oversee these protections, Trump picked a woman, Susan Combs, who had compared endangered species listings to "incoming Scud missiles" and worked to roll them back as Texas comptroller in order to facilitate more fossil fuel extraction.[9]

By the way, as we'll see in a few chapters, Scott Pruitt and Ryan Zinke are both as ethically challenged as they are environmentally destructive. Both men are power-hungry grifters cut from the Trump mold, and no mistake.

In any event, President Trump himself dealt the most severe blow to the environment. Having denied that climate change was real (except when it threatens his golf courses), he couldn't wait to run away from any world-wide efforts to fix it.

38. HE WITHDREW FROM THE PARIS CLIMATE ACCORDS

It was only a matter of time. For a while, there was faint hope that calmer heads, like then secretary of state Rex Tillerson, then chief economic advisor Gary Cohn, or even First Daughter Ivanka, might prevail and convince Donald Trump to stand with our allies in fighting climate change, even if as an unenthusiastic partner.

But who were they kidding? There was no way to stop Trump from being Trump. He revels in spouting conspiracy theories and abject nonsense—like questioning the legitimacy of Barack Obama's American citizenship—even on matters as obvious to all by now as the very existence of climate change. Take, for example, his tweet of November 6, 2012: "The concept of global warming was created by and for the Chinese in order to make U.S. manufacturing non-competitive."[10]

A year or so later, he upped his game by calling climate change a "hoax." On January 25, 2014, he tweeted: "NBC News just called it the great freeze—coldest weather in years. Is our country still spending money on the GLOBAL WARMING HOAX?"[11]

Again, four days later: "Snowing in Texas and Louisiana, record setting freezing temperatures throughout the country and beyond. Global warming is an expensive hoax."[12]

And even though he later insisted he just used the word *hoax* as a "joke," he never let up. On December 30, 2015, he told a campaign rally in Hilton Head, South Carolina, "Obama's talking about all of this with the global warming and . . . a lot of it's a hoax. It's a hoax. I mean, it's a moneymaking industry, okay? It's a hoax, a lot of it."[13]

Count 'em. That's *hoax* three times in one sentence. Donald Trump didn't misspeak; that was the word rolling around in his head at the time. And to this day, he continues to use *hoax* in his tweets.

So it was no surprise when, on June 1, 2017, President Trump walked into the Rose Garden to announce that he was fulfilling a campaign pledge to pull the United States out of the Paris climate accord. The accord was agreed to by nearly every country on the planet—195 in all—in December 2015. I bit my tongue as I sat there with my fellow members of the White House press corps, listening to Trump tell lie after lie about the Paris accord.

He claims the agreement undermines American sovereignty, preventing us from making our own energy and environmental decisions. No, it is nonbinding.

He claims Paris prevents the United States from building any new coal-fired power plants. No, it doesn't. Cheaper natural gas is what's killing new coal production.

He claims the climate accord punishes the United States, while letting India and China, the biggest polluters, off the hook. Wrong again. Despite only having 4 percent of the world's population, the United States is history's biggest carbon polluter. India and China have actually demonstrated a much stronger commitment to Paris.[14]

He claims the American people want him to put America first and ignore any global responsibilities. "It is time to put Youngstown, Ohio; Detroit, Michigan; and Pittsburgh, Pennsylvania, along with many, many other locations within our great country, before Paris, France," he said in the Rose Garden. To which Bill Peduto, the mayor of Pittsburgh, immediately responded, "I can assure you that we will follow the guidelines of the Paris Agreement for our people, our economy & future."[15]

Indeed, Trump's withdrawal of the Paris accord was widely condemned by scientists, world leaders, and leaders of the business community. Canadian prime minister Justin Trudeau and French president Emmanuel Macron each issued rebukes to Trump. "Make our planet great again," Macron challenged.[16]

Business leaders Elon Musk of Tesla, Jeffrey Immelt of General Electric, and Lloyd Blankfein of Goldman Sachs, among many others, said Trump's decision would ultimately harm, not help, the economy. Former vice president

Al Gore, one of the first politicians to really sound the alarm about climate change, called it a "reckless and indefensible action." Mohamed Adow, head of Christian Aid, a relief and development group, said, "It is immoral."[17]

Although the existence and impact of the Paris accord did not automatically disappear upon withdrawal of the United States, Trump's impetuous action has already had serious consequences, abroad and at home.

It has encouraged developing nations to take their own climate obligations less seriously. After all, if the world's number one polluter, which grew its economy to what it is today through fossil fuels, can thumb its nose at Paris, why can't they?

It has set back the efforts of our allies—particularly Germany, France, and the UK—who were counting, as in so many areas, on the leadership of the United States in confronting global warming.

And now it has left the United States in the embarrassing position of sole outsider. In June 2017, when Donald Trump pulled out of Paris, only two other countries in the world—Nicaragua and Syria—opposed the Paris accord, Nicaragua because they thought it didn't go far enough! But they signed in October 2017, and so did Syria a month later. Now the United States stands alone among the 197 nations of the world in joining together to combat climate change. But, of course, in Donald Trump's warped mind, he's right and everybody else on the planet is wrong.[18]

Meanwhile, each and every year, the United States experiences growing evidence of the serious consequences of climate change—rising sea levels, flooded city streets, record-high annual temperatures, crop losses, increased regularity and severity of hurricanes, tornadoes, rainfall, and wildfires—all with the federal government now turning a blind eye.

There is only one glimmer of hope. The way the pact is written, it will take three and a half years from the time Donald Trump made his announcement to the point where the United States is officially no longer part of the Paris climate accord. By sheer coincidence or God's grace, that would occur on the day after the 2020 presidential election.

With any luck, Donald Trump will be out of the White House before we're officially out of Paris.

39. HE'S BANNED THE EXPRESSION "CLIMATE CHANGE"

For Donald Trump, it wasn't enough that he pulled the United States out of any efforts to combat global warming. He has apparently decided he won't be satisfied until he has erased the phrase *climate change* from the English idiom, at least among the federal agencies he controls. Like a child who believes that if we just don't talk about something we can pretend it doesn't exist, Trump proceeded to memory-hole what is, next to nuclear weapons, the most significant threat to our planet's collective future today.

Administration officials try to dismiss the new language bans as merely "reflecting new priorities," "updating websites," or "removing outdated language," but they amount to nothing more than pure censorship. And that censorship cut across almost all government agency lines—not just among those, like the Environmental Protection Agency and Department of Energy, which deal directly with climate change, but also the Department of Health and Human Services, the Department of Agriculture, and the Department of Transportation.[19]

As Vox's Umair Irfan pointed out in November 2017, the watchdog group Environmental Data and Governance Initiative has been monitoring government websites and reporting on some of the most blatant out of hundreds of changes made. For example:[20]

Environmental Protection Agency. One of Director Scott Pruitt's first moves was to order removal of the entire Clean Power Plan, President Obama's signature climate policy initiative, from EPA's website. He then directed that the words *climate* and *climate change* be removed from all EPA websites. EPA scientists were blocked from attending a conference to present their work on climate change.[21]

Curiously, Pruitt still buried the Clean Power Plan, even after the White House in November 2017 released the *Climate Science Special Report* by thirteen federal agencies that concluded that "human activities, especially emissions of greenhouse gases, are the dominant cause of the observed warming." (By mistake? Presumably, nobody in the White House—chaotic on its best days—bothered to take the time to read it.)[22]

Department of Energy. In June 2017, the agency closed down its Office of

International Climate and Technology and replaced it with . . . nothing. Researchers were advised to remove the words *global warming* and *climate change* from grant applications. Staffers were ordered not to use the phrases *climate change, emissions reduction,* or *Paris Agreement* in written memos. Even before Trump was sworn in, all DOE staffers were asked whether or not they had ever attended any international conference on climate change—an interrogation later withdrawn under protest.[23]

Department of Transportation. In February 2017, the Federal Highway Administration, either anticipating or complying with Trump's edict, renamed its "Sustainable Transport and Climate Change" team the "Sustainable Transportation and Resilience" team.[24]

Department of Health and Human Services. The National Institute of Environmental Health Sciences removed many mentions of *climate change* from its web pages.[25]

Department of the Interior. Scientists said they were ordered to remove connections between climate change and rising sea levels in the press release for a study they published on coastal flooding. Joel Clement, an Interior scientist who studied the impact of rising seas on Native American tribes, was suddenly reassigned to a division that collects royalties from fossil fuel leases. He resigned.[26]

Department of Agriculture. Again, bowing to administration pressure, staffers combed through the department's website to change names of programs in order to remove any hint of taking climate change seriously. The department's "Soil Carbon Sequestration" project, for example, was rebranded "Building Organic Matter in the Soil to Improve Soil Health." In orders that could have been lifted right out of George Orwell, the phrases *climate change* and *climate change adaptation* were replaced by *weather extremes* and *resilience to weather extremes.* And *reduced greenhouse gases* was safely recast as *increase nutrient use efficiency.*[27]

Why does this matter? Because words matter! Scrubbing the phrases *climate change* or *global warming* out of government websites or documents amounts to more than a word change. It forces serious climate scientists to go underground. It puts a different set of priorities in place. It's a green light to ignore greenhouse gas emissions and rush back to a fossil fuel economy. It's the ostrich solution—sticking our head in the sand while the world burns around us.

One thing for sure: If the government can't, or won't, even talk about climate change, it won't do anything about it, either. Instead, it'll just make things worse, as Donald Trump has done in so many ways.

40. HE'S OPENED THE ALASKAN WILDERNESS TO OIL DRILLING

State senator Peter Behr, my former boss, was one of California's leading environmentalists. "The great sadness for us environmentalists," he used to say, "is that our defeats are so final, and our victories are so temporary."

Oh, so true. Look how many times environmentalists have beaten back attempts to open up the Arctic National Wildlife Refuge, or ANWR, to oil drilling—only to have it come back to life as a new threat under a new president. Republicans have tried nearly fifty times to destroy the Alaskan wilderness. Donald Trump's just the latest, but he's closer to succeeding than ever before.[28]

For those who care about the environment, there are not enough superlatives to describe ANWR. At twenty million acres, it is America's largest and wildest piece of publicly owned land and by far our largest wildlife refuge—established as wilderness by President Dwight Eisenhower in 1960. It is home to forty-two fish species, eight marine mammals, over two hundred bird species, and thirty-seven land mammals, including caribou and polar bears. It is a huge, unspoiled expanse of land of unparalleled natural beauty.[29]

But not to Donald Trump. To Trump, as he told his first cabinet meeting of 2018, ANWR is just "one of the great oil sites." And with Trump's approval, Republicans in Congress included a provision to lift the ban on oil drilling in ANWR as part of their 2017 tax cut bill.[30]

However, even with Trump's blessing, drilling in ANWR is no sure thing. While industry sources estimate the two thousand acres of coastal plain that would be open for drilling sit over 7.7–11.8 billion barrels of oil, several factors argue against oil companies rushing into ANWR. The price of oil is at an all-time low. Getting the oil to refineries could be prohibitively expensive. And there are cheaper fossil fuel alternatives available, including vast shale deposits in Texas and Oklahoma and enormous natural gas reserves now accessible by fracking.[31]

Indeed, the combination of those factors led one oil industry analyst, Pavel Molchanov of Raymond James Financial, to advise investors, "Our sense is that there is little to no current interest in the industry to invest in ANWR."[32]

The Arctic National Wildlife Refuge may have escaped a bullet again—for now—but no thanks to Donald Trump. Meanwhile, he's taken another whack not just at Alaska—he's going for the entire American coastline.

41. HE'S OPENED THE ENTIRE U.S. COASTLINE TO DRILLING

Often, the same government power can serve different purposes, some good, some bad. The awarding of permits to drill for oil, for example, is used primarily to make sure the country has enough oil in production to meet our defense needs and limit our dependence on foreign sources.

But when Donald Trump looked at the electoral college map of November 2016, he saw other uses for drilling permits: to reward his friends in the oil industry and punish his political enemies at the same time. After all, most red states, the states that voted for him, were located in the middle of the country. Most blue states were lined up on the Atlantic or Pacific Coast.

For Trump, under the guise of energy independence, it was a diabolical way to get even. You didn't want me as your president? I'll give you a good reason why not: That federal ban on drilling for oil off your coastline no longer exists. From now on, every state, every coastline, is open season.

In January 2018, Interior secretary Ryan Zinke unveiled the first draft of the biggest offshore lease sale ever, which would open up 90 percent of the Outer Continental Shelf, more than a billion acres, to new oil drilling—including the entire Atlantic and Pacific coasts, plus thirty-one new leases near Alaska and in the Gulf of Mexico.[33]

The Trump plan reversed an older Obama administration policy that closed off the Pacific and Atlantic coasts, as well as a "permanent ban" on drilling in the Atlantic continental shelf, which Obama issued in the final days of 2016.[34]

Of course, the Trump White House denied that politics had anything to do with the wholesale rape of the coast, but their story was soon undercut by Zinke himself. Just days after lifting the embargo—and after drawing an angry response from Florida Republican governor Rick Scott, who was preparing for a Senate run against incumbent Democrat Bill Nelson and therefore unusually political sensitive—Zinke suddenly announced his plan would apply to every state *but* Florida. He was taking Florida "off the table," he explained, in order to protect its tourism industry. And because, well, as he put it on CNN, "the coastal currents are different, the layout of where the geology is."[35]

And if you buy that, I have some coastal property in Kansas to sell you. This was politics, pure and simple. Too blatant, reportedly, even for Donald Trump, who let it be known he was not happy with Zinke's ham-handed approach.[36]

But Zinke's sudden change of heart about Florida didn't solve his political problems on the coast; it merely magnified them. After all, if Florida should be spared because of the economic importance of its tourist industry, what about California? Georgia? North Carolina? Delaware? New Jersey? Every one of them could, and did, make the same argument.

In the end, every coastal governor, Republican and Democrat, weighed in against offshore drilling. Well, every governor except one: Maine's Paul LePage, generally rated as one of the worst governors in the country.[37]

Interior will release its final offshore plan in 2019, at which time it will proceed to offer new drilling leases, but the early opposition of bipartisan coastal governors means that ending protection of the entire coastline won't be as easy as Donald Trump and Ryan Zinke first believed.

The fact is that, liberal or conservative, Americans like their beaches better than oil spills. So, despite his best efforts, President Trump may never achieve his revenge scenario of lining both coasts with offshore oil platforms.

42. HE'S CHAMPIONED NEW COAL MINING

If there's one idea even more unrealistic than planting offshore oil platforms up and down the coast, it's Donald Trump's dream of bringing back "King Coal."

"The war on coal is over," he's declared. To hear him talk, it's only a matter of time, thanks to his actions, when coal is back in full glory—reopened coal mines; new coal mines; coal miners back on their jobs; new coal-fired power plants; no restrictions on burning coal; freight trains full of coal crisscrossing the country; clouds of black soot choking the life out of towns and cities; a job boom in the chimney sweep market.[38]

Nonsense. It's not going to happen. For one reason. Because, thankfully for the polar ice caps and everyone who enjoys breathing, coal is a dying industry. And not even Donald Trump, no matter how many times he repeats the slogan *Trump Digs Coal,* can bring it back. The energy industry has changed dramatically. Cheaper, cleaner sources of energy—natural gas and renewables—are now available, and that's what the market wants. They don't want manual typewriters, and they don't want any more coal-fired power plants.[39]

Even Trump's own Department of Energy confirms what's actually slowing down the coal industry—it's not environmental regulations or the heavy hand of Obama; it's simply the market at work. An August 2017 DOE report concluded, "The biggest contributor to coal and nuclear plant retirements has been the advantaged economics of natural gas–fired generation."[40]

So why Trump's continuing infatuation with coal? Because, for Trump, coal is more than a source of energy. It's the essence of his political base. It brings together wealthy right-wing business executives who hate environmental regulations and working-class white men who flocked to his campaign. They helped him, he figures, so he'll help them. Forget about natural gas, wind, and solar. He'll bring coal back. Except he can't. Even coal miners know that. Everybody knows that except Donald Trump, who's doing everything in his power to resurrect the coal industry.

Those actions include rolling back limits on carbon pollution from existing or new coal-fired power plants; repealing rules against filling streams with coal debris; stacking environmental agencies with former coal executives; and citing its unfairness to the coal industry as one of his main reasons for withdrawing from the Paris climate accord.[41]

But the reality is, it's not working. As Michael Grunwald reported in *Politico* in October 2017:

> So far, coal is continuing its slump despite Trump's support. Utilities have announced the retirements of 12 more coal-fired power plants since he took office, including two massive ones in Texas . . . That announcement marked a milestone: Half of America's coal fleet has been marked for mothballs since 2010, a total of 262 doomed plants. And as jobs go, coal mining is now a tiny sliver of the U.S. economy, employing about 52,000 Americans last month, down 70 percent over three decades . . . By contrast, the solar and wind industries employed almost 10 times as many Americans last year, and they're both enjoying explosive growth.[42]

So where do things stand now? It's clear that Trump can't "save" coal, but, by championing it, he can make it possible for coal to do a lot more damage before it finally collapses entirely. Bruce Nilles, head of the Sierra Club's "Beyond Coal" campaign, sums it up: "Trump can't revive coal. What Trump can do is allow more pollution and death during the transition."[43]

Meanwhile, Donald Trump plows on, professing his ignorance about coal in two ways. First, he never talks about coal without using the phrase *clean coal*—as if there is such a thing. There's not! In fact, Trump seems to have no clue what even the industry euphemism *clean coal* actually refers to.

In February 2016, for example, President Trump effused at a campaign rally that "clean coal is coming back" and railed against China for not washing their coal. "Do you think they clean the coal? Believe me, they don't." The following year, President Trump crowed, "We've ended the war on beautiful, clean coal, and it's just been announced that a second, brand-new coal mine where they're going to take out clean coal—meaning they're taking out coal, they're going to clean it—is opening in the state of Pennsylvania."[44]

This is, in a word, ridiculous. "Clean coal" technology refers to various techniques that attempt to reduce pollution from mining and burning coal. But "very stable genius" Trump seems to think that "clean coal" involves scrubbing the coal with a toothbrush. "It sounds like he thinks that they're going to wash the coal," said one NOAA scientist. "It doesn't make any sense."

"Every time he refers to the word 'coal,' he puts the word 'clean' in front of it, or 'beautiful,'" noted Steve Clemmer of the Union of Concerned Scientists. "That signals to me that he doesn't understand what most people refer to 'clean coal' as."[45]

In short, all coal is dirty. It is the number one source of carbon contributing to greenhouse gases. The only way it becomes "clean coal" is by use of "clean coal technology" to remove carbon emissions from the coal when it is burned. In other words, the coal is not clean; the technology reduces the carbon emissions pumped into the atmosphere from burning—but never 100 percent. Again, there is no such thing as "clean coal."[46]

Second, Trump keeps bragging about how many new mining jobs he's created. "Everybody was saying, 'Well, you won't get any mining jobs,'" he told a rally in July 2017. "We picked up 45,000 mining jobs. Well, the miners are very happy with Trump and with Pence, and we're very proud of that."[47]

Except it's not true. In fact, according to monthly reports by the Bureau of Labor Statistics, since the beginning of Trump's presidency, just 1,200 new coal-mining jobs have been created. Not only that, the 1,200 coal jobs under President Trump through December 2017 are just 100 more than were created between August and December 2016 under President Obama. So much for the great general fighting against the "war on coal."[48]

No matter how hard he tries, and no matter how badly he lies, Donald Trump is not going to bring coal back. Yes, the war on coal is over. And coal lost. That's good news for the environment and for most Americans. For those coal miners who are now out of work, the right thing to do is to help them get back on their feet and acquire jobs in growing energy sectors like renewables, not keep lying to them about jobs that aren't, and won't ever, be coming back.

43. HE'S DESTROYED NATIONAL MONUMENTS

Trump may love "clean, beautiful coal," but clean, beautiful public lands? Not so much. Since President Ulysses S. Grant created our first national park at Yellowstone, and especially since Teddy Roosevelt signed the Antiquities Act into law, every president, Republican and Democrat, has made preserving America's most beautiful lands and creating new national parks and monuments part of his legacy. Some did not until the last year of their presidency, but they still did so.

We remember Lyndon Johnson for the Great Society, Medicare and Medicaid, and the War in Vietnam. But he also added fifty national park units, including Redwood National Park. Even Ronald Reagan, who once famously said, "A tree is a tree, how many more do you need to look at?" created a national park in American Samoa. Bill Clinton added nineteen national monuments and Joshua Tree National Park in California.[49]

In addition to expanding several national monuments, for his legacy, George W. Bush created the world's largest marine protected area, a group of remote Hawaiian islands called "America's Galápagos." Barack Obama used the Antiquities Act to establish or expand twenty-nine national monuments during his tenure, representing a total of about 553 million acres, more than any other president.[50]

Every president has wanted to be remembered as someone who put the most special of America's land aside for future generations to appreciate and enjoy. Every president until Donald Trump, who immediately set out not to add to America's national parks and monuments but to subtract from them.

Why? Does he really believe there are millions of Americans out there who believe, "We have too many national parks; let's get rid of a few of them"?

Trump began his assault on parks by naming Ryan Zinke as Interior secretary, who seems to believe that every piece of public land should have an oil rig on top of it or a mining shaft underneath it. With Trump's blessing, Zinke immediately proceeded to reopen federal lands to fossil fuel and mineral extraction and shrink the number and size of lands under protected status.[51]

Where other Interior secretaries set out to determine what special lands were worthy of being designated as a new national park or monument, Zinke set out to determine just the opposite. His first move was to order a review of twenty-seven national monuments created since 1966 to decide which ones might be reduced in size or eliminated entirely.[52]

In December 2017, Zinke revealed the next step in his plan to shrink the number and size of federal parks, rolling back protection on two million acres of land in two national monuments in Utah: the newly created Bears Ears monument and the Grand Staircase–Escalante monument.[53]

Bears Ears, designated by President Barack Obama, would lose 1.1 million acres, or 85 percent, of its land area. The Grand Staircase–Escalante monument would be reduced by 800,000 acres, or 45 percent. "Public lands will once again be for public use," Trump said in making the announcement. Sounds good, until you realize what he really meant—namely, that both monuments would thereby be opened up to coal and uranium mining, oil and natural gas drilling, and agricultural development.[54]

At the same time, Zinke unveiled other moves to undercut America's protected lands.

For one, opening up ANWR apparently wasn't enough damage to Alaska. Interior also announced plans to open up parts of Alaska's National Petroleum Reserve, a vast 22.8 million acres first set aside by President Warren Harding in 1923 as an emergency oil supply for the U.S. Navy. They've been protected ever since. Trump invited oil companies to rush in now, emergency be damned.[55]

On January 22, 2018, Secretary Zinke also approved a land swap deal that would allow a road to be built through Izembek National Wildlife Refuge in Alaska, marking the first time that a new road would be built through federally protected wilderness in violation of federal law.[56]

Elsewhere, Interior killed a plan developed during the Obama administration to protect threatened habitat for the sage grouse. Agreed upon by Interior, western states, environmentalists, and oil and gas companies, it has been called "the biggest conservation collaboration in U.S. history," involving fifteen planning areas in ten states. In June 2017, Zinke pulled the plug.[57]

And that is just the beginning of Donald Trump's assault on national parks and monuments, which 331 million visitors in 2017 believed would be protected forever. Little did they realize that, while they were enjoying our national monuments, Donald Trump was working to destroy them. Remember the lyrics from Woody Guthrie's "This Land Is Your Land"? Trump seems to think our lands are his, and he can just sell them off to his cronies at whim.[58]

President Teddy Roosevelt, perhaps our greatest conservationist president, made the strongest case for preserving our most precious lands. "We have fallen heirs to the most glorious heritage a people ever received," he once said, "and each one must do his part if we wish to show that the nation is worthy of its good fortune."[59]

Donald Trump is a different kind of Republican.

4

TRUMP FANS THE FLAMES OF RACISM

Ever since Richard Nixon first employed "the Southern Strategy," thereby bringing the conservative white South into the Republican column, racism has sadly been a weapon in the GOP arsenal. It's why Ronald Reagan railed on about "welfare queens" in 1976 and praised "states' rights" in Neshoba, Mississippi, in 1980, and why George H. W. Bush and Lee Atwater created the absurd Willie Horton ad in 1988. So in many ways, Trump's virulent racism represents the quintessence of a long-standing Republican tradition.

But it's also a deliberate choice made by a party on the cusp of demographic irrelevance. For decades, Republicans like Lindsey Graham and Chuck Hagel have warned that the Grand Old Party needed to become more inclusive or they would be wiped out as America grew more diverse. "The demographics race we're losing badly," a brutally honest Graham sighed in 2012. "We're not generating enough angry white guys to stay in business for the long term." But instead of opening their doors, Republicans have run the other direction, toward becoming an explicitly pro-white party. Such a sad closing chapter for the party of Lincoln.[1]

Either way, as we outlined in chapter 1, there's no doubt about where Donald Trump stands. He had a long history of racist statements and actions before being elected president, and he never changed once he got to the White House. If anything, he's just reinforced what we already knew: Donald Trump is a racist to the bone, and some of his more egregious offenses require their own listing here. For example:

44. HE LEAD THE BIRTHER MOVEMENT

Let's not forget: These two short statements speak volumes about Donald Trump.

In November 2008, America (finally!) elected its first African American president.

Donald Trump spent the next five years leading the movement to deny he was a legitimate president.

Does anybody really think he would have led such a movement against a white man? If John McCain—who was born in the Panama Canal Zone in 1936—had won the 2008 election instead, does anybody really think Trump would have spent the next half decade hollering about birth certificates?[2]

To be fair, Donald Trump did not start the "birther" movement— which asserted that Barack Obama was not eligible to be elected president because he was somehow born in Kenya, not the United States. (For the record, Obama was born in Hawaii in 1961.) It was led principally during the 2008 presidential campaign by right-wing extremist Orly Taitz, who was herself born in Moldova. The Obama campaign successfully shot the conspiracy theory down by releasing Obama's short-form birth certificate and contemporaneous announcements of Obama's birth in two Honolulu newspapers.[3]

The whole wacky theory might have died an ignominious death had not Donald Trump, considering a run against Obama in 2012, decided to resurrect it as a campaign issue.

In a speech to CPAC in February 2011, Trump first put on his "birther" hood. "Our current president came out of nowhere. Came out of nowhere," he claimed. "In fact, I'll go a step further: The people that went to school with him, they never saw him, they don't know who he is. It's crazy."[4]

Why, yes, it is crazy. But from that moment, the birther movement was back—with a new, high-profile, reckless leader with zero regard for the truth. For the next few months, Trump romped his way through cable television casting doubt on whether Obama was actually an American citizen. "If you are going to be president of the United States, you have to be born in this country," he told Bill O'Reilly on Fox News. "And there is a doubt as to whether or not he was . . . He doesn't have a birth certificate."[5]

Trump also nefariously suggested that Obama did not want to release his full birth certificate for religious reasons. "Maybe it says he's a Muslim," he told ABC's *Good Morning America*. He should have been laughed off the air then and there, never to return, but, since long before Trump became president, our press does love to indulge his crazy and repellent rants.[6]

In early April, Trump dramatically announced that he'd sent a team of investigators to Hawaii to find Obama's missing birth certificate. Later that month, he told CNN's Anderson Cooper, "I've been told very recently, Anderson, that the birth certificate is missing. I've been told that it's not there or it doesn't exist."[7]

By this time, the Obama White House had had it. I was in the White House briefing room on April 27, 2011, when aides distributed copies of Obama's *long-form* birth certificate to put the birther theory to rest once and for all. At which point, even Donald Trump accepted the final truth and moved on. Right?

Wrong! For the next *five* years, he continued raising the issue and raising doubts about Obama's birthplace, weaving an ever-more-complicated conspiracy theory, as on December 12, 2012: "How amazing, the state health director who verified copies of Obama's 'birth certificate' died in plane crash today. All others lived."[8]

"How amazing." Yes, how amazing that anybody believed that shit!

Even after he announced he was running for president in June 2015, Trump kept up the birther drumbeat. "I don't know. I really don't know," was all he would tell CNN.[9]

It was not until *five* years after initiating this racist nonsense that Donald Trump, now a candidate for president for real, buried the birther movement for good at his new hotel in Washington, D.C. There, on September 16, 2016, he finally admitted, "President Barack Obama was born in the United States." And then, never one to admit a mistake or doing anything wrong, he immediately blamed Hillary Clinton for having started the birther movement in the first place—for which he provided no evidence, nor does any such evidence exist.[10]

45. HE ATTACKS BLACK NFL PLAYERS

One of the many things in the world Donald Trump doesn't seem to understand: His tweets don't disappear. He doesn't get it because he always seems to think that whatever he's saying at the time is the new truth. But those old tweets will always be part of his online history, and sometimes—dare I say most of the time?—they will come back and bite him in the ass. As the saying goes, after not even two years of Donald Trump, "no matter the issue, there's always a tweet."[11]

In October 2013, for example, he blasted President Obama for weighing in on the issue of whether Washington's football team should change its racist name. "President should not be telling the Washington Redskins to change their name," Trump harrumphed. "Our country has far bigger problems! FOCUS on them, not nonsense."[12]

But as usual—there's always a tweet—Trump failed to follow his own advice. Instead, he decided to attack NFL athletes for not standing for the national anthem. Which was strange because, at the time, only a handful of players, led by 49ers quarterback Colin Kaepernick were "taking a knee," instead of standing, for the national anthem. Their reason? Protesting the systematic problem of police violence against unarmed, young black men.

Yet in Donald Trump's warped world, the kneeling in silent protest, not the epidemic of dead black civilians shot by police, was the national crisis. So much so that he had to make a big deal about it.

As a candidate in August 2016, he'd suggested that Kaepernick should leave the United States: "I think it's a terrible thing, and, you know, maybe he should find a country that works better for him." He also blamed the protests for the NFL's declining ratings.[13]

(As for the more likely culprit of football's ratings woes—the emerging definitive case that the sport is giving its veteran players massive brain damage through concussions and chronic traumatic encephalopathy [CTE]—Trump doesn't care. "The NFL has just barred ball carriers from using helmet as contact," he sniffed in 2013. "What is happening to the sport? The beginning of the end.")[14]

So, after 2016, did Trump change his tune, follow his earlier advice, and become more presidential about issues like this once he entered the nation's highest office? Of course not. Trump's not exactly known for sticking to the script. Still, on September 23, 2017, at a campaign rally for Alabama Senate candidate Luther Strange, he surprised everybody by suddenly taking on the NFL: "Wouldn't you love to see one of these NFL owners, when somebody disrespects our flag, to say, 'Get that son of a bitch off the field right now. Out. He's fired! He's fired!'"[15]

Setting aside for the moment whether it's appropriate for a president of the United States to be calling anybody a "son of a bitch" at a public forum—be they NFL players or journalists like Chuck Todd—Trump's verbal attacks backfired. He had made a mountain out of a molehill, bringing national media attention to what had been quietly going on for months, with little public notice and few players participating.

The next weekend, not just a handful but dozens of NFL players "took a knee" rather than stand for the national anthem. In response to which, Trump doubled down as always, escalating his attacks on the NFL and its players.

"If a player wants the privilege of making millions of dollars in the NFL or other leagues," he decreed on Twitter, "he or she should not be allowed to disrespect our Great American Flag (or Country) and should stand for the National Anthem. If not, YOU'RE FIRED. Find something else to do!" He also attacked NFL commissioner Roger Goodell for not cracking down on players. Soon thereafter, his obsequious vice president, Mike Pence, made a show of leaving a game in protest of the protests.[16]

It didn't escape anyone that there was an ugly racist reality hanging over Trump's sudden, angry attack on the NFL. The president was not just attacking professional football players. He was attacking African American football players who were protesting police brutality against young African American men and the country's failure to address that issue.

For Trump, it was clearly a racist attack. A racist twofer, in fact: against the players and against the community for whom they were kneeling in protest. And the players were right.

According to VICE, "African-American males are only six percent of the United States population, but comprise nearly 70 percent of the players in the National Football League." And, according to *The Washington Post,* "black Americans are 2.5 times as likely as white Americans to be shot and killed by police officers." In addition, *The Post* notes, "Unarmed black men are seven times more likely than whites to die by police gunfire." So as true leaders in the world of sports, Kaepernick and others were correct in using their stardom to shine the spotlight on those two issues.[17]

In any event, for many involved in pro football, Trump's war on protesting NFL players was just the latest battle in his long-standing war with the NFL—or "No Fun League" as he once called it. At one time, he owned the New Jersey Generals in the now-defunct United States Football League, which set out to be a competitor of the NFL. But the USFL collapsed in 1985, in no small part because Trump had pushed the league to sue the NFL for $1.2 billion in damages for monopolizing football—the NFL was ultimately fined all of three dollars. Trump then tried to buy the Buffalo Bills but lost the bidding war. In a sense, questioning the very patriotism of NFL players wasn't just another chance for Trump to dabble in racism. It was also Trump's revenge.[18]

In any event, by the end of the 2018 season, Trump's racist bluster had clearly alienated much of the NFL. When fewer than five members of the Super Bowl–winning Philadelphia Eagles planned to attend the usual White House ceremony in June, Trump disinvited the entire team in a huff, claiming that the Eagles "disagree with their President because he insists that they proudly stand for the National Anthem, hand on heart, in honor of the great men and women of our military and the people of our country." (In fact, no Eagles had kneeled during the season.)[19]

Instead, Trump declared he would throw his own party for the true patriotic Eagles fans. "We will proudly be playing the National Anthem and other wonderful music celebrating our Country today at 3 P.M., The White House, with the United States Marine Band and the United States Army Chorus," he decreed on Twitter. "Honoring America! NFL, no escaping to Locker Rooms!" At this sad rinky-dink jamboree, where most attendees wore suits rather than Eagles gear and reporters struggled mightily to find people who could even name the Eagles' quarterback, two onlookers took a knee in protest.[20]

Trump's White House lawn pity party was also notable for Trump the Super-Patriot obviously mangling the words to "God Bless America." In fact, Trump's sanctimony about the national anthem should have come to an inglorious end, ironically enough, at the NCAA National Championship football game on January 10, 2018, when Trump stood on the field with players to sing the national anthem—only to reveal he didn't know the words to the anthem, either. Or, at least, he didn't know all the words. He only mumbled along with the most well-known lines.[21]

Late-night comics had a field day. Trevor Noah noted the irony of the moment: "Trump attended last night's game, I assume, to hunt for unpatriotic black athletes," he quipped. "And, as it turns out, he may not even know the song that he has been so passionate about." And Seth Meyers piled on: "You would think that a man who ran on a platform of pure patriotism—and who's spent months lecturing athletes about respecting the national anthem—would at least know the words to the anthem."[22]

Meanwhile, of course, Trump has said or done nothing about the core issue of police brutality that triggered the NFL protests, while his attorney general has gone out of his way to make matters worse.

46. HE ATTACKS OTHER BLACK ATHLETES AND CELEBRITIES

It's not just NFL players. Or his attempts to lock away the Central Park Five. Or his intense jealousy and loathing of Barack Obama. It's a pattern. Clearly, Trump feels extremely insecure and threatened by black people, especially those more successful, celebrated, and well liked than he is.

True, as noted earlier in chapter 1, there's nothing Donald Trump loves more than picking a fight, usually on Twitter. It's a high school bully practice the White House repeatedly and predictably defends as: If you hit him, he'll hit you back even harder. But what's worth noting here, when talking about Donald Trump the racist, is how many times his attacks are directed against prominent African Americans.

Given what we've already discussed with the NFL, it's no surprise that he soon moved on to the NBA, where the same pattern unfolded.

In this case, the athlete that set off Trump's ire was Steph Curry, point guard for the Golden State Warriors, whom many fans, sportswriters, and veteran players have dubbed "the greatest shooter in NBA history." Curry was also spokesperson for Under Armour, the Baltimore-based sports apparel company. But when Armour's CEO Kevin Plank hailed President Trump as an "asset" to the country, Curry publicly broke with him and the company, saying he wanted nothing to do with Trump.[23]

When the Warriors won the NBA title again in 2017, Curry made clear he wasn't going to accept any White House invitation. "Somebody asked me about it a couple months ago, a hypothetical, if a championship were to happen: 'What would I do?'" Curry told reporters. "I answered that I wouldn't go. That hasn't changed."[24]

At which point, take a guess: petty Donald Trump pulled the plug. "Going to the White House is considered a great honor for a championship team," he tweeted on September 23, 2017. "Stephen Curry is hesitating, therefore invitation is withdrawn!"[25]

But, for once, Trump did not have the last word. Cleveland Cavaliers all-star LeBron James, believed by many to be the greatest basketball player ever, used Twitter to take on Trump directly: "U bum @StephenCurry30 already said he ain't going! So therefore ain't no invite. Going to the White House was a great honor until you showed up!"[26]

Houston Rockets guard Chris Paul suggested that, surely, the president of the United States had more important issues to focus on: "With everything that's going on in our country, why are YOU focused on who's kneeling and visiting the White House??? #StayInYoLane."[27]

Funnily enough, the following year, Curry's Golden State Warriors battled LeBron's Cleveland Cavaliers in the NBA Finals for the fourth year in a row. While the Warriors won the championship, one question was already a foregone conclusion before the games started—nobody was going to see Trump in the White House. "I mean, I know no matter who wins this series, no one wants the invite anyway," LeBron said before Game 3. "So it won't be Golden State or Cleveland going." Steph Curry and fellow Warriors star Kevin Durant quickly agreed.[28]

As crazy as his attacks on NFL and NBA players, Trump really went off the deep end in the case of three UCLA basketball players—Cody Riley, Jalen Hill, and LiAngelo Ball—arrested and temporarily jailed for shoplifting in China. After asking Chinese president Xi for their release, Trump was furious that the players and their families—especially LaVar Ball, father of LiAngelo—did not immediately thank and praise him for his intercession. "Now that the three basketball players are out of China and saved from years in jail, LaVar Ball, the father of LiAngelo, is unaccepting of what I did for his son and that shoplifting is no big deal. I should have left them in jail!"[29]

But the basis for his pretended outrage eventually fell apart when ESPN reported that charges against the UCLA players had already been dropped, their bail money was returned, their passports were given back, they were back at their hotel, and their return flight home was booked two days before White House chief of staff John Kelly called to tell them that Trump was going to intercede on their behalf.[30]

LaVar Ball could not resist a final taunt: "Thank you for what again @realdonaldtrump? #know your facts #stayinyolane."[31]

Trump goes after black sports players. Why not black sports commentators? ESPN's Jemele Hill also felt the president's wrath when she criticized Trump from her personal Twitter account on September 11, 2017, calling him "a white supremacist who has largely surrounded himself with other white supremacists."[32]

Even though her comments were not made on the air, ESPN suspended Hill. But that was not enough for Trump. He called for an apology from the network: "ESPN is paying a really big price for its politics (and bad programming). People are dumping it in RECORD numbers. Apologize for untruth!" White House press secretary Sarah Huckabee Sanders went even further, demanding that Hill be fired.[33]

Trump's persistent attacks on black celebrities have also reached beyond sports, into the fields of politics and entertainment.

In late 2017, rapper Snoop Dogg released a new album mocking Trump's slogan of "Make America Great Again." In his album, *Make America Crip Again*, Dogg criticized Trump's handling of race issues and accused him of neglecting communities of color. Not only that, in a music video for the album, he shot down a clown dressed as Trump, with a fake gun that released a banner reading BANG.[34]

Trump, unable to fathom that you can't fight satire, could not hold back and reacted like, well, a clown. "Can you imagine what the outcry would be if @SnoopDogg, failing career and all, had aimed and fired the gun at President Obama? Jail time!"[35]

Sidebar: Note how often Trump uses the word *failing* when blasting his critics: *The New York Times,* ESPN, Snoop Dogg, the NFL, CNN. The implication is clear—if you're not with him, you're bound to fail.

But in every case, Donald Trump's MO is clear: always deny, always attack. Now, to be fair, Donald Trump doesn't only attack African Americans. For example, he also attacked actress Meryl Streep, deriding her as "one of the most overrated actresses in Hollywood." Streep, by the way, has been nominated for a record twenty-one Academy Awards and won three of them: Best Supporting Actress in *Kramer vs. Kramer;* and Best Actress in *Sophie's Choice* and *The Iron Lady.* She's probably happy to be so "overrated."[36]

Nonetheless, the pattern is clear. Sure, sometimes Trump gets in a tiff with a Mark Cuban or a Jeff Bezos. And sometimes, he makes a black friend, like Don King or Kanye West. But much more often than not, Trump goes out of his way to disparage women and people of color, be they black like Colin Kaepernick, Steph Curry, and Congresswoman Frederica Wilson, Muslim like Khizr Khan and London mayor Sadiq Khan or Latino like "Little Marco" Rubio.

If you don't believe me, just look for yourself. Open Twitter or the local newspaper right now: Who is our racist president fighting with today?

47. HE STANDS WITH NEO-NAZIS

Thank you President Trump for your honesty & courage to tell the truth about #Charlottesville.[37]

That applauding tweet by former KKK leader David Duke tells all you need to know about Donald Trump's inherent racism. Every person, even a president, is known by the friends he keeps.

The entire country reacted with horror on Saturday, August 12, 2017, when white nationalists marched through Charlottesville, Virginia, to protest removal of a statue of Robert E. Lee from a city park. The night before, they had held a torchlit parade while chanting anti-Semitic and Nazi slogans "blood and soil" and "Jews will not replace us." The Saturday march turned violent when one longtime Nazi sympathizer drove his car through a crowd of counterprotestors, injuring nineteen people and killing thirty-two-year-old Heather Heyer.[38]

That horror was not relieved by President Trump's unfiltered and outrageous response. He began badly enough with a statement from his Bedminster, New Jersey, golf club, which blamed both sides for the violence: "We condemn in the strongest possible terms this egregious display of hatred, bigotry, and violence on many sides—on many sides."[39]

The Daily Stormer, a neo-Nazi website, was euphoric. "Trump comments were good. He didn't attack us," they crowed. "He just said the nation should come together. Nothing specific against us." When Trump walked out of the room without answering a question about white supremacists, they noted, "Really, really good. God bless him."[40]

But this failure to outright condemn white supremacists was met with howls of outrage from everyone else, even Republican members of Congress. Several business leaders resigned from the president's American Manufacturing Council in protest. At which point, he disbanded the council.

But true to form, Trump didn't back down. He doubled down. Three days later, at a Trump Tower news conference to talk about infrastructure, he returned to the same theme about Charlottesville: "What I'm saying is this: You had a group on one side and you had a group on the other and they came at each other with clubs and it was vicious and horrible. And it was a horrible thing to watch. But there is another side. There was a group on this side, you can call them the left. You have just called them the left, that came violently attacking the other group. So you can say what you want, but that's the way it is."[41]

Trump went out of his way to defend the neo-Nazi who descended on the quiet college town—insisting that "the press has treated them unfairly"—and to condemn those anti-racist individuals, mostly locals, who came out to protest their presence. Trump claimed, "They were very, very violent."[42]

He then expressed the moral equivalency argument that won praise from David Duke: "You had some very bad people in that group, but you also had people that were very fine people on both sides." Only Donald Trump, it seems, could look at a gang of skinheads, white supremacists, KKK, neo-Nazis, and anti-Semites marching in the streets of America, beating minorities and even murdering a woman with a car, and see "very fine people."[43]

Finally, reporters asked whether Trump might visit the troubled city to help the healing process. Without missing a beat, he showed how clueless he was about both what had happened in Charlottesville and the national outrage about his callous response. "I own one of the largest wineries in the United States," he volunteered. "And it's in Charlottesville."[44]

(Echoes of Trump's tone-deaf and reprehensible response to the destruction of the Twin Towers on 9/11, when he bragged on local TV about the size of his building at 40 Wall Street: "When they built the World Trade Center it became known as the second-tallest, and now it's the tallest." Not only was this a horrible thing to say, it still wasn't true—nearby 70 Pine Street was still taller.)[45]

No one should have been surprised, of course, that Donald Trump failed to condemn the alt-right for Charlottesville. They're an important part of his base. As slogan for his campaign, he chose "America First," the same slogan used by Nazi-sympathizer Charles Lindbergh and others in opposition to America's joining the fight against Hitler. And he began his campaign by promising to build a wall to keep out Mexican immigrants, whom he denigrated as criminals and rapists.[46]

Within a fortnight, Andrew Anglin, publisher of *The Daily Stormer,* wrote, "I urge all readers of this site to do whatever they can to make Donald Trump president."[47]

The KKK and neo-Nazis have been with Donald Trump from the beginning. And he, with them.

48. HE CONSIDERS NON-WHITE COUNTRIES "SHITHOLES"

After a year with the man in the Oval Office, we didn't really need yet one more example of Donald Trump's racist tendencies. But we got a particularly obscene one anyway on January 11, 2018, during an Oval Office meeting Trump held with several senators on immigration.

When the subject of "protected status" for immigrants from certain countries deemed especially dangerous—like El Salvador, Haiti, and multiple African nations—came up, the president complained, "Why are we having all these people from shithole countries come here?"

He followed up by suggesting that what we needed was more people from countries like Norway—all of whom, of course, would be white.[48]

His remarks were confirmed by Senator Dick Durbin of Illinois and quasi-confirmed by South Carolina's Republican senator Lindsey Graham, who, while not confirming the actual phrase *shithole countries*, said the president used a phrase so vile that he immediately chastised him for it.[49]

Reaction to Trump's comments was immediate, strong, and negative. His remarks were condemned by leaders of many African and Latin American countries, by the Congressional Black Caucus, and by members of Congress from both parties. Representative Bonnie Watson Coleman (D-NJ) put it in perspective: "It also reinforces the concerns that we hear every day, that the president's slogan Make America Great Again is really code for Make America White Again."[50]

True to form, Trump did not back down. "Certain Washington politicians choose to fight for foreign countries, but President Trump will always fight for the American people," deputy press secretary Raj Shah lamely explained, while refusing to deny Trump had actually called them *shithole countries*.[51]

Meanwhile, two other Republican senators also in the meeting came up with an even more tortured defense of Trump. Tom Cotton of Arkansas and David Perdue of Georgia flatly denied that Donald Trump uttered the phrase *shithole countries*. Privately, they suggested he said *shithouse countries* instead.[52]

When Republicans argue that describing countries as "shitholes" is not okay, but calling them "shithouses" is politically acceptable, you know the thread has been lost and that the Republican Party is morally bankrupt. But either way, what counts is that Donald Trump was clearly saying: We don't want any more people of color here. What's more racist than that?

49. HE ATTACKS NATIVE AMERICANS

So we know Donald Trump hates immigrants, unless they're from Norway. (Even though Norwegians themselves have no love for Trump.) So therefore he must love Native Americans, right? No, he hates them, too. You might think this is because, even though they were born here, they're also people of color, and you'd be right.

Trump's own Indian War, in fact, long predates his accession to the White House. It first surfaced when, as a wannabe gambling mogul himself, he led a massive lobbying effort against Indian gaming. In 1993, testifying before a House subcommittee, he publicly disparaged leaders of the Mashantucket Pequot Tribal Nation, operators of Connecticut's Foxwoods Resort Casino, one of the most successful casinos outside of Las Vegas. "They don't look like Indians to me," Trump grumbled, suggesting they might also be in collusion with the Mafia. Which, of course, is what a lot of people said about his own casino business in Atlantic City.[53]

Shortly afterward, Trump repeated his allegations in a radio interview with talk show host Don Imus. "I think I might have more Indian blood than a lot of the so-called Indians that are trying to open up the reservations." Referring to Foxwoods, Trump added, "I think if you've ever been up there, you would truly say that these are not Indians." As reported by *The Washington Post*, he also took out over $1 million in ads that, without any evidence, portrayed members of the Mohawk Indian tribe of Upstate New York as cocaine traffickers and career criminals. Sound familiar? This was basically his 2016 campaign strategy, with Mexicans taking the place of Native Americans.[54]

At the same time, showing what a hypocrite he is, Trump was secretly in negotiations with the Agua Caliente tribe to take over management of their casino in Palm Springs, California. The tribe wisely decided to partner with another operator.[55]

As was soon evident, Trump took all his bias against Native Americans with him into the White House. One of his first acts was to reverse President Obama's block on both the Keystone XL and Dakota Access Pipelines, both of which had been strongly opposed by tribal communities as a violation of their sovereignty and treaty rights. The Dakota project gained national attention when it was revealed that the pipeline had been originally designed to cross the Missouri River ten miles upstream, near the state capital of Bismarck, but had been rerouted to a half mile upstream from the Standing Rock reservation, whose inhabitants rely on the Missouri for drinking water, irrigation, and fish.[56]

The Trump administration has suggested deep cuts to the Indian Health Service and tried to flout decades of precedent regarding tribal sovereignty by letting states force their new Medicaid work requirements on Native Americans as well. This is "a remarkable departure from U.S. history, U.S. policy, and U.S law," said one legal expert of Trump's actions.[57]

As discussed earlier, Trump showed a similar disdain for Native American rights, history, and culture by his December 2017 decision to drastically cut the size of two national monuments in Utah: Grand Staircase–Escalante, designated by President Bill Clinton in 1996; and Bears Ears National Monument, created by President Obama in 2016.[58]

Trump's order cut the size of the Grand Staircase–Escalante almost in half, ignoring requests by Native American tribes, such as the Fremont and Pueblo, who sought protection for ancestral lands rich in ruins and rock art dating back thousands of years. Archaeologists and geologists also complained, noting its importance as one of the nation's most prominent sources of dinosaur fossils over seventy-five million years old. Both to no avail.[59]

Trump inflicted even a greater blow on Bears Ears, gutting the newest of our national monuments by 85 percent in a direct attack on Native Americans. Bears Ears, in fact, was known as "the first truly Native American monument," because five tribes—the Hopi, Ute Mountain Ute, Ute Indian, Zuni, and Navajo Nation tribes—had set its boundaries and pushed for its creation. As established, Bears Ears contained some one hundred thousand archaeologically significant sites, including dwellings, graveyards, shrines, ceremonial sites, and a record of rock art dating back at least five thousand years. It provided an archaeological record of the earliest human civilizations in North America, like the Clovis people, who lived within the Bears Ears region thirteen thousand years ago, when now-extinct megafauna like mammoths and ground sloths still roamed.[60]

Working together as the Bears Ears Inter-Tribal Coalition, the five tribes immediately filed a lawsuit, claiming that Trump's actions violated his presidential authority under the Antiquities Act. Unless they succeed, the gateway to those two great national monuments, and perhaps several more, will be opened to oil, gas, coal, and uranium companies. Kiss our Native American heritage goodbye.[61]

Even if Trump wasn't a fan of Native Americans, he didn't need to go out of his way to insult them. But on November 27, 2017, Donald Trump embarrassed himself and all of us with his idiotic antics.

On that day, he invited to the White House three Navajo Code Talkers, survivors of troops who used a singular, unbreakable language—Navajo!—to send top secret information during World War II. Their ingenuity, bravery, and sacrifice on behalf of the nation is worthy of praise. So far, so good.[62]

But then Trump gathered them in front of TV cameras while standing beneath a portrait of President Andrew Jackson, who signed the Indian Removal Act, seizing land from Native American tribes and forcing them to move to federal territory west of the Mississippi River—most notably along the Trail of Tears, where seventeen thousand Native Americans were forced to march from the ancestral homeland in Georgia through freezing temperatures and snow all the way to Oklahoma.[63]

Of all the presidential portraits in the White House—from George Washington to John F. Kennedy to Ronald Reagan to Bill Clinton—why Andrew Jackson? Did Donald Trump not know? Did he do it deliberately? Or did he just not care?

Worse yet, instead of using the occasion to recognize and thank the heroic efforts of the Navajo Code Talkers, Trump veered into a personal attack on Massachusetts senator Elizabeth Warren, resurrecting the slur he had repeatedly used against her. Native Americans in attendance were slack-jawed as Trump smirked and said, "I just want to thank you because you are very, very special people. You were here long before any of us were here. Although, we have a representative in Congress who has been here a long time . . . longer than you . . . they call her Pocahontas!" Actually, Donald, "they" don't—you do.[64]

To sum up, Trump invited Native Americans to the White House, forced them to stand before a portrait of a leading enemy, and used the occasion to disparage anyone of Native American ancestry. Only President Trump could suddenly turn a White House event to honor Native Americans into yet another occasion to insult their heritage.

The man has a knack for racism.

5

TRUMP'S CABINET OF THIEVES

If you can know a man by the company he keeps, you know a lot about Donald Trump by the men and women he named to his cabinet.

Two days before his inauguration, he described them as having "by far the highest IQ of any cabinet ever assembled." As always with Donald Trump, the truth is quite the opposite.[1]

From the Texas oilmen who don't know anything about their jobs to the billionaires who despise the poor and middle class to the conservative ideologues who want to destroy the agencies they lead while lining their own pockets, Donald Trump's cabinet is a rogues' gallery of ne'er-do-wells.

Together, they are, to paraphrase John F. Kennedy's famous witticism about Thomas Jefferson, the most extraordinary collection of hucksters, grifters, liars, ignoramuses, and right-wing nut jobs that have ever assembled in the White House, with the possible exception of when Donald Trump dines alone.

50. JEFFERSON BEAUREGARD SESSIONS

Almost two years into the Trump administration, it's still hard to believe that a man who was rejected by the United States Senate for a federal judgeship in 1986 because he was such an outright racist would be appointed, no less confirmed by the Senate, as attorney general of the United States—now responsible for enforcing the very laws he spent a lifetime opposing.[2]

It's even harder to believe that Jeff Sessions is still on the job. After Hillary Clinton, perhaps nobody has been more frequently and viciously pummeled by Donald Trump than his own attorney general. Trump has repeatedly denounced Sessions for recusing himself from the Russia investigation, blamed him for Robert Mueller, attacked him for not investigating Barack Obama's dealings with Russia and for not launching yet another investigation of Hillary Clinton's emails, and called him "weak" and "ineffective." He has publicly said several times he regrets nominating Sessions and wishes he had someone else in the job.[3]

As is his style, most of Trump's attacks on Sessions came in early-morning tweets from the White House residence.

On July 25, 2017, for example, Trump hit Sessions for not being tough enough on Hillary Clinton: "Attorney General Jeff Sessions has taken a VERY weak position on Hillary Clinton crimes (where are E-mails & DNC server) & Intel leakers!"[4]

In Donald Trump's mind, if Sessions was too easy on Clinton, he was also too easy on President Obama, as he fumed on February 21, 2018: "Question: If all of the Russian meddling took place during the Obama Administration, right up to January 20th, why aren't they the subject of the investigation? Why didn't Obama do something about the meddling? Why aren't Dem crimes under investigation? Ask Jeff Sessions!"[5]

A week later, he again publicly criticized Sessions for following the rules of the Justice Department: "Why is A.G. Jeff Sessions asking the Inspector General to investigate potentially massive FISA abuse. Will take forever, has no prosecutorial power and already late with reports on Comey, etc. Isn't the I.G. an Obama guy? Why not use Justice Department lawyers? DISGRACEFUL!"[6]

Again in June 2018: "The Russian Witch Hunt Hoax continues, all because Jeff Sessions didn't tell me he was going to recuse himself. I would have quickly picked someone else. So much time and money wasted, so many lives ruined . . . and Sessions knew better than most that there was No Collusion!"[7]

And yet, despite such continual criticism from the boss, Sessions is, as of this writing, still there. Why? As I see it, two reasons. One, because, although he's still nowhere near Mike Pence's league, Sessions is among the biggest ass-kissers in the cabinet. The occasional dinner with Rod Rosenstein to get under Trump's skin aside, he has rarely veered from supporting whatever Trump says or does. He was the first senator to back Trump in February 2016 and defended him even after release of the *Access Hollywood* tape in October. As for grabbing women by the genitals, "I don't characterize that as a sexual assault," Sessions explained. "I think that's a stretch."[8]

Second reason why Sessions has survived? Because no cabinet member, with the possible exception of EPA administrator Scott Pruitt, has done more to carry out Donald Trump's personal agenda or been more effective at it.

Under his "leadership," Jeff Sessions has, in fact, turned the Department of Justice upside down—from a government force whose historic mission is to defend civil rights to a nefarious power whose job is to undermine them; from an agency whose job is to enforce the law to a gang of lawyers whose job is to protect the president from the law.

In so doing, Sessions has reversed decades of progress in improving police–community relations, expanding voting rights, and achieving criminal justice and sentencing reform, while declaring war on states over sanctuary cities and relaxed marijuana laws.[9]

For anyone familiar with Sessions's background, his extreme right-wing record at DOJ came as no surprise. Just ask the ACLU, who published an overview of his dangerous record in May 2017.[10]

On sentencing reform: As senator, Sessions opposed legislation cosponsored by conservatives Charles Grassley and Mike Lee to eliminate mandatory minimum sentences and reduce sentences for nonviolent drug offenses. As attorney general, he instructed federal prosecutors to seek the maximum penalty in every case. "If I were attorney general," Sessions once told an Alabama newspaper decades ago, "the first thing I'd do is see if

I couldn't increase prosecutions by 50 percent." Under Trump, he's been working to make his dream come true.[11]

On policing reform: As senator, Sessions opposed efforts by the Obama Justice Department to improve police–community relations nationwide, which resulted in consent decrees signed with Chicago, New Orleans, Los Angeles, Baltimore, and other big cities that allow the Justice Department to get involved if serious police abuses occur. But, as the ACLU's David Cole points out, Sessions called these agreements "dangerous," and "an end run around the democratic process." As attorney general, Sessions ordered an end to the community relations program and declared existing consent decrees invalid.[12]

Sessions also suggested, early in his tenure as AG, "that the greatest increase in violence and murders in cities" is happening because "we undermined the respect for our police and made, oftentimes, their job more difficult." This is an oblique reference to what is called "the Ferguson effect"—the notion that crime is going up because police are more afraid to do their jobs if they are being more closely monitored for abuses.[13]

But there are a few problems with this line of thinking. First, despite Trump's and Sessions's continual claims that America is a crime-ridden hellhole thanks to Obama and that we now need to return to "law and order," crime rates in the United States remain at historic lows. In fact, both violent crime and the murder rate in 2017 were lower than they had been in nearly forty-five years, continuing a downward trend that, despite a brief blip in 2016, has been going on for a while. Second, as many policing experts have noted, there's no evidence that a "Ferguson effect" exists. And third, it wouldn't be an excuse to let police act like criminals regardless.[14]

On civil liberties: As senator, Sessions opposed legislation extending hate crimes protection to women and gays and lesbians. "I am not sure women or people with different sexual orientation face that kind of discrimination," he argued. "I just don't see it." Soon after becoming attorney general, he withdrew a Department of Justice rule protecting transgender students from discrimination.[15]

On freedom of religion: As senator, Sessions supported candidate Donald Trump's call for a ban on all Muslims coming to America and called one of the world's most practiced religions "a toxic ideology." He also opposed a resolution sponsored by Senator Patrick Leahy that simply affirmed that no religious discrimination should be allowed in the enforcement of immigration laws. The resolution passed, 94–6. As attorney general, he defended President Trump's first and second Muslim bans in federal court, insisting—despite Trump's many public statements to the contrary—that they were not a "ban" and were not "anti-Muslim."[16]

On voting rights: As Alabama's attorney general, Sessions prosecuted three black civil rights activists for the serious crime of encouraging people to vote by absentee ballot. A jury found all three not guilty. As senator, he called the Voting Rights Act "an intrusive piece of legislation" and cheered when the Supreme Court in 2013 gutted the act, calling it "good news . . . for the South." No surprise that, as attorney general, he immediately dropped a Justice Department challenge to a Texas voter ID law that a court later ruled was, in fact, a case of intentional racial discrimination.[17]

On separating families and rounding up children in detention camps: Sessions actually had the temerity to invoke "the clear and wise command in Romans 13 to obey the laws of the government because God has ordained them for the purpose of order." As historians soon pointed out, this dubious biblical reading—all laws are just because the Lord said so—last had its heyday in the Antebellum era, when it was used to uphold slavery. So naturally it rolled right off the tongue of racist Jefferson Beauregard Sessions, with no sense of irony whatsoever.[18]

Of course, none of that matters to Donald Trump, who will never forgive Sessions for recusing himself from the Russia investigation—when, in fact, Sessions was forced to do so. In his confirmation hearing for AG, he had denied under oath having any "communications with the Russians." Later, when it surfaced that he had actually met with Russian ambassador Sergey Kislyak at least twice while working on the campaign, Sessions, for once, had no choice but to recuse himself, whether Trump liked it or not. He's lucky he wasn't charged with perjury, and, in fact, FBI deputy director Andrew McCabe—before he was fired by Trump and Sessions—authorized an investigation into whether Sessions had perjured himself, but ultimately, it couldn't be proved.[19]

Having Jeff Sessions in any cabinet post would be bad enough, but having him serve as attorney general is a real disaster. The attorney general is the nation's top law enforcement officer. Under any president, his or her job is to serve as an independent defender of the rule of law, regardless of political party or rank. And with a president who doesn't care about the rule of law—who, in fact, believes himself above the law—the need for a strong, independent attorney general is now more important than ever. Weak Trump foot soldier Jefferson Beauregard Sessions is just the opposite.

51. REX TILLERSON

The position of secretary of state is considered the most prestigious and powerful job in any administration: the person who represents the United States and speaks for the president everywhere on the planet. Trump's filled the job twice so far but failed both times to nominate someone up to the job.

Rex Tillerson, his first pick, had zero diplomatic experience before taking the job, and even less when he left. In fact, it was soon clear that Tillerson wasn't a player in Donald Trump's foreign policy world at all. He was not included in White House meetings, he was absent from many sessions with world leaders, and he learned about many of Trump's foreign policy initiatives the same way the rest of us do—by watching television or Twitter.[20]

It's not that Tillerson didn't have a lot of experience dealing with foreign governments before becoming secretary of state. It's just that, as CEO of ExxonMobil, his experience with foreign governments consisted mainly in making deals, exploiting their resources, and cozying up with corrupt foreign leaders like Vladimir Putin, who honored him by inducting him into Russia's exclusive "Order of Friendship." So, on paper, sounds like a pretty good fit for Trump![21]

Indeed, senators found Tillerson's business practices so questionable that forty-three members of the Senate, both Republican and Democrat, voted against confirming him for secretary of state—more negative votes than any nominee for that position had received in fifty years.[22]

In a sense, they needn't have worried, because Tillerson—due both to Donald Trump's ignoring him and his own inability—never really took on the total job. It was obvious from the beginning that Tillerson's reliance on diplomacy was out of step with Trump's preference for bluster and nonsense. Tillerson never joined the "America First" crowd pushed by Steve

Bannon. Plus, Trump undercut Tillerson from the outset by carving one of the premier foreign policy goals—negotiating peace in the Middle East—out from under the State Department and handing it to his even more inexperienced son-in-law, Jared Kushner.[23]

Instead, Tillerson mostly just proceeded to carry out Trump's directive to gut the agency and leave the State Department an empty shell. Shortly after being sworn in, he announced his intention to cut the agency's budget by one-third, thereby eliminating some two thousand diplomatic jobs and billions of dollars in foreign aid.[24]

Promise made, promise kept. When Tillerson left office on March 31, 2018, eight of the top nine positions at the State Department, including his own, were vacant. The job titles themselves tell how those vacancies have crippled the agency. There was no under secretary for political affairs, no deputy secretary of state for management and resources, no under secretary for management, no under secretary of state for arms control and international security, no under secretary for civilian security, democracy, and human rights, no under secretary of state for economic growth, energy, and the environment, no counselor of the department—and, for a while, no secretary of state. With all the attention on the Korean Peninsula and the Middle East, there was no assistant secretary of state for East Asian and Pacific affairs and no assistant secretary of state for Near Eastern affairs.[25]

At the same time, seeing the writing on the wall, more than three hundred seasoned career diplomats quit, retired, or applied for sabbaticals. As of this writing in June 2018, five hundred days into the Trump presidency, at least forty top jobs at the Department of State remain empty, and Trump has failed to fill dozens of key ambassadorships, including ambassadors to the European Union, Mexico, Qatar, Turkey, and South Korea.[26]

Mostly all under Tillerson's watch. Ironically, for a man selected because he ran one of the world's biggest companies, Tillerson proved ineffective at the one thing he was supposed to be good at—executive leadership, or good management. As one State Department official quipped, "He took the job, and made it smaller."[27]

As the Trump administration gutted diplomatic efforts, it also proposed increasing defense spending by $54 billion—roughly equal to the entire budget of the State Department—reinforcing Trump's belief that force is more valuable than diplomacy in international affairs and that other countries, even allies, respond better to threats than to persuasion. As one senior White House official summed up the Trump approach to foreign policy in June 2018, "We're America, Bitch."[28]

Meanwhile, Trump undercut Tillerson at every turn. He ignored his advice to remain a partner in the Paris climate accord. He suggested a ten-fold increase in America's nuclear arsenal—which, no doubt among other things, prompted Tillerson to describe the president to friends as "a fucking moron." And back before his sudden pivot, he publicly ordered Tillerson to cease and desist from any talk of holding talks with North Korea. "I told Rex Tillerson, our wonderful Secretary of State, that he is wasting his time trying to negotiate with Little Rocket Man," Trump tweeted. "Save your energy Rex, we'll do what has to be done!"[29]

Later, of course, it was Trump himself who agreed to negotiate with Kim Jong-un, but by that time Tillerson was gone, fired in true Trumpian fash-ion—on Twitter. He learned he was fired upon picking up his iPhone on Tuesday morning, March 13, 2018, on his way back from Africa, to read the president's tweet:

> Mike Pompeo, Director of the CIA, will become our new Secretary of State. He will do a fantastic job! Thank you to Rex Tillerson for his service! Gina Haspel will become the new Director of the CIA, and the first woman so chosen. Congratulations to all![30]

Adding insult to injury, chief of staff John Kelly told reporters later that day how he had called Tillerson the previous Friday to inform him he might soon hear from the president about State Department matters. He de-lighted in adding, very likely at the behest of his boss, that Tillerson was suffering from a stomach bug when he called, and he reached him while the secretary was sitting on the toilet.[31]

He left office with scant praise from anyone. "Tillerson would be at or near the bottom of the list of secretaries of state, not just in the post–Second World War world but in the record of U.S. secretaries of state," said Paul Musgrave, foreign policy scholar at the University of Massachusetts–Amherst. Paul Krugman of *The New York Times* called him "surely the worst Secretary of State since William Jennings Bryan." Former Obama NSC spokesman Tommy Vietor proclaimed Tillerson "probably the worst

Secretary of State in modern history. He gutted and demoralized the department and delivered nothing for this country."[32]

But, as Jeet Heer sensibly noted in *The New Republic,* that raises an interesting question. While we criticize Tillerson because he was so ineffective, we also criticize some of his predecessors because they were so effective—in doing bad things. Certainly Tillerson did nothing to compare with Dean Rusk and the Vietnam War, Henry Kissinger and the secret bombing of Cambodia, or Colin Powell and the Iraq War.[33]

Is effective always better than ineffective? It's not just a rhetorical question, especially when you consider Tillerson's successor.

52. MIKE POMPEO

No doubt, Mike Pompeo started off as secretary of state with several advantages over Rex Tillerson, both in terms of experience—he's a former army officer, a skilled politician, and successfully led the CIA, a big, complex government agency—and in terms of political philosophy; he's a virtual clone of Donald Trump, who not only agrees with his bellicose approach to foreign policy but is willing to flatter the president shamelessly—which, as we now know beyond any doubt, is the key to success in the Trump administration. Pompeo also got a vote of confidence from Trump when he was secretly dispatched to North Korea to break the ice with President Kim Jong-un and lay the groundwork for a historic summit with the North Korean leader—and again when he went back to Pyongyang and returned with three Americans freed from a North Korean prison.[34]

On foreign policy, Pompeo and Trump are like peas in a pod. They both support keeping the Guantanamo Bay detention camp open. They both wanted to end the nuclear deal with Iran and did so early into Pompeo's tenure. They both supported the CIA's use of torture under President George W. Bush, with Pompeo declaring, "These men and women are not torturers, they are patriots." And they both insist that our intelligence agencies concluded that Russia's interference in the 2016 election made no difference in the results—when, in fact, the leaders of our intelligence agencies emphatically did not say that.[35]

All of which leads most foreign policy experts to believe that Mike

Pompeo could prove to be a far more effective secretary of state than Tillerson ever was. Which may be good news, but with an important catch: He may also be unwilling ever to stand up to Trump and thus amplify Trump's worst instincts instead of providing a badly needed voice of reason.

As one leading diplomat told *The Daily Beast,* "Pompeo will have the president's trust, but enable his worst foreign policy instincts."[36]

Pompeo is frightening for other reasons, too. As Senator Cory Booker made clear at Pompeo's confirmation hearing, our new secretary of state has long ties to, and refused to repudiate, rabidly anti-Muslim, right-wing organizations and leaders. (Previously, Pompeo has declared that Islamic terrorists will "continue to press against us until we make sure that we pray and stand and fight and make sure that we know that Jesus Christ is our savior is truly the only solution for our world.") He also, as Senator Booker pointed out, has called being gay a "perversion" and the Supreme Court's decision allowing same-sex marriage "wrong" and "a shocking abuse of power." Once again, Pompeo—now the chief diplomat of the United States—refused to repudiate these retrograde views.[37]

And then there's the small matter of the end of days. As Ken Klippenstein of *The Young Turks* reported in April 2018, Pompeo's colleagues at the CIA complained to watchdog organizations about the now secretary of state's penchant for Christian doomsday rhetoric. "They were shocked and then they were scared shitless," said Michael Weinstein of the Military Religious Freedom Foundation. Pompeo "is intolerant of anyone who isn't a fundamentalist Christian." We don't have to take his word for it— Pompeo has used similar rhetoric on the record many times, as when he declared, in 2015, that "evil is all around us" and politics is "a never-ending struggle . . . until the Rapture."[38]

Which gets us back to Jeet Heer's central question about Tillerson and Pompeo: Which is better, competence or incompetence? Is it better to be incompetent and have the right policies, as Tillerson did, or be competent but have more dangerous policies, like Pompeo?

I know my answer. I'd take Tillerson any day. Though, in the end, given the lasting damage both of Trump's secretaries have inflicted on the State Department, we will lose either way.

53. BETSY DEVOS AND ERIK PRINCE

In choosing his cabinet, Donald Trump apparently had one overarching goal in mind: Find the one person in the nation who is the archenemy of any agency—and put that person in charge of it. Not to lead but to destroy it.

As we will soon see, that seems to be how we got stuck with Scott Pruitt at the EPA, Ryan Zinke at Interior, Tom Price at HHS, and Ben Carson at HUD. And for the Department of Education, the nemesis in question is Betsy DeVos, who has long spent her career and considerable family fortune trying to destroy public schools—and now presides over them.

Betsy DeVos began life with both an impressive résumé in conservative circles and a massive fortune at her disposal, thanks to her father, Edgar Prince, an auto parts manufacturer and cofounder of the virulently right-wing Family Research Council. She also came into even more wealth and conservative cachet when she married Richard DeVos, heir of the Amway fortune.[39]

They are today the wealthiest people in Michigan, with an estimated family fortune of $5 billion. They are among Michigan's most politically prominent. Dick ran unsuccessfully for governor on a platform that added creationism to the public school curriculum. Betsy served as chair of the Michigan Republican Party and member of the Republican National Committee. They are also leading members of the religious Right, having given hundreds of thousands to two organizations, Focus on the Family and the aforementioned Family Research Council. Both the Prince family and the DeVos family operate under the principle that patriotism and politics are inseparable from Christianity.[40]

Dick and Betsy DeVos have also plowed their fortune into several other right-wing causes—making Michigan a right-to-work state; supporting a 1993 law setting up charter schools; donating over $100 million to conservative candidates; sponsoring a "school choice" ballot initiative in 2000 to legalize taxpayer-funded vouchers for use at private and religious schools; and establishing a PAC to support candidates who backed charter schools and vouchers.[41]

While all that DeVos money surely caught his eye, too, the ultraconservative, anti–public schools agenda is likely why Donald Trump named Betsy DeVos to the Department of Education. In effect, he turned the department upside down, placing an advocate of private Christian schooling at the helm of the nation's headquarters of public education. And clearly, DeVos's mission was his mission. "There's no failed policy more in need of urgent change than our government-run education monopoly," he said in September 2016. "It is time to break up that monopoly."[42]

Still, despite Donald Trump's full-throated endorsement, she almost didn't get the job. She demonstrated so little knowledge of fundamental education issues at her confirmation hearing—including suggesting that guns were needed in public schools to protect against attacks by grizzly bears—that every Senate Democrat and two Republicans—Susan Collins and Lisa Murkowski—voted against her. Only a tie-breaking vote by Vice President Mike Pence, the first ever for a cabinet member in Senate history, saved the day for her.[43]

Her dim-witted performance at her confirmation hearing was outdone, a year later, by her disastrous appearance on *60 Minutes*. After a year of flailing in the position, DeVos seized on the opportunity to patch up her reputation. Instead, she destroyed it. She made one gaffe after another. She lamented that so many schools were not doing well, yet admitted she had never visited any underperforming school. "Maybe I should," she admitted to veteran journalist Lesley Stahl. Her most embarrassing moment came when she asserted that public schools actually do better after a large percentage of students have left them for charter and privately run schools. When Stahl, posing the obvious follow-up question, asked her if that were true in her home state of Michigan, DeVos could only stutter in response, "I don't know. Overall, I—I can't say overall that they have all gotten better."[44]

That's been true of all America's public schools under Betsy DeVos. She has been quick to dismantle many critical programs of the Department of Education. For example, she rolled back new guidelines set by the Obama administration on campus sexual assault, thereby making it more difficult for victims of abuse to make their case. She scaled back investigations into civil rights abuses at public schools and universities and rescinded protections for transgender students and students with disabilities. She continued to undercut public schools by asking Congress for $1 billion to advocate charter schools and vouchers parents could use to send their kids to private schools. Fortunately, Congress rejected DeVos's request, as well as her attempts to cut funding for after-school programs, grants to low-income students, and mental health services.[45]

The combination of her disastrous media appearances and draconian cuts to public education made Betsy DeVos, at a 40 percent approval rating, the least popular member of Trump's cabinet. Which is quite an impressive feat when you consider the competition.[46]

But she's probably still more popular than her brother, Erik Prince.

He's not a member of Trump's cabinet—yet!—but Betsy's baby brother has a sordid reputation of his own and his own key part to play in the current fiasco in Washington. A former Navy SEAL, Prince first gained notoriety as the founder of Blackwater, the private security firm—in effect, mercenaries—employed by the Bush administration for various tasks during the second Iraq War. In 2007, five Blackwater employees fired into a crowd of civilians in Baghdad's Nisour Square, killing seventeen people and injuring twenty more.[47]

Prince defended his contractors, even after Blackwater was kicked out of Iraq by the Defense Department. Three years later, the company was in more trouble: five former executives had been indicted on federal weapons, conspiracy, and obstruction charges, and two former contractors faced murder charges in Afghanistan for firing into a civilian vehicle in May 2009 and killing two men. Sensing big trouble, Prince, who was not charged, nonetheless changed the name of Blackwater to Xe and moved with his family to Dubai. (Just coincidentally, I'm sure. The United Arab Emirates does not have an extradition treaty with the United States.)[48]

From there, Prince continues to promote the use of private security forces, or mercenaries—like those employed by his firm, now renamed once again as Academi—to replace American troops in fighting ISIS in Syria, the Taliban in Afghanistan, or other antiterrorist missions. Had Blackwater contractors been on the job in Benghazi, he insists, no Americans would have been killed and Ambassador Christopher Stevens would still be alive.[49]

Even more trouble awaited Erik Prince when he decided to throw in with Team Trump. Even as Donald Trump was busy denying that any of his associates had ever met with Russian operatives, *The Washington Post* reported that Erik Prince, in fact, had traveled to the Seychelles Islands in January 2017, the week before the inauguration. There, he identified himself as an official representative of Trump's and met with banker Kirill Dmitriev, an associate of Russian president Vladimir Putin, in order to establish, per reports, "a back-channel line of communication between Moscow and President-elect Donald Trump."[50]

Under oath before the House Intelligence Committee, Prince testified that this was nothing but a chance occurrence. He just happened to be in the Seychelles, and he just happened to run into one of Putin's best friends. Unfortunately for him, one of special counsel Robert Mueller's cooperating witnesses, businessman George Nader, told investigators that the meeting had been planned in advance. Meaning that Prince—for reasons that will no doubt become clear when Mueller finishes his investigation—perjured himself before the United States Congress.[51]

And then, thanks to Nader, the plot thickened even further. In late May 2018, reports emerged that Prince had organized a meeting at Trump Tower in August 2016 with Donald Trump Jr., Joel Zamel, an "Israeli specialist in social media manipulation," per *The New York Times,* and Nader, who was representing the leaders of Saudi Arabia and the United Arab Emirates. Prince introduced the pair to Junior, and they allegedly discussed ways that Saudi Arabia and the UAE could help Trump win the election, including through a multimillion-dollar social media effort run by Zamel's company, Psy-Group.[52]

Needless to say, and much as with the Russia example we will discuss in further detail later on, this incident if acted upon also constitutes illegal collusion by the Trump campaign to win the election with the aid of foreign powers. They sure are keeping Robert Mueller busy.

54. SCOTT PRUITT

People can and will have long arguments about who's the biggest crook in the Trump cabinet. To my mind, there's no doubt about it: Scott Pruitt is the worst member of the Trump cabinet and will have done the most lasting damage.

Even more than Betsy DeVos, Scott Pruitt personifies Donald Trump's

modus operandi in filling his cabinet. He looked for the most anti-
environmental zealot in the entire country, and he found him in the attorney general of Oklahoma. In that role, Pruitt had waged all-out war against
the environment on behalf of oil, gas, and coal companies. He had sued the
Environmental Protection Agency fourteen times. And today, in arguably
the biggest ever setback to environmental protection since the dawn of the
environmental movement, he's the head of the very agency his mission is to
destroy. "I've never known any administrator to go into office with such an
apparent disregard for the agency mission, definition, or science," said former New Jersey governor Christine Todd Whitman, EPA administrator
under President George W. Bush.[53]

Donald Trump has not succeeded in "Making America Great Again,"
but Scott Pruitt has succeeded, as a banner headline in *Mother Jones* well
put it in the spring of 2018, in MAKING AMERICA TOXIC AGAIN. Yet ironically, Pruitt has probably garnered more press for his various ethical problems than his catastrophic antienvironmental record.[54]

Indeed, while DeVos may be the least liked, Pruitt gets the award for
the Biggest Grifter in a cabinet full of grifters. His well-publicized and
comically corrupt ethical lapses so far include: contrary to EPA rules,
blowing millions of dollars on private planes and first-class airfare; spending $43,000 to have a soundproof phone booth installed in his office; hiring
a nineteen-person around-the-clock security detail at a cost of $2 million
annually and requesting a bullet proof limousine, just like the president's;
disobeying White House orders not to give a fat pay raise to two close
aides and doing it anyway; staying in a luxury hotel room paid for by developers for whom he promised to scuttle guidelines protecting wetlands; using
D.C.-stopping motorcades to get to restaurant reservations on time; forcing
employees to run personal errands for him; asking a staffer to secure a
$200,000 a year job for his wife; sending an employee to buy a used mattress
from the Trump Hotel; using his official position to push Chick-fil-A to
give his wife a franchise; and perhaps most notoriously, renting a room in a
Capitol Hill condo for fifty dollars per night from the wife of an oil industry lobbyist, at the same time her husband was lobbying the agency. Even
former New Jersey governor Chris Christie, who weathered his own
storm with Bridgegate, said, "I don't know how you survive this one."[55]

It's true. For anybody else, any one of those scandals would have been a fireable offense. HHS secretary Tom Price (as we'll see) and VA secretary David Shulkin were fired for a lot less. So why is Pruitt still on the job? Because he is doing exactly what Donald Trump wants at the EPA. As a candidate, Donald Trump promised to "get rid" of the EPA "in almost every form." Scott Pruitt is his one-man wrecking crew.[56]

In his inauguration address to EPA employees, Pruitt announced his goal of rolling back regulations adopted under President Obama—and he worked fast to do so, ordering EPA staffers to kill two existing regulations for every new one created. One year later, almost every positive step taken by Obama's EPA is gone, starting with the elimination of the landmark Clean Power Plan, imposing new limits on greenhouse gas emissions from new and existing coal-fired power plants. In addition, he weakened new rules for limits on methane emissions from oil and gas operations; rescinded rules giving the agency wider latitude to regulate pollution of drinking water; withdrew a 1995 policy imposing limits on nearly two hundred pollutants; and refused to ban certain dangerous pesticides. By early 2018, Pruitt had scuttled nearly fifty existing environmental regulations. And in March 2018, even as the signs of accelerating climate change became unmistakably clear, he unveiled plans to eliminate new fuel-efficiency standards adopted by President Obama with the support of the auto industry.[57]

On his first day on the job, Pruitt promised to "listen, learn, and lead." There's no doubt whom he's been listening to. In 2017, reports *The Washington Post,* Pruitt held 218 meetings in his office with representatives of industries he regulates. He met just a dozen times with environmental or public health groups.[58]

Meanwhile, Pruitt's efforts to reverse progress made under Obama had a twofold impact at the EPA. One, enforcement came to a standstill. Fines against polluters actually declined by 60 percent in the first seven months of 2017 and have not picked up since. Two, just like over at the State Department, some eight hundred career employees or scientists left the agency or were fired, replaced by industry officials handpicked by Pruitt and loyal to his agenda.[59]

As busy as he is driving the wrecking ball at the EPA, Pruitt already seems to be plotting his next move. He makes no secret that he'd like to be the next attorney general if Trump ever gets around to firing Jeff Sessions. And he has reportedly talked to friends about running for president in

2024. Again, from anybody else, that public display of ambition would anger Donald Trump. But not Scott Pruitt. In Trump's eyes, as long as Pruitt is taking care of his friends in the oil, gas, and coal business, Trump doesn't seem to care.[60]

Except when he's made to look bad. As this book was going to press, Pruitt resigned, the AP reporting that the "scandal-plagued" Pruitt "had become a constant source of embarrassment to a president who had entered Washington promising to "Drain the Swamp'." Trump nonetheless tweeted: "Within the Agency Scott has done an outstanding job."[61]

55. RYAN ZINKE

While Scott Pruitt is clearly Trump's number one climate denier and anti-environmental zealot, Secretary of the Interior Ryan Zinke is nipping at his heels. So, naturally, he was awarded the number two environmental slot in the Trump administration—where, like his brother-in-arms Scott Pruitt, he also emerged as one of the most corrupt and biggest grifters of the Trump cabinet.

Some people have compared Zinke to President Ronald Reagan's inept antienvironmental Interior secretary James Watt, but Zinke's far worse than Watt. A more accurate comparison is Albert Fall, Interior secretary under Warren G. Harding, who became the first cabinet official to go to prison. Like Fall in the infamous "Teapot Dome Scandal," Zinke's already starting to sell off public lands to the highest bidder.

And, again like Pruitt, Zinke earned the nickname the "Gulfstream Cowboy" for his use of charter planes to visit wealthy donors to the Trump campaign—for which he is now under investigation for violation of the Hatch Act. *Newsweek* later reported that Zinke paid for his luxury travel out of the department's wildfire preparedness fund. He chartered a helicopter to go horseback riding with Vice President Mike Pence. In one case, he even outdid Pruitt. As noted above, the EPA administrator spent $43,000 on a private phone booth. Zinke spent $139,000 for new doors to his office.[62]

Zinke, revealing an ego as big as Donald Trump's, went out of his way to show how "outdoorsy" and Rooseveltian he is. He rode a horse to work through the streets of Washington on his first day on the job. He ordered a specially designed flag to fly over the Interior Department whenever he's in his office. He had commemorative coins made to hand out to visitors and friends. He displayed his knife collection and a mounted bison head in his office and installed a *Big Buck Hunter* video game machine in the Interior cafeteria. He headlined a target practice fund-raiser for the NRA.[63]

It's all part of the con. As Interior secretary, Ryan Zinke is responsible for overseeing four hundred million acres of federal lands, including our national parks and monuments. To Zinke, all those lands are his—to exploit, sell, or give away to oil, gas, coal, and uranium companies. One of his first acts was to overturn a moratorium on new leases for coal mines on public lands. He's also opened up the Arctic National Wildlife Refuge to new drilling.[64]

As noted earlier, reversing decades of protection under both Democratic and Republican presidents, Zinke also announced he was opening up the entire American coastline—east, west, and south—to new offshore drilling, only to make a sudden exception for Florida because the Sunshine State was so dependent on coastal-related tourist dollars. Zinke never did explain why tourism won Florida special consideration but not California, Oregon, Washington, Maine, Massachusetts, New Hampshire, Connecticut, Rhode Island, New Jersey, Delaware, Virginia, North and South Carolina, Georgia, Louisiana, Mississippi, and Texas. But he insisted that the fact the Florida governor Rick Scott was preparing to run for U.S. Senate had nothing to do with his decision.[65]

Zinke also came under fire from several inland governors. Republicans Matt Mead of Wyoming, Brian Sandoval of Nevada, and Gary Herbert of Utah opposed Interior's plan to auction ten million acres to the oil industry on lands long protected as habitat of the endangered greater sage grouse. In a related action, Zinke announced in April 2018 that the Department would no longer enforce a century-old law holding people or companies responsible for killing birds. Over the years, 90 percent of the fines under the Migratory Bird Treaty Act had been paid by oil companies—after the *Exxon Valdez* oil spill, for example—so naturally the oil industry has been trying to get rid of the law for decades. They finally found their man in Ryan Zinke.[66]

And as seen earlier, Zinke will also be remembered and rebuked for gutting two of our great national monuments. If you took a survey today and asked one thousand people to name the most critical issues facing this country, not one of them would say, "We have too many national monuments. We have to get rid of a few or cut them down." But that's what Donald Trump and Ryan Zinke believe. So, at Trump's request, Zinke undertook a review of twenty-five national monuments and then rolled back federal protection on two of them: Utah's beautiful Grand Staircase–Escalante and Bears Ears National Monument. President Trump hailed this desecration as a move "to reverse federal overreach and restore the rights of this land to our citizens." Which makes sense, only if you define *citizens* as oil, gas, and coal companies.[67]

Adding insult to injury, Ryan Zinke carries on this destruction of our land and water even as he waxes poetic about President Teddy Roosevelt, whom he calls his role model. He's even described himself as TR's "unapologetic admirer and disciple." Yet Zinke must know it was Roosevelt himself who signed the Antiquities Act in 1906—which he then used to establish eighteen national monuments, and under which both Bears Ears and Grand Staircase–Escalante national monuments were created.[68]

Destroying this legacy is a strange way for Zinke to honor his alleged hero. Unless his real hero isn't Teddy Roosevelt at all, but Donald Trump.

56. TOM PRICE AND ALEX AZAR

Haven't we heard this song before? Third verse, same as the first and second. First, you find the biggest enemy of the agency involved. You give him the job, and he or she proceeds to do the most damage possible while at the same time lining their own pockets.

Enter Tom Price. HHS secretary. Archenemy of Obamacare, Medicare, and Medicaid. And another grifter. Like Pruitt and Zinke. But since, in Trump's eyes, Price mangled the attempted repeal of Obamacare, he got fired for it.[69]

After "the wall," ending Obamacare was the biggest promise of candidate Donald Trump. To champion that goal, he couldn't have picked a better (or worse?) crusader than Georgia congressman Tom Price. A physician himself, Price was arguably the most outspoken opponent of Obamacare in

Congress. But he didn't stop there. On health care, in fact, he was far more radical than Donald Trump. He advocated scaling back access to birth control, cutting funding for Planned Parenthood, and making abortion illegal again. He had also long fought for privatizing Medicare and turning Medicaid over to states through block grants—just the opposite of Trump's popular pledge not to touch either program.[70]

Still, Tom Price appeared to be Donald Trump's dream candidate for HHS secretary—until he ran into two potholes in the road. First, Senate Republicans couldn't round up enough votes to repeal Obamacare. True, Mitch McConnell was in charge, but Trump blamed Price for failing to deliver—as he telegraphed earlier in his memorable rambling to the Boy Scouts (!): "He better get the votes," Trump said. "Otherwise I will say, 'Tom, you're fired.'" Everybody thought he was kidding. He wasn't.[71]

And ultimately, Price was also caught with his hand in the cookie jar, giving Trump the out he needed. After *Politico* reported that his use of private planes had cost taxpayers over $400,000—in addition to over $500,000 on military aircraft to Africa, Europe, and Asia—President Trump ominously admitted to reporters on September 29, 2017, that Price was a "fine man," but he "didn't like the optics." By the end of the day, Price was out of a job.[72]

How do we know Trump wasn't actually livid about Tom Price's high-flying travel? Well, for one, Pruitt, Zinke, and Secretary of the Treasury Steve Mnuchin have all been racking up the frequent-flier miles as well, and, as of this writing, they all still have jobs. For another, this wasn't the first walk down the unethical highway for Tom Price.

As a congressman, he faced criticism in Congress for buying between $50,000 and $100,000 in stock in a biomedical firm that would benefit from legislation he was carrying—a transaction which, in Price's confirmation hearing, Senator Ron Wyden called "a conflict of interest and an abuse of position." Price also came under scrutiny for campaign contributions from health care industry organizations with matters pending before his committee. According to the Center for Responsive Politics, in his 2016 campaign for a seventh term in the House, Price accepted more than $700,000 from physicians, hospitals, drug companies, and health insurers.[73]

You'd think, given a do-over, that Trump might pick somebody a little more ethically grounded for his next HHS secretary. You'd think wrong. Soon a man with his own conflicts of interest was in the job.

When Donald Trump nominated Alex Azar to succeed Tom Price as secretary of Health and Human Services, he called him a "star for better healthcare and lower drug prices." Another big Trump lie. In fact, just the opposite is true.[74]

During Azar's tenure as president of Eli Lilly, the pharmaceutical company tripled the price of insulin and was fined for colluding to keep its drug prices high. "The last thing we need," observed Vermont senator Bernie Sanders, "is to put a pharmaceutical executive in charge of the Department of Health and Human Services." And yet here we are.[75]

By putting Azar at the helm of HHS, you wonder if Donald Trump forgot his campaign pledge to lower prescription drug prices or simply decided to ignore it. In either case, Azar's not the man to push for lower drug prices. He spent his time in Big Pharma trying to jack them up and thereby getting his company in serious legal trouble.

Just look at what happened with insulin, the key drug for treating diabetes. Drug companies usually justify high prices by claiming they need to recoup the cost of developing relatively new drugs. That's not the case with insulin. It was developed in Toronto in 1921 and today costs pennies on a dollar to produce. But instead of reducing prices to reflect the lower cost of production, drug companies have done just the opposite. Today, thanks to pharma executives like Alex Azar, those suffering from diabetes in the United States pay an average $571.69 per month on drugs—the highest of any other nation on earth. And Americans—like Shane Patrick Boyle, who perished after his GoFundMe for insulin came up fifty dollars short, and Alec Raeshawn Smith, who was rationing his insulin after falling off his parents' health insurance at age twenty-six—are literally dying because they can no longer afford the high price of a nearly hundred-year-old drug that should be completely affordable these days.[76]

As a candidate, Donald Trump accused big pharmaceutical companies of "getting away with murder." Nothing's changed. Big Pharma will continue to get away with murder—except now with the help of Alex Azar, one of their very own, as secretary of HHS.

57. BEN CARSON

Shortly after the 2016 election, conservative talk show host Armstrong Williams, a longtime friend and advisor of former Republican presidential candidate Dr. Ben Carson, told reporters, "Dr. Carson feels he has no government experience. The last thing he would want to do was take a position that could cripple the presidency." Which makes you wonder why he ran for the nation's top office in the first place.[77]

Yet, thanks to Donald Trump, he now sits in the cabinet anyway, as secretary of Housing and Urban Development.

Even in a cabinet filled with unqualified people, Ben Carson as secretary of Housing and Urban Development stands out. He may have been a leading brain surgeon, but what does he know about public housing? All the White House could offer was that he grew up in public housing. Which is not true. He grew up in Detroit *near* public housing. There's a big difference.[78]

Coming in with no qualifications for the job, Carson has basically ignored it. He's maintained the lowest profile of any cabinet member. In fact, coming into the position with no government experience, no political experience other than a comical run for president, and no desire to run a government agency, he has produced a situation at HUD that his predecessor, Julian Castro, describes as "benign neglect." One longtime employee described the scene at HUD to *New York Magazine*: "It was just nothing. I've never been so bored in my life. No agenda, nothing to move forward or push back against. Just nothing."[79]

But that doesn't mean he's avoided doing considerable damage. To be fair, HUD was already in bad shape when he arrived. Created in 1965 by President Lyndon Johnson as one prime hot spot of the Great Society, HUD's mission had shrunk and its workforce had fallen from over sixteen thousand to fewer than eight thousand by the time Carson got there. But rather than pump new blood into the agency, Trump's first budget proposed cutting HUD by $7 billion, or 15 percent.[80]

For an agency still responsible for overseeing rental subsidies for five million families and thirty-three hundred public housing authorities providing shelter to two million families, those cuts would mean real hardship.

OMB director Mick Mulvaney himself estimated that cutting HUD by 15 percent would mean that participants in the Section 8 low-income assistance, public housing voucher program would need to pay at least 17 percent more of their income toward rent, and there would likely be over two hundred thousand fewer vouchers available nationwide—thirteen thousand fewer in New York City alone.[81]

But Secretary Carson didn't seem to care. In a radio interview with his friend Armstrong Williams the day after Trump's budget was released, Carson pooh-poohed the importance of programs to help the poor, saying that poverty was largely a "state of mind." In other words, feel better, and no worries, your bills will be paid.[82]

A Republican-controlled Congress eventually rejected Trump's severe cuts to HUD, but that didn't stop Ben Carson from causing trouble elsewhere. On April 25, 2018, he unveiled a major overhaul of HUD's low-income rental housing program. Complaining that the current system, whereby poor families pay 30 percent of their adjusted income for housing, discourages "families from earning more income and becoming self-sufficient," Carson's new rules will effectively triple the rent. They require participants to contribute 35 percent of their gross income for rent and will authorize housing authorities to adopt work requirements for all participants, excluding those over sixty-five and the disabled.[83]

Meanwhile, Carson proceeded to cut back on what few agency initiatives remained. He canceled a survey testing how efforts to reduce homelessness for LGBT Americans were working in Cincinnati and Houston. He required employees to get executive approval before making any contacts with anyone outside the building. He scuttled guidelines to homeless shelters on providing access to transgender people.[84]

While comfortably slashing programs to help the poor, however, Carson still found a way to make life easier for his wealthy friends. In April 2018, as part of the FBI's investigation of Trump's personal attorney Michael Cohen, it was revealed that Cohen had also advised Fox News star anchor Sean Hannity on several real estate deals. *The Guardian* subsequently reported that, over the years, Hannity had built up a personal real estate empire—in part, with the help of $18 million in loans from HUD's National Housing Act—a special relationship Hannity failed to mention when interviewing Carson on his TV show.[85]

While these loans were first guaranteed during the Obama years, Carson's HUD had strongly supported Hannity's request and even increased the size of the loan by $5 million. Nor did Carson explain how he could preside over the decline of HUD's primary mission of providing low-income housing while finding resources to help the rich buy more real estate and then foreclose on struggling people. After a 152-unit apartment complex in Perry, Georgia, was acquired by Hannity through various shell companies, foreclosures and evictions shot up 400 percent.[86]

Meanwhile, like the other cabinet members we've visited, Carson also seized the opportunity to live higher on the hog. No charter jets, so far as we know, just a new dining room table, chairs, and hutch for his office—in clear violation of HUD spending guidelines—for which taxpayers shelled out $31,561. After at first insisting he knew nothing about the purchase, Carson later blamed it on his wife, Candy. "I invited my wife to come and help," he told reporters. "I left it to my wife, you know, to choose something. I dismissed myself from the issues." She chose the style and colors of the new furniture, he pointed out, while adding, "With the caveat that we were both not happy about the price." Still, the dining room set remains.[87]

The best that can be said about Ben Carson as HUD secretary is that he's in over his head. Which he himself admits. "There are more complexities here than in brain surgery," he candidly told *The New York Times*. He never should have been offered the job and never should have taken it.[88]

58. RICK PERRY

To give him credit, Rick Perry took Donald Trump's approach to filling his cabinet one step beyond anyone else. Not only was he, like DeVos and Pruitt, the number one enemy of his department and vowed to eliminate it, Perry couldn't even remember its name.

It was at the November 2011 GOP presidential debate in Detroit where candidate Perry, then the governor of Texas, infamously declared there were three government agencies that would no longer exist when he became president: "Commerce, Education, and . . . um . . . ah . . . um . . . ah." After an awkward forty-eight seconds (!), he finally admitted, "The third one I can't name . . . Oops!"[89]

That third one, of course, is the Department of Energy, at the head of which Rick Perry, God help us, is now secretary.

What soon became clear about Rick Perry at Energy was that he had no qualifying background for the job. In fact, even after he figured out its name, he still didn't know what the department was all about. As former governor of Texas, reported *The New York Times,* he believed "he was taking on a role as a global ambassador for the American oil and gas industry that he had long championed in his home state."[90]

And no doubt about it, Rick Perry has caught religion on fossil fuels. He's so bullish on them he told utility executives it was "immoral" to withhold fossil fuel–powered electricity from people around the world who don't have access to power (as if that's the only kind of power available). "You look those people in the eye and say, sorry you can't have electricity because we've decided that fossil fuels are bad."[91]

Not only that, Perry has argued that fossil fuels protect women from sexual abuse: "But also from the standpoint of sexual assault, when the lights are on, when you have light that shines, the righteousness, if you will, on those types of acts." In a way, it's impressive that Perry is even more clueless than his boss on the subject of "clean coal."[92]

In any event, Perry was no doubt surprised to learn that the Energy Department's threefold mission is much more complicated than "Yeah, fossil fuels!" Rather, the department works to advance the energy security of the United States; to promote scientific and technological innovation in support of that mission; and to oversee America's nuclear arsenal. It's a mission previously entrusted to very smart people, like Nobel Laureate Steven Chu and MIT professor Ernest Moniz. It's a mission that a failed politician who publicly questions the integrity of scientists, champions fossil fuels, opposes regulations on greenhouse gases, and insists "the science is still out" on climate change is particularly unqualified for. In fact, as governor, Perry's only experience with our nuclear stockpile was leading a campaign to bring a nuclear waste facility to the Lone Star State, at a time when every other state was rejecting them. (You can be the judge on whether sizable campaign donations to Governor Perry from the billionaire head of a Dallas-based waste control company had any influence on this stance.)[93]

Once at Energy, in addition to promoting fossil fuels and nuclear power,

Perry, like Donald Trump, became the champion of bringing back "clean coal" plants—in which, again like Trump, he soon proved himself ignorant of the market forces driving the energy economy. The fact is, as noted earlier, more and more utilities are abandoning coal, not just because it's dirty, and nuclear reactors, not just because we don't yet know how to dispose of the waste, but because cheaper alternatives—wind, solar, and natural gas—have become available. In 2017, that drove utilities to shut down more than twenty-two gigawatts of coal capacity across the country.[94]

Apparently, Perry didn't know that. One of his first acts was to put forth a plan to reward existing coal plants, which have a ninety-day pile of coal on hand, and therefore, he argued, were less likely to cause blackouts. Having first met fierce opposition by consumer and environmental organizations, as well as by utilities, which rely more and more on renewable sources of energy, his proposal was then unanimously rejected by the Federal Energy Regulatory Commission (FERC), of which four out of five members had been appointed by President Trump.[95]

But any mystery about why Perry was so gung ho on coal evaporated once one top DOE staffer, Simon Edelman, leaked unreleased photos of the secretary sitting down, just four weeks after taking office, with Robert Murray, CEO of Murray Energy, a large U.S. coal company. Murray had donated $300,000 to Donald Trump's presidential inauguration. At this meeting, he provided the administration with a coal industry wish list, which included, in addition to propping up failing coal power plants, replacing commissioners at three independent agencies, overturning safety and pollution regulations, and cutting the staff of the EPA in half.[96]

The meeting ended, as photos show, with Perry giving Murray a big hug. Eight months later, Perry made his ill-fated pro-coal industry proposal, as requested by Murray, to FERC. Perry called it a case of "energy realism," but even Donald Trump's own commissioners seemed to see it more as a case of "pay to play" and antithetical to market forces driving the energy industry. They rejected Perry's plan. And Perry immediately fired Simon Edelman.[97]

59. "GOVERNMENT SACHS"

Donald Trump hates Goldman Sachs. Or at least that's what we were led to believe. Indeed, during both the 2016 primary and general campaigns, he attacked them so often, we weren't sure whether he was running against Ted Cruz, Hillary Clinton, or Goldman Sachs CEO Lloyd Blankfein.

Trump frequently criticized Clinton for her paid speeches to Goldman Sachs audiences. He released a campaign ad featuring a photo of Clinton shaking hands with Blankfein. He accused Ted Cruz of being their puppet: "Goldman Sachs owns him, he will do anything they demand." And he called Goldman Sachs part of a "global power structure that is responsible for the economic decisions that have robbed our working class, stripped our country of its wealth, and put that money into the pockets of a handful of large corporations and political entities."[98]

If Donald Trump hated Goldman Sachs, then it also seemed Goldman Sachs hated Trump. As *Vanity Fair* reported, "He was the poster child of the kind of client that Goldman, which has always prided itself on superb risk management, warned its bankers to avoid." After at least four of his hotels and casinos went bankrupt, word went out that Goldman Sachs would never again do business with Trump.[99]

Then Donald Trump was elected president and the world turned upside down, or the mask dropped. Either way, suddenly, Trump loved Goldman and Goldman loved Trump.

As fast as an electronic transfer, Trump turned to Goldman Sachs to fill his administration's top financial posts. Steve Mnuchin, Gary Cohn, Dina Powell, Steve Bannon, and Anthony Scaramucci all did time at Goldman Sachs before joining Trump in Washington. Billionaire and Commerce secretary Wilbur Ross, while not a Goldman Sachs alum, belonged to the same elite Wall Street crowd.

Trump's newfound love for Goldman caused an exasperated Senator Elizabeth Warren, long a thorn in the side of Wall Street, to exclaim, "Donald Trump promised to drain the swamp. Then he put enough Goldman bankers on his team to open a branch office of Goldman in the White House."[100]

Together, they proceeded to fleece the public from Washington the same way they used to fleece the public from Wall Street.

STEVE MNUCHIN

During the 2016 campaign, Trump (rightfully) scorned hedge fund managers in particular. "The hedge fund guys didn't build this country," he told CBS. "These are guys that shift paper around and they get lucky." Yet he tapped Steve Mnuchin, a hedge fund mogul, to be his campaign finance chair. And when the dust settled, Trump made him secretary of the Treasury.[101]

It's not such a surprising choice, because Trump and Mnuchin have a lot in common. Both got started in business with a huge inheritance from their fathers. (Mnuchin's father was a partner at Goldman Sachs.) Both of their businesses had been accused of racial discrimination. Both men hedged their bets by donating to Democrats as well as Republicans. And like Trump, Mnuchin came to the administration with a shady business reputation, at best.[102]

After spending seventeen years at Goldman Sachs, Mnuchin worked for a couple of hedge funds before putting together a group of investors to buy the failed IndyMac Bank, which they renamed OneWest Bank. Within a year, according to the *Los Angeles Times,* Mnuchin and his fellow investors had paid themselves dividends of $1.57 billion, while foreclosing on tens of thousands of home mortgages, often for the tiniest of infractions. One judge called their treatment of a New York family "harsh, repugnant, shocking and repulsive." California housing counselors ranked OneWest among the worst mortgage servers in the state. Their track record was especially bad in communities of color. With a résumé of racism, thievery, and corruption like that, why wouldn't Donald Trump fall in love with the guy?[103]

Billionaire or not, it didn't take long at Treasury for Steve Mnuchin to join the ranks of Pruitt, Zinke, Price, and Veterans Affairs secretary David Shulkin in the money-grubbing private plane club. In this case, Mnuchin and his actress wife, Louise Linton, famously used a military plane to fly to Fort Knox, Kentucky, to view the 2017 solar eclipse. According to the watchdog group Citizens for Responsibility and Ethics in Washington, he spent $1 million in his first year on military aircraft, where previous Treasury secretaries have flown commercial. Reportedly, his request for a military aircraft to fly to Europe for his honeymoon was turned down.[104]

Pleasure trips aside, Mnuchin's main goal at Treasury was to give himself and his fellow billionaires a massive tax break. Unfortunately, with Donald Trump, Mitch McConnell, and Paul Ryan's help, he succeeded, with passage of the massive GOP tax cut bill in December 2017. In so doing, however, he made three big promises to the American people: that the tax cut bill would "pay for itself" and add nothing to the deficit; that everybody in the middle class would get a tax cut; and that the wealthy would not reap any special benefit—in his own words, there would be "no absolute tax cut for the upper class." All three were big fat obvious lies.[105]

In fact, according to the Congressional Budget Office, the GOP bill will add $1.7 trillion to the deficit over the next ten years. The Tax Policy Center estimates that while some middle-class taxpayers may see a small tax cut initially, their taxes will actually increase under the plan by 2027. Again, according to the Tax Policy Center, initially three-quarters of total tax cuts would go to the top 1 percent. By 2025, they would receive a remarkable 99.6 percent of benefits.[106]

This wasn't just Mnuchin breaking promises. He was straight-up lying the entire time. As *Slate*'s Jordan Weissman summed it up, "The man regularly says things that just aren't true." To take one more example, as the tax bill wended its way through Congress, Mnuchin promised everyone that experts at Treasury were working hard on assessing its impact on the American economy. "We have over 100 people working on this," he proclaimed, "and it will be a completely transparent process." Of course, it later emerged that no such comprehensive report or scoring existed. Instead, per *The New York Times*, the Treasury's Office of Tax Policy "have been largely shut out of the process." Mnuchin had just made the whole thing up.[107]

At a White House briefing the day after the tax cut bill was approved by Congress, I asked Secretary Mnuchin whether President Trump would release his tax returns so we might learn how much he benefited from the GOP bill. Mnuchin ducked, saying Trump's position on releasing his tax returns was well known. I regret not asking Mnuchin how much he himself would benefit. He probably would have just lied to me anyway.

WILBUR ROSS

If you had taken the candidate at his word, Wilbur Ross as secretary of commerce seemed another strange pick for Donald Trump. Ross was not only another of those hated billionaire hedge fund managers, he was known for buying up ailing businesses, selling off their assets, firing employees, and screwing their creditors while walking off with the profits—a practice that earned him the nickname "bottom feeder."[108]

A strange choice, indeed, for someone who campaigned as an "economic populist." But unlike Trump, Ross doesn't even pretend to be an economic populist. He showed his true colors in 2014 when he whined to a reporter that "the 1 percent is being picked on for political reasons."[109]

In Trump's eyes, however, Ross had several things going for him. For one, he was stupendously rich and had helped bail out Trump's failing Atlantic City casinos in the 1990s. For another, thanks to the Panama Papers leak, we now know he's got several shady connections with Russian oligarchs, among them a stake in a shipping venture, Navigator Holdings, partly owned by Vladimir Putin's son-in-law. (He shorted his position in Navigator Holdings days before *The New York Times* reported his Putin connection.) Ross also engineered the takeover of the Bank of Cyprus in 2014, which has now become a destination for iffier Russian and Eastern European elements—and their friends like Trump campaign manager Paul Manafort—to park their lucre. When asked whether or not his bank was transacting with customers sanctioned by the United States, Ross shrugged. "That's a question that is very complicated to answer."[110]

And he once owned a coal mine! Although, had Trump looked closer, he would have learned it was West Virginia's notorious Sago Mine, where a dozen miners lost their lives in January 2006, just months after the federal Mine Safety and Health Administration cited Sago for 208 "serious and substantial" safety violations.[111]

After the mine explosion, Ross declined to travel to West Virginia to inspect the damage or console the families of the dead miners. Instead, he sent $2 million for the twelve families to divide up. Two years later, he shut down the mine. That's the type of callous disregard for working people, and pathetic pursuit of profit above all else, that will get you far with Trump, so Ross for Commerce it was.[112]

GARY COHN

Among the Goldman Sachs bankers who took the plunge, COO Gary Cohn appeared the least likely to join the Trump administration. A lifelong Democrat, he was instrumental in arranging the infamous closed-door paid speeches for Hillary Clinton. Under his direction, Goldman's political PAC donated over $340,000 to the Clinton campaign and less than $5,000 to Trump.[113]

Yet reportedly, Cohn was getting restless at Goldman, tired of waiting for Lloyd Blankfein to step down so he could move up to CEO. Whether Cohn agreed with Trump's economic policies, or whether he even knew what they were, by dangling the position of head of the National Economic Council before him, Trump gave Cohn an easy way out of the waiting game at Goldman—and Cohn seized it.[114]

For a year or so, Cohn actually exercised a lot of influence in the White House. Together with Rex Tillerson, national security advisor H. R. McMaster, and Secretary of Defense James Mattis, he was known as one of the four grown-ups in the room. He was credited with talking Trump out of some crazy moves but still threatened to resign in summer 2017 after the Charlottesville fiasco, when Trump claimed there were some "very fine people" among the white supremacists.

In the end, Cohn decided to stay in order to keep the economic recovery (for the 1 percent) on track and avoid what he believed to be the looming threat of tariffs. For months, he'd been warning the president that bringing back tariffs would start another trade war and wreck the economy. But Trump rejected his advice.[115]

In March 2018 (with the tax giveaway now law), frustrated by Trump's decision to impose stiff tariffs on steel and aluminum imports and seeing his influence over Trump fade, Cohn finally resigned—which, to many, raised the question of why Cohn thought steel tariffs were a more important hill to die on than endorsing Nazis. By then, Tillerson and McMaster were also gone, leaving Secretary Mattis an ever-lonelier and increasingly ignored voice of reason in the room.[116]

LARRY KUDLOW

Looking for someone to replace Gary Cohn as chief economic advisor, President Trump turned to his favorite source of new hires. Avoiding leading economists in the financial industry or academia, he offered the job to someone who plays an economist on television.

Actually, he's not just a pretty face on television. Before hosting his own shows on CNBC, Larry Kudlow held several impressive economic posts: he was chief economist at Paine Webber and Bear Stearns and chief economist at the Office of Management and Budget, number two man to OMB director David Stockman, under President Reagan. But it's as a TV host that Kudlow's best known and where his talent for being so often dead wrong really shone through. If he's telling you to buy, sell. And vice versa.[117]

Kudlow's erroneous prognostications are legendary. In 1993, he predicted that Bill Clinton's tax hikes would kill any economic recovery. A boom happened instead. In 2002, he supported the war in Iraq, arguing that "the shock therapy of decisive war will elevate the stock market by a couple thousand points." We did invade Iraq, but the market did not soar. As late as December 2007, in the wake of George W. Bush's tax cuts, he was proclaiming that "the Bush boom is alive and well." That same month marked the beginning of the Great Recession.[118]

A doctrinaire supply-sider, Kudlow firmly believes in the now completely discredited trickle-down theory, a.k.a. "voodoo economics": that giving tax cuts to the 1 percent will rain down benefits on the 99 percent. As such, he was a strong supporter of the Trump tax cuts, predicting they would trigger 3–4 percent annual economic growth. (We'll see, of course, but consider Kudlow's track record here.)[119]

He, too, broke with Trump, however, on the question of tariffs. He even coauthored a column with Stephen Moore and Art Laffer denouncing Trump's proposed tariffs on steel and aluminum. "Trump should . . . examine the historical record on tariffs," they wrote. "If he does, he'll see they have almost never worked as intended and have almost always delivered an unhappy ending."[120]

In other words, Kudlow held the same position on tariffs as Gary Cohn. Both expressed their strong opposition. But once Trump rejected their advice and imposed tariffs, each responded differently. Cohn resigned. Kudlow changed his mind and came aboard—which doesn't bode well for his willingness to stand up to Trump on other important economic issues.

60. MICK MULVANEY

On April 25, 2018, Trump's OMB head and acting consumer financial watchdog Mick Mulvaney ripped the curtain off the way things work in Washington, and especially in Trumpworld. "We had a hierarchy in my office, in Congress," the former South Carolina congressman told leaders of the American Banking Association. "If you were a lobbyist who never gave us money, I didn't talk to you. If you were a lobbyist who gave us money, I might talk to you."[121]

That admission tells you all you need to know about Washington: it's strictly pay-for-play. And it tells you all you need to know about Mick Mulvaney: He's for sale.

Naturally, then, this is the man Donald Trump has entrusted with two top jobs—director of the Office of Management and Budget and acting director of the Consumer Finance Protection Bureau. He brings to OMB and CFPB the same extreme agenda he championed in Congress as co-founder of the House Freedom Caucus: ending Social Security and Medicaid; abolishing the Environmental Protection Agency; ending federal support for student loans, medical research, and "Meals on Wheels"; cutting back on foreign aid; demanding deep spending cuts as a price for raising the debt ceiling; defunding Planned Parenthood; and shutting down the government whenever conservatives don't get everything they want. Take it from the man himself. Mulvaney once jokingly introduced himself to Gary Cohn as a "right-wing nut job." That he is.[122]

Mulvaney got his first chance to enact his conservative wish list in Trump's 2018 budget, which he oversaw. It was a pure Freedom Caucus document, demanding deep cuts in domestic programs to offset $54 billion in new spending for the military. As proposed, the budget killed the National Endowment for the Arts, the Corporation for Public Broadcasting, the Children's Health Insurance Program, and the Legal Services Corporation; cut the EPA's budget by a third; cut the State Department by 29 percent; and stripped $7.7 billion out of the National Institutes of Health.[123]

On another front, Mulvaney led an effective administration effort to roll back regulations adopted across the board by the Obama administration, succeeding in rescinding 860 proposed regulations in year one of the Trump presidency.[124]

At the same time, in deference to Trump, Mulvaney agreed to go along with what would theoretically be a fiscal conservative's nightmare. Between the tax cuts of 2017 and the omnibus spending bill of January 2018, Trump added $2.4 trillion—and perhaps as much as $6 trillion—to the national debt: a repudiation of everything Trump promised as a candidate for president and Mulvaney had preached as a member of Congress. But, a loyal Trump foot soldier, Mulvaney simply talked out of the other side of his mouth for a while.

In fact, Mulvaney told a lie for Trump so brazen that economists outside the administration called for his immediate firing. While cutting deeply in services that help poor and working-class Americans, the Mulvaney–Trump budget also presumed that the new tax law will generate $2 trillion in revenue—a very, *very* unlikely proposition to any responsible economist—that will offset the cost of the ridiculous tax giveaways to the rich. That was bad enough. But then Mulvaney's OMB also argued that the same $2 trillion of magic money will balance the budget in ten years. In short, Mulvaney conjured up a ridiculous figure to make his budget work— and then double-counted it.[125]

Economists were appalled by Mulvaney's innumeracy. "This appears to be the most egregious accounting error in a Presidential budget in the nearly 40 years I have been tracking them," tweeted former Treasury head Larry Summers. "No business in the country would even try to get away with this type of phony accounting," another economist told *The Wall Street Journal*. In *Forbes,* Stan Collender said this fuzzy math "may well have been the biggest mistake in US history."[126]

But Mulvaney didn't care. He just wanted to please his boss, and Mick Mulvaney has already made it abundantly clear that he'll do anything for money.

And it worked. In Trump's eyes, in fact, Mulvaney did such a good job gutting essential government services in his proposed budget that he decided to give him yet another job. When Richard Cordray suddenly resigned as head of the Consumer Finance Protection Bureau (CFPB), Trump didn't search for a new director. In a classic Trumpian move, he just put Mick Mulvaney in charge. After all, as a member of Congress from South Carolina, Mulvaney had cosponsored a bill to eliminate the bureau.[127]

Now wearing two hats, instead of killing the CFPB, Mulvaney proceeded to turn the agency on its head: from adhering to its legislative mission of protecting consumers to following his own (bought-and-paid-for) agenda of protecting bankers and predatory lenders. In keeping with a memo he sent to CFPB staffers—"We don't just work for the government, we work for the people. And that means everyone: those who use credit cards, and those who provide those cards; those who take loans, and those who make them"—he immediately dropped a CFPB lawsuit against four payday lenders in Kansas that were charging rates as high as 950 percent and closed an investigation into a South Carolina payday lender that contributed to his congressional campaigns. With that and similar decisions, the agency's regulatory and enforcement work ground to a halt.[128]

Mulvaney then further weakened the bureau by asking Congress to rewrite its original congressional mandate to protect consumers by requiring that any new rules created by the bureau to help consumers first be approved by Congress before they could go into effect.[129]

Now, from all of this, you may think badly of Mick Mulvaney—I sure do. But even if he's proved himself an impressive liar, he's also at times been breathtakingly honest, arguably the most honest man in Donald Trump's cabinet. After all, the man flat-out told us himself—he works for lobbyists and the rich, not for us. If only the rest of Trumpworld were as honest about their mission.

6

TRUMP'S WHITE HOUSE STAFF

For most newly elected presidents, it's hard to decide among the hundreds of talented, experienced, and dedicated professionals clamoring for a top job in the White House.

But for Donald Trump, it was just the opposite. Hundreds of talented, experienced, and dedicated professionals didn't want anything to do with the Trump administration and had said so in writing. So he was stuck filling the White House with a motley gaggle of inexperienced, leftover campaign aides, family members, and second-rate political hacks. Trump didn't care—he didn't want competence, he wanted loyalty.

Within a year, things got even worse with the voluntary or forced departures of several members of the starting squad, leaving Trump with a C or D team at best, among them family members Ivanka and Jared; vampiric house elf Stephen Miller; human facepalm John Kelly; professional liars Sarah Huckabee Sanders and Kellyanne Conway; and dangerous fringe right-winger John Bolton, who would kill a rat in a trap with a tactical nuke.

61. FAIL TO THE CHIEF

After the president himself, there's nobody more important in the White House, not even the vice president, than the chief of staff. He's the man who imposes order on the White House, manages the president's time, oversees the entire staff, and sets the administration's priorities—a job for which he needs the president's ear, trust, and total confidence. If any of those are lacking, chaos ensues.

I'm sure you see where this is going. Since Donald Trump neither trusts nor listens to anyone but himself and resists any attempts to manage his time or tweets, chaos is exactly what we got in the Trump White House—under two chiefs and counting so far.

REINCE PRIEBUS

Priebus, the ultimate establishment party hack, was a misfit for Donald Trump from day one. Remove the vowels, as many have pointed out, and his very name says it all: "RNC-PR-BS."[1]

Priebus and Trump had nothing in common, except a desire to win. The difference was, Priebus wanted to win with anybody but Trump as the GOP nominee. He broke several times with Trump during the primary: over Trump's ridicule of primary opponents, his put-down of John McCain, and his attack on Khizr Khan. After release of the *Access Hollywood* tape, Priebus met with Trump at Trump Tower and urged him to drop out of the race.[2]

Still, once Trump won the nomination, Priebus totally rolled over in public. Like a true political patsy, he decided to no longer fight Trump but to embrace, coddle, enable, and empower him.

No doubt, Priebus was as surprised as anybody else when Trump actually won the presidency, which added up to a huge win for Priebus himself. As chair of the RNC, the party hack from Wisconsin had delivered the ultimate political prize to the Republican Party: the trifecta. Control of the House, Senate, and White House. And this was his reward: perhaps the worst job in Washington, chief of staff to Donald Trump! He was out of a job within six months.[3]

You could see this train wreck coming. Trump broadcast his distrust of Priebus from day one, announcing his appointment as chief of staff at the same time he appointed Steve Bannon his senior advisor, while making it clear that Bannon would report directly to him and not to Priebus.[4]

So why name him chief of staff at all? Because, even though Priebus wasn't his kind of guy, Trump saw him as the consummate D.C. insider who had lots of friends in Congress and knew how to get things done in Washington. For his part, Priebus saw Trump as a seriously unqualified and wildly undisciplined candidate who would follow advice and pivot to acting presidential once he got to the White House. They were both wrong.

It didn't take long for Priebus to fall out of favor. Privately, Trump told friends he didn't like Priebus's style of hovering over him like a butler in the Oval Office. He started calling him "Reincey." And once Priebus failed to deliver on his first assignment—repeal of Obamacare—Trump openly suggested making him ambassador to Greece. But in the end, Priebus didn't even get the satisfaction of that job. Instead, he was shoved out the door in the most humiliating fashion possible.[5]

Rumors had been swirling for weeks that he was on his way out. Daughter Ivanka and his son-in-law, Jared Kushner, reportedly didn't get along with him. Trump blamed him for Congress's failure to repeal Obamacare. But the sure sign he was dead meat came in July 2017, when Trump, over Priebus's objections, named hedge fund manager and publicity hog Anthony Scaramucci as the new White House communications director.[6]

Priebus having blocked him from getting a job earlier in the administration, "the Mooch" held a longtime grudge against Priebus and didn't wait to get even. On his first day on the job—as we'll see, already 9 percent of the way through his tenure—he called Priebus a "fucking paranoid schizophrenic." When Trump didn't defend Priebus or chasten Scaramucci, Reincey knew his goose was cooked.[7]

Two days later, Priebus accompanied Trump to a political event on Long Island, after which he basically got taken out like Tessio in *The Godfather*. When Air Force One returned to a rainy Andrews Air Force Base, Priebus deplaned and, in full view of reporters, climbed into a black Suburban with White House aides Stephen Miller and Dan Scavino. Moments later, as the motorcade sat there, President Trump, still on Air Force One, sent out a tweet announcing he was replacing Priebus with Homeland Security secretary John Kelly—at which point Miller and Scavino climbed out of the SUV, which soon pulled out of the presidential motorcade and left the base, taking the now former chief of staff home alone.[8]

JOHN KELLY

But forget about all the chaos under Reince Priebus. With John Kelly on the job, we were told, it would be a turbulent White House no more. He was a grown-up. He was a tough-ass general. He would impose order and discipline on the Trump White House where none existed before.[9]

Yet it wasn't long before Kelly's star—not to mention his dreams of a fifth star for his lapel—began to fade, and he eventually ended up just one more person sucked in, chewed up, and spit out by Donald Trump.

The problem is, as Reince Priebus discovered six months earlier, order and discipline were the last things Donald Trump wanted. *Chaos* is his middle name. He thrives on it. Which, in the beginning, even John Kelly was smart enough to recognize. He admitted he might be able to manage the White House staff but not the president himself. In fact, he said he wasn't even going to try controlling or curtailing Trump's twin addictions of Twitter and TV or convincing him to show up in the Oval Office before 11:00 or 11:30.[10]

Instead, Kelly focused on making the White House run smoothly. He set the president's daily schedule, monitored his phone calls, decided who was invited to meetings, made meetings shorter, cut down the number of people with access to the Oval Office, ordered staff to stay in their own lane, and began weeding out problem children.[11]

At first, Trump seemed pleased. He bragged about having a general in charge. He actually seemed to crave Kelly's approval, reportedly calling him as often as twelve times a day to seek his advice. Briefly, he even tried to adjust his freewheeling style to the more disciplined order Kelly was trying to introduce.[12]

That didn't last long. It was only a month before Trump began to chafe under Kelly's new rule, and rumors of another divorce leaked out of the West Wing. Trump actually told one friend, "I've got another nut job here who thinks he's running things." According to West Wing sources, Trump resented the fact that Kelly was telling people that he was the one running the government while Trump spent all his time watching TV and tweeting about it. He was especially angered when Kelly told Fox News anchor Bret Baier that Trump was "uninformed" in promising to build a wall and have Mexico pay for it.[13]

Soon, once again, Trump was floating names of possible replacements for his chief of staff. This time around it was budget director Mick Mulvaney, economic advisor Gary Cohn, or House majority whip Kevin McCarthy. How bad was it? So bad that Trump even called Reince Priebus to complain about Kelly.[14]

Kelly, meanwhile, didn't help his own case. His troubles managing the day-to-day White House were one thing, but whenever he injected himself in public policy, he fumbled badly, hurting both himself and the president.

It started when Kelly stepped into the dispute between Trump and Florida congresswoman Frederica Wilson over insensitive comments Trump made to the widow of army sergeant La David Johnson, killed in Niger. Stepping out of his role as chief of staff and into the role of White House attack dog, Kelly called Wilson an "empty barrel" and accused her of using the occasion of a speech at the dedication of a new FBI facility to take sole credit for the building. After checking the video, journalists reported that Wilson did no such thing. Kelly was lying.[15]

He got caught in another lie about firing his right-hand man, Rob Porter. When reports first surfaced that, even though he'd been on the job for thirteen months, Porter could not get a top security clearance because he'd been accused by two former wives of domestic abuse, Kelly called Porter a "man of integrity and honor" and urged him to stay. Days later, when a photo surfaced of one of his wives sporting a black eye received from Porter, Kelly changed his tune, insisting he'd known nothing about allegations of domestic abuse until being shown that photo. Even after the FBI blew Kelly's cover by confirming it had informed him of charges against Porter months earlier, Kelly ordered White House staff to back up his big lie that he'd just recently learned of Porter's problems.[16]

Over time, through a combination of Trump's obstinance and Kelly's incompetence, Kelly's influence and presence in the White House continued to erode. He was no longer consulted on key decisions, he didn't participate in key meetings, he was left behind on foreign travel. Nobody could understand why Trump hadn't fired him.[17]

In the end, Trump and Kelly were like an old couple whose marriage had ended a long time ago but who still lived in the same house together because they were too lazy to get a divorce.

62. SEAN SPICER

If chief of staff is the second-most important job in the White House, press secretary is right up there—and, by far, the most visible. It's the press secretary who's the public face of the administration. He or she serves as the president's link to the media and, through the media, to the American people: delivering the message, making the arguments, setting the agenda.

But that job becomes impossible when the president does not tell the truth. When he lies, he forces the press secretary, either knowingly or unknowingly, to lie for him—and that destroys the trust with the media on which the job of press secretary depends.

Thus is the case with both Sean Spicer and Sarah Huckabee Sanders. Whatever decent reputations they might have once enjoyed before, taking this job has destroyed them. Spicer's become a national joke, and Sanders has lasted longer only because she's a better liar.

To those of us who know him, Sean Spicer is a one-man Shakespearean tragedy. For years, he was one of the most well-known and well-liked conservative political figures in Washington. As communications director at the RNC, he was a man who could spin as well as anybody in the business, but a man you could trust never to tell an outright lie. Then he hooked up with Donald Trump, who quickly told him to dress better so he looked the part. Six months later, he resigned with a closetful of nattier clothes and a reputation as the biggest liar ever to stand at the White House podium every day (that is, until Sarah Sanders came along).

At first, reporters were relieved to hear that Spicer would be Trump's press secretary. After Trump's own relentless attacks against the media—"the enemy of the American people"—and those of Steve Bannon—"the opposition party"—members of the White House press corps believed they'd at least have a straight shooter as press secretary. But Spicer burst that bubble of optimism on his first appearance in the briefing room.[18]

On the day after Trump's inauguration, Spicer famously stepped up to the podium to declare that it had been "the largest audience to ever witness an inauguration. Period." Of course, it wasn't. And that was just the first of many lies.[19]

Spicer's problem was that he'd lie about anything for his boss. And he didn't just lie, he was so bad at it. He defended Trump's lie about how three million people voted illegally for Hillary Clinton. He insisted Trump was right about Barack Obama wiretapping Trump Tower. He argued that the famous June 2016 meeting at Trump Tower was about adoption, even after Donald Trump Jr. had admitted it was about gathering dirt on Clinton. And he defended Trump's missile attack on Syria by explaining, "You had someone as despicable as Hitler, who didn't even sink to using chemical weapons"— news to anyone who knew anything about the Holocaust.[20]

Those of us who cover the briefings soon began to dismiss Spicer as a hopeless con man, who would say anything to please his obvious audience of one. Meanwhile, his temper tantrums, awkwardness at the podium, and antagonism toward reporters inspired the brilliant parody of Spicer on *SNL* by Melissa McCarthy. Everybody found it funny except Donald Trump, who didn't like the fact that his press secretary was portrayed by a woman.[21]

Trump's hiring of Anthony Scaramucci as his new boss finally pushed Spicer off the edge. He resigned on July 21, 2017. Although, even after leaving the White House, he continued to defend his lies. A few weeks later, asked by Jimmy Kimmel if he regretted his claim about the size of the inauguration audience, Spicer declined. "Look, your job as press secretary is to represent that president's voice," he explained, "and to make sure that you are articulating what he believes . . . Whether or not you agree or not isn't your job."[22]

Spicer concluded, "That's what you sign up to do." How sad. And far from how most every other White House press secretary before him saw the job.[23]

Months later, Spicer seemed to have some regrets about taking the job. When I ran into him in April 2018 at one of many parties surrounding the White House Correspondents Dinner, I jokingly asked, "Aren't you glad you got out when you did?"

"Fuck yeah!" Spicer shot back.

"Off the record?"

"On the record!" he said.

At any rate, Sean Spicer will be remembered as a bad liar. What we should really fear is a press secretary who will be remembered as a good liar. She came next.

63. SARAH HUCKABEE SANDERS

There's always a certain tension at White House briefings. In fact, you can't avoid it. It's inevitable. Reporters want to know more, and the press secretary wants to say as little as possible. So one side pushes and the other side pushes back. That's healthy. It goes with the territory.

As a member of the White House press corps, I've experienced, and contributed to, that tension under press secretaries Robert Gibbs, Jay Carney, Josh Earnest, and Sean Spicer. But with Sarah Huckabee Sanders, it's different. It's way beyond tension. Every day with Sanders is all-out war.

She snarls, she ridicules, she drips with sarcasm, she cuts people off, belittles them, and talks down to them. And above all, she lies. You have the feeling she doesn't mind being sent out to defend Donald Trump's most outrageous lies. She actually looks forward to it. In fact, she routinely expands and compounds his lies. Little wonder that, in June 2018, the Red Hen restaurant in Lexington, Virginia, refused to serve her.

Asked if she agreed with Trump that the women who accused him of sexual harassment were all lying, she replied, "Yeah, we've been clear on that from the beginning, and the president's spoken on it."[24]

Asked if Trump should apologize for calling Senator Elizabeth Warren "Pocahontas," she insisted it was "not a racial slur" and accused Warren of using her Native American heritage "to advance her career."[25]

Asked why Trump fired Comey, she said she'd talked to "countless" FBI agents who complained of Comey's leadership of the FBI. Yet we all saw President Trump specifically tell NBC's Lester Holt he fired Comey because of that "Russia thing."[26]

Asked if Trump's comment that Senator Kirsten Gillibrand would come to his office and "do anything" for a campaign contribution was a sexist remark, she snipped, "Your mind is in the gutter."[27]

Of course, Sanders is not the first White House spokesperson to tell a lie. We just talked about Spicer lying up a storm, and Nixon press secretary Ron

Ziegler once had to famously concede that his earlier statements were "inoperative." But Spicer and Ziegler aside, with other press secretaries, it was a rare occurrence and, more often than not, unwitting: merely repeating something they were told was true but turned out not to be. Most secretaries would never deliberately tell a lie because they know that, in dealing with the press, truthfulness is the coin of the realm.[28]

Sarah Sanders doesn't care. She lies like she means it. PolitiFact, which, as of this writing, rated 69 percent of Donald Trump's statements as False, Mostly False, or Pants on Fire!, has also identified several whoppers told by Sarah Sanders. She's lied about everything from gun laws in Chicago to the vetting of immigrants who receive diversity visas to Trump's infamous comments suggesting President Obama ordered him wiretapped. Over and over again, she insisted President Trump had no role in drafting a memo to *The New York Times* stating the purpose of Donald Jr.'s Trump Tower meeting in June 2016 was about adoption. When Trump's attorneys, in June 2018, admitted that Trump himself had actually dictated the phony memo, Sanders refused to acknowledge that she had lied to the press corps.[29]

In May 2018, after Rudy Giuliani revealed that Trump had been lying all along about his dalliances with adult film actress Stormy Daniels—he *did* know she'd been paid $130,000 in hush money, and he *did* reimburse his bagman Michael Cohen for the money—lies dutifully repeated by Sarah Sanders, former Clinton press secretary Joe Lockhart had some advice for her. "I think at this point," Lockhart told CNN, "I'd go into the Oval Office and tell the president that if he lies to me again, I have to quit."[30]

Lockhart doesn't understand. Sanders would never do that. By all appearances, she loves lying as much as Donald Trump does. And like everyone else in this wretched White House, she knows that the only way to stay in Trump's good graces is to constantly demonstrate her loyalty to him. If that gets her kicked out of a few restaurants along the way, so be it.

64. ANTHONY SCARAMUCCI

You can distill the chaos and incompetence swirling about the Trump White House with one sad story: the brief saga of Anthony Scaramucci, or "the Mooch." He represents all the Trump White House is: nasty, brutish, and short. With apologies to Russian Revolution chronicler John Reed, the Mooch's tenure as communications director, which actually lasted eleven days, became wryly known in Washington as "Ten Days That Shook the World."[31]

One thing you can say about Scaramucci: He wasn't always a Trump loyalist. In fact, politically, he's been all over the place. He raised money for Barack Obama in 2008. He backed Mitt Romney in 2012. In 2016, he first backed Scott Walker and Jeb Bush, deriding Donald Trump as a "hack politician," a "big-mouthed bully," and "an inherited money dude from Queens County."[32]

But after Bush faded, the political chameleon emerged from a ninety-minute meeting with Trump and praised him as "a results-oriented entrepreneur capable of delivering bipartisan solutions to common-sense problems."[33]

With Trump's win, Scaramucci sold his asset management firm, SkyBridge Capital, to jockey for a top job in the Trump White House—director of the White House Office of Public Liaison or ambassador to the Organization for Economic Co-operation and Development or senior vice president of the U.S. Export-Import Bank. But he was shot down for all three by chief of staff Reince Priebus. Ironically, Scaramucci was better qualified for any one of those jobs than the one Trump finally gave him: White House communications director, an odd choice for someone with zero experience in either journalism or communications.[34]

His days at the White House may have been brief, but they were also eventful, starting with a bizarre solo appearance in the briefing room, where he said four times, "I love the president." By that time, press secretary Sean Spicer had resigned rather than report to Scaramucci. At first, the Mooch insisted he and Reince Priebus "are a bit like brothers"—until he phoned an old friend, *The New Yorker*'s Ryan Lizza, called Priebus "a fucking paranoid schizophrenic," and said he'd sicced the FBI on him for leaking his financial disclosures.[35]

Scaramucci may have been successful in pushing Priebus out the door, but that also proved to be his undoing. When he announced that he would not be reporting to John Kelly, the new chief of staff, but would report directly to the president, Kelly seized the opportunity to show who was in charge. His very first act was to fire Scaramucci, eleven days after the Mooch arrived at the White House and fifteen days before his official start date. He never should have been hired in the first place.[36]

65. STEVE BANNON

After Donald Trump himself, Steve Bannon may be one of the most dangerous and repellent personalities to work in the White House in modern times. It's scary he ever got that close to the center of power, and we should all feel relieved that he self-destructed as soon as he did.

After a peripatetic and lucrative career as naval officer, investment banker, and Hollywood producer, Bannon turned to politics and immediately made his mark as a radical, antiestablishment bomb thrower. In 2011, he was introduced to Donald Trump, who was then considering a run for president in 2012, by Trump advisor David Bossie. When Trump dropped out, Bannon went on to shake up the political scene as chief executive of the right-wing website *Breitbart News*—so much so that in October 2015, *Bloomberg* called him "the Most Dangerous Political Operative in America." Dangerous to some, perhaps, but just the man Donald Trump was looking for. In August 2016, now running for president for real, Trump brought Bannon back as CEO of his campaign, replacing Paul Manafort.[37]

Later, when things between them soured, Trump belittled Bannon's role in the campaign, insisting Bannon had "very little to do with our historic victory" and he'd already won the nomination before Bannon came on board. But there's no doubt that, early on, Bannon played a key role in Trump's positions and actions—through the last three months of the campaign, the transition, and the early months of Trump's presidency as "chief strategist."[38]

The isolationist, nativist, extremist Bannon, in fact, reinforced Trump's worst instincts and helped augment every one of Trump's most outrageous campaign promises—from building a wall and making Mexico pay for it to ripping up both the Paris accord on climate change and the Iran nuclear deal. After release of the *Access Hollywood* "grab 'em by the pussy" tape, Bannon urged Trump not to back down, but to double down, dismissing it as "locker room talk." And, at least for a while, in the White

House, he had unlimited access to Trump and was the only one Trump listened to. He even engineered himself a seat on the National Security Council Principals Committee, the first White House political staffer to be so honored.[39]

In the first months of the Trump administration, Bannon's influence was so powerful that rumors began about how he, not Trump, was really running the country. Cynics started talking about "President Bannon," and writing Trump off as "Bannon's puppet." That story gained such credence that Trump finally felt compelled to shoot it down with a pathetically insecure tweet: "I call my own shots, largely based on an accumulation of data, and everyone knows it." When the president of the United States has to remind everyone that he's still in charge, you know he's in trouble.[40]

No matter which one was actually elected, it soon became clear that Bannon saw Trump as a player in his overall agenda, not the other way around. He compared himself to notable forces of evil. "Darkness is good," he told author Michael Wolff. "Dick Cheney. Darth Vader. Satan. That's power." And he called himself a "Leninist" because, he said, "Lenin wanted to destroy the state, and that's my goal, too. I want to bring everything crashing down, and destroy all of today's establishment."[41]

In the end, what brought Bannon crashing down was a clash of egos. When Trump saw all the good publicity Bannon, the ultimate self-promoter, was getting as the "brains" of the White House, he rebelled. Bannon was out the door in August 2017, but not without a searing parting shot: "The Trump presidency that we fought for, and won, is over."

"Steve Bannon has nothing to do with me or my Presidency," Trump desultorily responded six months later, after some choice Bannon quotes found their way into Michael Wolff's *Fire and Fury*. "When he was fired, he not only lost his job, he lost his mind."[42]

Once outside the White House, Bannon immediately set out to take on the Republican Party establishment, vowing to support and elect antiestablishment candidates for the U.S. Senate, starting with Alabama's Roy Moore. But with Moore's defeat, Bannon's power and influence soon fizzled. He may have talked about running for president himself in 2020, if Donald Trump did not run for reelection, but nobody took him seriously anymore.[43]

Except, oddly enough, for Donald Trump—who continues to talk to

Bannon on a regular basis. They may have publicly broken up, but in their zeal to destroy everything America has always stood for, Trump and Bannon remain soul mates.

66. JARED KUSHNER

You might think that Jared Kushner and Ivanka Trump have no credentials for top jobs in the White House, and you'd be right. But, in Trumpworld, which, as former FBI chief James Comey pointed out, runs like a Mafia family, they have the only two credentials that count: Ivanka is Donald's daughter, and Jared is Donald's son-in-law. Both of them have leveraged those family connections not only to snare access and influence in the White House but to use their presence in the administration to advance their own personal fashion and real estate careers.[44]

Jared Kushner's résumé is not long. He's thirty-seven years old. He's in good shape. He's a good dresser. He's rich. He went to Harvard, thanks entirely to his daddy's donations. And he acquired a New York newspaper as a graduation present. Oh, yeah—and he's married to the president's daughter.[45]

With those creds, who cares if he has zero government experience? His father-in-law immediately put him in charge of several of the administration's top priorities. Add 'em up. At one time or another, Kushner's been in charge of negotiating peace in the Middle East; solving America's opioid epidemic; diplomatic relations with Mexico and China; revamping the Department of Veterans Affairs; reforming the criminal justice system; and reinventing government. And to this date, he's failed at every one.[46]

So far as we know, Kushner has succeeded at only two things. First, he's used his position to settle personal scores: convincing Trump to fire James Comey and Steve Bannon, and to deny any job to Chris Christie, because Christie had sent Kushner's father to prison. And second, he's worked to help his family's real estate business.[47]

The New York Times has reported on several occasions where the Kushner Companies got big loans from U.S. financial institutions shortly after their executives attended meetings arranged by Kushner in the White House. And both federal and state prosecutors have been kept busy investigating connections between Kushner-led White House meetings with officials from Qatar and other countries, subsequent investments in the Kushner family business, and foreign policy decisions of the Trump administration.[48]

Driving that narrative is the well-known fact in New York real estate that, like his father-in-law, Jared never totally divorced himself from his family business—and that, also like Trump, he's been lousy at running it. Most notably, Kushner Companies faces a $1.2 billion mortgage payment in February 2019 on a high-rise at 666 Fifth Avenue, which Jared Kushner himself bought in 2006 and which has never been fully occupied.[49]

At the same time, special counsel Robert Mueller has also been investigating Kushner's many ties with Russian government and financial officials. Kushner attended the ill-fated Trump Tower meeting with Russian representatives on June 9, 2016, to gain dirt on Hillary Clinton and subsequently met with Russian ambassador Sergey Kislyak—a meeting, like so many others, that at first he failed to disclose.[50]

Kushner's apparent conflicts of interest and questionable dealings with foreign governments are of such concern that to date, even though he's been in the Trump White House from day one, he didn't receive a permanent top secret security clearance until May 2018, and that was at Trump's discretion.

Yes, that's right. The man Donald Trump has put in charge of peace in the Middle East couldn't get a top security clearance for nearly eighteen months. That's in part because of his many undisclosed meetings with foreign officials, as well as the constant revisions and updates he's made to his financial disclosure and security clearance paperwork as new information comes to light. It's also because, according to news reports in February 2018, a number of countries—including China, Mexico, Israel, and the UAE—have figured out that Kushner is eminently bribable and easily manipulated if and when they want anything out of Trump.[51]

Even though he's Trump's son-in-law, who knows how long Jared Kushner will last or what will happen to him. In this case, perhaps Steve Bannon has the best insight. "You realize where this is going," Bannon told Michael Wolff in *Fire and Fury*. "This is all about *money laundering*. Mueller chose [Andrew] Weissmann first and he is a money laundering guy. Their path to fucking Trump goes right through Paul Manafort, Don Jr., and Jared Kushner ... It's as plain as a hair on your face ... It goes through

Deutsche Bank and all the Kushner shit. The Kushner shit is greasy. They're going to go right through that."[52]

Time will tell, but as the conflicts of interest and investigations mount, it's looking increasingly like Bannon will get the last laugh over his old White House nemesis and that Jared may well follow the path of his father, in prison.

67. IVANKA TRUMP

Even as Jared Kushner is tied up in some "greasy shit," his wife clearly appears to be his partner in crime. And their very presence in the White House is awkward. Clearly, they're only there because they're family. Yet they've been given prominent roles and significant responsibilities for which neither one is qualified. The couple was quickly nicknamed "Javanka," and, behind her back, staffers deride Ivanka as "princess royal"—a part she readily plays and enjoys.[53]

But the awkwardness surrounding Ivanka predates her father's presidency. To say the least, the relationship between Donald Trump and his daughter has always been complicated. He clearly regards her as a sex object and readily admits it.

At the Miss Teen USA pageant in 1997, when Ivanka was only sixteen, Trump turned to the then Miss Universe and asked, "Don't you think my daughter's hot? She's hot, right?" Six years later, he bragged to shock jock Howard Stern about Ivanka, now twenty-two: "You know who's one of the great beauties of the world, according to everybody? And I helped create her. Ivanka." The very next year, speaking of Ivanka yet again, he and Stern had the cringing exchange:

STERN: "By the way, your daughter . . ."
TRUMP: "She's beautiful."
STERN: "Can I say this? A piece of ass."
TRUMP: "Yeah."[54]

When asked on *The View* in 2006 how he'd feel if Ivanka chose to appear in *Playboy,* Trump responded, "I don't think Ivanka would do that, although she does have a very nice figure. I've said if Ivanka weren't my daughter, perhaps I'd be dating her."[55]

Yeeach. In Ivanka's defense, Trump's extremely off-putting remarks sexualizing her are obviously not her fault. But she's proved herself her father's daughter in other ways as well.

At first, it was believed that Ivanka would be a moderating influence on Daddy, protecting him from doing anything crazy, like pulling out of the Paris accord, for example. That didn't last long. She uttered no public protest when he did, in fact, trash the Paris accord. She remained silent after he praised the white supremacists who marched in Charlottesville. She even defended him after some twenty women accused him of sexual misconduct. "He's not a groper," she told CBS. "He treats women and men equally"—as if Trump has been running around grabbing men by the crotch. She's become an enabler, not an enforcer.[56]

Plus, as a "point person" for the Trump Organization, Ivanka has her own set of sleazy business practices and a record of hanging out with some pretty unsavory characters. Among them are Felix Sater, who pleaded guilty in 1998 to a $40 million stock fraud scheme run by the Russian mafia, and Russian businessman Tamir Sapir, involved in a 2004 racketeering conspiracy with the Gambino crime family. She also oversaw development of the Trump Ocean Club in Panama City, whose owner was arrested for money laundering. And the FBI is investigating possible financial irregularities involving the Trump International Hotel and Tower in Vancouver, Canada, another project led by daughter Ivanka.[57]

And all the while she's serving at the White House, the Ivanka Trump collection continues to offer her line of clothing, shoes, jewelry, and accessories—not only with the, at least implied, official White House stamp of approval but with the active involvement of both father and daughter.[58] According to required financial forms, Ivanka made five mllion from her product brand in 2017, plus an additional $43.9 million on her share of Washington's Trump International Hotel. Together, Ivanka and Jared Kushner reported $82 million in outside income for 2017.

As was widely reported, Ivanka received three new trademarks from China for her fashion brand on the same day she dined with Chinese president Xi Jinping at Mar-a-Lago in her official capacity as White House advisor. In April 2018, when President Trump announced a second round of tariffs against products made in China, he specifically exempted clothing, like his daughter's line of clothing, made in China—thereby saving her millions of dollars. And the following month, Ivanka secured several more lucrative Chinese trademarks both right before and right after Trump suddenly and publicly took a strange interest in saving the Chinese telecom company ZTE.[59]

Like father like daughter. Both are using the White House to promote their personal business interests, sometimes with the help of friends. "Go buy Ivanka's stuff is what I would tell you," presidential counselor Kellyanne Conway told *Fox & Friends,* in violation of ethics regulations. "I hate shopping. I'm going to go get some myself today."[60]

From the beginning, there have been rumors that Javanka would soon tire of the Washington rat race and return to the much more comfortable (for them) New York social scene. But no matter how short their stay—and for now, they're still there—the damage has already been done, and the image of paternal favoritism has already been established. Cindy McCain, wife of Senator John McCain, summed it up best on *The View.* "This is nepotism," she said. "And I truly believe that in the White House nepotism should not play a role in any of this. You have two people whose purpose in the White House is not the country, whose purpose is the man. And that's a problem."[61]

Cindy McCain is right. And unlike, say, Robert Kennedy, Jared and Ivanka have time and again proved themselves terrible at politics. Even before arriving at the White House, Ivanka and Jared showed their political naïveté. Shortly after Trump's election, they invited Cecile Richards, president of Planned Parenthood, for a meeting at Trump Tower and presented her with what they believed was an ideal compromise. If Planned Parenthood would agree to drop abortion from one of the services provided at its clinics, Trump would drop his demand to defund the organization. Which is as wrongheaded as asking Al Sharpton to drop demands for racial equality.[62]

What have Javanka accomplished in the White House? After eighteen months on the job, most observers cite as their sole contribution three personnel decisions made by Trump on their advice: the firing of James Comey and the hiring of Michael Flynn and Anthony Scaramucci. On that basis alone, they should be sent back to New York.[63]

68. KELLYANNE CONWAY

You have to give Kellyanne Conway credit for one thing: Of all the non-truth-tellers in the Trump White House, she, as "counselor to the president of the United States," came up with perhaps the most creative defense for Trump's whoppers. Trump wasn't telling lies, she insisted; he was just presenting "alternative facts."[64]

Outside of the official daily briefings, Conway's the most visible Trumper on television. And if the measure is being fast and loose, or shamelessly defending your boss by telling any lie about any topic, she's the best. She will say anything, no matter how far it is from the truth.

As reporter Molly Ball noted in *The Atlantic,* she insisted, all evidence to the contrary, that Trump "doesn't hurl personal insults" and that Donald Trump wasn't the one who led the birtherism issue but the one who put it "to rest." To defend Trump's Muslim ban, she cited what she called "the Bowling Green massacre." "Most people don't know that because it didn't get covered." Yes, most people don't know that because those rumored tragic events at Bowling Green never occurred. At one time, Conway spewed forth such a blatant string of lies that she got banned from CNN, but the network soon welcomed her back as a frequent guest—probably for entertainment value.[65]

As with Sarah Huckabee Sanders, PolitiFact has also tracked some of the more notable lies told by Kellyanne Conway. They include such greatest hits as:

- "Just 6 percent of Americans say Russia is the country's most important issue, yet the story receives 75 percent of the coverage in the media." MOSTLY FALSE

- "Here's the fact: the number one source of income into Mexico are Mexicans working here and sending the money back." FALSE

- The Donald J. Trump Foundation's money "is his money." FALSE

- There "are no cuts to Medicaid" in the GOP health care proposals. MOSTLY FALSE.[66]

On occasion, Conway's glib TV talk has also gotten her in legal trouble. According to the Office of the Special Counsel, during the 2017 Alabama Senate contest, she twice violated the Hatch Act, which prohibits federal employees from engaging in overtly political activities, like speaking out on national television against Democrat Doug Jones and in favor of Republican Roy Moore. As noted earlier, she was also chastised by a top federal ethics official for touting Ivanka's clothing line.[67]

One curious side note to Kellyanne Conway's spirited defense of the president is that even as she's saying one thing about Trump, her husband, George Conway, is often saying just the opposite. While she's praising Trump, he's dumping on him.

It didn't start out that way. Initially, George Conway was a serious contender for several top administration jobs, including solicitor general and head of the Department of Justice's Civil Division. But suddenly he dropped his name from consideration, and it wasn't long after that that he started tweeting out critical comments about President Trump.

Conway, for example, shared articles on how difficult it was for Donald Trump to find a lawyer willing to represent him. He warned that the Stormy Daniels lawsuit against Trump could open him up to discovery and possible deposition under oath. He even retweeted an article about the difficulty White House staffers faced dealing with a president who routinely says one thing and does another. (Was he talking about his wife?) And when Trump for the thousandth time called the Mueller investigation a "witch hunt," Conway retweeted the image of an old *Washington Post* headline reading, NIXON SEES WITCH-HUNT. None of which sat well with the Trump White House.[68]

At the same time, Conway insisted he still "VERY, VERY STRONGLY" supported the president. Which he may have felt necessary in order not to be locked out of his house.[69]

69. STEPHEN MILLER

If nothing else, much like a cockroach, Stephen Miller is a survivor. Outside of family members, he's one of the few original Trump staffers to survive. His old mentor Steve Bannon's gone, as are Reince Priebus, Sean Spicer, Sebastian Gorka, Rob Porter, Hope Hicks, and Katie Walsh. But Stephen Miller remains in place and in power.

No one, not even Javanka, seems to have more influence with Donald Trump, especially on the issue of immigration. He's the one effectively driving the train—for building the wall and making Mexico pay for it, for imposing a ban on Muslims, for ending the DREAMers program, for breaking up families, locking up kids, and deporting the parents. It's an anti-immigrant passion he somehow developed in the liberal enclave of Santa Monica High School, honed at Duke University, perfected in the U.S. Senate, where he led efforts by Senator Jeff Sessions to kill the bipartisan 2014 deal on immigration reform, made the centerpiece of Donald Trump's campaign for president, and took with him to the White House.[70]

Every time it looked like President Trump might be willing to compromise with Republican or Democratic members of Congress on some aspect of immigration policy, Miller stepped in to shoot it down—forcing some to give up. After one such encounter, an exasperated Senator Lindsey Graham told reporters, "As long as Stephen Miller is in charge of negotiating immigration, we are going nowhere. He's been an outlier for years."[71]

Indeed, he has, schooled as a political outlier by among the nation's most extreme right-wing political figures—David Horowitz, Andrew Breitbart, Steve Bannon, Michele Bachmann, and Ann Coulter—all of whom he calls his mentors.

On the persecution of immigrants, Miller doesn't stand alone, of course. He not only has the president's ear, he has a soul mate in chief of staff John Kelly, who's known for being a zealot on immigration. Peter Baker of *The New York Times* reports that in the summer of 2017, shortly after Kelly's arrival at the White House, administration officials were debating whether to lower the cap on refugees admitted to the United States from 110,000 to 50,000, or somewhere in between. If it were up to him, Kelly said, the number would be between zero and one. A man after Stephen Miller's heart.[72]

But it's not just on immigration that Miller's dangerous. He's a sick man, one of the most extreme fringe political figures ever to serve in any White House. This is a guy who got his start in high school campaigning for student government by denouncing janitors. "Am I the only one," he asked, "who is sick and tired of being told to pick up my trash when we have plenty of janitors who are paid to do it for us?" For which he was rightfully booed off the stage.[73]

At Duke, Miller perfected his brand of extreme politics by denouncing the school's antismoking policy, criticizing black students for what he called their racial "paranoia," cheerleading the war in Iraq, and ridiculing the women's rights movement. "Women already have equal rights in this country," he wrote in a column. "Sorry, feminists. Hate to break this good news to you."[74]

After college, Miller only needed to find a Republican star he could hitch his wagon to. He found two of them in Jeff Sessions and Donald Trump. And Trump couldn't have found a more loyal acolyte. On January 7, 2018, the White House tapped Miller to go on CNN's *State of the Union* with Jake Tapper and refute critical comments made by Steve Bannon in Michael Wolff's *Fire and Fury*.

After bashing his former colleague Bannon as being "out of touch with reality," Miller effusively praised his boss: "The reality is that the President is a political genius who won against a field of 17 incredibly talented people, who took down the Bush dynasty, who took down the Clinton dynasty," he said.[75]

After Miller droned on and on, Tapper accused Miller of trying to please only "an audience of one" and cut off the interview—whereupon Miller refused to leave the set until escorted out of the studio by CNN security agents. But Tapper was right. Watching from the White House, Trump immediately put out a tweet praising Miller's performance and bashing Tapper as a "CNN flunky."[76]

Yes, others may leave the White House. But a staffer as craven, obsequious, and filled with hate as Stephen Miller is going nowhere.

70. JOHN BOLTON

How appropriate that John Bolton learned he'd been named national security advisor—Donald Trump's third in sixteen months—while he was sitting in the green room at Fox News, waiting to go on the air. It's Fox News, after all, that Trump uses as his headhunter firm and there that he'd come to admire Bolton's hard-line views on foreign policy. At one time, he'd even considered naming Bolton secretary of state.[77]

Trump had apparently grown tired of foreign policy advisors like Rex

Tillerson and H. R. McMaster, who kept telling him no. No, you can't bomb Iran. No, you can't launch a preemptive strike against North Korea if the recent talks go south. He wanted somebody who would robotically say, "Yes, Mr. President," every time he wanted a war. Someone who would actually advocate bombing both Iran and North Korea, which Bolton had done—where else?—on Fox News.

He got his yes-man in John Bolton (even if he didn't like his mustache). And within a week of Bolton's joining the White House, Trump bombed Syria. Mission accomplished.[78]

If that sounds like a joke, unfortunately, it isn't. When Trump tweeted news that he'd fired H. R. McMaster and hired John Bolton, Joe Cirincione, president of the Ploughshares Fund, tweeted in response: "This is the moment that the administration has officially gone off the rails." In an article for *Slate* entitled "It's Time to Panic Now," foreign policy writer Fred Kaplan proclaimed that Bolton's hiring "puts the United States on a path to war."[79]

Of course, Trump could only get Bolton on his team by naming him to a post that didn't require Senate confirmation. Bolton had already famously failed at that, when George W. Bush appointed him to be under secretary of state for arms control.[80]

Then, Bolton stunned members of the Senate Foreign Relations Committee by asserting, without doubt, that Iraq had weapons of mass destruction hidden throughout the country and that Cuba had an active biological weapons program. Several people who had worked with him at the State Department under George H. W. Bush spoke of extreme bullying of staffers under him, including one woman who testified, "Mr. Bolton proceeded to chase me through the halls of a Russian hotel—throwing things at me, shoving threatening letters under my door and, generally, behaving like a madman."[81]

Bolton's views and behavior proved so extreme that not even a Republican-controlled Senate would rally behind him. President Bush retaliated by giving Bolton a recess appointment as U.S. ambassador to the United Nations. Which was, indeed, a very Trumpian move since Bolton not only didn't like the UN, he opposed its very existence. "There is no such thing as the United Nations," he famously said shortly after being appointed. "If the U.N. Secretariat building in New York lost ten stories, it wouldn't make a lot of difference."[82]

With Bolton at his side, Donald Trump is more free to follow his most hawkish instincts in Syria, Iran, Yemen, Afghanistan, and anywhere else that strikes his fancy. Even North Korea. While Trump was ridiculing North Korean president Kim Jong-un as "Little Rocket Man" and threatening to release "fire and fury" if North Korea fired another ballistic missile, Bolton was openly advocating a preemptive strike against the rogue nation. "Pre-emption opponents argue that action is not justified because Pyongyang does not constitute an 'imminent threat,'" Bolton wrote in *The Wall Street Journal.* "They are wrong. It is perfectly legitimate for the United States to respond to the current 'necessity' posed by North Korea's nuclear weapons by striking first."[83]

Bolton was so outspoken about a preemptive strike against North Korea, many wondered how he would react when President Trump suddenly changed his tune and decided to hold a summit with Kim Jong-un in Singapore. Would Bolton suddenly cave, as Larry Kudlow did on tariffs, or would he bite his tongue? He didn't help himself by publicly suggesting that Kim Jong-un follow the "Libya model" of nuclear disarmament. Bolton theoretically meant a verification system that North Korea has already rejected, but, especially given his prior stances, both Trump and North Korea took "the Libya model" to mean eventual and humiliating regime change after the nukes are gone.[84]

I'm not a diplomat, but it seems unlikely that Kim, or any other world leader, would accede to a "model" of disarmament that ultimately resulted in being dragged from a drainpipe, sodomized with a bayonet, and dying horribly. In any event, due to his belligerent nature, Bolton was mainly sidelined at the Singapore summit. Let's hope it stays that way.[85]

71. THE SEXUAL AND PHYSICAL ABUSERS

Given Donald Trump's own, self-proclaimed record of sexual abuse it should come as no surprise that several male Trump staffers would be charged with sexual and physical abuse of women. They learned from their boss, the poster boy for the assaults that galvanized the #MeToo movement, that they, too, could engage in such behavior with impunity. At least for a while.

COREY LEWANDOWSKI

After Trump himself, the first one to get in trouble was campaign manager Corey Lewandowski, accused by *Breitbart News* reporter Michelle Fields of roughly grabbing her as she attempted to ask Trump a question in March 2016 at Trump International Golf Club in Jupiter, Florida.[86]

At first, Lewandowski denied touching Fields, but surveillance video showed that he clearly did grab her. Lewandowski then alleged he had grabbed her because she had reached out to touch Trump's coat, which he considered a threat to the candidate.[87]

In the end, neither the Secret Service nor the Palm Beach County police decided to file charges. Lewandowski offered no apology. Fields resigned from *Breitbart News* because her editors sided with Lewandowski, not her. And Lewandowski was fired as campaign manager.[88]

Old habits apparently die hard, however. In November 2017, Republican activist Joy Villa accused Lewandowski of slapping her on the butt—"really hard, almost violent in nature"—at the Grammy Awards.[89]

She filed a sexual assault report against Lewandowski but ended up saying she'd settle for an apology—which, again, never came.

ROB PORTER

Things were much more serious with White House staff secretary Rob Porter—a scandal in which, once again, Corey Lewandowski played a leading role.

Porter wasn't well known outside the administration, but he held a very important job inside the White House: he was the last person to see any documents placed before the president, including the most top secret papers coming from the intelligence agencies. As such, it was curious and troubling that, after thirteen months on the job, Porter had still not received a top security clearance. He was still acting under a temporary okay.[90]

And then the bombshell hit. *The Daily Mail* first reported that Porter's security clearance had been held up because he'd been accused by two former wives of domestic violence. Porter at first denied the accusations, and chief of staff John Kelly, who praised Porter as "a man of true integrity and honor," urged him to "stay and fight" the charges. At which point, *The Daily Mail* published a photograph, taken by Porter, of ex-wife Colbie Holderness with a black eye, given to her by Porter.[91]

In no time, Porter was out the door, and White House aides scrambled for days trying to get their story straight. In the same briefing, deputy press secretary Raj Shah said Porter had resigned and had been fired. John Kelly claimed this was all new information to him and that he'd fired Porter within forty minutes of learning it. The White House also claimed that because the FBI had not completed its background investigation, they were kept in the dark. But FBI director Christopher Wray told Congress that Kelly and other top White House officials had first been informed of Porter's problems five months earlier.[92]

Meanwhile, how did the boss take the news that one of his aides was a domestic abuser? "We certainly wish him well," Trump said, shrugging. "It's obviously a very tough time for him. He did a very good job while he was in the White House. We hope that he will have a wonderful career." Within a month, Trump was reportedly telling aides he wanted to bring Porter back into the fold.[93]

Since Porter's history of domestic violence had occurred years earlier, how did it finally become public? Enter Corey Lewandowski and the love triangle. At the time the scandal broke, Porter was dating White House communications director Hope Hicks, who had earlier been romantically involved with Lewandowski. She broke up with him and started dating Porter, and apparently Lewandowski never got over it.[94]

According to Porter's former wife Jennifer Willoughby, Porter called her in January 2018, asking her to remove a blog post in which she accused him of physical abuse because someone close to the White House knew about it and was threatening to send it to the media. At first, she thought Porter was talking about Steve Bannon. She later figured out it was Corey Lewandowski—who finally got his revenge.[95]

So Porter was gone. Soon Hope Hicks was gone. The matter of physical abuse by White House staffers—the president himself notwithstanding, of course—could finally be put to rest. Oh, no. There was more to come.

DAVID SORENSEN

Only two days after Rob Porter resigned amid charges of domestic abuse, White House speechwriter David Sorensen was forced to resign for the same reason.[96]

The Washington Post was the first to learn of charges leveled against Sorensen to the FBI by his ex-wife, Jessica Corbett, as part of the routine background check of Sorensen for the White House job. As reported by *The Post,* "She said that during her marriage to Sorensen, he ran a car over her foot, put out a cigarette on her hand, threw her into a wall and grasped her menacingly by her hair while they were alone on their boat in remote waters off Maine's coast."[97]

Like Porter, Sorensen denied the charges—he even accused Corbett of assaulting him!—but nevertheless resigned once contacted by *The Post* because, he said, he "didn't want the White House to have to deal with this distraction." Sadly, assault and abuse seem less a distraction in this White House than a way of life, one set by the president himself.

7

TRUMP'S "AMERICA FIRST!" MEANS "AMERICA LAST"

If you thought Donald Trump wasn't dangerous . . . If you thought we had nothing to worry about and we could all ride this out because he was just some clown who ended up in the Oval Office through a fluke in the electoral college and could do nothing worse than tweet out insults and nonsense ten times a day . . . Think again. Rich or poor, American or not, this man is dangerous to us all.

That's because as president, Donald Trump's obviously also in charge of our foreign policy. And he has been a disaster. Under the banner of "America First!" he has recklessly proceeded to rescind scores of treaties, scuttle longtime alliances with our closest allies, reject diplomacy in favor of military threats, and alienate almost every other nation on the planet, friend or foe.

For Donald Trump—who believes every negotiation is about winners and losers and who only has one diplomatic setting: bullshit and bluster— "America First" apparently means "America Stands Alone," which we now do on many important fronts. On climate change, as we've seen, every other nation on the planet has agreed to come up with a plan to meet the goals of the Paris accord. Only the United States now stands alone in rejecting the agreement. Trump told us he alone could fix our problems. Now we are alone and stuck with him.[1]

See also: nuclear proliferation. The UK, France, Germany, Russia, China, and the EU originally joined the United States in persuading Iran to abandon its nuclear weapons program in return for lifting economic sanctions against the country. Among the eight signatories, only the United States today stands alone—a move that could have horrific consequences.[2]

72. HE SHREDDED THE IRAN NUCLEAR DEAL

Indeed, by unilaterally shredding the Iran nuclear deal in May 2018, Donald Trump made one of the most dangerous moves not just in his administration but in the history of the American presidency—triggering the resumption of a nuclear arms race and exposing the planet to the very real risk of nuclear war.

But let's first be clear why Trump did this. No matter what he claims, from his point of view, there was only one reason behind pulling the United States out of the Iran deal. Not because it was a bad deal. Not because he had a better deal up his sleeve. But solely because it was made by Barack Obama.

Donald Trump pulled the plug on the Iran nuclear deal for the same reason he tried to repeal the Affordable Care Act, withdrew the United States from the Paris accord on climate change, revoked every new antipollution regulation of the EPA, and, allegedly, paid prostitutes to urinate on a Moscow hotel bed once slept in by his predecessor: Because he's obsessed with undoing anything connected with former President Barack Obama, good or bad. If Obama had been against the Iran nuclear deal, Trump would be for it.

While driven by pique and patently idiotic, Trump's action came as no surprise. As candidate, he promised to cancel the deal. As president, he did nothing but condemn it as "insane" and something that "should have never,

ever been made." What was somewhat surprising is that, even after eighteen months in the White House to think about it, he could come up with no better case for withdrawal than a string of lies.[3]

Lie number one: It's a lousy deal. Not true. As former UN ambassador Susan Rice wrote in *The New York Times,* according to terms of the deal, "Iran relinquished 97 percent of its enriched uranium stockpile, dismantled two-thirds of its centrifuges and its entire plutonium facility, abided by the most intrusive international inspection and monitoring regime in history, and forswore ever producing a nuclear weapon." What more do you want? That's why, in a poll of more than 1,500 international relations scholars and experts, a whopping 94 percent thought Trump had made a big mistake reneging on the agreement.[4]

Lie number two: Iran was not in compliance. Not true. The International Atomic Energy Agency; the State Department; the director of national intelligence, Dan Coats; and the CIA all certified that Iran was living up to the terms of the agreement. The then CIA director, Mike Pompeo, told Congress, "I have seen no evidence that they are not in compliance today." Trump's secretary of defense, Jim Mattis, has said of the deal that "the verification, what is in there, is actually pretty robust."[5]

Lie number three: Trump will come up with a better deal. This is a classic Trumpism. Every time he breaks a deal, he promises a new one but never delivers. He made the same promise when trying to repeal Obamacare, pulling out of the Paris accord, scrubbing the Trans-Pacific Partnership trade agreement, going after NAFTA, and ending DACA. Each time, the promise of a better deal. Each time, nothing. Same with Iran. There is no plan B.

Lie number four, which actually came at the beginning of a cabinet meeting the day after Trump's announcement—that other countries are "all very happy with his decision." How could he say that after, in one week, the president of France, the chancellor of Germany, and the foreign secretary of the UK all came to Washington and pleaded with him *not* to pull out of the deal? And, once he did so anyway, issued a joint statement condemning his decision?[6]

Lie number five: His action made the world a safer place. No, no, no. Just the opposite. The world is today a much more dangerous place. Because a rogue nation, which had agreed to abandon any efforts to build a nuclear weapon for at least seven years, and maybe fifteen, was given a green light by Donald Trump to resume production of nuclear weapons, which will only further destabilize the entire Middle East.

Admittedly, it was not a perfect deal—what compromise between nations with completely different agendas is? There were other important issues, like Iran's support of radical organizations like Hezbollah, which were not included. But as I sat in the East Room, I heard French president Emmanuel Macron eloquently explain to Trump that the answer was to fix and improve the original agreement—which all other signatories were willing to do—not scuttle the whole thing. Trump wasn't listening.[7]

To complicate things further, Trump's decision to shred the Iran nuclear deal came on the threshold of his summit with North Korean president Kim Jong-un and a potential deal with North Korea. Ironically, conservatives have always warned against making any such deal because, they argued, you can't trust North Koreans to live up to the terms of any agreement.

Thanks to Donald Trump, it's now just the opposite. After what happened with the Paris accord and the Iran nuclear deal, it's no longer the North Koreans who can't be trusted to stick to a deal. It's the United States. Now more than ever, our word means nothing.[8]

73. NORTH KOREA

If you find it hard to figure out Donald Trump's relationship with North Korea's Kim Jong-un, don't feel bad. Nobody can figure it out. Kim Jong-un is at once the world leader most insulted by Trump—"short and fat," "maniac," "madman," "bad dude," "sick puppy," "Little Rocket Man"—and the one most praised (after his man-crush on Vladimir Putin, of course)—"very honorable" and a "pretty smart cookie"—all in less than one year.[9]

In that same short time span, Trump went from threatening to "totally destroy" North Korea by unleashing "fire and fury like the world has never seen before" to, after various on-again, off-again shenanigans, sitting down with Kim on June 12, 2018, in a summit that will always be deemed historic, no matter what comes of it.[10]

Even many of Trump's harshest critics give him some credit for sitting down with North Korea and negotiating on abandoning their nuclear weapons program, something pursued but never achieved by Bill Clinton,

George W. Bush, or Barack Obama. Reluctantly, some admit it could be Trump's "Nixon in China" moment. But other, cooler heads say, "Not so fast," and point to China and Kim's increased nuclear capability as the main factors involved.[11]

The beginning of the Trump administration coincided with North Korea's most militarily active year yet. In 2017, Kim Jong-un personally oversaw the launch of twenty-three missiles, including two intercontinental missiles that experts determined capable of reaching mainland United States as far as Los Angeles, Denver, or Chicago. After conducting their sixth nuclear test, North Korea also said they were close to developing the technology to fit a nuclear warhead on their long-range missiles.[12]

Then, suddenly in 2018, the mood shifted. Instead of launching more missiles, Kim Jong-un launched a public relations campaign. In rapid order, he agreed to let North Korean athletes join forces with South Korean athletes in the Winter Olympics. He traveled to Beijing to meet with President Xi, his first meeting with a foreign leader. He announced the suspension of all missile tests and promised to shut down one main testing site. In a historic summit, he met in the DMZ with South Korean president Moon Jae-in. He met again with President Xi. He released three Americans from prison. And he agreed to put "denuclearization," whatever he means by that, on the table at the summit with President Trump in Singapore. At which point, even Kim's friend Dennis Rodman's head must have been spinning, not just Donald Trump's.[13]

Continuing his bluster, Trump promised to get up and walk away from the table if things don't go well. He even sent a letter to Kim officially canceling the summit because of "tremendous anger and open hostility," before he changed his mind and rescheduled the meeting. It probably helped that Kim sent his reply to Trump in a cartoonishly large envelope—because, for Trump, big means good and important.[14]

And then, the big moment in Singapore. In an historic summit on June 12, Trump and Kim came together, shook hands, smiled for the cameras, had lunch, took a stroll, inspected the presidential limousine, watched a video, patted each other on the back, shook hands again, and left.[15]

And just like that—Shazam!—everything changed! "There is no longer a nuclear threat from North Korea," Trump boasted on Twitter the next day. In fact, North Korea was now our new best friend—"we now have a very good relationship with North Korea," he declared. And Trump and Kim were *definitely* BFFs. "He's got a very good personality, he's funny, and he's very, very, smart," Trump gushed to Sean Hannity. "He's a great negotiator, and he's a very strategic kind of guy." Naturally, Trump also admired Kim's authoritarian bent. "He speaks and his people sit up at attention. I want my people to do the same."[16]

But of course, this was all Trump's usual bluster. In fact, the summit brought no agreement on concrete steps or a timetable moving forward. Instead, it concluded with the blandest of statements: "President Trump committed to provide security guarantees to the DPRK, and Chairman Kim Jong Un reaffirmed his firm and unwavering commitment to complete denuclearization of the Korean peninsula." Where's the beef?[17]

Even if the Singapore summit turns out to be a true turning point in US–North Korea relations, it will only be the beginning of a long road of continued negotiations on demilitarization of the Korean Peninsula, if not outright denuclearization. And the prospect that North Korea will agree, as did South Africa and Libya, to totally destroy its nuclear arsenal remains very remote. As Joe Cirincione, president of the Ploughshares Fund, told me: "Donald Trump is permanently booked at the Grand Delusion Hotel." It'll take more than one handshake to get rid of the most serious nuclear threat facing the planet.

Indeed, instead of popping the champagne, many experts like Cirincione hold up a caution sign. No matter how open and reasonable Kim Jong-un may have suddenly appeared, they warn, he could just be repeating a familiar pattern of behavior perfected by his father, Kim Jong-il. Jung H. Pak of the Brookings Institution's Center for East Asia Policy Studies likens it to cycles: "North Korea comes to dialogue, then retracts, using the U.S.'s 'hostile policy' as an excuse to conduct missile or nuclear tests, then re-enters dialogue to dampen sanctions implementation or reduce tension." And before the month of the summit was even out, U.S. intelligence agencies reported ominous signs of North Korea enriching more uranium and improving infrastructure at their nuclear sites.[18]

Bottom line: While we all hope for the best, there's no reason to trust North Korea to live up to the terms of the Singapore meeting. But then again, based on the withdrawal of the United States from the Paris accord and the Iran nuclear deal, there's no reason to trust Donald Trump, either.

74. HE'S CONTINUED AND EXPANDED AMERICA'S WARS

When it comes to ending wars, as we all know from long, sad experience, presidential promises can't always be trusted. Barack Obama campaigned on a promise to end the "bad" war in Iraq and to work toward shutting down the "good" war in Afghanistan. Except, when he left office eight years later, we were not only still fighting the "good" war and the "bad" war, we were also fighting a new war in Syria.

With Donald Trump, it's more of the same. "Ron Paul is right that we are wasting trillions of dollars in Iraq and Afghanistan," he tweeted in 2011. "Afghanistan is a complete waste. Time to come home!" he wrote the next year. In 2016, he (rightly) blamed George W. Bush for the "big fat mistake" of the Iraq War, which "destabilized the Middle East," during a GOP presidential debate.[19]

And yet the Iraq War, now under the banner of Operation Inherent Resolve against ISIS, lingers on. He has sent more American troops to Afghanistan. There are more American support troops in Syria, and we are also secretly militarily engaged in several countries in northern Africa—with most of that activity taking place under the radar and barely, if ever, reported.[20]

In other words, like Barack Obama, Donald Trump hasn't ended any of America's wars, he's just started new ones.

Most Americans would be surprised to learn, for example, that civilian deaths in the Middle East have soared under Donald Trump. The media's been so consumed with Trump tweets, Stormy Daniels, Roseanne Barr, or whatever the newest daily outrage is, they never talk about civilian casualties anymore. Yet according to the watchdog group Airwars, 2017, Trump's first year in office, was the deadliest year ever for civilian casualties in Iraq and Syria, with as many as six thousand people killed in strikes by the U.S.-led coalition.[21]

In March 2018, for example, as media columnist Margaret Sullivan pointed out in *The Washington Post,* the press went wild over former Trump campaign official Sam Nunberg's meltdown on CNN—where he admitted, "Trump may well have done something during the election with the

Russians." That's news, sure. But they spent virtually no time reporting on 150 civilians, including scores of children, killed when U.S. forces repeatedly bombed a school in Syria, or dozens of other civilians killed in bombings of mosques and markets.[22]

Without a doubt, the uptick in civilian casualties was a direct result of Trump's campaign promise to "bomb the shit out of 'em"—a directive he gave the Pentagon once in the White House. Lieutenant General Stephen Townsend, the top U.S. officer during the coalition buildup in Syria, admitted that the Trump administration "freed us up a bit to prosecute the war in a more aggressive manner."[23]

Indeed, in direct contravention of the Geneva convention, Trump has been cheering on more collateral damage. "We're fighting a very politically correct war," he complained during the election campaign. The "thing with the terrorists—you have to take out their families. When you get these terrorists, you have to take out their families!" Here's one bloody promise he kept. On his first day in office, when he was told by the CIA that they had waited on a drone strike until the target was away from his family, Trump angrily harrumphed, "Why did you wait?"[24]

While much of it takes place in the shadows, here's what we know, as of this writing, of military operations in the Middle East.

SYRIA

Having a hard time understanding what's happening in Syria? No wonder. There are actually not one but three wars ongoing in Syria—beginning in 2011, the civil war between rebel forces and the Assad government, assisted by its longtime ally Russia; Israel's war against Iran-backed forces; and the U.S. war, with the assistance of Kurd fighters, against ISIS. Though ISIS has lost most of its territory, two thousand American ground troops remain in Syria to prevent their return. In April 2017 and April 2018, the Trump administration launched cruise missile attacks in Syria to punish President Assad for his use of chemical weapons. Meanwhile, the civil war drags on with no end in sight, and President Obama's goal of removing Bashar al-Assad from power has been long forgotten.[25]

AFGHANISTAN

It started out in October 2001 as Operation Enduring Freedom. It endures today as Operation Never Ending. The war in Afghanistan is already the longest of all American wars overseas, and it shows no promise of slowing down. Like Obama, Trump promised to end it. But like Obama, all Trump has done is send in more troops.[26]

Most people don't remember, but the original purpose of the war, in the wake of the September 11 attacks, was to overthrow the Taliban in order to find and destroy al-Qaeda. It took only a few weeks to oust the Taliban and drive the remaining al-Qaeda forces into Pakistan. Since then, the war in Afghanistan has still gone on, but without any clear mission. Meanwhile, the Taliban has enjoyed a resurgence. NBC reports there are now sixty thousand Taliban fighters active in 70 percent of the country.[27]

The war has taken its toll in lives and dollars. Through May 2018, 2,411 American troops had been killed in Afghanistan. According to the Costs of Wars project at Brown University, the war has cost $2 trillion so far—plus an additional $45 billion for 2018—which does not include interest on war debt that Americans taxpayers will have to pay, nor the cost of VA medical treatment for veterans.[28]

An even more tragic cost: In early 2015, three international watchdog organizations—Physicians for Social Responsibility, Physicians for Global Survival, and International Physicians for the Prevention of Nuclear War—estimated the number of civilians killed since the beginning of the conflict at between 106,000 and 170,000. Those numbers have only grown since.[29]

In August 2017, with no announced plan for withdrawal from Afghanistan and claiming that "decisions are much different when you sit behind the desk of the Oval Office," Donald Trump increased the number of American troops from 8,400 to 14,000. According to the air force, his first year in office saw more than three times as many bombs dropped in the country as 2016, and early 2018 saw no signs of slowing down. Our longest war drags ever on.[30]

IRAQ

Oh, yes, even though it was officially declared over on December 18, 2011, that war continues, too. Or at least its second phase—or even third, if you count the first Gulf War back in 1991.[31]

George W. Bush's Iraq War began in 2003 under the pretext, later proved false, that Saddam Hussein possessed weapons of mass destruction and posed a direct threat to the United States. Taking Baghdad and toppling Hussein proved relatively easy. Helping a weak government and ragtag army take back control of the country proved far more difficult. In October 2007, the number of American troops peaked at 170,000. As conditions on the ground improved, they were gradually withdrawn until combat operations in Iraq were declared over.[32]

But in 2014, it was discovered that ISIS forces, taking advantage of the absence of U.S. and Iraqi troops, had seized large swaths of Iraq and Syria. This began the second phase of this Iraq War, to push them back. In December 2017, Iraq announced that all Iraqi territory had been fully liberated from ISIS control and yet, for now, U.S. troops remain in the region.[33]

Obviously, the war in Iraq has also taken a serious toll. According to Brown University's Costs of War project again, the initial phase of the war cost American taxpayers $1.7 trillion—which, again, could balloon to $3–$6 trillion when interest rates and veterans costs are included. That number is even more significant when we remember that Lawrence Lindsey, head of President Bush's National Economic Council, was forced to resign in 2003 when he told Congress the total cost of the war in Iraq might reach $200 billion. Secretary of Defense Donald Rumsfeld predicted it would cost "something under $50 billion."[34]

Overall, Costs of War estimated that between 176,000 and 189,000 were killed in the Iraq War, including 134,000 civilians. In phase one, 4,424 American troops were killed and 31,052 wounded in action. Phase two casualties include 73 Americans killed and 1,295 wounded.[35]

As of early 2018, there were still 5,200 American forces in Iraq, mainly in support and training missions. And that war, too, drags on.[36]

NORTHERN AFRICA

Sadly, it won't surprise you to learn the United States still has troops in Iraq, Afghanistan, and Syria. But you may be surprised to learn that, under Donald Trump, American troops are also on the ground in Niger, Chad, Cameroon, the Central African Republic, Uganda, and South Sudan. This is Trump's "Shadow War" in Africa.[37]

All these operations are questionably and quietly being conducted under the sweeping Authorization for the Use of Military Force (AUMF) passed by Congress in the aftermath of September 11, but they all have two things in common: none of them have ever been specifically authorized by Congress; and they're almost totally ignored by the media, even though thirty-six American soldiers have been killed in Africa since 2001.[38]

Americans wouldn't even have known of these troops until four Special Forces members—including Sergeant La David Johnson, whose widow felt insulted by Donald Trump—were killed on patrol there in October 2017. At which point most people were asking, "Where is Niger, and what are American troops doing there?"[39]

The administration's answer is that American troops are there in a support capacity only, to help African nations deal with a variety of Islamic jihadists who have fled to northern Africa from Iraq, Syria, Libya, and other hot spots. They argue, in words that should haunt anybody who lived through Vietnam or any other recent American war, that it's cheaper for us to train local forces how to shut down terrorist operations than to send in American troops to do it later.[40]

Which sounds good in theory, except for the fact that just by being in the combat zone means that American troops are in harm's way, and, as happened in Niger, any reconnaissance mission can suddenly become a fight for survival.

At this point, June 2018, there are 1,500 American troops throughout North Africa, three times the number on the ground in Syria—and unless Congress steps in, that number's only going to grow. "The war is morphing," Senator Lindsey Graham told reporters after a briefing on Africa by defense secretary James Mattis. "You're going to see more actions in Africa, not less; you're going to see more aggression by the United States toward our enemies, not less; you're going to have decisions being made not in the White House but out in the field."[41]

TRUMP'S WARS

On one front, the Trump administration started out on a positive foot. Allegedly speaking for the president, Secretary of State Rex Tillerson defended chopping the foreign operations budget by 31 percent because, he said, "There will be fewer military conflicts that the U.S. will be directly engaged in."[42]

Obviously, he had not talked to his boss. In fact, we've seen just the opposite. As Micah Zenko wrote in *Foreign Policy,* "In reality, the Donald Trump administration has demonstrated no interest in reducing America's military commitments and interventions, nor committed itself in any meaningful way to preventing conflicts or resolving them."[43]

The reality is, as Zenko and Jennifer Wilson also pointed out in an August 2017 column entitled "Donald Trump Is Dropping Bombs at Unprecedented Levels," Trump had already learned to love the bomb. As soon as he was in office, he immediately approved a disastrous, ill-thought-out Special Forces mission in southern Yemen that Obama had rejected, resulting in the death of Navy SEAL Ryan Owens and multiple civilian casualties. Then, in April 2017, he dropped a MOAB—a.k.a. Massive Ordnance Air Blast, or "Mother of All Bombs," America's largest nonnuclear bomb—on Taliban targets in Afghanistan. It's big—it must be good and important, right?[44]

"Within eight months of assuming office," Zenko and Wilson wrote, "Trump—with the announcement of six 'precision airstrikes' in Libya—had bombed every country that former President Barack Obama had in eight years. One month after that, the United States surpassed the 26,172 bombs that had been dropped in 2016. Through the end of December 2017, Trump had authorized more airstrikes in Somalia in one year (33), than George W. Bush and Obama had since the United States first began intervening there in early 2007."[45]

At least we ducked one new war. As first reported by the Associated Press, in August 2017, Trump surprised his foreign policy team by suddenly suggesting an American invasion of Venezuela. A stunned Defense Secretary James Mattis, backed up by then-DHS Secretary H. R. McMaster and UN Ambassador Nikki Haley, talked him out of it. Catastrophe averted. For now.[46]

So much for the populist maverick. Donald Trump clearly loves war, and he now has the United States engaged in more wars than ever.

75. HE'S ALIENATED OUR NEAREST NEIGHBORS

"Since we're neighbors, let's be friends." Good slogan. It works for Safeway. And for a long time, it worked for the United States and our neighbors Canada and Mexico, who are also the top two largest foreign markets for U.S. goods. Until Donald Trump. He treats them both, and especially Mexico, like dirt. He's gone out of his way to alienate both nations, on immigration and trade. And having lost faith in the United States, they both have begun to reach out for new partners they can count on.[47]

MEXICO

Of course, things got off to a disastrous start between Trump and Mexico on June 16, 2015, when he infamously announced he was running for president by denouncing Mexican immigrants—"When Mexico sends its people, they're not sending their best . . . They're bringing drugs. They're bringing crime. They're rapists."—and promising to build a wall on the southern border and make Mexico pay for it.[48]

Things only went downhill from there. In May 2018, Enrique Peña Nieto, the president of Mexico, tweeted that there was no way, no how, they were going to pay for the wall. And according to the Pew Research Center, 94 percent of Mexicans opposed the border wall, and confidence in the American president fell among the Mexican people to a historic low of 5 (!) percent.[49]

As president, too, Trump has been pissing off Mexico from the start. Just days after his inauguration, a group of top Mexican officials came to the White House to meet with Jared Kushner, who, as one of his many foreign policy assignments, had been tasked to smooth over relations with Mexico. The ostensible purpose of the meeting was to plan a summit between President Trump and President Nieto, but as they were meeting, Trump chose that moment to sign two executive orders—one calling for "immediate construction of a physical wall on the southern border"; the other expanding the categories of undocumented immigrants who would be prioritized for deportation.[50]

That evening, a furious Nieto went on national television to declare again, "Mexico will not pay for any wall." The next morning, Trump tweeted that if Mexico would not agree to pay for the wall, they might as well cancel the summit. Which Nieto did. The two leaders finally met face-to-face at a G20 meeting.[51]

Since then, relations with Mexico have not improved. Turning back the clock on decades of partnership with Mexico on many issues, Trump treats Mexico like an American colony, not a sovereign nation. He's threatened to unilaterally scuttle NAFTA, continues to blame Mexico for doing nothing to stem illegal immigration, calls all immigrants criminals, threatens to impose tariffs or a border tax on Mexican imports, and still insists he'll find some way to make Mexico pay for the wall. In fact, by May 2018, a note of Trump's past as a serial sexual assaulter had crept into the diplomatic discussion. "They're going to pay for the wall," he boasted at a rally in Nashville, Tennessee, "and they're going to enjoy it." Charming.[52]

Despite his differences with Donald Trump, the sitting president of Mexico has tried to be polite. Not so the former president. In a video jokingly announcing he might run for president of the United States in 2020, former president Vicente Fox probably spoke for the majority of Mexicans when he said, "Donald, you suck so much at this job. If they ever do a Mt. Rushmore for shitty presidents, it will just be your bloated, orange head—four times."[53]

Meanwhile, relations with our neighbor to the north went south, too.

CANADA

I saw them together myself at the White House. If there were ever any two national leaders who connected, it was Barack Obama and Justin Trudeau. Both young, charismatic, articulate, progressive, driven by a global perspective.

How times have changed. If there were ever two leaders who have nothing in common, it's Justin Trudeau and Donald Trump. One is a leader in efforts to combat climate change; the other's a climate change denier. One committed $241.5 million to reproductive health and contraception programs; the other cut $600 million from family planning programs in the developing world. One believes in exercising global leadership; the other preaches "America First!" One takes the day off from work every year to celebrate his wedding anniversary. The other has cheated on his wife with multiple porn stars.[54]

As in Mexico, once Trump took office, approval ratings for America among Canadians sank to an all-time low. Their favorable view of the United States dipped from 65 to 43 percent. Confidence in the American president plummeted from 83 to 22 percent.[55]

Rather than do battle with the Trump administration, meanwhile, the Canadian government decided to chart a more independent course—as reflected in a June 2017 statement issued by foreign affairs minister Chrystia Freeland: "The fact that our friend and ally has come to question the very worth of its mantle of global leadership puts into sharper focus the need for the rest of us to set our own clear and sovereign course. For Canada that course must be the renewal, indeed the strengthening, of the postwar multilateral order."[56]

Relations between the United States and Canada also quickly soured over trade issues. Again, Trump unilaterally trashed NAFTA but has still not come up with what he insisted would be a better deal. Meanwhile, he slapped punitive U.S. duties on Canadian softwood lumber—which Canada appealed to the World Trade Organization. He also announced tariffs on Canadian steel, only to suspend them pending the outcome of NAFTA negotiations, and then slap them back on again. And Trump still insists the United States has a trade deficit with Canada, even though the opposite is true. When all products are included, the U.S. actually has a small trade surplus with Canada.[57]

In only eighteen months, what was once a close, positive working relationship between Canada and the United States has turned distant and negative. Trump accuses Canada of unfair trade practices. "People don't realize Canada has been very rough on the United States," he said in announcing his tariffs on steel. "They've outsmarted our politicians for many years."[58] But Canada isn't just rolling over. "We are going to defend our industries and our workers," Justin Trudeau declared on June 7, 2018, in a joint appearance with France's Emmanuel Macron, and "show the U.S. president that his unacceptable actions are hurting his own citizens. American jobs are on the line because of his actions." When Trudeau reiterated this stance after the G7 summit, Trump threw a hissy fit on Twitter. "PM Justin Trudeau of Canada acted so meek and mild during our @G7 meetings only to give a news conference after I left . . . Very dishonest & weak." Larry Kudlow, Trump's economic advisor, added that Trudeau had "stabbed us in the back."[59]

And that's why Canada is looking to enter new trade partnerships with other Asian, Pacific, and European nations, and Mexico is now buying ten times more corn from Brazil than before. After all, when your next-door neighbor is an asshole like Donald Trump, you're probably going to turn your attention elsewhere.[60]

76. HE'S ALIENATED OUR CLOSEST EUROPEAN ALLIES

Mexico and Canada do have this consolation: They're not the only close and longtime allies with whom Trump has damaged relations. Even as a candidate, he began to alienate France, Germany, and the UK, our longest and strongest allies, to the point where he's not welcome anywhere.

It was no surprise, then, that aside from extremists like France's Jean-Marie Le Pen, most European opinion-makers reacted with horror even at the remote possibility that someone like Donald Trump might be elected president of the United States. J. K. Rowling tweeted that he's worse than Voldemort, the Big Bad of her Harry Potter books. David Cameron called his proposed Muslim ban "divisive." Germany's *Der Spiegel* called him the most dangerous man on the planet. It featured his election victory on the cover with the words *Das Ende Der Welt*—"The End of the World."[61]

Once he was elected, European leaders acted with dismay. Germany's Angela Merkel said she would cooperate with Trump, but only if he agreed to respect common values: "democracy, freedom, respect for the law and for human dignity, regardless of ancestry, skin color, religion, gender, sexual orientation or political leanings." Which may be the first time a foreign leader had to inform an American president about what our Constitution stands for. Trump repaid her by famously refusing to shake her hand at the press avail during her first visit to the Trump White House.[62]

Others were not even that hopeful. Gérard Araud, French ambassador to the U.S., warned, "The world is crumbling in front of our eyes."[63]

Still others saw a potential silver lining—that disgust at Trump would force members of the EU, no longer able to depend on the United States, to band together more strongly. Former U.S. ambassador to Germany John Kornblum put it bluntly: "The American umbrella over Europe is gone forever. Trump's election marks the end of the postwar order."[64]

For European leaders expecting Trump to be difficult to work with, he did not disappoint. As already covered, he broke with 197 nations by pulling the United States out of the Paris accord on climate change. He also ignored the personal pleas of Emmanuel Macron, Angela Merkel, and Boris Johnson to mend, not end, the Iran nuclear deal—and even threatened sanctions against the UK, France, and Germany if any of their firms continued to do business with Iran. Then, on May 31, 2018, he enacted steel and aluminum sanctions against the EU, Canada, and Mexico, quickly prompting calls for retaliation.[65]

A few months earlier, in November 2017, Trump accomplished what no other British politician has been able to do in the age of Brexit: He actually united Brits across the political spectrum—in outrage! Trump had retweeted anti-Muslim videos from a far-right British hate group as part of a direct rebuke of Prime Minister Theresa May, whom he accused of being soft on terrorism. As *The New York Times* reported: "One member of Parliament called him a 'fascist.' Another described him as 'stupid.' A third wondered aloud whether President Trump was 'racist, incompetent or unthinking—or all three.'" The resulting flap stirred up such universal condemnation that Trump canceled a planned first visit to the UK scheduled for early 2018. So much for the special relationship.[66]

Instead, it was also early in 2018 that Trump attacked Britain's system of universal health care. Referring to efforts by some congressional Democrats to expand Obamacare into "Medicare for All," Trump tweeted: "The Democrats are pushing for Universal HealthCare while thousands of people are marching in the UK because their U system is going broke and not working."[67]

To most Brits, them were fightin' words. Britain's health secretary, Jeremy Hunt, fired back: "I may disagree with claims made on that march but not ONE of them wants to live in a system where 28 million people have no cover." Theresa May added that she was "proud" of Britain's health care system.[68]

For a while, it seemed that, even after reneging on the Paris accord,

Trump might still be able to make friends with French president Emmanuel Macron. In April 2018, Macron visited Trump at the White House, and the two exchanged a series of awkward backslaps, hugs, and handshakes that one would need Jane Goodall to fully decipher. ("I like him a lot" and "he is perfect," Trump cooed then of his new man-crush.)[69]

But only about a month later, the passions had cooled and all the primate signaling was for naught—especially after Trump announced his proposed tariffs on European aluminum and steel. When Macron told Trump on a phone call that the tariffs were "not only illegal" but "a mistake on many points," Trump flipped out. "Just bad. It was terrible," said one White House official to CNN of the call. "Macron thought he would be able to speak his mind . . . but Trump can't handle being criticized like that." Later that week, with Trudeau by his side, Macron called the tariffs "unilateral and illegal . . . A trade war doesn't spare anyone" and will "first of all hurt U.S. workers," he warned.[70]

The G7 summit the following week turned out to be an outright disaster, with Trump showing up late to a working meeting on gender equality, urging everyone else to let Russia back in after they were booted from the group for illegally annexing Crimea, railing on about tariffs and fairness, and further alienating Macron, Merkel, May, Trudeau, and the rest of America's closest friends.[71]

So none of our closest allies in Europe can abide Trump. And, once again, by June 2017, the Pew Research Center noted a plunge in approval ratings for the American president. Compared to Barack Obama's 90 percent approval rating in Western Europe, Donald Trump scored only 22 percent in the UK, 14 percent in France, and 11 percent in Germany.[72]

Of course, to Donald Trump, a man who lives by ratings at home, his low approval numbers in Western Europe meant nothing at all. After breaking with the UK, Germany, and France on every issue from trade to climate change to the Iran nuclear deal, it's clear that he doesn't care about maintaining good relations with our allies. He doesn't seem to see the importance of maintaining any of our traditional alliances at all. As we'll see in a moment, he wants to make a whole new set of friends, more like him.

77. HE'S ENDANGERED NATO

With all the talk about President Trump canceling America's participation in the Paris accord and the Iran nuclear deal, we tend to forget the first international organization he undermined: the North Atlantic Treaty Organization, or NATO.

Created in 1949 at the beginning of the Cold War by the United States, Canada, and ten Western European nations to defend against aggression by the former Soviet Union, NATO, solid as a rock, was considered our primary national security alliance—until Donald Trump came along.

He didn't wait till he got to the White House. As a candidate, he called NATO "obsolete," complained it was costing us too much money, and said he'd consider pulling out of it. As president, he's backed off somewhat—the United States is still a member!—but he's still critical, still pushing other nations to pay more so we can pay less, and still gives the impression he's not solidly committed to NATO's Article 5, which declares that an attack on one member is an attack on all.[73]

In May 2017, Trump tellingly deleted a specific pledge to honor Article 5 from his speech to the first NATO summit he attended in Brussels, causing consternation among aides like James Mattis and H. R. McMaster. The next month, he finally climbed on board, committing the United States to Article 5 in a random aside, not exactly putting to rest the fears of our allies.[74]

Trump made (at least) two other faux pas at that first NATO summit of his. He claimed he was feeling more positive about NATO because, at his insistence, leaders had agreed to start fighting terrorism. (Actually, NATO has been engaged in fighting terrorism since the 1980s.) Then, arriving for the family photo, he rudely—and on camera—pushed Montenegro's prime minister, Duško Marković, aside so he could stand in the front line alongside NATO head Jens Stoltenberg.[75]

But the news wasn't all bad for NATO. In a move that both surprised and reassured European leaders, the Trump administration reversed course and actually increased funding for more U.S. troops and hardware in Eastern Europe and for more drills with NATO partners.[76]

Nevertheless, Trump's negative comments about and threats of cutting back support or leaving NATO have badly shaken any confidence European leaders had in continued partnership with the United States on self-defense. Alexander Vershbow, former NATO deputy secretary general, has said, "The transatlantic relationship may be scarred for a long time to come." After all, if Russian tanks start rolling west toward Europe, would you want Donald Trump next to you in the foxhole?[77]

According to Ivan Krastev, founding member of the European Council on Foreign Relations, after a year and a half of Trump's waffling support of NATO, "many European leaders basically believe they cannot simply rely on the United States' guarantees and that Europe should develop a military power of its own."[78]

With Donald Trump, the outcome could well be: Out of the Paris accord and the Iran nuclear deal today. Out of NATO tomorrow.

78. HE HEARTS STRONGMEN

Both during the campaign and the early months of his presidency, there was a lot of confusion over Donald Trump's relationship with Russian president Vladimir Putin. While other Republicans condemned him as "dangerous" and "evil," Trump praised him. "He does have an 82 percent approval rating," Trump told NBC.[79]

We'll talk more about Trump and Putin's special relationship in the next chapter. But in one sense, no one should have been surprised by the duo's budding bromance. Putin—and, recently, Kim Jong-un—are just two of many notorious dictators Trump has showered with lavish praise. As Domenico Montanaro of NPR pointed out in a worthy rundown, some of the others include:

RODRIGO DUTERTE, PHILIPPINES

Duterte is accused of having more than seven thousand Filipinos killed in his extra-legal war on drugs, which he has justified by arguing, "Hitler massacred three million Jews. Now, there is three million drug addicts. I'd be happy to slaughter them." Nor did he exclude journalists: "Just because you're a journalist, you are not exempted from assassination, if you're a son of a bitch."[80]

Trump praised Duterte for his war on drugs and invited him to the White House.[81]

ABDEL FATTAH AL-SISI, EGYPT

After the promise of the Arab Spring, Sisi came to power in a coup that saw eight hundred protestors killed in a single day. Once in power, he rounded up scores of opposition leaders, shut down independent media, forbade freedom of religion, criminalized sex outside of marriage, and tracked down and prosecuted gays.[82]

In response to which Donald Trump said, "I will tell you, President al-Sisi has been somebody that's been very close to me from the first time I met him . . . He's done a fantastic job in a very difficult situation. We are very much behind Egypt and the people of Egypt."[83]

RECEP TAYYIP ERDOĞAN, TURKEY

Erdoğan is one of the most brutal dictators on the planet. He accused anti-government protestors of being "arm-in-arm" with terrorists. More than 50,000 people have been detained since an attempted coup in 2016, one he blames on Fethullah Gülen, a septuagenarian Muslim cleric living in exile in Pennsylvania. Turkey has the most jailed journalists of any country in the world, and some 120,000 public servants, deemed not supportive of the Erdoğan regime, have been fired. He pushed through a referendum giving himself dictatorial powers. "You cannot put women and men on an equal footing," Erdoğan preaches. "It is against nature." He even had the temerity, while on a visit to Washington in May 2017, to sic his bodyguards on peaceful protestors near the Turkish embassy, right here in the United States.[84]

Donald Trump has never criticized Erdoğan. Au contraire. He called to congratulate him on his referendum victory and thanked him for supporting the United States in its bombing of Syria.[85]

XI JINPING, CHINA

It's like an ongoing Tiananmen Square in China, except undercover. Among other abuses, Xi is accused of extrajudicial detention, where detainees are tortured and mistreated; leading the world in executions; and enforced disappearance of critics. Until surpassed by Turkey, China was known as "the world's worst jailer of journalists." It ranks 176 out of 180 on the World Press Freedom Index. Access to the internet is very limited and censored. Only members of five "licensed" religions are allowed freedom to worship.[86]

Trump has entertained President Xi at Mar-a-Lago, played golf with him, and called him a good friend. "He certainly doesn't want to see turmoil and death," Trump told Reuters on April 28, 2017. "He doesn't want to see it. He is a very good man and I got to know him very well."[87]

When Xi secured a change in party rules allowing him to rule indefinitely, Trump was thrilled. "He's now president for life. President for life. No, he's great," he told a fund-raiser at Mar-a-Lago. "And look, he was able to do that. I think it's great. Maybe we'll have to give that a shot someday."[88]

And, speaking of Tiananmen Square, when that peaceful protest was put down in bloody fashion in 1989, Trump declared China's response "shows you the power of strength." In 2016, he even called the massacre a "riot."[89]

AND MORE FROM THE PAGES OF HISTORY

As long as they're ruthless enough, Trump doesn't care whether dictators are dead or alive. He'll praise them regardless.

In 2016, he opined that Libya would be better off "if Muammar Gaddafi were in charge right now."

He has also defended tweeting out a quote by fascist leader Benito Mussolini: "It's better to live one day as a lion than 100 years as a sheep." After all, argued Trump, "Mussolini was Mussolini . . . It's a very good quote. It's a very interesting quote . . . What difference does it make whether it's Mussolini or somebody else?" You just wouldn't believe this is the same guy who, according to his first wife, Ivana Trump, allegedly kept a book of Hitler's speeches by his bedside.[90]

And, believe it or not, Trump once even praised Saddam Hussein—on the campaign trail—for killing terrorists. "He did that so good," Trump said in July 2016. "They didn't read them the rights. They didn't talk. They were terrorists. Over."[91]

When you look at all the thugs Trump has praised and befriended, especially compared to how he has treated democratically elected allies, it's clear that he loves strongmen because he wants to be like them. As American president, his role model is not Abraham Lincoln, FDR, or Ronald Reagan. His role model and favorite dictator, whom we'll get to in the next chapter, is Vladimir Putin.

79. JERUSALEM AND ISRAEL

When we said earlier that Donald Trump began his foray into foreign politics by alienating all our longtime allies, I misspoke. I should have said, "By alienating all our longtime allies but one: Israel."

It didn't seem like it should be that way at first. During the GOP presidential primary in 2016, Trump stood out for not giving a wholehearted endorsement of Israel, instead describing himself as "sort of a neutral guy" between Israelis and Palestinians. He even refused to repudiate the endorsement of former KKK leader David Duke. Nonetheless, he was surprisingly popular in Israel. In early 2016, even before Republicans had chosen a candidate, Trump came in second (26 percent) to Hillary Clinton (38 percent) among all contenders, and, when asked which candidate would best represent Israel's interests, he came in first, 25 percent to 24 percent.[92]

As it turns out, the Israeli public was right. Today, Trump is so 100 percent Israel that it's hard to know whether it's he or Israeli prime minister Bibi Netanyahu who's in charge. Or, more likely, Sheldon Adelson, Las Vegas casino mogul, major Trump financial backer, and owner of *Israel Hayom,* Israel's most widely read and archly pro-Netanyahu newspaper.[93]

In fact, Trump began doing Bibi's bidding even before he got elected. According to news reports based on findings from the Mueller investigation, Trump aide Michael Flynn, apparently under orders from Jared Kushner, lobbied Russia and other countries to delay or block a UN vote against Israel's continued and illegal settlement expansion into the occupied territories. This despite the fact that President Obama's administration—still in charge of our foreign policy at the time—had said they would abstain from the vote and announced America's opposition to the settlements.[94]

A year later, at a public event in December 2017, Jared Kushner was personally thanked by billionaire Haim Saban for "taking steps to try and get the United Nations Security Council to not go along with what ended up being an abstention by the U.S." As Mehdi Hasan of *The Intercept* summed up this incident, "The Trump transition team reached out to the Russian government in order to undermine the U.S. government because the Israeli government asked them to."[95]

Whoever's calling the shots, it ends up the same: Whatever Bibi wants, Bibi gets, whether it's ignoring the continuing illegal building of settlements on the West Bank, scuttling the Iran nuclear deal, supporting without complaint Israel's killing of unarmed protestors at the Gaza border, or, long Bibi's wet dream, relocating the American embassy from Tel Aviv to Jerusalem.[96]

There's a reason that moving the embassy is a promise made by every recent president, Republican and Democrat, while running for office, and broken once they got to the White House. Because cooler heads pointed out that, for several very good reasons—since both Israelis and Palestinians consider Jerusalem their capital; and since Jerusalem contains sites considered sacred by both Jews and Muslims, not to mention Catholics; and since deciding the future of Jerusalem outside the context of Israeli–Palestinian negotiations would make the goal of a two-state solution even more difficult to achieve—this was a matter that should be left for Israel and the Palestinian National Authority to resolve as part of the peace process.[97]

For President Trump, caution be damned. On December 6, 2017, defying the advice of everyone from Rex Tillerson to James Mattis and Mike Pompeo to Pope Francis, President Trump declared that the United States now officially recognizes Jerusalem as the capital of Israel and would soon relocate its embassy there from Tel Aviv.[98]

To the relief of most foreign policy experts, the only saving grace was he did not say Jerusalem was the capital of a "united Israel"—thereby leaving the door open to negotiations that could result, down the road, in Jerusalem being established as the capital of both Israel and the Palestinian National Authority (which de facto is what it is today), with shared jurisdiction over holy sites. But that is cold comfort to the dozens of Palestinian protestors murdered, and thousands injured, by the Israel Defense Forces on the day Jared and Ivanka helped open the new embassy in May 2018.[99]

In short, Trump's rash action forever changed the role of the United

States in the Middle East. We can no longer pretend to be the "honest broker" in peace negotiations (which we have not been for a long time). We are now clearly on Bibi's team. But again, in the World of Trump, whatever Bibi wants, Bibi gets. Meanwhile, according to four State Department officials, having helped convince Trump to make the move, Sheldon Adelson also offered to pay for building the new American embassy in Jerusalem.[100]

In the long run, perhaps even more significant than Netanyahu's efforts to persuade Donald Trump to move the embassy to Jerusalem was his success in convincing Trump to scuttle the Iran nuclear deal. Netanyahu had long opposed the deal. He was furious and felt betrayed when Obama made it, and he pushed Trump from the beginning to end it. Just a week before Trump made his announcement, Netanyahu held a news conference at which he displayed notebooks seized by Israeli intelligence, which Bibi said proved that Iran "has" an ongoing nuclear weapons program. Then, to further reach his audience of one and manipulate our ignorant dupe of a president, Bibi went on *Fox & Friends* to further plead his case.[101]

It turned out to be nothing but a phony photo op. Reporters soon discovered that the documents proved that Iran "had" a nuclear weapons program, which we all knew anyway, and not that they "have" one today. But of course, Donald Trump didn't care. He'd already made up his mind. Whatever Bibi wants, Bibi gets.[102]

80. SAUDI ARABIA

As strange as it may seem, by pulling the United States out of the Iran nuclear deal, Donald Trump did something no other president had been able to do: He at least momentarily brought together Israel and Saudi Arabia—because both countries perceive Iran as their principal threat.

One of the very few ideological positions that defines Donald Trump is his constant attacks on Muslims. In his mind, they're all terrorists. As a candidate, he told Anderson Cooper, "I think Islam hates us." He berated Clinton and Obama because they would not utter the words *radical Islamic terrorism*. His Muslim ban was one of his first actions as president.[103]

Which is why his support for the corrupt monarchy of Saudi Arabia, home country of fifteen out of the nineteen 9/11 attackers, is all the more surprising and all the more dangerous. Evidently, Trump loves money more than he hates Muslims. And recall that Erik Prince brokered a meeting between Saudi and UAE reps and Donald Jr. during the campaign, where the Saudis allegedly pledged their troth and offered their resources to Trump. That likely helped as well.

In any case, where other allies reacted with alarm or hesitation at Trump's election, Saudi Arabia rushed to embrace him, winning the loyalty of both Trump and his Middle East envoy, Jared Kushner. In return, Trump chose Saudi Arabia as the destination for his first trip overseas. And he has since totally embraced the agenda of King Salman, or more particularly the direction of young crown prince Mohammed bin Salman, or MBS, including his purge of political rivals, his fierce feud with Qatar, and his ongoing war of destruction in Yemen.[104]

Count the Saudi king and his son among the other authoritarian human rights violators that Trump loves to tongue-bathe. When MBS rounded up and detained dozens of prominent wealthy Saudis, including several royal princes, issued travel bans, and seized their assets, Trump praised him for recognizing "the need to build a moderate, peaceful, and tolerant region," which is "essential to ensuring a hopeful future for the Saudi people."[105]

When King Salman convinced Egypt, the United Arab Emirates, Bahrain, and other Arab countries to join in a boycott against Qatar because of reports that Sheikh Tamim, leader of Qatar, had expressed support for the Muslim Brotherhood and ISIS—which turned out to be "fake news" attributed to foreign hackers—Trump quickly sided with Saudi Arabia and threw Qatar under the bus.[106]

For Trump, it was another impulsive, shoot-from-the-hip move and alienation of another ally. Qatar has been one of America's most steadfast friends in the Arab world. It is home to the United States Central Command and an airbase where eleven thousand U.S. military are based. Just months earlier, Trump had enlisted Qatar as part of a pan-Arab nation coalition to develop a new peace plan for the region.

And yet, just one hour after Rex Tillerson had defended Qatar and publicly urged Saudi Arabia and others to "de-escalate the situation and put forth a good faith effort to resolve the grievances they have with each other," Trump bloviated, "The nation of Qatar, unfortunately, has been a funder of terrorism at a very high level. I've decided, along with Secretary of State Rex Tillerson, our great generals, and military people, the time has come to call on Qatar to end its funding. They have to end that funding. And its extremist ideology in terms of funding." The very stable diplomatic genius strikes again.[107]

Most seriously, Trump has been Saudi Arabia's biggest supporter in its brutal war against Houthi rebels in Yemen. Using more than $40 million in American weapons supplied by both the Obama and Trump administrations, plus extensive intelligence and logistical assistance, Saudi armed forces have bombed the hell out of Yemen, attempting to restore deposed former president Abdo Rabo Mansour Hadi to power.[108]

Over the last three years, according to Vox, the Saudi military have conducted more than 145,000 bombing missions over Yemen. So far, the conflict has claimed more than 13,500 lives. And UN officials estimate more than 20 million people, including more than 11 million children, need basic humanitarian assistance, and at least 14.8 million lack basic medical care.[109]

Apparently confronted with photos of the Yemen war's carnage in December 2017, Trump surprised everyone by suddenly admonishing Saudi Arabia and calling for humanitarian aid to get through to civilians on the ground. But this epiphany didn't last—only a few months later, it was back to business as usual. In April 2018, as that war waged on, Crown Prince Mohammed visited Donald Trump at the White House, where, as Vox's Zack Beauchamp reports, "the crown prince of an absolute monarchy—a country where dissent and homosexuality are punishable by death—was received less like a human rights abuser and more like a visionary civil rights hero." Trump was full of nothing but praise for his new BFF: "We really have a great friendship, a great relationship."[110]

81. HE'S GUTTED THE STATE DEPARTMENT

We previously discussed Trump's inability to staff his government way back in chapter 2 (#28), as well as the disastrous impact of Rex Tillerson on our diplomatic infrastructure (#51), but here, it must be said, is where the rubber really hits the road.

Under Donald Trump, it's been a string of foreign policy blunders in many different parts of the globe. But there's one common thread that's been exacerbating them all—the lack of a State Department. There is simply nobody home.

This is, after all, the president who explained to *Forbes* magazine in October 2017 why there were still so many key jobs left vacant in his administration: "I'm generally not going to make a lot of the appointments that would normally be—because you don't need them." And that's been true, most of all, of the State Department.[111]

Okay, go to Foggy Bottom. The building's still there. But it's an empty shell—its core staff of career foreign policy experts decimated, most of its top officer positions sitting empty, and its budget cut by one-third—all at the direction of President Trump, with the gleeful support of then secretary of state Rex Tillerson and now Mike Pompeo.[112]

As of this writing, eighteen months into the administration, problems at the State Department have not gotten any better, only worse. As noted earlier, after Tillerson's firing on March 13, 2018, eight of the top nine jobs at State were unfilled. Not only was there no secretary of state (until Pompeo's confirmation), there was no assistant secretary for arms control, or international security and nonproliferation, or Near East affairs, nor South and Central Asian affairs.[113]

Two months later, there was still no American ambassador in 38 out of 188 key international organizations or countries, including Mexico, the European Union, Turkey, South Korea, South Africa, or Saudi Arabia—even though a lot's going on in every one of those countries.[114]

Even more damaging in the long run is the fact that so many experienced, career State Department veterans—who've been there, representing the United States, under presidents Democratic and Republican—have either been shown the door or decided to walk out of it voluntarily rather than serve under Donald Trump. According to the American Foreign Service Association, 60 percent of our highest-ranked diplomats have departed in Trump's first year alone. That has left veteran diplomats to conclude that the State Department is, in the words of writer Evan Osnos, in "its most diminished condition since the nineteen-fifties, when Joseph McCarthy called it a hotbed of 'Communists and queers.'"[115]

At the same time, the State Department accepted the lowest number of new Foreign Service officers in years. Indeed, many in the diplomatic service lament that due to resignations, firings, and failure to fill so many positions, the United States is losing its next generation of foreign policy leaders. The diplomatic problems we're having now will continue for decades.[116]

But don't tell that to Donald Trump. In his view, that's no problem at all. We "don't need them."

8

TRUMP'S RUSSIAN CONNECTIONS

A foreign government interfering in an American presidential election? Secret meetings in London, Prague, Washington, and the Seychelles with Russian operatives? One candidate under criminal investigation by the FBI for colluding with Russians? And the Russian-backed candidate wins?

If this were a Daniel Silva or Ted Bell spy novel, we'd easily buy into it. But it's still hard to believe it happened in real life: right here, in the United States of America, with the 2016 presidential campaign of Donald J. Trump.

Someday soon, perhaps even as you're reading this, special counsel Robert Mueller will have completed his investigation, and we'll know the full extent to which Trump or members of his campaign team actually cooperated with Russian operatives and whether criminal activity was involved. But we already know without a doubt:

1. As determined by our top U.S. intelligence agencies and confirmed by the Senate Intelligence Committee, the Russian government

intervened in the 2016 presidential election in order to undermine Hillary Clinton and help elect Donald Trump.[1]

2. Various Trump campaign officials—including Paul Manafort, Rick Gates, Carter Page, George Papadopoulos, Michael Flynn, Jared Kushner, Donald Trump Jr., and Jeff Sessions—met on several occasions with Russian operatives. And at first lied about every meeting.[2]

3. As of this writing, four Trump campaign officials known to have held meetings with Russian agents—Paul Manafort, Rick Gates, Michael Flynn, and George Papadopoulos—have been indicted by special counsel Robert Mueller, as well as Manafort-linked lawyer Alex van der Zwaan and a host of Russian nationals and companies.[3]

4. Many wealthy Russians with criminal records have bought condos or established offices in Trump properties in Toronto, New York, Panama City, Vancouver, and other places around the world. And for over twenty years, Trump has aggressively sought Kremlin assistance in building projects in Russia.[4]

5. As president, Trump has withheld enforcement of tougher, congressionally approved sanctions on Russia, while continuing to shower praise on Russian president Vladimir Putin.[5]

When you add all those facts together, we may not know where the fire is yet—but there sure is a lot of smoke. Especially after you throw in Trump's constant and increasingly unhinged rants on Twitter about "NO COLLUSION" and "WITCH HUNTS." Let's take it frame by frame.

82. HE'S PUTIN'S PUPPET

If her intention was to get under Donald Trump's skin in their debate on October 19, 2016, Hillary Clinton clearly seemed to have succeeded. Suggesting that his over-the-top praise of Vladimir Putin would prevent him from standing up to the Russian leader, she said Putin "would rather have a puppet as president of the United States." Trump's reaction was sharp, furious, and typical playground logic. "No puppet," he shot back. "You're the puppet."[6]

Decades from now, Russian foreign policy analysts will still be shaking their heads over the strange but indisputable bromance between Trump and Putin. Whether they've actually ever met or not, they clearly form a mutual admiration society. For Putin, Trump's his dream candidate—a useful and easily bought idiot to help rupture longtime Western alliances. For Trump, Putin's his ideal strongman—whom, for years now, he's tried desperately to buddy up to.

First, let's be clear: Putin is a brutal dictator. We know about his continued arrests and persecutions—and in some cases murders—of critics, opponents, and journalists, his poisoning of political enemies, his invasion of the sovereign country of Ukraine and annexation of Crimea, and his support for President Assad's use of chemical weapons in Syria. Add all that up, and you have all the makings of the world's most ruthless tyrant—in the eyes of everybody except Donald Trump.

Where others see evil, Trump sees strength. On September 7, 2016, he told NBC News about Putin: "If he says great things about me, I'm going to say great things about him. I've already said, he is really very much of a leader. I mean, you could say, oh, isn't that a terrible thing . . . the man has very strong control over a country. Now, it's a very different system, and I don't happen to like the system. But certainly, in this system, he's been a leader, far more than our president has been a leader."[7]

It's also crystal clear who's using whom in this mutual admiration society. As David Remnick described their relationship in the August 3, 2016, *New Yorker,* before its full republic-threatening ramifications became known: "Trump sees strength and cynicism in Putin and hopes to emulate him. Putin sees in Trump a grand opportunity. He sees in Trump weakness and ignorance, a confused mind. He has every hope of exploiting him."[8]

And Trump, whose crush on Putin began well before the 2016 election, is an easy mark. At least nine times between 2013 and July 2016, as reported by CNN, Trump asserted he had met or spoken to Putin (even though no record of such a meeting or conversation exists). Trump invited Putin to the 2013 Miss Universe contest in Moscow, after which he told *Fox & Friends:* "Putin contacted me and was so nice." He described Putin as "somebody who can be dealt with," and also told Fox he'd give Putin an A for leadership.[9]

In Trump's eyes, no matter how ruthless he is, Putin's better than Obama. He told *Morning Joe* in December 2015, "He's running his country and at least he's a leader, unlike what we have in this country." Trump doesn't even mind how many political opponents or journalists Putin has killed. After all, he told Fox's Bill O'Reilly, "There are a lot of killers. Do you think our country is so innocent?"[10]

And there you have candidate Donald Trump's Russia policy in a nutshell: Putin's better than Obama, and America's no better than Russia. As *Slate*'s Franklin Foer concluded, that's worse than being a puppet. That's "slavish devotion." "If Putin wanted to concoct the ideal candidate to serve his purposes," Foer writes, "his laboratory creation would look like Donald Trump."[11]

Of course, it's no secret why Trump was showering Putin with such lavish praise; we've already seen how much Trump loves and admires authoritarian leaders. And more to the point, Trump was trying to make money off him! His business dealings with Russia go back thirty years. He tried five different times to build projects—hotels, apartments, retail, even an ice rink—in Russia. He marketed his own brand of Trump Vodka. He partnered with the Bayrock Group, a front for wealthy Russian investors, two of whose leaders, Tevfik Arif and Felix Sater, had an office in Trump Tower. And as noted earlier, even as other investors backed away from the "King of Debt," Russian oligarchs have invested heavily in Trump properties around the globe. A study by McClatchy found that buyers connected to Russia or former Soviet Republics paid $109 million to Trump—in eighty-six all-cash transactions—at ten Trump properties in Florida and New York over the years.[12]

In many ways, the entire Trump business empire was built on Russian money. Donald Trump Jr. let the cat out of the bag at a real estate conference in New York in 2008. He and his daddy weren't too worried about the Great Recession because "Russians make up a pretty disproportionate cross-section of a lot of our assets," he told the crowd. He added, "We see a lot of money pouring in from Russia."[13]

As the saying goes, follow the money. That's what drives both Putin and Trump. And that's why Putin helped Trump win the presidency. With money, Putin bought the Olympic Games and the World Cup. With enough money, he apparently figured he could buy an American president, too. As David Remnick summed it up, "Putin sees the ready benefit in having the United States led by an unlettered narcissist who believes that geostrategic questions are as easy to resolve as a real estate closing. Putin knows a chump when he sees one."[14]

Putin's gamble paid off—"bigly." Having already seized Crimea, Russian troops remain in Eastern Ukraine. Trump does nothing, unless you count destabilizing NATO. Congress passes tough new sanctions against Russia. Trump says we don't need them and refuses to enact them. Putin directs Russian operatives to meddle in the 2016 presidential election to help Donald Trump. Trump not only hasn't condemned their actions, he's left America unprotected for the next wave of interference.

A classic case of Trump's supplication to his Russian idol happened in early 2018, after Putin had staged a phony election, which he won with over 75 percent of the votes (after locking up all opponents), and Trump placed a call to his Kremlin pal. Several White House sources confirm that at the very top of his briefing book for the call, security analysts had advised in all caps: DO NOT CONGRATULATE FOR WINNING ELECTION! Effort wasted. True to form, the first thing Trump did was to congratulate Putin for winning the election. A few short months later, Trump once again embarrassed himself, the United States, and the world by begging the other G7 nations to reinstate Russia. Soon thereafter, and shortly before he announced a July 14 summit with Putin in Helsinki, Trump tweeted: "Russia continues to say they had nothing to do with Meddling in our Election!"[15]

Meanwhile, according to intelligence agencies, Russia's already up to their old tricks in influencing the midterm elections of 2018. "Frankly, the United States is under attack," Dan Coats, the director of national intelligence, testified to Congress in February 2018. And where is our president?[16]

Yes, Putin found just the chump he was looking for.

83. HE'S REVEALED STATE SECRETS

As any Washington journalist can tell you, the Trump White House leads all others in one particular way: It has more leakers, and provides more leaks, than any other administration ever. The sieve-like nature of Trump's administration reached comic proportions on May 11, 2018, when a furious Sarah Huckabee Sanders scolded her communications teams for leaking the derogatory remarks made behind closed doors about Senator John McCain by aide Kelly Sadler. (To wit, who cares what he thinks "because he's dying anyway.") The next day, Axios reported Sanders's harangue as it went down "according to five sources in the room."[17]

But in a way, what can you expect? The fish rots from the head down, and it is well known that Donald Trump has always been an inveterate leaker. For decades, he even pretended to be his own fake spokesman using the name John Barron.[18]

In any event, not even top-level meetings in the Oval Office are secure, as we learned on May 10, 2017, the day after President Trump fired FBI director James Comey. And this time, the White Horse's biggest leaker, Donald J. Trump doing something so much more nefarious than leaking to the press. He was revealing state secrets to two of Vladimir Putin's top diplomats.[19]

It sounds crazy, but it's true. During a meeting with Russia's foreign minister Sergey Lavrov and the Russian ambassador to the United States, Sergey Kislyak, for the first time since he became president, Trump first unloaded on why he'd fired Comey. The official White House line, issued just the day before, was that Trump dumped Comey because he had violated Justice Department procedures in his conduct of the Hillary Clinton email investigation.[20]

Nobody believed that, anyway, but . . . having lied to the American people, Trump decided to tell the Russians the truth: Comey's firing had nothing to do with Clinton. It was all about getting Comey off his back and shutting down the Russia investigation.

"I just fired the head of the FBI. He was crazy, a real nut job," Trump told Lavrov and Kislyak, according to an internal document summarizing the meeting, leaked to *The New York Times*. Then, as if to reassure the Russians they had nothing to worry about, that he'd taken care of everything, Trump added, "I faced great pressure because of Russia. That's taken off."[21]

Revealing his secret reasons for firing Comey was bad enough, but then Trump blabbered on to reveal state secrets, informing the Russians about intelligence received from a top secret Israeli counterterrorism operation.

"I get great intel," Trump bragged to the Russians. "I have people brief me on great intel every day." At which point he told them the broad outlines of an ISIS plan uncovered by Israeli spies to turn laptop computers into bombs terrorists could carry onto commercial planes, including the city in Syria where the operation was located—information given the United States exclusively by Israel but not yet shared with Congress or foreign allies—information that Trump, like any old office gossip, now shared with our longtime adversary.[22]

The May 10 meeting was one more example of the danger of having an uninformed, loose-lipped, bigmouth amateur in the White House, especially when dealing with matters of national security. National security experts agree that Israel and other allies will now be much more careful about what intelligence they share with the United States, and intelligence agencies will think twice about what they share with the White House.[23]

Of course, there remains the open question of whether Trump just slipped up in divulging this intel or whether he was doing a favor for Russia, his biggest patron.

84. PAPADOPOULOS AND THE RUSSIANS

Donald Trump continues to claim that the Russia investigation began when the Clinton campaign hired former British intelligence officer Christopher Steele to prepare his famous dossier. (More on that coming up.) But we know that's not the case. The FBI confirms that the whole mess began when the bureau first learned that a Trump campaign operative was going around London bragging about getting dirt on Hillary Clinton from Russian operatives.[24]

The braggart in question was one George Papadopoulos, a member of the Trump campaign's National Security Advisory Committee led by Jeff Sessions, once praised by Trump as an "excellent guy." In fact, Papadopoulos holds a dubious distinction. He's not only the reason the Russian investigation began in July 2016; in October 2017, he also became the first person to plead guilty in that investigation and has been cooperating with special counsel Robert Mueller ever since.[25]

In many ways, Papadopoulos is a carbon copy of Donald Trump—little political experience, even less foreign policy experience, loose-lipped, and a braggart. After volunteering for two months in the Ben Carson campaign, he had gone to work as an energy consultant in London when he was recruited by the Trump campaign as a foreign policy advisor in March 2016. Weeks later, while vacationing in Italy, he met Joseph Mifsud, a London professor with close ties to Russia, who in turn introduced him to two Russian operatives.[26]

Seizing the opportunity to be an important player, Papadopoulos immediately started working with his Russian contacts on connecting the

Trump campaign with the Russian government, including trying to set up a meeting between Trump and Putin. In so doing, Papadopoulos also learned that Russian government hackers had uncovered "dirt" on Hillary Clinton from her emails, a fact he shared with campaign officials.[27]

But just like Trump, Papadopoulos talked too much. And unlike Trump, he also drank too much. In May 2016, over too many libations at London's upscale Kensington wine bar, Papadopoulos regaled his guest Alexander Downer, Australia's ambassador to the UK, with tales of all the dirt on Hillary the Trump campaign was about to obtain from Kremlin sources. That proved to be his undoing.[28]

Two months later, when WikiLeaks started releasing the Clinton emails, Downer informed American officials of his conversation with Papadopoulos. The FBI, upon learning that Russian operatives were interfering in the 2016 presidential campaign with the knowledge, and perhaps assistance, of the Trump campaign—on top of earlier reports of meetings between Russian officials and Trump aide Carter Page, which we will see shortly—opened their investigation into possible collusion between the Trump operation and Russia.[29]

In January 2017, in his first interview with the FBI, Papadopoulos denied any efforts to cooperate with the Russians and claimed his meetings with Mifsud amounted to a big "nothing." But that October 2017, he was charged with lying to the FBI and pleaded guilty.[30]

Bottom line: As of this writing, we have as yet seen no concrete evidence that Donald Trump himself colluded with the Russians in the 2016 campaign, but there is no doubt that George Papadopoulos did and that he reported back to the Trump campaign about it.

But he may get off yet. In June 2018, Papadopoulos's wife, Simona Mangiante, made the TV news rounds to beg Trump for a pardon for her husband. And as we'll discuss more later on, Trump definitely isn't above abusing the pardon power to cover his tracks.[31]

85. THE TRUMP TOWER MEETING

Of course, as we later learned, George Papadopoulos wasn't the only one meeting with Russian operatives to get dirt on Hillary. There was at least one other big meeting, much closer to home, in Trump Tower itself, hosted by Donald Trump Jr. and attended by Trump's campaign manager Paul Manafort and his son-in-law, Jared Kushner.[32]

Whatever happened at that summit, and however the involved parties tried to spin it afterward, there's no doubt what it was all about. It was proposed—in writing!—to Donald Jr. by Rob Goldstone, the publicist for Aras and Emin Agalarov, a wealthy father–son pair who financed the 2013 Miss Universe pageant in Moscow—with the promise of "documents and information that would incriminate Hillary and her dealings with Russia and would be very useful to your father." Without hesitation, Junior immediately responded, "If it's what you say, I love it!"[33]

Even after thousands of pages of testimony about it to the Senate Intelligence Committee have been released, much is still unknown about that June 9, 2016, meeting. Robert Mueller's still investigating its details and consequences. But here's what we do know.[34]

In attendance from the Trump campaign: Donald Trump Jr.; Paul Manafort; Jared Kushner.[35]

In attendance from Russia: Rob Goldstone; Natalia Veselnitskaya, Russian lawyer with ties to the Kremlin; Irakly Kaveladze, the Georgian American president of Agalarov's real estate company; Rinat Akhmetshin, Russian American lobbyist; and Anatoli Samochornov, translator.[36]

The purpose of the meeting: Judging from Goldstone's promise to Donald Jr., the Russian team was expected to divulge their hacker-acquired dirt on Hillary, which, as Goldstone put it, was "part of Russia and its government's support for Mr. Trump." For the Trump team, getting that dirt on Hillary was their goal, no matter where it came from.[37]

What happened at the meeting: Again, much is still unknown, but apparently Veselnitskaya spent much of the meeting droning on and on about problems with sanctions against Russia under the Magnitsky Act, in response to which Russia had placed a ban on adoption of Russian children by American parents. (It came out in the Senate testimony that Jared Kushner, evidently "agitated" and "infuriated," in Goldstone's words—presumably because the promised Hillary dirt wasn't immediately forthcoming—left the meeting in a huff.)[38]

What else happened at the meeting: Who knows? Was there a deal cut on releasing Hillary's emails? On getting the Russian government's help on ads and fake news on social media? Or on easing off on Russian sanctions in return for campaign help? Did Trump join the meeting, which was held just below his office in Trump Tower? That's part of what Robert Mueller is investigating.

What happened after the meeting: Again, Mueller's on the case. But we do know of two things that followed. One, Donald Jr. made two phone calls to a blocked number. Was he reporting on the meeting to his father? He now says he can't remember to whom he placed the calls—convenient!—but Corey Lewandowski told investigators that Trump's primary residence utilized a blocked number.[39]

That leads to one big question: How much did Trump himself know about the Trump Tower confab with Russians, either before or after the meeting?[40]

For almost a year, there was another big question: Once *The New York Times* was on the verge of revealing the Trump Tower meeting in July 2017, who wrote the statement—drafted on Air Force One as the president was flying home from Europe—that asserted that the meeting was all about adoption and had nothing to do with the campaign? According to *The Times,* in an article several months later, the author of that big lie was . . . none other than Trump himself:

"The president supervised the writing of the statement, according to three people familiar with the episode, with input from other White House aides. A fierce debate erupted over how much information the news release should include. Mr. Trump was insistent about including language that the meeting was about Russian adoptions, according to two people with knowledge of the discussion."[41]

Michael Wolff corroborated *The Times*'s account in *Fire and Fury:* "The president insisted that the meeting in Trump Tower was purely and simply about Russian adoption policy. That's what was discussed. Period."[42]

But, of course, we already knew from Don Jr.'s emails that he had originally called the meeting for the express purpose of receiving the alleged dirt on Hillary Clinton dug up by Russian hackers. Which raises another question: If Donald Trump was so eager to lie about the true nature of the June 9 meeting, what was he trying to hide?

Clearly, something. In a memo sent to special counsel Robert Mueller in January 2018 and made public in June, White House attorneys Jay Sekulow and John Dowd finally admitted that it was, in fact, President Trump himself, as first reported by *The Times,* who insisted upon and personally dictated the phony "adoption" statement—his own version of "fake news." In that same memo, Dowd and Sekulow argue that, even if writing that memo amounted to obstruction of justice, Trump could not be charged with the crime because he's president of the United States.[43]

Bottom line: Again, as of this writing, we have seen no evidence that Donald Trump himself colluded with the Russians. But even if his meeting didn't produce the damning evidence he was looking for, there is no doubt that Donald Trump Jr. did. And so did Paul Manafort and Jared Kushner, by attending the same meeting.

86. SESSIONS, JARED, AND THE RUSSIANS

Secret meetings in London. A big secret meeting at Trump Tower. That's already a lot of circumstantial evidence of Russian connections. But they're just the tip of the iceberg. The Moscow Project has documented seventy-five contacts between Russian officials and members of the Trump team, including at least twenty-two meetings. They've also identified twenty-two high-ranking Trumpers who had direct contacts with Russians during the campaign or transition, or knew about such contacts. And—*quelle coïncidence!*—they initially lied about all of them.[44]

Among those, per the Moscow Project, engaging in contact with Russian representatives and not disclosing them: Michael Cohen, Roger Stone, Donald Trump Jr., Jeff Sessions, Paul Manafort, J. D. Gordon, Jared Kushner, Carter Page, Michael Flynn, Erik Prince, George Papadopoulos, Anthony Scaramucci, and Rick Gates.

And don't forget the Trump aides who knew of contacts with Russia-linked operatives: Corey Lewandowski, K. T. McFarland, Tom Bossert, Hope Hicks, Reince Priebus, Sam Clovis, Steve Bannon, Stephen Miller, and Sean Spicer.

As you can see, we're talking about a who's who of Trumpworld here, all engaging in the same illicit activity and then refusing to properly disclose it. Two names stand out because of the top roles they played in both the campaign and the new administration.

JEFF SESSIONS

During his confirmation hearing for attorney general, Jeff Sessions denied under oath ever meeting any Russian officials during the campaign or after. He also denied knowing about any other contacts between the Trump team and Russian operatives. Both of these statements have proved to be big fat lies.[45]

Sessions, in fact, met with Russian ambassador Sergey Kislyak three times during the campaign. He also attended the meeting at which George Papadopoulos reported on his meetings with Russian officials trying to arrange a Trump–Putin meeting. In June 2016, he had dinner at the Capitol Hill Club with Papadopoulos, Carter Page, and J. D. Gordon, another Trump campaign advisor, during which Page, whom we'll get to in a moment, informed Sessions of his upcoming trip to Moscow.[46]

Far from zero, Sessions had so many contacts with Russians he was eventually forced to recuse himself, much to Donald Trump's everlasting chagrin, from anything having to do with the Russia investigation, turning the whole thing over to Deputy Attorney General Rod Rosenstein. Except, of course, when Trump sought his help in firing James Comey.[47]

Recusing himself from the Russia investigation was a move—the correct move for Sessions—for which Donald Trump will never forgive his attorney general. He's stated several times publicly that he's sorry he ever appointed Sessions, wishes he hadn't, and that if he had known Sessions would end up recusing himself from the Russia investigation, he would have asked somebody else to be AG.

JARED KUSHNER

At first, his son-in-law, Jared Kushner, also denied meeting with, or knowing of, any campaign staffer's contacts with Russian officials—until the FBI helped him "refresh" his memory. In the end, along with the thirty-nine late changes to his financial disclosures, he had to update his national security clearance paperwork to list more than one hundred foreign officials, including Russians, he met before joining the White House.[48]

As reported above, Kushner attended the June 9 meeting at Trump Tower with Donald Trump Jr. and Kremlin representatives. He also held private meetings with Ambassador Kislyak and with Sergey Gorkov, the head of the Russian state-owned bank VEB—both of which he failed to disclose on the initial forms he filed with the FBI for a security clearance.[49]

In testimony before the Senate Judiciary Committee, Kushner also testified he knew nothing about secret communications between Donald Trump Jr. and WikiLeaks—until Junior revealed he'd informed Kushner about his emails. He was also criticized by the committee for failing to reveal emails related to a planned meeting between Trump and Alexander Torshin, deputy head of Russia's central bank, and a further thread of emails to and from Sergei Millian, president of the Russian American Chamber of Commerce.[50]

Kushner also had a hard time remembering his business ties with Russia. In July 2017, in response to the Russia investigation, he put out a statement declaring his innocence: "I have not relied on Russian funds to finance my business activities in the private sector. I have tried to be fully transparent."[51]

Not so. It was later revealed that Kushner was a business partner with Russian oligarch Yuri Milner in a company called Cadre—which Kushner conveniently forgot to mention on financial disclosure forms when he went to work in the White House.[52]

At this late juncture, there are two possibilities to explain all this. Either Sessions, Kushner, and the rest of Team Trump all have the memories of goldfish and probably shouldn't be anywhere near the top corridors of power . . . or they're all lying.

87. MICHAEL FLYNN AND THE RUSSIANS

He may have been the first high-level Trump nominee to leave the administration, but Michael Flynn can say he lasted longer than Anthony Scaramucci. The Mooch was fired after only eleven days in the White House. Flynn lasted all of twenty-four. And, of course, once again, Russians were right in the middle of it.[53]

Long before stepping in as President Trump's first national security advisor, Michael Flynn was no stranger to controversy. As a three-star general, he was fired as director of the Defense Intelligence Agency for, among other reasons—and not unlike his future boss—constantly telling and repeating what everybody knew were lies. (His colleagues euphemistically called them "Flynn Facts.")[54]

After leaving the military, he went on an anti-Islam speaking tour. Naturally, as a hysterical anti-Muslim with a tortured relationship to the truth, he soon found a home on the Trump campaign. At the 2016 Republican National Convention, he led the crowd in chants of "Lock her up!"—a hyperpartisan rant about Hillary Clinton that shocked his former army colleagues, but not Donald Trump.[55]

Trump didn't hesitate to name Flynn his national security advisor, even after no less than President Obama warned Trump against that. And that's when his troubles really started. For one, Flynn had failed to report payments received as a lobbyist for the corrupt government of Turkey. For another, a January 12 report by *The Washington Post* disclosed that Flynn had made a series of phone calls to Russian ambassador Sergey Kislyak—yes, he's the Zelig of the Trump administration and somehow just keeps popping up everywhere—on December 29, 2016, the same day the Obama administration had announced tough new sanctions on Russia in retaliation for their sadly successful meddling in the 2016 election.[56]

In one sense, Flynn's conversations with Kislyak came as no surprise. Flynn had known ties to Russia. He'd even previously been given an award by RT, Russia's American propaganda cable network, at a Moscow dinner, where he sat at the head table with Vladimir Putin. But Flynn insisted his calls to Kislyak had nothing to do with U.S. sanctions against Russia and were, in fact, nothing more than friendly holiday greetings—which didn't really add up, since the Russian Orthodox celebration of Christmas doesn't take place until January 9.[57]

Nonetheless, Vice President Mike Pence and press secretary Sean Spicer dutifully defended Flynn by insisting the friendly holiday call had nothing to do with sanctions. But a month later, that cover story fell apart. On February 9, *The Post* followed up with another story confirming that Flynn and Kislyak had, indeed, discussed sanctions—with Flynn reassuring Kislyak he had nothing to worry about, because Trump would not enforce them.[58]

When Trump fired Flynn on February 13, allegedly for lying to Vice President Pence, he clearly did so reluctantly, telling reporters Flynn was a "wonderful man" and saying that "it's really a sad thing" that Flynn was treated "very, very unfairly" by the media. For months, Trump insisted that any reports that Flynn had done anything improper were nothing but "fake news."[59]

He didn't just say this for our benefit. As recounted by James Comey in congressional testimony and his book, Trump summoned the then FBI director to the Oval Office the day after Flynn's firing, Valentine's Day 2017. After asking Mike Pence and Jeff Sessions to leave the room (!), Trump said to Comey, "I want to talk about Mike Flynn. He is a good guy and has been through a lot. I hope you can see your way clear to letting this go, to letting Flynn go. He is a good guy. I hope you can let this go."[60]

Comey, of course, refused, and now there was a whole new can of worms open and wriggling everywhere. Flynn lying to the FBI about the nature of phone calls with the Russian ambassador is bad enough, but now the president of the United States was asking the FBI director to look the other way.

As such, Michael Flynn poses a much, much bigger problem for Donald Trump, something we'll talk about more next chapter—obstruction of justice! This became especially true on December 1, 2017, when Michael Flynn, he of the infamous "Lock her up!" chant, pleaded guilty to lying to the FBI about the nature of the Kislyak calls and announced that he was cooperating with special counsel Robert Mueller in his criminal investigation of the Trump campaign and administration.[61]

Which is probably why the White House immediately changed its story, claiming that Flynn's guilty plea implicated Flynn alone and no one else in the White House, certainly not the president himself. That, of course, depends on whether or not Trump knew the true nature of Flynn's conversations with Kislyak, or perhaps even directed him to make them—questions certain to be investigated by Mueller.

We'll see what the final report says, but as always, Trump has protested too much. "I had to fire General Flynn because he lied to the Vice President and the FBI," he tweeted on December 2, 2017, the day after Flynn's guilty plea. In other words, according to the president himself, Trump now says he knew Flynn had committed the crime of lying to the FBI when he fired him, *before he asked Comey to drop his investigation.* If that's not obstruction of justice, what is?[62]

88. MANAFORT, GATES, AND THE RUSSIANS

Throughout his career, whether it was prosecuting mobster John Gotti or serving as the longest FBI head since J. Edgar Hoover, Robert Mueller has always been a respected figure in Washington. But perhaps the first sign that Mueller was conducting a very serious investigation with potentially dire consequences for Donald Trump was his October 2017 indictments of Trump campaign manager Paul Manafort and deputy campaign manager Rick Gates. Outside of immediate family, few were closer to the heart of the Trump operation from March to August 2016 than these top campaign officials. And Manafort, remember, attended the infamous June 9 meeting with Russian operatives in Trump Tower organized by Donald Trump Jr. to get dirt on Hillary Clinton.[63]

That's why both Manafort and Gates are so key to Mueller's investigation. Even though the twelve charges against both men are related to money laundering and other financial crimes committed before they joined the Trump campaign, few likely know better where the bodies were buried or what connections might have occurred between the Trump campaign and Russian officials.[64]

Compounding the threat for Donald Trump is the fact that, even though Paul Manafort, who has been involved in corruption and skullduggery for decades, is as of this writing still fighting the charges from his prison cell, Rick Gates is cooperating with the special counsel. If he knows anything, he's talking.[65]

In many ways, and just like Trump and Flynn, Trump and Manafort were made for each other. Both have a history of shady business deals and a mutual attraction for strongmen. For Manafort, a veteran political operative who first emerged on the scene during the Gerald Ford campaign, that led to partnering with Roger Stone in a political consulting firm whose clients included dictators Ferdinand Marcos of the Philippines and Jonas Savimbi of Angola. Always chasing increasingly dirty money to support an increasingly lavish lifestyle, Manafort also courted Russian oligarchs with close ties to Vladimir Putin, notably Oleg Deripaska, who later sued Manafort for allegedly cheating him of millions. It was Deripaska who introduced Manafort to Ukrainian politician Viktor Yanukovych, who later became president of Ukraine and a major Manafort benefactor.[66]

No doubt, then, that Manafort and his protégé Gates felt right at home in the Trump campaign. They were lifelong grifters who had found themselves yet another rich mark. They brought their own Russian contacts with them and met even more in Trump Tower. And whatever black deeds were committed with Russian help during those spring and summer campaign months, Manafort and Gates would have the receipts. Now Gates is talking to Mueller. And, as of June 15, 2018, Manafort is cooling his heels in federal prison, awaiting trial.[67]

89. CARTER PAGE AND THE RUSSIANS

The Best and the Brightest, David Halberstam's magnificent history of the Vietnam War, shows the colossal mistakes that can be made even by the smartest of people. Any history of the Trump administration—*The Worst and the Dullest?*—will similarly show the colossal mistakes made by the dumbest of people, of whom, even among considerable competition, there may be none dumber than Carter Page. Like a character out of central casting, he's a small-time yet wannabe-big player, whose clumsy attempts to establish connections with Russia ultimately triggered events that could bring down the whole Trump operation.[68]

From early on, Page had deep Russian ties. He studied in Moscow as a navy midshipman in 1991 and worked there for three years in the 2000s. But the FBI didn't begin looking into Page's Russian ties until 2013, long before the Trump campaign got under way, after he'd held several meetings back in New York with Russian intelligence agent Victor Podobnyy. Page insisted they only talked energy policy. The FBI suspected the Russian may have recruited Page as a spy. For his part, Podobnyy said of Page on a recorded conversation, "I think he's an idiot."[69]

Two years later, with zero experience, Page was named, along with George Papadopoulos, as a foreign policy advisor to the Trump campaign. ("Anyone who came to us with a pulse, a résumé, and seemed legit would be welcomed," one Trump official later conceded.) In this new capacity, after informing Jeff Sessions of his plans, Page soon jetted off to Moscow, where he gave a speech critical of Obama foreign policy, met with several top Russian officials, including deputy prime minister Arkady Dvorkovich, and again attracted the attention of the FBI, who'd had their eyes on him since the idiot episode. Except that now the idiot was wearing a Trump campaign hat.[70]

Recall that, based on suspicious contacts between Russians and George Papadopoulos, the FBI had already launched its Russian investigation in July 2016. (When asked in October 2017 by MSNBC's Chris Hayes if he and Papadopoulos had discussed Russia, Page shrugged and said, "It may have come up, yeah.") The FBI became even more suspicious of Page in the fall of 2016 after they were informed by former British intelligence agent Christopher Steele that his opposition research on candidate Trump revealed possible connections with Russia to influence the outcome of the election. Steele's report, or "dossier," prompted the FBI to seek a FISA warrant to monitor Page's communications, which it obtained after convincing the court there was probable cause to believe Page was acting as an agent of a foreign power—namely, Russia.[71]

To say it again, since Trump keeps trying to muddy the waters on this: The investigation was not started by Democrats in Congress, or Hillary Clinton, or Barack Obama. It was triggered by questions raised with the FBI about questionable dealings with Kremlin operatives by Trump aide George Papadopoulos and, later, Carter Page.

Perhaps to his dismay, Page remains a small-time player, even in the Mueller investigation, which he helped launch. He has not been charged with any crime. For the most part, he's been ignored by the FBI and congressional committees. His book proposal went unsold. He's largely been forgotten, except on cable TV, where he still occasionally pops up to proclaim his innocence and his continued loyalty to Donald Trump—appearances so bizarre that many people now question not only his competence but his sanity, as well. Every tragedy has a fool or two.[72]

90. THE PEE TAPE

Speaking of the Steele dossier, I regret it is now time to talk about what is known as the "pee tape."

You think your job is tough? Think about this. As he recounts in his book, *A Higher Loyalty,* James Comey first met Donald Trump when he went to Trump Tower during the transition to brief the president-elect on the FBI's Russia investigation. Having sketched out the broad outlines of the ongoing probe, Comey informed Trump there was something else the FBI had been told about but had not seen—a videotape of Trump in a Moscow hotel room in 2013, where he had allegedly paid prostitutes to perform a "golden shower" show in front of him, urinating on the bed used by President and Mrs. Obama on their last visit to Russia.[73]

According to Comey, Trump neither affirmed nor denied the event described, responding instead, "Do I look like a guy who needs hookers?" And Comey moved on to other subjects.[74]

Asked by ABC's George Stephanopoulos in his first book interview if he thought the rumor was true, Comey would only say, "I honestly never thought these words would come out of my mouth, but I don't know whether the current president of the United States was with prostitutes peeing on each other in Moscow in 2013. It's possible, but I don't know."[75]

And thus was born the famous pee tape, which none of us have seen, but which many of us just know exists and which all of us, thanks to its absurd specificity, believe is true. It hangs over the Russia investigation like Chekov's gun or the proverbial other shoe, just waiting to drop on Donald Trump's head.

So what do we know about the pee tape? We know Trump was in Moscow in 2013 for his Miss Universe contest. We know, as Steele writes in his dossier, that the "Russian regime has been cultivating, supporting and assisting Trump for at least 5 years" as a witting or unwitting ally in their efforts to sow dissent in the West. And we know that Russian intelligence agents were more than capable of setting up and secretly videotaping Trump in embarrassing activities so they could blackmail him with it later. In Moscow, as every tourist knows, a hidden microphone and camera are included in the price of virtually every hotel room.[76]

We also know how the dossier came about. As first reported by David Corn of *Mother Jones,* a firm named Fusion GPS was originally hired by *The Washington Free Beacon,* a right-wing website funded by hedge fund operator Paul Singer, to do opposition research on Donald Trump. When Trump won the nomination, Singer dropped the project. Hired next by the

Clinton campaign and the DNC to continue their oppo research on Trump, Fusion GPS brought on board a top investigator from the British firm Orbis, former MI6 intelligence officer and Russian expert Christopher Steele.[77]

Most troubling for Donald Trump, we know that, according to CNN, U.S. intelligence sources who interviewed Steele found both him and his dossier very "credible"—even if they had not seen the pee tape.

In fact, as the Mueller probe progressed, the existence of, or veracity of, the pee tape, which was never the main focus of the Steele dossier nor the center of the FBI investigation, has taken on even less significance. As Jane Mayer reported in *The New Yorker* of March 12, 2018, much more significant, and much more damning to Trump, other findings of the dossier have been confirmed, including:

- The Kremlin favored Trump over Hillary in 2016.
- The Kremlin was offering the Trump campaign dirt on Hillary.
- The Kremlin and WikiLeaks worked together to release the DNC emails.
- Carter Page had secret Moscow meetings with Kremlin officials.[78]

Bottom line: No matter how salacious, whether the golden shower rained on Trump's orders or not, the Steele dossier still holds up as a convincing description of a determined effort by several members of the Trump team, and perhaps Trump himself, to collude with Russian operatives, influence the outcome of the 2016 presidential campaign, and improve Donald Trump's chances of becoming president over Hillary Clinton.

Despite desperate attempts by Republicans in Congress to smear Christopher Steele and question his motives, the dossier he prepared has proved solid. As the investigation continues, Steele's credibility increases, while Donald Trump's diminishes. Let's just pray that, when the hour of reckoning finally comes for this administration, we don't have to screen any grainy and rainy videos from Moscow hotel rooms in the halls of Congress.

9

TRUMP'S IMPEACHABLE OFFENSES

Let's be honest. The sad truth is, even though several Democrats have introduced articles of impeachment, there's no rush in a Republican-controlled Congress, or even among most Democrats, to impeach President Trump.

When it comes to impeachment, every single Republican and the majority of Democrats, including House minority leader Nancy Pelosi, make the same argument: As incompetent and obnoxious as he may be, there's no evidence yet that he's committed any crime. So let's wait and see what special counsel Robert Mueller comes up with. In other words, the usual congressional response to most problems these days—let's kick the ball in somebody else's court and see what happens.

The fallacy with that argument, of course, is that, ultimately, under the Constitution, only Congress and the Supreme Court have the power to be a check on the president. In fact, Congress could have already reined Trump in, if they wanted to. Most constitutional scholars agree that under the language of the Constitution—"Treason, Bribery, or other high Crimes and

Misdemeanors"—grounds for impeachment don't necessarily require commission of a crime.

Just ask Andrew Johnson or Bill Clinton. Impeachment has always been considered, and exercised, as a political, not a criminal matter. It's up to Congress to decide what is impeachable and what is not. In the famous words of then House minority leader Gerald Ford, who failed in his attempts to impeach Supreme Court justice William O. Douglas, "An impeachable offense is whatever a majority of the House of Representatives considers it to be at a given moment in history." A few years later, President Ford found out the costs of standing in the way of the public desire for presidential justice when he pardoned Richard Nixon and thereby ensured he'd be a less-than-one-term president.[1]

By that admittedly low standard, Congress doesn't have to wait for Robert Mueller to find Donald Trump guilty of breaking the law to proceed with impeaching him. As I hope this book has pointed out, there are already plenty of solid reasons for doing so.

But even aside from the question of electoral collusion with Russia—which is not something easily put aside—Trump is also clearly guilty of several offenses against the Constitution and our system of government that rise to the level of impeachment.

91. HE'S VIOLATED THE EMOLUMENTS CLAUSE

On this point, the Constitution is clear. Article I, Section 9: "No Person holding any Office of Profit or Trust under them, shall, without the consent of the Congress, accept of any present, Emolument, office, or Title, of any kind whatever, from any King, Prince, or foreign State."[2]

Translation: No president, without specific permission of Congress, shall accept any gift or payment from any foreign government or individual. Period.

It's the same throughout the government—that's why members of Congress and their staff can't even accept gifts from potential lobbyists worth more than fifty dollars. And in the past, whether it's Jimmy Carter putting his peanut farm in a blind trust or Barack Obama converting his investments into treasury bonds and index funds, every other president has gone out of his way to avoid any appearance of impropriety.

But Donald Trump pockets money from foreigners every day and has done so since day one of his administration. Every time any foreigner checks into a Trump hotel anywhere in the world . . . Every time foreign embassies hold events in Washington's Trump International Hotel . . . Every time a foreigner plays golf at any Trump golf course or buys a condo in any Trump property . . . part of that money goes right into Trump's pocket. Donald Trump is in violation of the Emoluments Clause thousands of times a day.[3]

We're talking big money. *USA Today* reported that President Trump earned $40.4 million from Washington's Trump International Hotel in 2017, the first year of its operation, and $246 million from his fifteen golf courses. The Grand Old Party pays him, too—in just the first two months of 2018, the Republican National Committee spent $424,000 at Trump properties.[4]

Note: The president's hardly the only member of the Trump family to reap financial benefits from being in the White House. So does First Daughter Ivanka, as we've seen. And so does the First Lady. According to financial forms, Melania Trump herself made between $100,000 and $1 million in 2017, through Getty Images, from selling media outlets permission to publish family photos—but only if they were used as part of "positive coverage" of the Trump family. If there's any way to turn the White House into a money-making machine, the Trumps have found it.

There's also the related issue of those fat cats who pay hundreds of thousands of dollars at Mar-a-Lago—to join his golf club for the chance of running into Trump in the clubhouse or on the links, or just to tell him or his staff in lobbying meetings that they're lining the Trump family's pockets. Also from *USA Today:*

> Members of the clubs Trump has visited most often as president—in Florida, New Jersey and Virginia—include at least 50 executives whose companies hold federal contracts and 21 lobbyists and trade group officials. Two-thirds played on one of the 58 days the president was there, according to scores they posted online.[6]

And there's also the enormous issue of the many—and, since Trump refuses to release his tax returns, largely unknown—deals between the

Trump empire and foreign governments, including loans from the Chinese government and tens of millions of dollars in building projects in Saudi Arabia. Since his election, by many accounts, Trump and his sons have engaged in business negotiations with several foreign governments, including India, the Philippines, Japan, and Scotland. A bank owned by the Chinese government is a tenant in Trump Tower. Violations of the Emoluments Clause are everywhere. In the words of a May 2018 *Slate* headline, IT'S AMAZING HOW MANY COUNTRIES APPEAR TO BE TRYING TO BRIBE OUR PRESIDENT RIGHT NOW.[7]

How does Trump deal with this problem? For one, he argues that he's exempt from the conflict-of-interest laws governing every other federal employee. But while that's true, he is not exempt from the restrictions of the Constitution. It's just that so far, because every other president has decided to do right by the Emoluments Clause, Trump's indirect taking of gifts from foreigners through their patronage at his international business properties has not been tested in court. Put another way, Trump's flouting of the Constitution has been so brazen that there are few legal precedents to challenge him.[8]

When and if there are such legal challenges—and three lawsuits against Trump for violating the Emoluments Clause have been winding their way through the courts—Trump will surely lose. As Jordan Libowitz, communications director for Citizens for Responsibility and Ethics in Washington (CREW), put it bluntly before the inauguration, "The president cannot get a gift from a foreign government. And it looks like he's going to do exactly that." And so he has, a thousand times over.[9]

One dangerous consequence of Trump's ongoing business deals is the potential influence of foreign investments in Trumpworld on American foreign policy. In the *Slate* article just mentioned, Ben Mathis-Lilley has identified several countries now engaged in major business deals with the Trump Empire that have significant diplomatic dealings with the United States, including Qatar, Turkey, Russia, the United Arab Emirates, Saudi Arabia, the Philippines, and India. There's no way of knowing whether President Trump—who may or may not be aware of each transaction, depending on what his children choose to tell him—adjusts his foreign policy decisions to reflect, respect, and reward such deals.[10]

In at least one major case, there's reason to suspect that he did. One of Trump Inc.'s biggest deals is in Indonesia, where the Chinese government invested $500 million in a new resort that includes a Trump hotel and golf course. Days after that financial commitment was finalized, Trump suddenly announced he was stepping in to rescue from bankruptcy the giant Chinese telecom company ZTE, which had been under U.S. sanctions for doing business with Iran. As noted earlier, both before and after that surprising announcement, the Chinese government granted new trademarks to Ivanka Trump to market her clothing and jewelry line in China.[11]

Pure coincidence? Only a fool would believe that. It's the ultimate quid pro quo. And it proves the wisdom of the Founding Fathers in prohibiting presidents from accepting gifts or cash benefits from foreign entities.

So, if Congress were looking for a place to start impeachment hearings, independent of the Mueller investigation's ultimate findings, the Emoluments Clause is a good place to start. And so is . . .

92. HE'S OBSTRUCTED JUSTICE

Donald Trump continues to insist that the Robert Mueller "witch hunt" has found no evidence of collusion, which is misleading for a couple of reasons. One, we don't know what Mueller has discovered on the matter of collusion, and we won't know until he releases his final report. Two, that's now only one focus of Mueller's investigation. Another is the issue that felled Richard Nixon—obstruction of justice, which is far more serious and for which there is already substantial evidence, most of it provided by Donald Trump himself. Once again, it's the cover-up more than the crime itself that has put the president in legal jeopardy.

Obstruction of justice is any attempt to hinder, interfere with, or kill a criminal investigation by the Justice Department of the president of the United States, whether or not it's successful. You don't have to be a criminal attorney to think of the many ways Donald Trump has done, and continues to do, just that:

- He asked James Comey to drop the investigation into Michael Flynn, who lied about his discussions about sanctions with the Russian ambassador.[12]

- He fired James Comey when he refused to play along.[13]

- On at least two occasions—once in a meeting with the same Russian ambassador, the other time on national television with Lester Holt—he admitted that he fired Comey in order to get rid of the Russia investigation.[14]

- He has often criticized, and threatened to fire, Attorney General Jeff Sessions for recusing himself from the Russia investigation.[15]

- At least four times, he explicitly pressured Sessions to change his mind on recusal and resume control of the investigation, in order to shut it down.[16]

- He has constantly denounced the Mueller investigation as a "witch hunt," initiated by Democrats in the wake of Hillary Clinton's loss at the polls.[17]

- He personally dictated a misleading public statement on the nature of a meeting with Russian operatives at Trump Tower on June 9, 2016.[18]

- He also admitted on Twitter to obstructing justice, declaring, "No Collusion or Obstruction (other than I fight back!)" As ThinkProgress's Aaron Rumar deadpanned after this incident, "There is no 'fighting back' exception to obstruction of justice charges."[19]

- He has shamelessly and erroneously accused the FBI of planting a spy in his campaign.[20]

- Trump lawyer John Dowd intimated to attorneys for Paul Manafort and Michael Flynn that Trump might pardon them.[21]

- Trump himself has used presidential pardons—pardoning Dick Cheney consigliere Scooter Libby for perjury and obstruction of justice, for example—in a way that clearly sends a message to Manafort, Flynn, or other Trump aides charged by Mueller that they, too, could be pardoned.[22]

The case is cut-and-dried. Indeed, as much as Trump routinely attacks Robert Mueller, he often ends up helping him make the case for obstruction of justice. Shortly after firing Comey, for example, he plainly admitted to NBC's Lester Holt that he fired the FBI chief because he felt "this Russia thing with Trump and Russia is a made-up story." Case made: Firing Comey had nothing to do with his handling of Hillary's emails, as the White House pretended, and everything to do with getting rid of the Russia investigation.[23]

As noted earlier, Trump also did Mueller a big favor when tweeting about his firing of Michael Flynn. In December 2017, the day after Flynn entered a plea deal with Robert Mueller, Trump tweeted: "I had to fire General Flynn because he lied to the Vice President and the FBI. He has pled guilty to those lies. It is a shame because his actions during the transition were lawful. There was nothing to hide!"

The closer you examine it (and you can be sure Mueller did), what sounds at first like nothing more than a typical Trump boast takes on more serious meaning. Trump admits he knew Flynn had committed a crime by lying to the FBI when he asked Comey to drop the investigation of Flynn. In essence, he was asking Comey to let Flynn get away with lying to the FBI. That's clear obstruction.[24]

And so, apparently, as we'll discuss more next chapter, is his flagrant abuse of the pardon power in two ways—by instructing his attorney to tell lawyers for Paul Manafort and Michael Flynn that they might receive a presidential pardon and by the exclusive use of his pardon power to take care of friends or supporters like Dinesh D'Souza, Joe Arpaio, or Scooter Libby, thereby sending a clear signal to any of his associates who get charged by Robert Mueller that they don't have to worry about prison time, because he has their backs.[25]

On the subject of Trump's questionable use of pardons, Vox interviewed eleven legal experts, all of whom basically agreed with Fordham University law professor Jed Shugerman: "If a president sold pardons for money, the president would be guilty of bribery. If a president sold nominations for money, he would be guilty of bribery. So, too, if the president offered pardons in order to corruptly obstruct justice, that would be a felony. Those who say the president is immune for his official acts are essentially saying the president is uniquely above the law."[26]

By June 2018, the case for Trump's obstructing justice was so blatant that this ridiculous, Nixonian notion—the president is so above the law that he could even pardon himself—had become Trump's legal fallback position. Suffice it to say, even Republicans weren't buying it. "There's no doubt that the president is not above the law," an alarmed Senator Susan Collins told reporters. "It would be a tremendous abuse of his authority if he were to do so, as well as remarkably unwise." As Iowa's Chuck Grassley put it, "If I were president and somebody, some lawyer told me that I could do that, I'd hire a new lawyer."[27]

But as of this writing, Trump still seems committed to blowing this up by any means necessary. One of his most blatant attempts to undermine the Mueller investigation, and thereby obstruct justice, was his accusing the FBI in late May, with zero evidence, of planting a spy in his campaign headquarters. He even gave the scandal a name: Spygate.[28]

Of course, as even Republican members of Congress had to admit after a special briefing by the Department of Justice, there was no such spy. The FBI did, however, employ retired professor Stefan Halper as an "informant" to help determine whether there was any truth to reports that certain members of the Trump campaign team were having suspicious meetings with Russian officials, in violation of the law.[29]

In other words, the FBI was conducting a criminal investigation into candidate Trump's alleged Russian connections at the same time it was conducting a criminal investigation into candidate Clinton's use of a private email server. The difference is: We knew about the Clinton investigation, because Director Comey chose to make it public; we did not know about the Trump investigation, because Comey chose to keep it secret—which certainly helped Trump in the election, and hurt Clinton. Had voters known that Trump was also under investigation by the FBI, the outcome of 2016 may have turned out differently. All of which makes the Spygate notion that the FBI was out to get Trump all the more absurd.[30]

Yes, the Russians did help Donald Trump. But so did James Comey and the FBI. Instead of attacking the FBI, Donald Trump should be thanking them.

Add it all up: Being charged with obstruction of justice is the biggest legal and political threat Donald Trump faces. Why? Because there's stronger evidence on obstruction than on collusion. And because, while the laws on collusion are somewhat murky, obstruction is clearly an out-and-out crime other presidents have been charged with. Allegations of obstruction of justice were included in articles of impeachment against both Richard Nixon and Bill Clinton. Will Donald Trump be next? The only thing missing now is the congressional will to do what is right.

93. STORMY DANIELS

While Congress may be afraid to stand up against Trump, one woman clearly isn't. How ironic if, after all the charges of collusion with Russians and obstruction of justice, it's not a special counsel named Robert Mueller that brings Donald Trump down but an adult film actress named Stephanie Clifford, better known as Stormy Daniels.

If so, it won't be his fling with Daniels, which started at Lake Tahoe in July 2006, that does it. As we learned under Bill Clinton, cheating on your wife, even when she's still recovering from the birth of your child, is not an impeachable offense—nor should it be. It won't be the fact that he paid her $130,000 in hush money, either. That in and of itself is not a crime. Nor would it even be the fact that Trump lied for four months about knowing anything about paying Stormy Daniels until "outed" by his new lawyer, Rudy Giuliani.[31]

What could be impeachable, if proved, is paying Stormy Daniels to keep quiet in order to influence the outcome of the election, possibly paying her out of campaign funds, and not reporting it as a campaign expense, as required by federal election law.

There's no need to go into the sleazy details of Trump's affair with Daniels. She's already recounted it in full color for *In Touch* magazine and again on *60 Minutes*. For impeachment purposes, the story only gets relevant in early October 2016, just before the election, when Daniels starts talking to reporters again about her dalliances with Trump. Once he heard of that, Trump's attorney—or fixer—Michael Cohen jumped in and, using a shell company called Essential Consultants, negotiated a $130,000 nondisclosure agreement with Daniels, finalized on October 28, just ten days before the election.[32]

For a while, it worked. Daniels did keep quiet. Trump was elected. Then, on January 12, 2018, *The Wall Street Journal* dropped a bomb, reporting for the first time the news of Daniels's nondisclosure agreement, $130,000 arrangement, and the role of Michael Cohen. At first, Daniels denied receiving hush money from Trump, and Cohen denied that either the Trump campaign or Trump Organization had anything to do with the payment and did not reimburse him. In fact, Cohen said, as a favor for his friend Donald, he actually took out a home equity line of credit to pay Daniels—some friend! Meanwhile, for his part, Donald Trump told reporters on Air Force One he knew nothing about the payment.[33]

Then things started to unravel. Daniels hired a new lawyer, Michael Avenatti, who is every bit as media-savvy as Donald Trump. She filed a lawsuit to get out from under the nondisclosure agreement. Cohen sent Daniels a cease and desist letter, while continuing to insist that he and he alone was involved in paying Daniels $130,000 and that Trump had nothing to do with it.[34]

But he was soon undercut by his own team. President Trump, perhaps inadvertently, admitted to *Fox & Friends* that Cohen represented him in the Stormy Daniels matter. His new attorney, Rudy Giuliani, then followed up by telling Fox News the president did, indeed, pay Cohen back the $130,000, in $35,000 installments. Giuliani even volunteered that Trump might even have paid other women to keep quiet about their affairs with him, and probably did—"if necessary."[35]

Bottom line: Trump and Cohen were lying all along, and Stormy Daniels was telling the truth. Trump did have an affair with Stormy Daniels. Trump did agree for Michael Cohen to pay her $130,000 to keep quiet. Trump knew all about it. And Trump did pay him back.

But still the big question is: So what? Is that itself an impeachable offense? The big answer: No, the extramarital affair is not. But the payment of hush money to Stormy Daniels could be. It all depends on what funds were used, and why, and whether or not they were reported—and that's one of the things the U.S. attorney for the Southern District of New York, to whom Robert Mueller referred the Stormy Daniels scandal, is now looking into.

Was it paid for with campaign funds and not reported? If so, the 2016 Trump campaign is in trouble. Even if it wasn't paid for by the Trump campaign, if it was in fact paid out of Michael Cohen's private resources, then it's likely an illegal, over-the-limit donation to the Trump campaign. Again, the Trump campaign and Michael Cohen are in trouble.[36]

With Stormy Daniels, President Trump now faces legal jeopardy on two fronts: Robert Mueller's investigation into collusion and obstruction of justice; and the U.S. attorney's investigation into violations of campaign law on money paid to Stormy Daniels. The only question is: Who nails Donald Trump first?

94. MICHAEL COHEN AND
THE ART OF THE SHAKEDOWN

Which brings us to Michael Cohen, another longtime rogue in Trump's gallery. As if Cohen weren't in enough legal jeopardy because of his handling of hush money for Donald Trump, he's also in plenty of trouble on his own. In a surprising move that shocked all of Washington, D.C., allegations of crooked business deals drove the U.S. attorney's office to seize documents and computers from Cohen's home, office, and hotel room and begin a criminal investigation into his legal practice.[37]

But, of course, if Donald Trump's personal attorney is in serious legal trouble, so is Donald Trump. And if there was enough evidence for the courts to agree that a raid on the president's lawyer's home was necessary, who knows what manner of dirt Trump and Cohen were up to?

What we do know is that the two go back awhile. Cohen hooked up with the Trump Organization in the early 2000s, buying up Trump properties in New York and helping Trump explore development projects in Georgia, Kazakhstan, and Moscow.[38]

When Trump decided to run for president in 2015, Cohen signed on as fixer—handling hush payments to Stormy Daniels and other women who claimed to have had affairs with Trump—according to Steve Bannon in Michael Wolff's *Fire and Fury,* "What did we have, a hundred women?"—and even, according to Christopher Steele's dossier, traveling to Prague to meet with Russian officials—which Cohen has denied.[39]

But it soon emerged that the U.S. attorney was interested in much more than Cohen's role in the Stormy Daniels scandal. In May 2018, Stormy Daniels's attorney, Michael Avenatti, released documents showing that, as Trump's "personal attorney," and acting through the same Essential Consultants shell company, Cohen had charged corporations millions of dollars for access to Donald Trump—and delivered nothing. Among those who signed up with Cohen, according to *Huffington Post:*

- AT&T paid Cohen $600,000 for "insights" into the new administration.
- Columbus Nova, with close ties to Russian oligarch Viktor Vekselberg, paid Cohen $500,000 as a "consulting fee."

- Novartis, pharmaceutical giant, paid $1.2 million for advice on "healthcare policy matters."
- Korea Aerospace Industries paid $150,000 for advice on "local accounting standards."[40]

At this point, we do not know if Cohen's business deals were illegal. That's what the U.S. attorney is investigating. But the very nature of the deals, and Cohen's relationship with Trump, raises very serious questions: What did these companies get for their money? What did Donald Trump know about Cohen's contracts? Did Trump and Cohen collude to provide them special access? What percentage of this money was kicked back to Trump? Were these, in effect, bribes?[41]

Real estate, hush payments, and selling access to the president aren't the only shady deals Michael Cohen's up to his armpits in. Long before he connected with Donald Trump, he also got involved in the taxi business, buying up taxi medallions when they sold for over $1 million apiece. Because of competition from Uber and Lyft, they're now worth about $200,000. Reportedly, that's another area the U.S. attorney is interested in.

Any ties between Donald Trump and Cohen's taxi troubles remain to be seen. What we do know is that any inquiries into how Trump and Cohen have been running his business over the years will undoubtedly unearth reams of impeachable illegalities. All of which is bad news for Donald Trump. Any hopes he had that Michael Cohen would remain a loyal acolyte evaporated in July 2018. Asked by ABC's George Stephanopoulos if he were still willing to "take a bullet" for Trump, Cohen replied: "To be crystal clear, my wife, my daughter, and my son, and this country, have my first loyalty." Cohen was clearly sending a message to federal prosecutors that he was open to making a deal.[42]

Where this leads is still to be determined. But as journalist Adam Davidson well put it in *The New Yorker:*

> I am unaware of anybody who has taken a serious look at Trump's business who doesn't believe that there is a high likelihood of rampant criminality . . . Of course Trump is raging and furious and terrified. Prosecutors are now looking at his core. Cohen was the key intermediary between the Trump family and its partners around the world; he was chief consigliere and dealmaker throughout its period

of expansion into global partnerships with sketchy oligarchs. He wasn't a slick politico who showed up for a few months. He knows everything, he recorded much of it, and now prosecutors will know it, too. It seems inevitable that much will be made public. We don't know when. We don't know the precise path the next few months will take. There will be resistance and denial and counterattacks. But it seems likely that . . . we are now in the end stages of the Trump Presidency.[43]

Which would be great! Although, as we'll conclude in the next chapter: Remarkably, what comes after Trump could be even worse.

10

CLOSING ARGUMENTS

By now, we've outlined a lot of reasons why Trump must go, but we've hardly exhausted the list. Indeed, the reasons he's such a menace far exceed those we have room for here.

But to round it off, here are a few more to complete the list of the top hundred.

95. HE AND HIS ALLIES HAVE SUPPRESSED THE VOTE

Spend five minutes in the same room with Donald Trump—anytime, anywhere—and he's bound to tell you all about the time he won the 2016 election. Even now, more than five hundred days into his presidency, he can't let it go. When he brought it up yet again in a press avail with Norwegian prime minister Erna Solberg in January 2018, CNN's Jake Tapper likened it to "Donald Trump's 'Free Bird,'" the greatest hit he can't stop trotting out at every occasion.[1]

This penchant for reveling in past glory would normally just be sad, like a middle-aged adult always talking about the touchdown he scored back in high school. But as with everything Trump, his nostalgia has become actively pernicious, because, from the beginning, he's tried to rewrite the story of the election with lies. For one, he likes to say he won the popular vote in 2016—a yuuuge victory, believe me—because three to five million people voted illegally for Hillary Clinton. For another, he'll invariably tell you he scored the biggest electoral college victory of any president since Ronald Reagan.[2]

Like most things Donald Trump says, both statements are demonstrably false.

Actually, Clinton crushed Trump in the popular vote, 48.2 percent to 46.1 percent. More Americans voted for her than any other losing presidential candidate in U.S. history. She even received 389,944 more votes than Barack Obama's 2012 winning total, while Donald Trump lost the popular vote by the biggest margin of any president—nearly 2.9 million votes. That's more than five times the 544,000-vote margin that Al Gore received over George W. Bush in 2000. And overall, fewer than one in four voting-age Americans voted for Trump.[3]

As for the electoral college, not only did Donald Trump not roll up a landslide in electoral votes, he, in fact, ended up near the bottom. In 1984, running for reelection against Walter Mondale, Reagan won 525 electoral votes. Trump only won 306: fewer than George H. W. Bush in 1988 (426); fewer than Bill Clinton in 1992 (379) and 1996 (370); and fewer than Barack Obama in both 2008 (332) and 2012 (365). According to John J. Pitney of Claremont University, Trump won 56.97 percent of the electoral count. That places him forty-sixth out of fifty-eight elections held since George Washington.[4]

And there's zero—zero!—evidence of any voter fraud, let alone five million illegal voters, despite Trump's whining post-election tweets:

> In addition to winning the Electoral College in a landslide, I won the popular vote if you deduct the millions of people who voted illegally.[5]

Serious voter fraud in Virginia, New Hampshire and California—so why isn't the media reporting on this? Serious bias—big problem![6]

Clearly, the media weren't reporting on it because it didn't happen. But that didn't stop Donald Trump from trying to make a big deal of it. On January 25, 2017, he announced:

I will be asking for a major investigation into VOTER FRAUD, including those registered to vote in two states, those who are illegal and . . . even, those registered to vote who are dead (and many for a long time). Depending on results, we will strengthen up voting procedures.[7]

Of course, the White House was never able to provide any evidence of such voter fraud. The bipartisan National Association of Secretaries of State issued a report saying its members, representing all fifty states, are "not aware of any evidence that supports the voter fraud claims made by President Trump." Even Trump's lawyers conceded that there was no relevant voter fraud when they pushed back against a requested recount by Green Party candidate Jill Stein. "All available evidence," they argued, "suggests that the 2016 general election was *not* tainted by fraud or mistake."[8]

Who cares about the facts? Trump went ahead and named a voter fraud commission headed by Mike Pence and Kris Kobach, the disreputable Kansas secretary of state, who has long been a leading advocate of restricting voting rights. Kobach's group got off to a bad start by demanding that states turn over all information on registered voters, including Social Security numbers—a massive invasion of privacy that the majority of fifty secretaries of state refused to comply with. In less than a year, when at most a couple of hundred cases of voter fraud could be verified out of hundreds of millions of votes cast, Trump quietly disbanded the commission.[9]

Unfortunately, the uproar over Kobach and the phony voter fraud commission obscured the most important, and most underreported electoral issue in 2016, which was not voter fraud but voter suppression. New restrictive voting laws in several states not only made it more difficult to vote but prevented tens of thousands of people from voting—enough Americans to swing the election to Trump.[10]

As *The New Republic* reported, citing research on voter suppression by *Mother Jones,* "45,000 people in Wisconsin were deterred from voting due to the state's new voter ID law, possibly costing Hillary Clinton the election." In fact, black Wisconsinites, who went for Hillary by nearly 90 percent, were three times more likely to say the voter ID law prevented them from voting. A 2014 study found that nearly 10 percent of registered voters would be blocked because of the law. And statewide, Wisconsin experienced its lowest voter turnout since 2000, in a presidential election that generated tons of publicity.[11]

Clearly, Clinton's widely criticized failure to campaign in Wisconsin wasn't the only reason she lost the state. And in fact, even Republicans in the state admit as much. "Now we have photo ID," one Wisconsin Republican bragged before the election, "and I think photo ID is going to make a little bit of a difference as well." "How many of your listeners," another told a right-wing radio host in April 2018, "really honestly are sure that Senator [Ron] Johnson was going to win reelection or President Trump was going to win Wisconsin if we didn't have voter ID"?[12]

It gets worse. Again, from *TNR:* "An MIT study found that 12 percent of all voters—an estimated 16 million people—encountered at least one problem voting in 2016. MIT estimates there were more than 1 million lost votes because people had to deal with ID laws, long lines at the polls, and registration problems. Overall, fourteen states"—including Wisconsin, Florida, Arizona, North Carolina, and Ohio—"had new voting restrictions in place for the first time in 2016, many of them adopted after the Supreme Court's 2013 decision to gut the Voting Rights Act."[13]

If you'd never heard about problems with voter suppression, you're not alone. Media Matters for America reported that only 8.9 percent of TV segments on voting rights from July 2016 to June 2017 "discussed the impact voter suppression laws had on the 2016 election," while more than 70 percent "were about Trump's false claims of voter fraud and noncitizen voting." As Ari Berman noted in *Mother Jones,* there were twenty-five presidential debates in 2016, but not one single question about voter suppression.[14]

96. HE'S ABUSED THE PARDON POWER

It's true that the job of president of the United States is the most powerful position in the world. But given the brilliantly conceived separation of powers and limits written into the Constitution, there are in fact few things that a president can do on his own. He or she can't declare war (unless Congress abdicates its own responsibility, which it has ever since passing the Authorization for the Use of Military Force, or AUMF, after 9/11), adopt a budget, or hire a cabinet member without Senate approval. But he or she can issue presidential pardons.

Even with pardons, there's a whole process in place: there are dozens of attorneys in the Justice Department whose job it is to review cases where someone may have been unjustly convicted and to recommend candidates worthy of a pardon to the president. There are now some ten thousand cases pending presidential approval.[15]

But for Donald Trump, that process may as well not exist. He completely ignores the Justice Department. He wastes no time reviewing and acting on their recommendations. Instead, he takes glee in using his presidential power exclusively to take care of his friends: the bigots, liars, criminals, frauds, and sexual abusers he loves to hang out with.

The roster of those friends pardoned by Donald Trump reads like the Rogues' Gallery of America. Among their numbers are:

SHERIFF JOE ARPAIO

Can you get away with breaking the law in America? For most people, the answer is no. Unless . . . you're a friend of Donald Trump's. Then, anything goes. Just ask Joe Arpaio.

For some twenty-five years, Arpaio ruled as the racist sheriff of Arizona's Maricopa County, until he was finally ousted by voters in November 2017. As the proud warden of what he himself proclaimed a "concentration camp," Arpaio housed prisoners in flimsy tents under the scorching desert sun, made men wear pink underwear and handcuffs, reinstated chain gangs, and presided over a prison hellscape notorious for human rights abuses and brutal mortality rates.[16]

He also became known for out-and-out racism, ordering his officers to target anybody with dark skin. Over the years, he and his department faced many lawsuits for police misconduct, which cost Arizona taxpayers over $146 million. In 2011, in fact, a federal court ordered Arpaio to cease patrols that racially profiled Latinos and stopped them on suspicion of being in the country illegally—an order he proudly and publicly ignored until a federal court convicted him of contempt of court in July 2017.[17]

But Arpaio, who had endorsed Trump for president in 2015, just before the Iowa caucuses, didn't have to worry about serving any time. Before he was even sentenced, President Trump granted Arpaio a full pardon on August 25, 2017, praising him for "more than 50 years of admirable service to our nation." It helps to have friends in high places.[18]

SCOOTER LIBBY

By this time in his presidency, we have all given up expecting any consistency out of President Trump. Still, veteran Washington heads were spinning once more on April 13, 2018, when, in the morning, Trump again attacked James Comey for being a "leaker" and "liar," and then, in the afternoon, issued a presidential pardon to Lewis "Scooter" Libby, convicted for "leaking" and "lying" about former CIA agent Valerie Plame.[19]

Libby, then chief of staff to Vice President Dick Cheney, became the only person charged in the leaking of the identity of CIA agent Plame to columnist Robert Novak after her husband, Ambassador Joseph Wilson, had written a column critical of George Bush's arguments for launching a war against Iran. A jury convicted him on four of five counts of perjury and obstruction of justice—and he was sentenced to two and a half years in prison and a $250,000 fine.[20]

Thanks to a commutation from President Bush, Libby never had to serve any time. He got his law license back in 2016 and was comfortably lawyering away in a D.C. law firm, making lots of money, until suddenly, Donald Trump issued him a pardon.

Why? Libby didn't need it. He hadn't even been lobbying for it. Why did Trump do it? Only for one reason—to send a message to Paul Manafort, Michael Flynn, Jared Kushner, to anybody else charged in the Mueller investigation: Don't worry, I've got your back. Valerie Plame, now writing spy novels in Santa Fe since Libby ruined her CIA career, summed it up: "The message being sent is you can commit perjury and I will pardon you if it protects me and I deem that you are loyal to me."[21]

But if Trump sent a clear message with his pardon of Libby, he sent an even stronger message with his next one.

DINESH D'SOUZA

If there was no compelling reason to pardon Joe Arpaio or Scooter Libby, there was even less of a reason to pardon Dinesh D'Souza—except to reward another friend and enrage people in the process.

Long one of the most risible right-wing commentators, D'Souza has a sordid history of racist, sexist, homophobic, fringe, and conspiratorial comments, so naturally he was a regular on Fox News. He's argued that black people actually owe white people reparations for abolishing slavery. Which, incidentally, he sees nothing wrong with. "The American slave was treated like property," he wrote, "which is to say pretty well." Among other ignorant and incendiary statements, D'Souza also called Obama a "boy" from the "ghetto" and a "grown-up Trayvon," ridiculed the survivors of the Parkland massacre, and deemed Rosa Parks "an overrated Democrat."[22]

But for the purposes of this discussion, there are two things you need to know about him. One, he broke the law. Two, he pleaded guilty. In granting him a pardon, President Trump asserted he was "treated very unfairly by our government"—allegedly because the Obama administration was not happy with his aggressively dumb and dishonest documentary, *2016: Obama's America*.[23]

No. He broke the law, and he pleaded guilty.

Here's what happened. In 2014, D'Souza's friend Wendy Long was running for senator from New York against Kirsten Gillibrand. Despite Long's having no chance of winning, D'Souza persuaded a couple of friends to write a $10,000 check to Long, promising to reimburse them out of his own pocket—which is a felony. He pleaded guilty. He paid a $30,000 fine and was sentenced to eight months in a halfway house (hardly the Hanoi Hilton) near his home in San Diego.[24]

After serving his time, D'Souza was back on the lucrative political trail, publishing articles and books, producing documentaries, and endorsing candidates, including Donald Trump. He was, in other words, no hard-luck case whose life had been ruined. He was a racist Trump supporter whom Trump decided to pardon, again, in order to let other friends know—friends who either have gotten or might get in trouble with Robert Mueller—that if he could pardon D'Souza out of the blue, he could pardon them, too.

Just in case they still didn't get the message, Trump, apparently infatuated with his new pardon toy, also said he was considering a pardon for Martha Stewart and a commutation for Rod Blagojevich, two former contestants on *The Apprentice.* Both Stewart and Blagojevich were convicted of lying to federal investigators.[25]

And wait, wait, it gets better: As noted last chapter, his lawyers also sent a memo to special counsel Mueller insisting that Trump also, under the Constitution, has the power to pardon himself!

97. HE'S A POLITICAL LOSER—BIGLY

With their party facing an uphill battle in 2018, many Republican primary candidates came to an early conclusion: One sure way to win was to have Donald Trump endorse their opponent. In state after state, he's demonstrated he doesn't have any political coattails. Instead, he's actually poison.

VIRGINIA

Poor Ed Gillespie. As the former chair of the Republican National Committee, he's not really a Trump Republican. But he definitely wasn't above pretending to be one in order, with Trump's support, to get elected governor of Virginia. In his campaign against moderate Democrat Ralph Northam, Gillespie invested in Trump and Willie Horton–style ads effectively painting Northam as an MS-13 gang member. And while Gillespie did not have Trump appear at any campaign events, Trump nonetheless endorsed and made robocalls for him—which proved to be toxic for Gillespie in a purple, tending toward blue, state.[26]

So what did Gillespie ultimately get for abasing himself? The back of Trump's hand. Minutes after the networks announced that Northam had defeated Gillespie, Trump sent out a tweet blaming him: "Ed Gillespie worked hard but did not embrace me or what I stand for."[27]

ALABAMA

Even in deep-red Alabama, Trump was a two-time loser. To fill the Senate seat vacated by Attorney General Jeff Sessions, Trump first traveled to Alabama to endorse Luther Strange, who'd been appointed provisional senator until a special election could be held. When Strange lost the primary, even with Trump's endorsement, the president immediately jumped on Roy Moore's bandwagon—and stayed there after Moore was accused of preying on and molesting teenage girls. While most of America was aghast at the revelations about Moore, who had praised the pro-slavery era and had reportedly once been banned from a local mall for stalking young girls, Trump even held a pro-Moore rally in Pensacola, Florida, just over the Alabama border.[28]

But not even Trump could save a full-fledged creep like Roy Moore. Instead, he helped deliver what nobody expected: the first Democratic senator elected in Alabama since 1986. When Jones won, Trump could not resist tweeting "I was right!"—for endorsing Luther Strange.[29]

PENNSYLVANIA

Having failed to deliver in races for governor and senator, Trump also tried to work his magic in a key House race—and lost again. A special election in Pennsylvania's Eighteenth Congressional District pitted veteran GOP state legislator Rick Saccone against a young political newcomer, Democrat Conor Lamb. The district is classic, blue-collar, working-class Trump territory. He carried the district over Hillary Clinton in 2016 by twenty points. But whatever appeal he once had was lost. Even after holding a rally in the Eighteenth, Trump could not pull Saccone over the finish line. It was one more special election won by Democrats.[30]

The day after Lamb's win, pollster Harry Enten reported that in the seven special elections since 2016, Democrats were overperforming their predicted baseline by 16 percentage points, the best performance in at least twenty-four years. Overall, given his dismal record of endorsing losing candidates, instead of running with President Trump in 2018, many Republicans will be running away from him. Trump is such a loser. Sad![31]

98. HE CONSORTS WITH TERRIBLE PEOPLE

You know what they say: By their friends, you shall know them. If true, Donald Trump's don't reflect well on him. Throughout his life, he's hung out with and been close to some of the most disgusting, reprehensible lowlifes on the planet. Here are just a few of them.

ROY COHN

Roy Cohn's been out of the public eye for so long, most people forget or don't know what an evil man he was. As Frank Rich pointed out in an April 2018 essay on Donald Trump's mentor, he is probably best known today as a character in Tony Kushner's *Angels in America,* one variously described as "the polestar of human evil" and "the worst human being who ever lived."[32]

Kushner has the right of it. Cohn was as vile as they come. And sadly, the evil that he did lived after him and now haunts us all, in the form of his protégé.

Cohn first came to national attention as one of Senator Joseph McCarthy's loyal acolytes—specifically as chief counsel to the Senate Permanent Subcommittee on Investigations, through which McCarthy, during the "Red Scare" of the 1950s, conducted his crusade against "Communist sympathizers" in the State Department, U.S. Army, and universities. With Cohn at his side, McCarthy also led his "Lavender Scare" campaign to identify and root out suspected homosexuals in government: a homophobic, hatefilled exercise in which the closeted Cohn gleefully participated.[33]

With McCarthy's censure by the Senate and fall from power, Cohn moved back to New York, where he quickly became what *Vanity Fair* called "the premier practitioner of hardball deal-making," and where he quickly hooked up with the perfect, young, and equally corrupt client, Donald Trump. From then on, the former prosecutor was Trump's mentor in the dark arts and ruthless fixer, always standing by—again, in the words of *Vanity Fair*—"to help with the shady tax abatements, the zoning variances, the sweetheart deals, and the threats to those who might stand in the way" of any Trump project. Cohn also taught Trump to lie and bluster his way through any crisis and always double down, never concede an inch.[34]

"You knew when you were in Cohn's presence you were in the presence of pure evil," is how lawyer Victor A. Kovner, a contemporary of Cohn's, described him. Even Trump seemed to recognize his evil. He confided to a friend in 1980: "All I can tell you is he's been vicious to others in his protection of me." As gossip columnist Liz Smith summed up their relationship, "Donald lost his moral compass when he made an alliance with Roy Cohn."[35]

But Cohn's ethical lapses meant nothing to Donald Trump. After all, they were partners in crime. Cohn, who introduced Trump to the mob figures who backed his career for the next several decades, was indicted four times on charges ranging from extortion and blackmail to bribery, conspiracy, securities fraud, and obstruction of justice. He was acquitted each time. Trump and his father were sued by the Justice Department for refusing to rent apartments to African Americans. Trump was indicted for bribery in 1996. Both times, Cohn got him off.[36]

In his Cohn postmortem, Frank Rich noted how closely the two resembled each other. Like Cohn, Rich wrote, Trump "also flourished for decades despite being a shameless lawbreaker, tax evader, liar, racist, bankruptcy aficionado, and hypocrite notorious for his mob connections, transactional sexual promiscuity, and utter disregard for rules, scruples, and morals." Which, you must admit, is an accurate portrait of developer Trump back then—and President Trump today.[37]

In the end, Trump proved he had all of Roy Cohn's bad qualities but barely an ounce of his good one: loyalty. After Cohn was diagnosed with AIDS and later disbarred for "dishonesty, fraud, deceit, and misrepresentation," Trump dropped him like a hot potato and started moving his legal business elsewhere. Cohn was not surprised at Trump's suddenly dumping him. As he reportedly told journalist friend Wayne Barrett, "Donald pisses ice water." And despite their long association, upon Cohn's death, Trump was not invited to be a pallbearer or speak at his funeral.[38]

Nonetheless, Roy Cohn served another key function for Donald Trump. He introduced him to another total sleazebag, Roger Stone.

ROGER STONE

Only twenty-seven years old, Roger Stone already had a reputation as one of Richard Nixon's "ratfuckers," a.k.a. dirty tricksters, when he met Roy Cohn in 1979. Stone, then the campaign manager for Ronald Reagan in New York, Connecticut, and New Jersey, needed office space. So Cohn hooked him up with his client Donald Trump—and thus was born another insidious political relationship, and one that still poisons American politics.[39]

Once Reagan was elected, Stone formed a lobbying and political consulting firm with GOP operative Charlie Black and—wait for it—Paul Manafort!—and together they started lining up clients and charging them big bucks for access to and favors from the Reagan White House, much as Michael Cohen and, for a while, Paul Manafort were doing for the Trump White House. As Franklin Foer convincingly argued in a March 2018 Manafort profile for *The Atlantic,* this firm, deemed the "ultimate supermarket of influence-peddling" by *Time* and "institutionalized conflict of interest" by government reformer Fred Wertheimer, helped transform Washington into the lobbyist-riddled K Street corridor of illicit cash and quid pro quos it is today.[40]

And who was Manafort and Stone's first client? Who else? Donald Trump! Already used to the political game of "pay to play."[41]

In the early 1980s, Stone and Roy Cohn hatched another sweet political deal. After managing his campaign, Stone was senior advisor to New Jersey governor Tom Kean—at the same time Donald Trump was beginning to buy up property in Atlantic City to open a casino. Trump helped Kean win. And, of course, Kean helped Trump build. Through the Reagan White House, Stone even secured federal funding to dredge the Atlantic City canal so it could accommodate Trump's yacht.[42]

In 2000, Stone and Trump were off on another political adventure. By this time, Trump was so smitten with politics, and probably so tired of writing checks to someone else, he decided to try it on his own—launching an exploratory campaign for president as a Reform Party candidate. Trump soon tired of that gig, only to toy with running again in 2008 and 2012. And, no surprise, when he decided to do it for real in 2016, Roger Stone was at his side from the very beginning.[43]

This time, he didn't last long. Stone left the campaign—meaning Donald

Trump probably fired him—in August 2015. But clearly Nixon's dirty trickster played some role in Trump's campaign afterward.

Stone is apparently under investigation by Robert Mueller for any role he may have played in the hacking of the DNC's emails by Kremlin operatives, including his liaising with the hacker Guccifer 2.0. One of Stone's associates, social media advisor Jason Sullivan, has already been questioned by the grand jury. And Stone himself reportedly told friends he had met in London with Julian Assange of WikiLeaks, who released the DNC emails. Days before that release, Stone was tweeting things like "Wednesday @ HillaryClinton is done. #WikiLeaks." and "I have total confidence that @wikileaks and my hero Julian Assange will educate the American people soon. #LockHerUp."[44]

Stone's possible troubles with Mueller don't bother Trump. The two of them reportedly still talk often, and Trump still follows Stone's political playbook, especially when it comes to dealing with the media. It's pure Nixonian. Of course! First, you wrap yourself in the flag, then you attack. As Stone himself described it to *Vanity Fair*'s Marie Brenner, "Pro-Americanism is a common threat for McCarthy, Goldwater, Nixon, and Reagan. The heir to that tradition is Donald Trump. When you combine that with the bare-knuckled tactics of Roy Cohn—or a Roger Stone—that is how you win elections. So Roy has an impact on Donald's understanding of how to deal with the media—attack, attack, attack, never defend."[45]

Vintage Roy Cohn, vintage Roger Stone, vintage Donald Trump.

TED NUGENT

Of course, not all of Trump's buddies are world-historical assholes. Some of them are just your run-of-the-mill assholes, like Dinesh D'Souza, Joe Arpaio, and Roy Moore. Or to take another chip off the same vile, racist, despicable block, like musician and Trump supporter Ted Nugent. For decades, Nugent has been spewing hate every time he opens his mouth. Of course, he and Trump get along swimmingly.

For example, in 1994 when asked about then First Lady Hillary Clinton, Nugent told *Westword* magazine, "You probably can't use the term 'toxic cunt' in your magazine, but that's what she is. Her very existence insults the spirit of individualism in this country. This bitch is nothing but a two-bit whore for Fidel Castro."[46]

And yet, surprisingly, not a single conservative completely beside themselves over Kathy Griffin's unfortunate anti-Trump cover shoot in May 2017, which got her fired from CNN, said a word when Nugent was a guest of honor in Trump's White House the month before.[47]

Nor did Trump, who publicly called on the TBS network to fire comedienne Samantha Bee for calling Ivanka Trump a "feckless cunt"—which Bee did in anger over the administration's patently evil policy of separating immigrant children from their parents at the border—seem to engage in much self-reflection about his Nugent invite.[48]

And Nugent is not a one-time offender. During the Democratic primary between Barack Obama and Hillary Clinton, Nugent lashed out at both candidates. After earlier calling Obama a "subhuman mongrel," he told a 2007 audience, "Obama, he's a piece of shit. I told him to suck on my machine gun. Hey Hillary, you might want to ride one of these into the sunset, you worthless bitch."[49]

Nugent's violent speech is not limited to politicians. Also in 2008, appearing on *Hannity & Colmes,* he advocated shooting to kill anybody who crossed the southern border illegally. "In an unauthorized entry, armed, like they are right now, invading our country, I'd like to shoot them dead."[50]

In 2010, in a column for *The Washington Times,* he offered his alternative to building a mosque near Ground Zero in New York City: "Killing more Muslim terror punks would make the world a more peaceful place to live—and safer for Muslims—and we all know Islam is the religion of peace. Yeah, right. Let's call a spade a spade here. If Islam is the religion of peace, then I'm a malnourished, tofu-eating anti-hunter."[51]

And at the 2012 convention of the NRA, when Obama was campaigning for reelection, Nugent seemed to threaten America's first black president with assassination: "If Barack Obama becomes the president in November, again, I will either be dead or in jail by this time next year."[52]

And yet that history of the ugliest language possible didn't deter Donald Trump. He welcomed Ted Nugent's endorsement in 2016. He welcomed him onstage at campaign rallies and featured him in TV ads. And then, once elected, he invited him to the White House for dinner and proudly posed for photographs with him.

That's not a double standard. As Nugent himself might say, that's a fucking outrage!

99. HE DOESN'T HAVE A DOG

This may be the most straightforward reason why Trump must go. He's the only president in modern times not to have a First Dog. In fact, he's the first president since William McKinley not to have a dog, and even McKinley had two kittens and a parrot.[53]

But, really, this should come as no surprise.

After all, dogs—and most animals, really—are excellent judges of character. Dogs are also kind, good-natured, friendly, hardworking, and loyal. Just the opposite of Donald Trump, in other words. So no wonder he can't stand them.

Dogs also need love and care. They want to be petted, talked to, and played with. Donald Trump wouldn't even take care of his own children. "There's a lot of women out there that demand the husband act like the wife," he once told radio hosts Opie and Anthony. "It's just not for me." Or to Howard Stern: "I won't do anything to take care of them. I'll supply funds and she'll take care of the kids."[54]

And it's not that he didn't have a dog's chance. Soon after he was elected, a devoted friend and fan searched for the perfect dog for President Trump and surprised him at Mar-a-Lago by introducing him to Patton—a gentle, beautiful goldendoodle named after Trump's favorite general. But Trump wasn't impressed. He said he was too busy to have a dog.[55]

Not only does Donald Trump not like dogs, he also demeans them every chance he gets. During the primary, he accused Marco Rubio of "sweating like a dog." He said former director of intelligence James Clapper, in testimony before Congress, choked "like dogs." He laughed about NBC's David Gregory getting "fired like a dog." And he joked that Tennessee senator Bob Corker, were he to run for reelection, "couldn't get elected dogcatcher in Tennessee."[56]

Apparently, Trump doesn't realize that other presidents had dogs as pets not just because they liked having them around but because they improved the image of the whole First Family. Whatever we think of their politics, we all fondly remember George W. Bush's Barney, Bill Clinton's Buddy, George H. W. Bush's Millie, and Barack Obama's Bo and Sunny. And Americans, conservative and liberal alike, howled in outrage when Lyndon Johnson picked up his two beagles, Him and Her, by the ears.

A dog running around the South Lawn can humanize any president. But all you need to know about Donald Trump is that he seems to hate dogs—and that alone is a sign of his bad character.

100. HE'S ALREADY MADE THIS BOOK OBSOLETE

This book lists a hundred reasons why Trump must go. I know what you're thinking: Why only a hundred? Believe me, it's not because that exhausts the list. It's only because that's all we have room for.

Which means that, in a way, this book is already obsolete from the day it's published. By the time you read it, Trump will no doubt have told more lies, hired more cronies, killed more environmental protection regulations, sent out a thousand more outrageous tweets, made more money off his hotels and golf courses, cracked down on more immigrants, insulted more allies, and launched war against another country or three.

The endless reasons Trump must go are almost impossible to keep up with. Which is why I need your help.

Once you've finished this book, please go to my website—billpress show.com—click on the link "Trump Must Go"—and add your personal reason(s) why it's important to get Trump out of the White House.

Let's make this an interactive project.

Let's build the next hundred reasons together.

You add your reasons, and I'll continue adding more of mine as long as he's in the White House.

Warning: Trump does so many things wrong, you'll probably be adding a new reason every day. But let's keep at it.

Hopefully, before we reach two hundred, we will have accomplished our goal of being able to say at last, not "Trump Must Go" but "Trump Is Gone."

EPILOGUE: AND ONE REASON TRUMP MUST STAY

MIKE PENCE

Everything we've said about Donald Trump is true. He's the most ignorant, unqualified, inexperienced, and utterly obnoxious person ever elected president. He knows nothing about issues and has no interest or patience to learn. He listens to and respects no one's opinion but his own, which is invariably wrong, if not deluded. He's rude, crude, gross, and mean. Even conservative commentator George Will calls him the worst of all forty-five presidents so far.[1]

But as frustrated, angry, or embarrassed as you may be that Donald Trump is the forty-fifth president of the United States, it could still be worse. We could be stuck with Mike Pence.

He's the one argument—and a strong, compelling argument, too—for keeping Trump right where he is.

Not everybody gets that. Pence has buffaloed a lot of people, liberal and conservative. After all, he seems so disciplined where Trump is so unruly; so soft-spoken where Trump is loudmouthed; so grown-up where Trump is so childish. A lot of people wish something bad would happen to Trump so Pence could take over.

When Trump at one time agreed to an immigration compromise with Democratic leaders (which he later abandoned), conservative pundit Ann Coulter tweeted: "At this point, who DOESN'T want Trump impeached? If we're not getting a wall, I'd prefer President Pence."[2]

Some on the left fell for the same story line. *New York Times* columnist Gail Collins praised Pence as someone who "seems less likely to get the planet blown up." And the headline on a *Washington Post* column by Dana Milbank declared, PRESIDENT PENCE IS SOUNDING BETTER AND BETTER.[3]

No, he's not. Don't be fooled. Because as dangerous as Trump is, Pence would be even more dangerous. He's even more conservative than Trump—former GOP congressional staffer Mike Lofgren calls him "as far right as you could go without falling off the earth"—and a lot more effective.[4]

Where Trump doesn't really believe in anything, Pence is a committed, doctrinaire ideologue and right-wing extremist. Where Trump is a know-nothing, Pence is a total, deeply conservative policy wonk. Where Trump has no apparent religious convictions, Pence is a full-fledged evangelical zealot. Where Trump has no idea how to govern, Pence knows how things work, both at the state and federal level. Where Trump is chaotic evil, Pence is lawful evil.

And make no mistake about it: Pence's show of low-key humility is just a front. He burns with political ambition and high aspirations, as was already evident when he was just involved in local politics in his hometown of Columbus, Indiana. Harry McCawley, editor of *The Republic,* Columbus's local paper, told *The New Yorker*'s Jane Mayer, "Mike Pence wanted to be President practically since he popped out of the womb."[5]

Elected to Congress in 2000, Pence served six terms without authoring a single successful bill. His eyes were always on the national scene, according to colleagues at the time. In fact, he gained national attention by bucking President George W. Bush and fellow congressional Republicans when he thought they were not conservative enough—opposing expansion of Medicaid to cover the cost of prescription drugs, for example.

It was also as a member of Congress that he followed "the Billy Graham rule," now better known as "Pence's rule": He does not eat alone with a woman who is not his wife, or attend an event where alcohol is being served unless his wife, Karen, whom he reportedly calls "Mother," is also present. Needless to say, Donald Trump does not abide by the same rule.[6]

Now, as vice president, Pence enjoys a twofold shot at the big job he's always coveted. First, just by being where he is (which, he believes, was ordained by God). Of his forty-seven predecessors, nine vice presidents eventually assumed the presidency either because of death or a resignation. Second, Pence is vice president to Donald Trump, whom many believe will be convicted, impeached, or forced to resign before he completes his first term.[7]

Reportedly, very quietly—so as not to spook his boss—Pence is already preparing for that possibility, assembling his own team of experts, developing his own relations with foreign leaders, staying in close touch with leaders of Congress, and hosting dinners for major Republican donors at the vice president's mansion—many of whom, like Charles and David Koch, can't stand Trump. But Pence is so close to the Kochs, says Rhode Island senator Sheldon Whitehouse, that "if Pence were to become President for any reason, the government would be run by the Koch Brothers— period. He's been their tool for years." Even Steve Bannon agrees and has expressed his concern that Pence would be "a president that the Kochs would own."[8]

You only have to look at his record to know what kind of president Pence would be: the candidate of the religious Right, and further to the right than any president so far. His political agenda comes right out of Franklin Graham's playbook. In fact, he proudly declares, "I am a Christian, a conservative, and a Republican, in that order." Richard Land, president of the Southern Evangelical Seminary, told The New Yorker's Mayer, "Mike Pence is the 24-karat-gold model of what we want in an evangelical politician."[9]

In short, his America would be straight out of Margaret Atwood's The Handmaid's Tale. Pence believes in the criminalization of abortion and wants to deny unmarried women access to birth control. He campaigned for Congress in 2000 vowing to oppose "any effort to recognize homosexuals as a discrete and insular minority entitled to the protection of anti-discrimination laws."[10]

As governor of Indiana, Pence signed a bill requiring burial or cremation of aborted fetuses and slashed funding for Planned Parenthood. He opposed resettlement of any Syrian refugees in this state. He helped exacerbate the worst HIV outbreak in state history by slashing health spending and, until the damage was done, opposing needle exchanges. And he achieved national notoriety by signing the so-called Religious Freedom Restoration Act, allowing business owners to cite their religious beliefs as justification for refusing service to LGBTQ Americans—which stirred up such a backlash, Pence was forced to back down and sign a weaker version of the bill. In fact, Pence's extreme social agenda proved so unpopular in Indiana, it looked like he could never get reelected and his political career was over—until Donald Trump saved him by making him his running mate.[11]

Now, mix that extreme policy agenda with a bland, nonthreatening public persona and an undeserved reputation for making government work, and you have a very dangerous combination, indeed. You have Mike Pence, who is, again, far, far more dangerous than that shoot-from-the-hip, bull-in-the-china-shop Donald Trump.

You also have in Mike Pence a total and unrepentant hypocrite. In August 2016, when the *Access Hollywood* tape surfaced, on which Trump bragged about grabbing women "by the pussy," pundits were sure that the devout Christian Pence would break with Trump and resign from the ticket. But they didn't know Pence. After allegedly trying to see if he could dislodge Trump from the top of the ticket, he not only stuck with Trump, he praised him publicly, saying, "I am grateful that he has expressed remorse and apologized to the American people." Put to the test, Pence's Christian beliefs proved far less long-standing than his political ambition.[12]

And today, Pence is the most disgusting suck-up to Trump of anybody else in the White House. If George Will, as noted above, is no fan of Trump's, he's even less of a fan of Pence's. "The oleaginous Mike Pence, with his talent for toadyism and appetite for obsequiousness," Will writes, has become "America's most repulsive public figure."[13]

Will's distrust and disgust with Trump is shared by former *Apprentice* contestant and White House aide Omarosa Manigault, who knows both men well. "As bad as y'all think Trump is, you would be worried about Pence," she said on *Celebrity Big Brother.* Nor does Manigault buy Pence's belief that he and Trump are all part of God's plan: "I'm Christian. I love Jesus, but he thinks Jesus tells him to say things. And I'm like, 'Jesus ain't say that.' He's scary."[14]

So for those of you in a hurry to replace Donald Trump with Mike Pence, I issue one word of warning: "Be careful what you wish for, you just might get it." And you just might want Donald Trump back again.

After all, with Trump in office, some now pine for the disastrous days of George W. Bush. Then again, when he was president, my 2004 book *Bush Must Go* only listed ten reasons. At this rate, we may well need a thousand reasons to deal with His Holiness Mike Pence of Indiana.

ACKNOWLEDGMENTS

I'm not just being humble when I tell you: I did not write this book.

No, it's true. I did not write this book. Donald Trump did. Thanks to Donald Trump, all I had to do every day was go online, watch cable TV, read the paper, capture the latest outrage—and add one more reason why Trump must go. With his help, this book wrote itself.

Still, I had a lot of valuable help along the way. Again, it was a joy to work with publisher Thomas Dunne, executive editor Stephen S. Power, and their talented team at St. Martin's Press, including Samantha Zukergood, Michelle Cashman, and Joseph Rinaldi.

I was also fortunate to reassemble the winning combination of research assistant Kevin Murphy and literary agent Ronald Goldfarb. This is our ninth book together. It's a winning team, so don't expect us to stop now.

And, of course, I couldn't have disappeared into another book-writing black hole without the patience and counsel of my long-suffering wife, Carol.

In a way, *Trump Must Go* is the stepchild of my 2004 book *Bush Must Go*. However, as much fun as I had writing both, I really don't feel like making this a trilogy. I have no desire to add another sequel to this dismal series—*Ivanka Must Go?*—in 2024 or 2028.

So I close by saluting every American who's out there today, all over the country, standing up against the policies of Donald Trump: making phone calls, knocking on doors, registering voters, writing checks, running for office. Keep it up! Your enthusiasm is contagious. Together we can make a difference. Together we can make sure, one way or the other, Trump does go—the sooner, the better.

NOTES

INTRODUCTION: ENOUGH IS ENOUGH

1. Jen Kirby, "Trump Has the Lowest Approval of Any Modern President at the End of His First Year," Vox, December 21, 2017, https://www.vox.com/policy-and-politics /2017/12/21/16798432/trump-low-approval-december-first-year; Gary Langer, "Trump Seen by 66 Percent in US as Doing More to Divide Than Unite Country (POLL)," ABC News, September 24, 2017, https://abcnews.go.com/Politics/deep-challenges -trump-north-korea-home-front-poll/story?id=50032349.

2. John Parkinson, "6 Democrats Introduce 5 Articles of Impeachment Against President Trump," ABC News, November 15, 2017, https://abcnews.go.com/Politics /democrats-introduce-articles-impeachment-president-trump/story?id=51167864; Eric Garcia, "House Votes to Table Trump Impeachment," Roll Call, January 12, 2018, https://www.rollcall.com/news/politics/house-votes-to-table-impeachment; Greg Price, "Trump Impeachment Petition Has More Than 4 Million Signatures After President's First Year," Newsweek, January 17, 2018, http://www.newsweek.com /trump-impeachment-petition-millions-first-year-783674.

3. Lois Beckett, "Grounds for Impeachment if Trump Lied About Trying to Fire Mueller—Ken Starr," *The Guardian,* January 28, 2018, https://www.theguardian .com/us-news/2018/jan/28/trump-robert-mueller-russia-ken-starr.

4. NCC Staff, "How a National Tragedy Led to the 25th Amendment," National Constitution Center, February 10, 2018, https://constitutioncenter.org/blog/how-jfks -assassination-led-to-a-constitutional-amendment-2.

5. Olivia Beavers, "Dem Lawmaker: Trump Showing Signs of 'Mental Instability,' Must Be Removed," *The Hill,* August 16, 2017, http://thehill.com/homenews/administration /346863-dem-lawmaker-trump-showing-signs-of-mental-instability-must-be.

6. "Declaration of Independence—A Transcription," National Archives, https://www .archives.gov/founding-docs/declaration-transcript.

7. Ibid.

1: TRUMP'S UNFIT FOR THE JOB

1. Michael Wolff, "Donald Trump Didn't Want to Be President," *New York,* January 3, 2018, http://nymag.com/daily/intelligencer/2018/01/michael-wolff-fire-and-fury-book -donald-trump.html.

2. David Smith, Lauren Gambino, Ben Jacobs, and Sabrina Siddiqui, "The Conservatives Turning Against Donald Trump," *The Guardian,* August 8, 2017, https://www .theguardian.com/us-news/2017/aug/08/the-conservatives-turning-against-donald -trump.

3. Philip Rucker and Karoun Demirjian, "Corker Calls White House 'an Adult Day Care Center' in Response to Trump's Latest Twitter Tirade," *The Washington Post,* October 8, 2017, https://www.washingtonpost.com/news/post-politics/wp/2017/10/08 /trump-attacks-gop-sen-corker-didnt-have-the-guts-to-run-for-reelection/.

4. Jonathan Landay, "Republican National Security Experts: Trump Would Be 'Dangerous' President," Reuters, August 8, 2016, https://www.reuters.com/article/us-usa -election-trump-security/republican-national-security-experts-trump-would-be -dangerous-president-idUSKCN10J2EH.

5. Dexter Filkins, "Rex Tillerson at the Breaking Point," *The New Yorker,* October 16, 2017, https://www.newyorker.com/magazine/2017/10/16/rex-tillerson-at-the-breaking-point.

6. Zack Beauchamp, "H. R. McMaster Reportedly Thinks Trump Is an 'Idiot' with the Brain of a 'Kindergartner,'" Vox, November 20, 2017, https://www.vox.com/world /2017/11/20/16680190/hr-mcmaster-trump-idiot-kindergartner.

7. Quinnipiac University, "Trump Is Intelligent, But Not Fit or Level-Headed, U.S. Voters Tell Quinnipiac University National Poll; First Year Was 'Disaster,' 'Cha-

otic,' 'Successful,'" January 10, 2018, https://poll.qu.edu/national/release-detail?Rele
aseID=2511.

8. Ibid.

9. Patrick Henry, "Speech Before Virginia Ratifying Convention," June 5, 1788,
http://teachingamericanhistory.org/library/document/patrick-henry-virginia
-ratifying-convention-va/.

10. Donald Trump (@realDonaldTrump), Twitter, February 1, 2018, 7:02 a.m., https://
twitter.com/realdonaldtrump/status/959034299222843394.

11. Manuela Tobias, "Trump's State of the Union Ratings Are Not the Highest in History," PolitiFact, February 1, 2018, http://www.politifact.com/truth-o-meter/statements
/2018/feb/01/donald-trump/trump-state-union-ratings-not-highest-history/.

12. Ibid.

13. Jessica Taylor, "Trump Administration Goes to War with the Media Over Inauguration Crowd Size," NPR, January 21, 2017, https://www.npr.org/2017/01/21/510994742
/trump-administration-goes-to-war-with-the-media-over-inauguration-crowd-size;
German Lopez, "Donald Trump Keeps Lying About the Size of His Electoral
College Victory," Vox, February 16, 2017, https://www.vox.com/policy-and-politics
/2017/2/16/14639058/trump-electoral-college-win; Donald Trump (@realDonald-
Trump), Twitter, November 27, 2016, 3:30 p.m., https://twitter.com/realdonaldtrump
/status/802972944532209664; Billy House and Steven T. Dennis, "Trump Says Undocumented Immigrants Cost Him Popular Vote," *Bloomberg,* January 24, 2017,
https://www.bloomberg.com/news/articles/2017-01-24/trump-again-claims
-undocumented-immigrants-cost-him-popular-vote.

14. Josh Dawsey, Damian Paletta, and Erica Werner, "In Fundraising Speech, Trump
Says He Made Up Trade Claim in Meeting with Justin Trudeau," *Washington Post,*
March 15, 2018, https://www.washingtonpost.com/news/post-politics/wp/2018/03/14
/in-fundraising-speech-trump-says-he-made-up-facts-in-meeting-with-justin
-trudeau/; Morgan Gstalter, "Trump: If I was wrong about Kim, 'I'll find some kind
of an excuse,'" *The Hill*, June 12, 2018, http://thehill.com/homenews/administration
/391774-trump-if-i-was-wrong-about-kim-ill-find-some-kind-of-an-excuse.

15. Mary Ann Georgantopoulos, "Here's a Running List of President Trump's Lies and
Other Bullshit," BuzzFeed, January 26, 2017, https://www.buzzfeed.com/mary
anngeorgantopoulos/president-trump-lie-list.

16. "In 365 Days, President Trump Has Made 2,140 False or Misleading Claims," *The
Washington Post,* January 19, 2018, https://www.washingtonpost.com/graphics/politics
/trump-claims-database/; David Leonhardt and Stuart A. Thompson, "Trump's

Lies," *The New York Times,* June 23, 2017, https://www.nytimes.com/interactive /2017/06/23/opinion/trumps-lies.html.

17. Ibid; Daniel Dale, "Donald Trump Said 71 false things in 14 days. His Dishonesty Is Increasing," *Star,* June 21, 2018, https://www.thestar.com/news/world/analysis/2018/06 /21/trump-said-71-false-things-in-14-days-his-dishonesty-is-increasing-over-time .html; Daniel Dale, "Donald Trump Made 103 False Claims Last Week, Shattering His Dishonesty Record," *Star,* June 26, 2018, https://www.thestar.com/news/world/analysis /2018/06/26/donald-trump-made-103-false-claims-last-week-shattering-his-dishonesty -record.html.

18. David Leonhardt, Ian Prasad Philbrick, and Stuart A. Thompson, "Trump's Lies vs. Obama's," *The New York Times,* December 14, 2017, https://www.nytimes.com /interactive/2017/12/14/opinion/sunday/trump-lies-obama-who-is-worse.html.

19. Leonhardt and Thompson, "Trump's Lies."

20. Ibid.; Jens Manuel Krogstad and Antonio Flores, "Unlike Other Latinos, About Half of Cuban Voters in Florida Backed Trump," Pew Research Center Fact Tank, November 15, 2016, http://www.pewresearch.org/fact-tank/2016/11/15/unlike-other -latinos-about-half-of-cuban-voters-in-florida-backed-trump/.

21. Glenn Kessler, Meg Kelly, and Nicole Lewis, "President Trump Has Made 1,628 False or Misleading Claims Over 298 Days," *The Washington Post,* November 14, 2017, https://www.washingtonpost.com/news/fact-checker/wp/2017/11/14/president -trump-has-made-1628-false-or-misleading-claims-over-298-days.

22. Ibid.

23. Christina Willkie, "Trump Walks Back His Pledge That Tax Reform Won't Make Him Richer," CNBC, October 11, 2017, https://www.cnbc.com/2017/10/11/trump -walks-back-his-pledge-that-tax-reform-wont-make-him-richer.html; Dylan Matthews, "The Republican Tax Bill Got Worse: Now the Top 1% Gets 83% of the Gains," Vox, December 18, 2017, https://www.vox.com/policy-and-politics/2017/12/18 /16791174/republican-tax-bill-congress-conference-tax-policy-center.

24. Maya Rhodan, "President Trump Said His Win Was the 'Biggest Since Reagan.' It Wasn't," *Time,* February 16, 2017, http://time.com/4673993/donald-trump-campaign -electoral-college-win/.

25. Robert Farley, "Fact Check: No Evidence of Busing Voters to New Hampshire," *USA Today,* February 14, 2017, https://www.usatoday.com/story/news/politics/2017 /02/14/fact-check-no-evidence-busing-voters-new-hampshire/97896228/.

26. Donald Trump (@realDonaldTrump), Twitter, March 4, 2017, 6:35 a.m., https:// twitter.com/realdonaldtrump/status/837989835818287106; Eugene Kiely, "Revisit-

ing Trump's Wiretap Tweets," FactCheck, September 22, 2017, https://www.factcheck .org/2017/09/revisiting-trumps-wiretap-tweets/.

27. Leonhardt and Thompson, "Trump's Lies"; Jon Greenberg, "Donald Trump Wrongly Repeats That Chicago Has Strongest Gun Laws," PolitiFact, November 7, 2017, http://www.politifact.com/truth-o-meter/statements/2017/nov/07/donald-trump /trump-wrongly-repeats-chicago-has-strongest-gun-la/.

28. Leonhardt and Thompson, "Trump's Lies"; Louis Jacobson, "Donald Trump Wrong That Murder Rate Is Highest in 47 Years," PolitiFact, February 8, 2017, http://www .politifact.com/truth-o-meter/statements/2017/feb/08/donald-trump/donald -trump-wrong-murder-rate-highest-47-years/.

29. Leonhardt and Thompson, "Trump's Lies"; Michelle Ye Hee Lee, "What Trump Got Wrong on Twitter This Week (#4)," *The Washington Post,* February 3, 2017, https://www.washingtonpost.com/news/fact-checker/wp/2017/02/03/what-trump -got-wrong-on-twitter-this-week-4/.

30. Leonhardt and Thompson, "Trump's Lies"; Alicia Parlapiano, Karen Yourish, Larry Buchanan, and Wilson Andrews, "What All the Russia Investigations Have Done and What Could Happen Next," *The New York Times,* May 10, 2017, https://www.nytimes .com/interactive/2017/05/10/us/politics/fbi-congress-trump-russia-investigations.html.

31. Donald Trump (@realDonaldTrump), Twitter, January 6, 2018, 7:27 a.m., https:// twitter.com/realdonaldtrump/status/949618475877765120.

32. Donald Trump (@realDonaldTrump), Twitter, January 6, 2018, 7:30 a.m., https://twitter .com/realdonaldtrump/status/949619270631256064.

33. Peter Dreier, "Trump Is 'Very Intelligent.' Just Ask Him," *Los Angeles Times,* October 30, 2017, http://www.latimes.com/opinion/opinion-la/la-ol-dreier-trump-intelligence -20171030-story.html; Chris Cillizza, "Donald Trump's IQ Obsession, in 22 Quotes," CNN, October 10, 2017, https://www.cnn.com/2017/10/10/politics/donald-trump -tillerson-iq/index.html.

34. Robert Reich, "Seriously, How Dumb Is Trump?," *HuffPost,* January 9, 2018, https:// www.huffingtonpost.com/entry/seriously-how-dumb-is-trump_us_5a525a1ee 4b003133ec8cb66.

35. Wolff, "Donald Trump Didn't Want to Be President"; David A. Graham, "The President Who Doesn't Read," *The Atlantic,* January 5, 2018, https://www.theatlantic .com/politics/archive/2018/01/americas-first-post-text-president/549794/.

36. Dreier, "Trump Is 'Very Intelligent.'"

37. Ashley DeJean, "Exclusive: Classified Memo Tells Intelligence Analysts to Keep Trump's Daily Brief Short," *Mother Jones,* February 16, 2017, https://www.motherjones

.com/politics/2017/02/classified-memo-tells-intelligence-analysts-keep-trumps
-daily-brief-short/; Jonathan Swan, "1 Big Thing: Scoop: Trump's Secret, Shrinking Schedule," Axios, January 7, 2018, https://www.axios.com/newsletters/axios
-sneak-peek-a7c58480-bc9e-4580-93c1-6358a6102b93.html; Carol D. Leonnig, Shane
Harris, and Greg Jaffe, "Breaking with Tradition, Trump Skips President's Written
Intelligence Report and Relies on Oral Briefings," *The Washington Post,* February 9,
2018, https://www.washingtonpost.com/politics/breaking-with-tradition-trump
-skips-presidents-written-intelligence-report-for-oral-briefings/2018/02/09
/b7ba569e-0c52-11e8-95a5-c396801049ef_story.html.

38. Maya Rhodan, "President Obama on the *Daily Show*: Without Proper Intelligence
'You Are Flying Blind,'" *Time,* December 13, 2016, http://time.com/4598778/obama
-daily-show-noah-trump/.

39. Emily Babay, "Trump Remarks on Frederick Douglass Draw Ridicule," *The Phila-
delphia Inquirer,* February 2, 2018, http://www.philly.com/philly/blogs/real-time
/Trump-remarks-on-Frederick-Douglass-draw-ridicule.html; Jesse Berney, "Trump's
Terrifying Nuke Answer at the Debate Should End His Campaign (But It Won't),"
Rolling Stone, December 16, 2015, https://www.rollingstone.com/politics/news
/trumps-terrifying-nuke-answer-at-the-debate-should-end-his-campaign-but-it
-wont-20151216; Mack Lamoureux, "Donald Trump Sure Does Like to Talk About
How 'Invisible' F-35 Fighter Jets Are," VICE, November 24, 2017, https://www.vice
.com/en_nz/article/mb3zzy/donald-trump-sure-does-like-to-talk-about-how
-invisible-f-35-fighter-jets-are; Madeline Conway, "Trump: 'Nobody Knew That
Health Care Could Be So Complicated,'" *Politico,* February 27, 2017, https://www
.politico.com/story/2017/02/trump-nobody-knew-that-health-care-could-be-so
-complicated-235436.

40. Tal Koplan, "Trump Contradicts Self Repeatedly in Immigration Meeting,"
CNN, January 10, 2018, https://www.cnn.com/2018/01/09/politics/donald-trump
-immigration-contradictions/index.html.

41. Todd Gilman, "Trump Threatens Federal Shutdown Over Demand for Border Wall
and Immigration Curbs; Pentagon Chief Chilly to the Idea," *The Dallas Morning News,*
February 6, 2018, https://www.dallasnews.com/news/politics/2018/02/06/trump
-threatens-federal-shutdown-demand-border-wall-immigration-curbs; Mike DeBo-
nis and Erica Werner, "Brief Government Shutdown Ends as Trump Signs Spending
Bill," *The Washington Post,* February 9, 2018, https://www.washingtonpost.com
/powerpost/congress-passes-sweeping-budget-bill-ending-brief-shutdown/2018/02
/09/6021367e-0d69-11e8-8890-372e2047c935_story.html.

42. Glenn Thrush, Michael D. Shear, and Eileen Sullivan, "John Kelly Quickly Moves to Impose Military Discipline on White House," *The New York Times,* August 3, 2017, https://www.nytimes.com/2017/08/03/us/politics/john-kelly-chief-of-staff-trump .html; Gabriel Sherman, "'I've Got Another Nut Job Here Who Thinks He's Running Things': Are Trump and Kelly Heading for Divorce?," *Vanity Fair,* January 22, 2018, https://www.vanityfair.com/news/2018/01/are-trump-and-kelly-heading-for -divorce.

43. Daniel Drezner, "White House Aides Can't Stop Talking About President Trump Like He's a Toddler," *The Washington Post,* August 21, 2017, https://www.washingtonpost .com/news/posteverything/wp/2017/08/21/the-trump-as-toddler-thread-explained -and-curated.

44. Michael Wolff, "'You Can't Make This S— Up': My Year Inside Trump's Insane White House," *Hollywood Reporter,* January 4, 2018, https://www.hollywoodre- porter.com/news/michael-wolff-my-insane-year-inside-trumps-white-house -1071504.

45. Susan B. Glasser, "'People Here Think Trump Is a Laughingstock,'" *Politico,* May 19, 2017, https://www.politico.com/magazine/story/2017/05/19/trump-first-foreign -trip-europe-215163; Robbie Gramer, "NATO Frantically Tries to Trump-Proof President's First Visit," *Foreign Policy,* May 15, 2017, http://foreignpolicy.com/2017 /05/15/nato-frantically-tries-to-trump-proof-presidents-first-visit-alliance-europe -brussels/.

46. Swan, "1 Big Thing"; Brandon Carter, "Trump Watches Up to 8 Hours of TV Every Day; Report," *The Hill,* December 9, 2017, http://thehill.com/homenews/administration /364094-trump-watches-at-least-four-hours-of-tv-per-day-report.

47. Maggie Haberman, Glenn Thrush, and Peter Baker, "Inside Trump's Hour-by- Hour Battle for Self-Preservation," *The New York Times,* December 9, 2017, https:// www.nytimes.com/2017/12/09/us/politics/donald-trump-president.html; Abdullah al-Shihri, "Worldwide Effort Set to Keep Trump Happy on 1st Trip Abroad," ABC News, May 19, 2017, http://abcnews.go.com/amp/Politics/wireStory/worldwide -effort-trump-happy-1st-trip-abroad-47506485; Michael Scherer and Zeke Miller, "Donald Trump After Hours," *Time,* May 2017, http://time.com/donald-trump -after-hours/.

48. David Leonhardt and Ian Prasad Philbrick, "Donald Trump's Racism: The Defini- tive List," *The New York Times,* January 15, 2018, https://www.nytimes.com/interactive /2018/01/15/opinion/leonhardt-trump-racist.html.

49. Ibid.

50. Ibid.; Sarah Burns, "Why Donald Trump Doubled Down on the Central Park Five," *The New York Times,* October 17, 2016, https://www.nytimes.com/2016/10/18/opinion/why-trump-doubled-down-on-the-central-park-five.html; Ron Stodghill, "True Confession of the Central Park Rapist," *Time,* December 9, 2002, http://content.time.com/time/magazine/article/0,9171,397521,00.html; Matt Fuller, "John McCain (Un)Endorses Donald Trump, *HuffPost,* October 8, 2016, https://www.huffingtonpost.com/entry/john-mccain-unendorses-trump_us_57f95fc1e4b0e655eab4f273.

51. Leonhardt and Philbrick, "Donald Trump's Racism."

52. Ibid.

53. Ibid.

54. Ibid.

55. Ibid.; Katie Reilly, "Here's All the Times Donald Trump Has Insulted Mexico," *Time,* August 31, 2016, http://time.com/4473972/donald-trump-mexico-meeting-insult/.

56. Leonhardt and Philbrick, "Donald Trump's Racism"; Matt Zapotosky, "Federal Judge Blocks Trump's Third Travel Ban," *The Washington Post,* October 17, 2017, https://www.washingtonpost.com/world/national-security/federal-judge-blocks-trumps-third-travel-ban/2017/10/17/e73293fc-ae90-11e7-9e58-e6288544af98_story.html.

57. Ibid.

58. Leonhardt and Philbrick, "Donald Trump's Racism"; Asawin Suebsaeng and Andrew Desiderio, "'Clean-Up on Aisle Trump': President Reverses Course on Neo-Nazis, Slams the 'Alt-Left,'" *The Daily Beast,* August 15, 2017, https://www.thedaily beast.com/clean-up-on-aisle-trump-president-reverses-course-on-neo-nazis-slams-the-alt-left.

59. Philip Bump, "Roy Moore: America Was Great in Era of Slavery, Is Now 'Focus of Evil in the World,'" *The Washington Post,* December 8, 2017, https://www.washingtonpost.com/news/politics/wp/2017/12/08/roy-moore-america-was-great-in-era-of-slavery-is-now-focus-of-evil-in-the-world/.

60. Leonhardt and Philbrick, "Donald Trump's Racism"; Ray Stern, "Sheriff Joe Arpaio's Office Commits Worst Racial Profiling in U.S. History, Concludes DOJ Investigation," *Phoenix New Times,* December 15, 2011, http://www.phoenixnewtimes.com/news/sheriff-joe-arpaios-office-commits-worst-racial-profiling-in-us-history-concludes-doj-investigation-6655328; Alexander Nazaryan, "Donald Trump and Joe Arpaio: A Bromance Forged in Birtherism and Xenophobia," *Newsweek,* August 28, 2017, http://www.newsweek.com/trump-arpaio-pardon-arizona-maricopa-immigration-655995.

61. Miriam Jordan, "Trump Administration Says Nearly 200,000 El Salvadorans Must

Leave," *The New York Times,* January 8, 2018, https://www.nytimes.com/2018/01/08/us/salvadorans-tps-end.html.

62. Leonhardt and Philbrick, "Donald Trump's Racism"; Josh Dawsey, "Trump Derides Protections for Immigrants from 'Shithole' Countries," *The Washington Post,* January 12, 2018, https://www.washingtonpost.com/politics/trump-attacks-protections-for-immigrants-from-shithole-countries-in-oval-office-meeting/2018/01/11/bfc0725c-f711-11e7-91af-31ac729add94_story.html.

63. Richard Wolf, "Trump's 87 Picks to Be Federal Judges Are 92% White with Just One Black and One Hispanic Nominee," *USA Today,* February 13, 2018, https://www.usatoday.com/story/news/politics/2018/02/13/trumps-87-picks-federal-judges-92-white-just-one-black-and-one-hispanic-nominee/333088002/.

64. Ibid.; Nina Totenberg, "Jeff Sessions Previously Denied Federal Judgeship Amid Racism Controversy," NPR, January 9, 2017, https://www.npr.org/2017/01/09/509001314/jeff-sessions-previously-denied-federal-judgeship-amid-racism-controversy.

65. Alec MacGillis, "Is Anybody Home at HUD?," *New York,* August 22, 2017, http://nymag.com/daily/intelligencer/2017/08/ben-carson-hud-secretary.html.

66. Helena Andrews-Dyer, "Omarosa Says She Wouldn't Vote for Trump Again 'in a Million Years,'" *The Washington Post,* February 8, 2018, https://www.washingtonpost.com/news/reliable-source/wp/2018/02/08/omarosa-says-she-wouldnt-vote-for-trump-again-in-a-million-years/; Devon Ivie, "Omarosa Likens Her White House Experience to Working at a Plantation," Vulture, February 25, 2018, http://www.vulture.com/2018/02/omarosa-likens-her-white-house-experience-to-a-plantation.html.

67. Nick Anderson and Moriah Balingit, "Trump Administration Moves to Rescind Obama-era Guidance on Race in Admissions," *The Washington Post,* July 3, 2018, https://www.washingtonpost.com/local/education/trump-administration-moves-to-rescind-obama-era-guidance-on-race-in-admissions/2018/07/03/78210e9e-7ed8-11e8-bb6b-c1cb691f1402_story.html.

68. Chris Cillizza, "Half the Country Thinks Donald Trump Is a Racist. HALF," CNN, July 4, 2018, https://www.cnn.com/2018/07/04/politics/donald-trump-quinnipiac-poll/index.html.

69. Emily Crane, "Ex-White House Staff Secretary Rob Porter 'Told Staffers His Ex-Wife's Black Eye Was an Accident' as He Tried to Downplay Domestic Abuse Allegations," *Daily Mail,* February 13, 2018, http://www.dailymail.co.uk/news/article-5384603/Rob-Porter-told-staffers-wifes-black-eye-accident.html.

70. Jenna Johnson, "Trump Lavishes Praise on Rob Porter, Former Top Aide Accused of

Domestic Violence," *The Washington Post,* February 9, 2018, https://www.washington post.com/news/post-politics/wp/2018/02/09/trump-lavishes-praise-on-rob-porter -former-top-aide-accused-of-domestic-violence/.

71. Ibid.

72. Chris Cillizza, "A Timeline of the White House's Head-Scratching Responses to the Rob Porter Debacle," CNN, February 13, 2018, https://www.cnn.com/2018/02 /13/politics/rob-porter-trump-analysis/index.html.

73. Jake Tapper (@JakeTapper), Twitter, February 10, 2018, 10:59 a.m., https://twitter .com/jaketapper/status/962355261238398976.

74. Claire Cohen, "Donald Trump Sexism Tracker: Every Offensive Comment in One Place," *The Telegraph,* July 14, 2017, http://www.telegraph.co.uk/women/politics /donald-trump-sexism-tracker-every-offensive-comment-in-one-place/.

75. Ibid.; Libby Nelson, "Donald Trump's History of Misogyny, Sexism, and Harassment: A Comprehensive Review," Vox, October 12, 2016, https://www.vox.com/2016 /10/8/13110734/donald-trump-leaked-audio-recording-billy-bush-sexism.

76. Cohen, "Donald Trump Sexism Tracker."

77. Ibid.; Paul Solotaroff, "Trump Seriously: On the Trail With the GOP's Tough Guy," *Rolling Stone,* September 9, 2015, https://www.rollingstone.com/politics/news /trump-seriously-20150909.

78. Cohen, "Donald Trump Sexism Tracker."

79. Daniel Victor, "'Access Hollywood' Reminds Trump: 'The Tape Is Very Real,'" *The New York Times,* November 28, 2017, https://www.nytimes.com/2017/11/28/us/politics /donald-trump-tape.html.

80. Cohen, "Donald Trump Sexism Tracker."

81. Cohen, "Donald Trump Sexism Tracker"; Ashley Parker, John Wagner, and Ed O'Keefe, "Trump Attacks Gillibrand in Tweet Critics Say Is Sexually Suggestive and Demeaning," *The Washington Post,* December 12, 2017, https://www.washingtonpost .com/news/post-politics/wp/2017/12/12/trump-sends-sexually-suggestive-and -demeaning-tweet-about-gillibrand/.

82. "Transcript: Donald Trump's Taped Comments About Women," *The New York Times,* October 8, 2016, https://www.nytimes.com/2016/10/08/us/donald-trump -tape-transcript.html.

83. Victor, "'Access Hollywood.'"

84. Catherine Pearson, Emma Gray, and Alanna Vagianos, "A Running List of the Women Who've Accused Donald Trump of Sexual Misconduct," *HuffPost,* December 12, 2017, https://www.huffingtonpost.com/entry/a-running-list-of-the-women

-whove-accused-donald-trump-of-sexual-misconduct_us_57ffae1fe4b0162c043a7212; Chris Riotta, "When Has Trump Been Accused of Rape or Attempted Rape? Allegations Include a Child, His Wife and a Business Associate," *Newsweek,* November 16, 2017, http://www.newsweek.com/donald-trump-rape-sexual-assault-minor -wife-business-victims-roy-moore-713531.

85. Pearson, Gray, and Vagianos, "A Running List of the Women."

86. Ibid.; Frances Stead Sellers, "The Trump Accuser Who Refuses to Go Away," *The Washington Post,* February 13, 2018, https://www.washingtonpost.com/politics/the -trump-accuser-who-refuses-to-go-away/2018/02/13/3b62f02c-f6ce-11e7-a9e3 -ab18ce41436a_story.html; Julia Marsh and Bruce Golding, "Trump Must Sit for Deposition in Zervos Defamation Case: Judge," *New York Post,* June 5, 2018, https:// nypost.com/2018/06/05/trump-must-sit-for-deposition-in-zervos-defamation-case -judge/.

87. Eli Saslow, "Is Anyone Listening?," *The Washington Post,* February 19, 2018, https:// www.washingtonpost.com/news/national/wp/2018/02/19/feature/trump-accuser -keeps-telling-her-story-hoping-someone-will-finally-listen/ .

88. Ibid.; Rachel Crooks (@RachelforOhio), Twitter, February 20, 2018, 8:22 a.m., https://twitter.com/RachelforOhio/status/965984922933628928.

89. Nick Gass, "Trump Says He Won't Tweet Anymore as President," *Politico,* April 25, 2016, https://www.politico.com/blogs/2016-gop-primary-live-updates-and-results /2016/04/trump-no-tweeting-president-222408.

90. Jonathan Swan, "1 Big Thing."

91. Ibid.; Rich McCormick, "Donald Trump Is Using an iPhone Now," The Verge, March 29, 2017, https://www.theverge.com/2017/3/29/15103504/donald-trump-iphone -using-switched-android; Eliana Johnson, Emily Stephenson, and Daniel Lippmann, "'Too Inconvenient': Trump Goes Rogue on Phone Security," *Politico,* May 21, 2018, https://www.politico.com/story/2018/05/21/trump-phone-security-risk-hackers -601903.

92. Matthew Gertz, "I've Studied the Trump-Fox Feedback Loop for Months. It's Crazier Than You Think," *Politico,* January 5, 2018, https://www.politico.com/magazine /story/2018/01/05/trump-media-feedback-loop-216248.

93. Donald Trump (@realDonaldTrump), Twitter, February 12, 2018, 4:54 a.m., https://twitter.com/realdonaldtrump/status/963033580107653120.

94. Sonam Sheth and Natasha Bertrand, "Trump Bucked His Own White House on a Controversial Surveillance Law After Watching Fox News," *Business Insider,*

January 11, 2018, http://www.businessinsider.com/trump-attacks-fisa-white-house-pass-warrant-702-2018-1.

95. Ibid.

96. Miriam Valverde, "Trump Says It's a Travel Ban, Despite What His Own Team Says," PolitiFact, June 5, 2017, http://www.politifact.com/truth-o-meter/article/2017/jun/05/trump-says-his-immigration-executive-order-travel-.

97. Andrew Restuccia, "Trump's Uncontrollable Tweeting Triggers Deeper Anxiety Among Advisers," *Politico,* December 3, 2017, https://www.politico.com/story/2017/12/03/trump-twitter-flynn-advisers-277296.

98. Ibid.; Lachlan Markay, Asawin Suebsaeng, and Spencer Ackerman, "Even Trump's Aides Blame Him for Obstruction Probe: 'President Did This to Himself,'" *The Daily Beast,* June 14, 2017, https://www.thedailybeast.com/even-trumps-aides-blame-him-for-obstruction-probe-president-did-this-to-himself; Lachlan Markay and Asawin Suebsaeng, "Trump Manages Not to Screw Up for a Day, Stunning His Aides," *The Daily Beast,* June 9, 2017, https://www.thedailybeast.com/aides-celebrate-trumps-quiet-day-brace-for-hate-tweets-when-hes-alone.

99. Alison Main, "A Complete Breakdown of Trump's Tweets Since He Was Elected President," Mashable, November 7, 2017, https://mashable.com/2017/11/07/trumps-twitter-addiction-since-election; John Parkinson, "500 Days of Trump: His Presidency, by the Numbers," ABC News, June 4, 2018, https://abcnews.go.com/Politics/500-days-trump-presidency-numbers/story?id=55635385.

100. Markay and Suebsaeng, "Trump Manages Not to Screw Up."

101. Sean Rossman, "'He Went to Play Golf, While They Held Funerals,' Anderson Cooper Lays into Trump," *USA Today,* February 20, 2018, https://www.usatoday.com/story/news/nation-now/2018/02/20/he-went-play-golf-while-they-held-funerals-anderson-cooper-lays-into-trump/354131002/.

102. Ibid.

103. Dalton Ross, "Celebrity Big Brother: Omarosa Compares the White House to a Plantation," *EW,* February 24, 2018, http://ew.com/tv/2018/02/24/omarosa-white-house-celebrity-big-brother/.

104. Yoni Appelbaum, "I Alone Can Fix It," *The Atlantic,* July 21, 2016, https://www.theatlantic.com/politics/archive/2016/07/trump-rnc-speech-alone-fix-it/492557/.

105. James Hamblin, "Is Something Neurologically Wrong with Donald Trump?," *The Atlantic,* January 3, 2018, https://www.theatlantic.com/health/archive/2018/01/trump-cog-decline/548759/.

106. Bandy X. Lee, *The Dangerous Case of Donald Trump* (New York: Thomas Dunne Books, 2017), 36–39.

107. Julie Hirschfeld David, "Trump's Cabinet, with a Prod, Extols the 'Blessing' of Serving Him," *The New York Times,* June 12, 2017, https://www.nytimes.com/2017/06/12/us/politics/trump-boasts-of-record-setting-pace-of-activity.html.

108. Caleb Ecarma, "Trump Claims Orrin Hatch Said He's the Greatest Pres Ever: Better Than 'Lincoln and Washington,'" Mediaite, February 1, 2018, https://www.mediaite.com/trump/trump-claims-orrin-hatch-said-hes-the-greatest-prez-ever-better-than-lincoln-and-washington/; David A. Graham, "Does Trump Believe His Own Hype?," *The Atlantic,* October 22, 2017, https://www.theatlantic.com/politics/archive/2017/10/why-wont-the-world-recognize-trumps-greatness/543126/.

109. Erin Durkin, "Here's How Much Donald Trump Loves Naming Things After Himself," *New York Daily News,* July 27, 2016, http://www.nydailynews.com/news/politics/donald-trump-loves-naming-article-1.2728810; Brett Neely, "Trump Doesn't Own Most of the Products He Pitched Last Night," NPR, March 9, 2016, https://www.npr.org/2016/03/09/469775355/trump-doesnt-own-most-of-the-products-he-pitched-last-night.

110. David, "Trump's Cabinet"; John Wagner, "Praise for the Chief: Trump's Cabinet Tells Him It's an 'Honor' and 'Blessing' to Serve," *The Washington Post,* June 12, 2017, https://www.washingtonpost.com/politics/praise-for-the-chief--trumps-cabinet-tells-him-its-an-honor-privilege-blessing-to-serve/2017/06/12/ddd3919e-4fa4-11e7-91eb-9611861a988f_story.html.

111. David, "Trump's Cabinet"; Wagner, "Praise for the Chief."

112. Aaron Blake, "In Cabinet Meeting, Pence Praises Trump Once Every 12 Seconds for Three Minutes Straight," *The Washington Post,* December 20, 2017, https://www.washingtonpost.com/news/the-fix/wp/2017/12/20/in-cabinet-meeting-pence-praises-trump-once-every-12-seconds-for-3-minutes-straight/.

113. John Dickerson, "President Trump's Interview in the Oval Office: Full Transcript," CBS News, May 1, 2017, https://www.cbsnews.com/news/president-trump-oval-office-interview-cbs-this-morning-full-transcript/; Jena McGregor, "Trump Had a Puzzling Answer to this CBS Interview Question About a Basic Leadership Concept," *The Washington Post,* May 1, 2017, https://www.washingtonpost.com/news/on-leadership/wp/2017/05/01/trump-had-a-puzzling-answer-to-this-cbs-interview-question-about-a-basic-leadership-concept.

114. Zeeshan Aleem, "China Isn't the First Country to Flatter Its Way to Trump's Heart. It Won't Be the Last," Vox, November 8, 2017, https://www.vox.com/world/2017/11/8/16614136/trump-china-xi-jinping-asia-visit-flatter-honor.

115. Deena Zaru, "9 Celebrity Feuds of 2017, Starring Donald Trump," CNN, December

30, 2017, https://www.cnn.com/2017/12/30/politics/trump-celebrity-twitter-feuds-2017 /index.html.

116. Ibid.

117. Chris Cillizza, "The Definitive Rankings of Donald Trump's Nicknames for His Political Enemies," CNN, January 5, 2018, https://www.cnn.com/2018/01/05/politics /trump-nickname-rankings/index.html.

118. Jasmine C. Lee and Kevin Quealy, "The 426 People, Places and Things Donald Trump Has Insulted on Twitter: A Complete List," *The New York Times,* January 3, 2018, https://www.nytimes.com/interactive/2016/01/28/upshot/donald-trump-twitter -insults.html.

119. Ibid.; Cillizza, "The Definitive Rankings."

120. Lee and Quealy, "The 426 People, Places and Things."

121. Ibid.; Zaru, "9 Celebrity Feuds."

122. Madeline Conway, "In Awkward Exchange, Trump Seems to Ignore Merkel's Handshake Request," *Politico,* March 17, 2017, https://www.politico.com/story/2017 /03/trump-angela-merkel-no-handshake-236175; Jennifer Hassan, "'I'm Just Waiting for a Call from the White House with an Apology.' Britain's 'Wrong' Theresa May Speaks Out," *The Washington Post,* November 30, 2017, https://www.washingtonpost .com/news/worldviews/wp/2017/11/30/donald-trump-blasted-theresa-may-on -twitter-unfortunately-he-got-the-wrong-woman/; "Donald Trump Cancels February Visit to UK," BBC, January 12, 2018, http://www.bbc.com/news/uk-42657954.

123. Ryan Teague Beckwith, "Forget the Nuclear Button. Trump's Tweet Button Is the Real Threat," *Time,* January 3, 2018, http://time.com/5085979/donald-trump-nuke -button-nuclear-north-korea/.

124. Danielle Paquette, "Donald Trump Insulted a Union Leader on Twitter. Then the Phone Started to Ring," *The Washington Post,* December 7, 2016, https://www .washingtonpost.com/news/wonk/wp/2016/12/07/donald-trump-retaliated-against -a-union-leader-on-twitter-then-his-phone-started-to-ring; Andrew Joseph, "The LaVar Ball–Donald Trump Feud Was the Dumbest Sports Controversy of 2017," *USA Today,* December 19, 2017, http://ftw.usatoday.com/2017/12/lavar-ball-donald -trump-year-in-review-feud-big-baller-brand-controversy-twitter-ucla-2017.

125. Julia Manchester, "First Lady's Spokeswoman on Trump Attacking Brzezinski: 'He Will Punch Back 10 Times Harder,'" *The Hill,* June 29, 2017, http://thehill.com /homenews/administration/donald-trump-mika-brzezinski-attack-looks-melania -trump-cyberbulling.

126. Ben Schreckinger, "Trump Attacks McCain: 'I Like People Who Weren't Captured,'"

Politico, July 18, 2015, https://www.politico.com/story/2015/07/trump-attacks-mccain
-i-like-people-who-werent-captured-120317.

127. Ibid.

128. Ibid.

129. Ibid.

130. Ibid.

131. Ibid.

132. Katie Bo Williams, "Trump-Khan Feud: A Timeline," *The Hill,* August 1, 2016,
http://thehill.com/policy/national-security/290049-trump-khan-feud-a-timeline.

133. Ibid.

134. Ibid.

135. Ibid.

136. Ibid.; Fuller, "John McCain (Un)Endorses."

137. Lachlan Markay, Asawin Suebsaeng, and Sam Stein, "How Trump Created His
Sickest Self-Own," *The Daily Beast,* October 18, 2017, https://www.thedailybeast
.com/donald-trump-dug-himself-a-mighty-hole-on-the-deaths-of-us-soldiers-then
-he-kept-digging.

138. Ibid.

139. Ibid.

140. Ibid.

141. Ibid.

142. Ibid.

143. Lachlan Markay and Asawin Suebsaeng, "Donald Trump Feels Zero Remorse
Over How the Week Went, Friends and Allies Say," *The Daily Beast,* October 20,
2017, https://www.thedailybeast.com/donald-trump-feels-zero-remorse-over-how
-the-week-went-friends-and-allies-say.

144. Alana Horowitz Satlin, "Parkland Survivor: 'I've Never Been So Unimpressed by a
Person' After Trump Call," *Huff Post,* February 23, 2018, https://www.huffingtonpost
.com/entry/parkland-survivor-trump-unimpressed_us_5a8fc5f0e4b01e9e56ba318a.

145. Jason Kurtz, "Jake Tapper: Donald Trump Just 'Can't Quit' Hillary Clinton,"
CNN, January 10, 2018, https://www.cnn.com/2018/01/10/politics/donald-trump
-hillary-clinton-jake-tapper-the-lead-he-cant-quit-her-cnntv/index.html; Amy Davidson Sorkin, "Trump's Never-Ending Complaint about Hillary Clinton and the
F.B.I.," *The New Yorker,* January 11, 2018, https://www.newyorker.com/news/our
-columnists/trumps-never-ending-complaint-about-hillary-clinton-and-the-fbi.

146. Parkinson, "500 Days of Trump."

147. Ken Meyer, "Morning Joe on Why Trump Is 'So Obsessed' with Clinton: 'She Crushed Him,'" Mediaite, January 11, 2018, https://www.mediaite.com/tv/morning -joe-on-why-trump-is-so-obsessed-with-clinton-she-crushed-him/.

148. German Lopez, "Conway Said 'Nobody' at White House Talks About Clinton. These 75 Trump Tweets Say Otherwise," Vox, January 11, 2018, https://www.vox.com /policy-and-politics/2018/1/11/16878354/trump-white-house-clinton-kellyanne -conway; Gideon Resnick, "These Stats Prove Trump Is Still Obsessed with Hill-ary," The Daily Beast, January 16, 2018, https://www.thedailybeast.com/totally-not -obsessed-with-hillary-donald-trump-has-mentioned-her-hundreds-of-times-as -president; Lee and Quealy, "The 426 People, Places and Things."

149. Zack Schonfeld, "Every Time Trump Tweeted About Hillary Clinton During the First Year of His Presidency," Newsweek, January 19, 2018, http://www.newsweek.com /donald-trump-hillary-clinton-tweets-presidency-first-year-783843; Donald Trump (@realDonaldTrump), Twitter, September 13, 2017, 7:47 p.m. https://twitter.com /realdonaldtrump/status/908160218995068928.

150. Schonfeld, "Every Time Trump Tweeted"; Donald Trump (@realDonaldTrump), Twitter, November 3, 2017, 7:28 a.m., https://twitter.com/realDonaldTrump/status /926456069047582721.

151. Schonfeld, "Every Time Trump Tweeted"; Donald Trump (@realDonaldTrump), Twitter, January 11, 2018, 3:33 a.m., https://twitter.com/realDonaldTrump/status /951416674808467461.

152. Schonfeld, "Every Time Trump Tweeted"; Donald Trump (@realDonaldTrump), Twitter, March 27, 2017, 8:26 p.m., https://twitter.com/realDonaldTrump/status /846533818811080704; Donald Trump (@realDonaldTrump), Twitter, March 27, 2017, 8:35 p.m., https://twitter.com/realDonaldTrump/status/846536212362018816.

153. Lopez, "Conway Said 'Nobody.'"

154. Patrick Monahan (@pattymo), Twitter, December 8, 2017, 12:45 p.m., https://twitter .com/pattymo/status/939189181653405696.

155. Peter Baker, "Can Trump Destroy Obama's Legacy?," The New York Times, June 23, 2017, https://www.nytimes.com/2017/06/23/sunday-review/donald-trump-barack-obama .html; Daniel Halper, "Trump: 'I Inherited a Mess,'" New York Post, February 16, 2017, https://nypost.com/2017/02/16/trump-i-inherited-a-mess/.

156. Matthew Yglesias, "Last February, Trump Signed a Bill Making It Easier for People with Mental Illness to Buy Guns," Vox, February 15, 2018, https://www.vox.com /policy-and-politics/2018/2/15/17016036/trump-guns-mental-illness; Avery Anapol, "White House Refused to Release Photo of Trump Signing Bill Overturning

Obama Gun Rule: Report," *The Hill,* February 15, 2018, http://thehill.com/homenews
/administration/374133-white-house-refused-multiple-requests-to-release-photo-of
-trump.

157. Baker, "Can Trump Destroy Obama's Legacy?"

158. George F. Will, "Trump's Moore Endorsement Sunk the Presidency to Unplumbed
Depths," *The Washington Post,* December 13, 2017, https://www.washingtonpost
.com/opinions/trumps-moore-endorsement-sunk-the-presidency-to-unplumbed
-depths/2017/12/13/3c245482-e036-11e7-bbd0-9dfb2e37492a_story.html.

159. Charles Blow, "Trump—Chieftain of Spite," *The New York Times,* October 15, 2017,
https://www.nytimes.com/2017/10/15/opinion/columnists/trump-spite-obama-legacy
.html.

160. Ryan Sit, "Trump's Obsession with Obama and Clinton Even Extends to His Campaign Website's Error Messages," *Newsweek,* December 28, 2017, http://www.newsweek
.com/donald-trump-barack-obama-hillary-clinton-2016-election-coding-obsession
-golf-763109.

161. Ibid.; Jamiles Lartey, "Three TVs, a Phone and a Cheeseburger: Tell-All Book
Reveals Donald's Bedtime," *The Guardian,* January 4, 2018, https://www.theguardian
.com/us-news/2018/jan/04/donald-trump-white-house-domestic-life-cheeseburger.

162. Jen Hayden, *"Evangelical President Reportedly Complains that He Can't Watch Porn
Videos in the White House,"* Daily Kos, June 7, 2018, https://www.dailykos.com/stories
/2018/6/7/1770081/-Evangelical-president-reportedly-complains-that-he-can-t-watch
-porn-videos-in-the-White-House.

163. Kelly Swanson, "Trump: The White House Is a Real Dump," Vox, August 2, 2017,
https://www.vox.com/policy-and-politics/2017/8/2/16082988/trump-white-house
-dump; Trump Golf Count, http://trumpgolfcount.com/.

164. Allison Graves, John Kruzel, and Manuela Tobias, "Who Plays More Golf: Donald
Trump or Barack Obama?," PolitiFact, October 10, 2017, http://www.politifact.com
/truth-o-meter/article/2017/oct/10/who-plays-more-golf-donald-trump-or-barack
-obama/.

165. Trump Golf Count, https://www.trumpgolfcount.com/; Parkinson, "500 Days of
Trump."

166. Hayley Miller, "Past Presidents Volunteered on MLK Day. Donald Trump Is
Spending It at His Golf Club," *Huff Post,* January 15, 2018, https://www.huffingtonpost
.com/entry/donald-trump-mlk-day-golf_us_5a5cc0b2e4b03c418967bad2; Rossman,
"'He Went to Play Golf.'"

167. Bill Press, *Buyer's Remorse: How Obama and the Democrats Let Progressives Down*

(New York: Threshold, 2016), 15–16; Donald Trump(@realDonaldTrump), Twitter, September 19, 2012, 7:01 a.m., https://twitter.com/realDonaldTrump/status/248421632413147136; Ryan Sit, "Trump Told Obama to Golf with Republicans but He Hasn't Golfed with a Single Democratic Lawmaker," *Newsweek,* December 21, 2017, http://www.newsweek.com/donald-trump-golf-rounds-played-barack-obama-comparison-755588.

168. Dylan Dethier, "LPGA Star on Golf with Trump: 'He Cheats Like Hell,'" *Golf,* January 30, 2018, http://www.golf.com/tour-news/2018/01/30/president-trump-cheats-hell-golf-course-according-suzann-pettersen.

169. Ibid.

170. Hamblin, "Is Something Neurologically Wrong?"

171. Jamie Ducharme, "Donald Trump's Former Doctor Says Trump Dictated Letter That Claimed He'd Be 'Healthiest Individual Ever Elected,'" *Time,* May 11, 2018, http://time.com/5262611/harold-bornstein-donald-trump-doctor-letter/.

172. Wolff, "'You Can't Make This S— Up.'"

173. Charles Pierce, "Trump's *New York Times* Interview Is a Portrait of a Man in Cognitive Decline," *Esquire,* December 29, 2017, https://www.esquire.com/news-politics/politics/a14516912/donald-trump-new-york-times-michael-schmidt/.

174. Hamblin, "Is Something Neurologically Wrong?"

175. "Excerpts of Trump's Interview with the *New York Times,*" *New York Times,* December 28, 2017, https://www.nytimes.com/2017/12/28/us/politics/trump-interview-excerpts.html.

176. Ibid.

177. Ibid.

178. Hamblin, "Is Something Neurologically Wrong?"

179. Ibid.

180. Ibid.

181. Pierce, "Trump's *New York Times* Interview."

182. Jen Christiansen, "Did President Trump Slur His Speech?," CNN, December 7, 2017, https://www.cnn.com/2017/12/06/health/did-trump-slur-his-speech-bn/index.html; Graham Lanktree, "White House Solved Mystery of Donald Trump's Slurred Speech—And It Has Nothing to Do with His Teeth," *Newsweek,* December 7, 2017, http://www.newsweek.com/white-house-claims-have-solved-mystery-donald-trumps-slurred-speech-and-it-has-740829; Hannah Perry, "Fresh Dementia Concerns After Donald Trump Drinks Glass of Water with Two Hands," *Daily Mail,* December 20, 2017, http://www.nzherald.co.nz/world/news/article.cfm?c_id=2&objectid=11962973.

183. Laura Bradley, "Does Donald Trump Really Not Know the Words to the National Anthem?," *Vanity Fair,* January 10, 2018, https://www.vanityfair.com/hollywood/2018/01/donald-trump-national-anthem-late-night; "Morning Joe Hosts Mock Trump for Thanking John Cornyn and Then Immediately Forgetting," *The Week,* February 2, 2018, http://theweek.com/speedreads/752729/morning-joe-hosts-mock-trump-thanking-john-cornyn-immediately-forgetting. Ephrat Livni, "Watch Donald Trump Totally Forget the Name of SCOTUS Justice Anthony Kennedy," QZ, June 27, 2018, https://qz.com/1316345/watch-donald-trump-forget-the-name-of-scotus-justice-anthony-kennedy.

184. Terence Cullen, "Joe Scarborough Says His Sources Doubt Trump's Mental Fitness 'and It's Getting Worse,'" *New York Daily News,* January 8, 2018, http://www.nydailynews.com/news/politics/joe-scarborough-sources-doubt-trump-mental-fitness-article-1.3744401.

185. Josh Delk, "Trump Touts High Score on Cognitive Test," *The Hill,* January 17, 2018, http://thehill.com/blogs/blog-briefing-room/369426-trump-touts-high-scores-on-cognitive-test; Gina Kolata, "Trump Passed a Cognitive Exam. What Does That Really Mean?," January 19, 2018, *The New York Times,* https://www.nytimes.com/2018/01/19/health/trump-cognitive-screening-dementia.html.

186. Kate Taylor, "Donald Trump Jr.'s Wife Once Called Trump the R-Word After He Introduced Them Twice in One Night," *Business Insider,* March 15, 2018, http://www.businessinsider.com/donald-trump-jr-wife-vanessa-once-called-trump-retarded-2018-3; "Morning Joe Hosts Mock Trump."

187. Lee, *The Dangerous Case of Donald Trump;* Sunlan Serfaty and Ryan Nobles, "Yale Psychiatrist Briefed Members of Congress on Trump's Mental Fitness," CNN, January 5, 2018, https://www.cnn.com/2018/01/04/politics/psychiatrist-congress-meeting-trump/index.html.

188. James Gilligan, "The Issue Is Dangerousness, Not Mental Illness," in Lee, *The Dangerous Case of Donald Trump,* 170–180.

189. Serfaty and Nobles, "Yale Psychiatrist."

190. Rosemary K. M. Sword and Phillip Zimbardo, "The Dangerous Case of Donald Trump," *Psychology Today,* September 28, 2017, https://www.psychologytoday.com/blog/the-time-cure/201709/the-dangerous-case-donald-trump; Rosemary K. M. Sword and Phillip Zimbardo, "The Elephant in the Room," *Psychology Today,* February 28, 2017, https://www.psychologytoday.com/blog/the-time-cure/201702/the-elephant-in-the-room.

191. Serfaty and Nobles, "Yale Psychiatrist"; Hamblin, "Is Something Neurologically Wrong?"

192. Ibid.; John Bowden, "More Dems Sign On to Bill to Impeach Trump," *The Hill,* July 1, 2017, http://thehill.com/homenews/administration/340392-more-dems-sign-onto-bill-to-impeach-trump.

193. Sword and Zimbardo, "The Elephant in the Room."

2: TRUMP'S DISASTROUS ACTS AS PRESIDENT

1. Jordan Fabian, "Trump Says He's Accomplished More Than Anyone but FDR in Six Months," *The Hill,* June 12, 2017, http://thehill.com/homenews/administration/337421-trump-says-hes-accomplished-more-than-anyone-but-fdr-in-six-months; Lauren Gill, "Trump Has Signed Fewest Bills into Law of Any Modern President, Research Shows," *Newsweek,* December 21, 2017, http://www.newsweek.com/trump-has-signed-fewer-bills-law-any-modern-president-research-shows-756111.

2. Gregory Krieg, "Trump's History of Anti-Muslim Rhetoric Hits Dangerous New Low," CNN, November 30, 2017, https://www.cnn.com/2017/11/29/politics/donald-trump-muslim-attacks/index.html.

3. Jenna Johnson, "Trump Calls for 'Total and Complete Shutdown of Muslims Entering the United States,'" *The Washington Post,* December 7, 2015, https://www.washingtonpost.com/news/post-politics/wp/2015/12/07/donald-trump-calls-for-total-and-complete-shutdown-of-muslims-entering-the-united-states.

4. Jaweed Kaleem, "From 'See You in Court!' to the Supreme Court: Who's Up and Down in the History of Trump's Travel Ban," *Los Angeles Times,* December 5, 2017, http://www.latimes.com/nation/immigration/la-na-travel-ban-history-2017-htmlstory.html.

5. Ibid.

6. Ibid.

7. Ibid.

8. Mark Sherman, "Supreme Court Upholds Trump Travel Ban," AP, June 26, 2018, https://www.apnews.com/3a20abe305bd4c989116f82bf535393b.

9. Ana Campoy, "Trump's Tweets Have Sunk His Own Travel Ban—Again," Quartz, October 18, 2017, https://qz.com/1105690/travel-ban-a-maryland-federal-judge-cited-trumps-tweets-as-evidence-to-block/; Amrit Chan, "Trump's Lawyers Say the Muslim Ban Has No Bias, but His Tweets Show Otherwise," ACLU, November 30, 2017, https://www.aclu.org/blog/immigrants-rights/trumps-lawyers-say-muslim-ban-has-no-bias-his-tweets-show-otherwise.

10. Campoy, "Trump's Tweets Have Sunk."

11. Ibid.

12. Ibid.

13. Katie Reilly, "President Trump Praises Fake Story About Shooting Muslims with Pig's Blood-Soaked Bullets," *Time,* August 17, 2017, http://time.com/4905420/donald -trump-pershing-pigs-blood-muslim-tweet/; Matt Zapotosky, "Trump's Tweets Could Again Complicate," *The Washington Post,* November 29, 2017, https://www.washingtonpost .com/news/post-nation/wp/2017/11/29/thanks-see-you-in-court-trumps-tweets-could -again-complicate-effort-to-defend-travel-ban/.

14. Ariane de Vogue, "Judges in Travel Ban Case Concerned About Trump Tweets," CNN, December 8, 2017, https://www.cnn.com/2017/12/08/politics/travel-ban-trump -tweets/index.html; Zapotosky, "Trump's Tweets Could Again."

15. Chris Sommerfeldt, "President Trump's Muslim Ban Excludes Countries Linked to His Sprawling Business Empire," *New York Daily News,* February 1, 2018, http:// www.nydailynews.com/news/politics/trump-muslim-ban-excludes-countries -linked-businesses-article-1.2957956.

16. Ibid.

17. Ibid.

18. Ryan Grim and Alex Emmons, "How Sudan Got Off Donald Trump's Latest Travel Ban List," *The Intercept,* September 25, 2017, https://theintercept.com/2017/09 /25/sudan-trump-travel-ban-uae-yemen/.

19. Jordan Fabian, "Trump Says He Has 'Great Love' for Dreamers," September 5, 2017, http://thehill.com/homenews/administration/349295-trump-says-he-has-great-love -for-dreamers.

20. Amanda Holpuch, "Dreamers React to Trump's DACA Dispute: 'We Feel Like Bargaining Chips,'" *The Guardian,* January 11, 2018, https://www.theguardian.com /us-news/2018/jan/11/confusion-over-fate-of-daca-leaves-dreamers-in-limbo.

21. Ibid.

22. Gregory Korte, Alan Gomez, and Kevin Johnson, "Trump Administration Struggles with Fate of 900 DREAMers Serving in the Military," *USA Today,* September 7, 2017, https://www.usatoday.com/story/news/politics/2017/09/07/trump-administration -struggles-fate-900-dreamers-serving-military/640637001/.

23. Scott Clement and David Nakamura, "Survey Finds Strong Support for 'Dream- ers,'" *The Washington Post,* September 25, 2017, https://www.washingtonpost.com/pol itics/survey-finds-strong-support-for-dreamers/2017/09/24/df3c885c-a16f-11e7-b14f -f41773cd5a14_story.html; Max Greenwood, "Poll: Nearly 9 in 10 Want DACA Recipients to Stay in US," *The Hill,* January 8, 2018, http://thehill.com/blogs/blog

-briefing-room/news/369487-poll-nearly-nine-in-10-favor-allowing-daca-recipients-to-stay.

24. Sara Wise, "Trump's DACA Flip-Flops: A Timeline," Roll Call, January 30, 2018, https://www.rollcall.com/news/politics/tracking-trumps-daca-flip-flops; Miriam Valverde, "Timeline: DACA, the Trump Administration and a Government Shutdown," PolitiFact, January 22, 2018, http://www.politifact.com/truth-o-meter/article/2018/jan/22/timeline-daca-trump-administration-and-government-/.

25. Valverde, "Timeline: DACA."

26. Ibid.; Holpuch, "Dreamers React."

27. Valverde, "Timeline: DACA."

28. Ibid.

29. Ibid.

30. Tal Kopan, "A Timeline of DACA Offers Trump Has Rejected," CNN, March 23, 2018, https://www.cnn.com/2018/03/23/politics/daca-rejected-deals-trump/index.html.

31. Alan Gomez and David Agren, "First Protected DREAMer Is Deported Under Trump," *USA Today,* April 18, 2017, https://www.usatoday.com/story/news/world/2017/04/18/first-protected-dreamer-deported-under-trump/100583274/.

32. Eric Levitz, "Paul Ryan Scrambles to Block Vote on DREAM Act," *New York,* May 17, 2018, http://nymag.com/daily/intelligencer/2018/05/paul-ryan-scrambles-to-block-discharge-petition-on-dreamers.html.

33. Holpuch, "Dreamers React"; Dylan Scott, "The Senate Put 4 Immigration Bills Up for a Vote. They All Failed," Vox, February 15, 2018, https://www.vox.com/policy-and-politics/2018/2/15/17017682/senate-immigration-daca-bill-vote-failed; Dara Lind, "DREAMers Are at Risk Because of Donald Trump. Period," Vox, February 16, 2018, https://www.vox.com/policy-and-politics/2018/2/16/17017908/immigration-congress-fault-daca.

34. Emma Lazarus, "The New Colossus," quoted in Walt Hunter, "The Story Behind the Poem on the Statue of Liberty," *The Atlantic,* January 16, 2018, https://www.theatlantic.com/entertainment/archive/2018/01/the-story-behind-the-poem-on-the-statue-of-liberty/550553/.

35. Miriam Jordan, "Trump Administration Says That Nearly 200,000 Salvadorans Must Leave," *The New York Times,* January 8, 2018, https://www.nytimes.com/2018/01/08/us/salvadorans-tps-end.html.

36. Ibid.; Tal Kopan, "DHS Ends Protections for Nearly 90,000 Central Americans," CNN, May 6, 2018, https://www.cnn.com/2018/05/04/politics/immigration-tps-honduras/index.html.

37. Kopan, "DHS Ends Protections"; Kathryn Johnson, "Trump Has Ended Temporary Protected Status for Hundreds of Thousands of Immigrants. Here's What You Need to Know," American Friends Service Committee, May 4, 2018, https://www.afsc.org/blogs/news-and-commentary/trump-has-ended-temporary-protected-status-hundreds-thousands-immigrants.

38. "'Temporary' Status But Long-Term US Lives," Human Rights Watch, April 4, 2018, https://www.hrw.org/news/2018/04/04/temporary-status-long-term-us-lives.

39. Miriam Jordan, "Trump Administration Ends Temporary Protection for Haitians," *The New York Times,* November 20, 2017, https://www.nytimes.com/2017/11/20/us/haitians-temporary-status.html.

40. Jordan, "Trump Administration"; Raymond Bonner, "America's Role in El Salvador's Deterioration," *The Atlantic,* January 20, 2018, https://www.theatlantic.com/international/archive/2018/01/trump-and-el-salvador/550955/.

41. Jordan, "Trump Administration"; Ted Hesson, Seung Min Kim, and Heather Caygle, "Trump to End Protected Status for Salvadorans," *Politico,* January 8, 2018, https://www.politico.com/story/2018/01/08/trump-end-salvadorans-protected-status-327570.

42. Jordan, "Trump Administration"; Micaela Sviatschi, "By Deporting 200,000 Salvadorans, Trump May Be Boosting Gang Recruitment," *The Washington Post,* February 12, 2018, https://www.washingtonpost.com/news/monkey-cage/wp/2018/02/12/by-deporting-200000-salvadorans-trump-may-be-boosting-gang-recruitment.

43. Nick Miroff, "9,000 Nepalis Face Deportation as Trump Administration Prepares to Cancel Residency Permits," *The Washington Post,* April 25, 2018, https://www.washingtonpost.com/world/national-security/9000-nepalis-face-deportation-as-trump-administration-prepares-to-cancel-residency-permits/2018/04/24/e6cd7594-4800-11e8-9072-f6d4bc32f223_story.html; Kopan, "DHS Ends Protections."

44. Mark Joseph Stern, "Domestic Abuse Victims Need Not Apply," Slate, March 13, 2018, https://slate.com/news-and-politics/2018/03/jeff-sessions-looks-poised-to-bar-domestic-abuse-victims-from-getting-asylum-in-america.html; Natasha Lennard, "The Misogynistic Logic of Jeff Sessions's Horrifying New Asylum Policy for Domestic Violence Victims," *The Intercept,* June 15, 2018, https://theintercept.com/2018/06/15/domestic-violence-asylum-jeff-sessions/.

45. Serena Marshall, "Obama Has Deported More People Than Any Other President," ABC News, August 29, 2016, http://abcnews.go.com/Politics/obamas-deportation-policy-numbers/story?id=41715661; Nick Miroff and Maria Sacchetti, "ICE Arrests of 'Noncriminal' Immigrants Double Under Trump," *The Washington Post,* February 12, 2018, https://www.mercurynews.com/2018/02/12/trump-takes

-shackles-off-ice-which-is-slapping-them-on-immigrants-who-thought-they-were-safe/.

46. Miroff and Sacchetti, "ICE Arrests of 'Noncriminal' Immigrants"; Alastair Boone and Tanvi Misra, "Immigration Raids, Coming to a Store Near You," CityLab, January 18, 2018, https://www.citylab.com/equity/2018/01/immigration-raids-coming-to-a-store-near-you/550289/.

47. Miroff and Sacchetti, "ICE Arrests of 'Noncriminal' Immigrants."

48. Brian Tashman, "Congress Needs to Hold ICE Accountable for Abuses," ACLU, February 2, 2018, https://www.aclu.org/blog/immigrants-rights/ice-and-border-patrol-abuses/congress-needs-hold-ice-accountable-abuses.

49. Tania Unzuetta Carrasco, "Trump Is Going After Immigration Activists Like Me. Will You Be Next?," *USA Today,* February 7, 2018, https://www.usatoday.com/story/opinion/2018/02/07/trumps-ice-going-after-immigration-activists-like-me-whos-next-tania-unzueta-carrasco-column/1080396001/.

50. Kate Mettler, "'This Is Really Unprecedented': ICE Detains Woman Seeking Domestic Abuse Protection at Texas Courthouse," *The Washington Post,* February 16, 2017, https://www.washingtonpost.com/news/morning-mix/wp/2017/02/16/this-is-really-unprecedented-ice-detains-woman-seeking-domestic-abuse-protection-at-texas-courthouse.

51. Lizzy Acker, "Watch ICE Agents Arrest Man After Entering Portland Home Without Warrant," *Oregonian,* October 20, 2017, http://www.oregonlive.com/portland/index.ssf/2017/10/watch_ice_agents_arrest_man_af.html.

52. Maryam Saleh, "Excessive Force: ICE Shackled 92 Somalis for 40 Hours on a Failed Deportation Flight. That Was Just the Start of the Abuse," *The Intercept,* March 4, 2018, https://theintercept.com/2018/03/04/somali-deportation-flight-ice-detention-center/.

53. Clio Chang, "ICE Allegedly Puts Woman in Solitary Confinement to Get Her to Recant Claims of Sexual Assault," Splinter News, February 14, 2018, https://splinternews.com/ice-allegedly-puts-woman-in-solitary-confinement-to-get-1822993354; John Washington, "ICE Wants to Destroy Its Records of In-Custody Deaths, Sexual Assault, and Other Detainee Files," *The Nation,* September 13, 2017, https://www.thenation.com/article/ice-wants-to-destroy-its-records-of-in-custody-deaths-sexual-assault-and-other-detainee-files/.

54. Robin Urevich, "Deadly Detention: Why Are Immigrants Dying in ICE Custody?," Capital and Main, December 20, 2017, https://capitalandmain.com/deadly-detention-why-are-immigrants-dying-in-ice-custody-1220.

55. Cindy Carcamo, "ICE Launches New Immigration Sweep in L.A. Area; At Least

100 Detained So Far," *Los Angeles Times,* February 14, 2018, http://www.latimes
.com/local/california/la-me-ice-raids-20180213-story.html.

56. Megan Flynn and Avi Selk, "ICE Spokesman Resigns, Citing Fabrications by
Agency Chief, Sessions About California Immigrant Arrests," *The Washington Post,*
March 13, 2018, https://www.washingtonpost.com/news/morning-mix/wp/2018/03
/13/ice-spokesman-resigns-over-false-statements-by-top-officials-about-calif
-immigrant-arrests.

57. Dara Lind, "The Trump Administration's Separation of Families at the Border, Explained," Vox, June 15, 2018, https://www.vox.com/2018/6/11/17443198/children
-immigrant-families-separated-parents.

58. Ibid.; Philip Bump, "Why the Trump Administration Bears the Blame for Separating Children from their Families at the Border," *The Washington Post,* June 15,
2018, https://www.washingtonpost.com/news/politics/wp/2018/06/15/why-the-trump
-administration-bears-the-blame-for-separating-children-from-their-families-at-the
-border/. Adam Edelman, "Trump Says He Won't Sign GOP Immigration Bill that
Would Stop Separating Families at Border," NBC News, June 15, 2018, https://www
.nbcnews.com/politics/immigration/trump-says-he-won-t-sign-gop-immigration
-bill-would-n883526.

59. Laura Bush, "Laura Bush: Separating Children from Their Parents at the Border
'Breaks My Heart'," *The Washington Post,* June 17, 2018, https://www.washingtonpost
.com/opinions/laura-bush-separating-children-from-their-parents-at-the-border
-breaks-my-heart/2018/06/17/f2df517a-7287-11e8-9780-b1dd6a09b549_story.html.

60. Michael E. Miller, Emma Brown and Aaron C. Davis, "Inside Casa Padre, the con-
verted Walmart where the U.S. is holding nearly 1,500 immigrant children," *The
Washington Post,* June 14, 2018, https://www.washingtonpost.com/local/inside-casa
-padre-the-converted-walmart-where-the-us-is-holding-nearly-1500-immigrant
-children/2018/06/14/0cd65ce4-6eba-11e8-bd50-b80389a4e569_story.html; Jacob
Soboroff, Courtney Kube, and Julia Ainsley, "Administration Will House Migrant
Kids in Tents in Tornillo, Texas," NBC News, June 14, 2018, https://www.nbcnews
.com/politics/immigration/trump-admin-will-house-migrant-kids-tents-tornillo
-texas-n883281.

61. Abby Vesoulis, "Here's the Constitutional Problem With Trump's Call to Deport
Immigrants Without Seeing Judges," *Time,* June 25, 2018, http://time.com/5321318
/donald-trump-immigration-due-process/.

62. Jared McBride, "The Next Time ICE Rounds Up Workers, Remember That We
Didn't Do the Same with Nazi-Era War Criminals," *Los Angeles Times,* February 4,

2018, http://www.latimes.com/opinion/op-ed/la-oe-mcbride-nazi-immigrants-in-america-20180204-story.html.

63. Ron Nixon and Linda Qui, "Trump's Evolving Words on the Wall," *The New York Times,* January 18, 2018, https://www.nytimes.com/2018/01/18/us/politics/trump-border-wall-immigration.html.

64. "Everything We Know About Donald Trump's Proposed Border Wall," *Fortune,* January 19, 2018, http://fortune.com/2018/01/19/donald-trump-border-wall/.

65. Jorge Ramos, "Donald Trump's Wall Is Totally Useless," *Time,* January 28, 2017, http://time.com/4652648/jorge-ramos-donald-trump-wall-useless/.

66. Ibid.

67. Michael Dear, "5 Problems the Wall Won't Solve," *Politico,* February 28, 2017, https://www.politico.com/magazine/story/2017/02/trump-wall-mexico-problems-immigration-214837.

68. Ariane de Vogue and Joan Biskupic, "How the Trump White House and GOP Senators Fast-Track Judicial Nominees," CNN, December 15, 2017, https://www.cnn.com/2017/12/15/politics/trump-judges-nominees/index.html.

69. Shira A. Scheindlin, "Trump's New Team of Judges Will Radically Change American Society," *The Guardian,* November 30, 2017, https://www.theguardian.com/commentisfree/2017/nov/30/donald-trump-legacy-judiciary.

70. Rebecca Savransky, "80 of Trump's First 87 Judicial Nominees Are White," *The Hill,* February 13, 2018, http://thehill.com/homenews/administration/373676-80-of-trumps-first-87-judicial-nominees-are-white.

71. Jennifer Bendery, "Donald Trump Renominates Court Picks Rated 'Not Qualified' to Serve," *HuffPost,* January 8, 2018, https://www.huffingtonpost.com/entry/donald-trump-judicial-nominees-not-qualified_us_5a4fc2cae4b01e1a4b14e51d.; Philip Bump, "How Unusual Are Trump's 'Not Qualified' Judicial Nominations?," *Washington Post,* December 15, 2017, https://www.washingtonpost.com/news/politics/wp/2017/11/10/how-unusual-are-trumps-not-qualified-judicial-nominations/.

72. Bump, "How Unusual"; Aaron Blake, "That Painful Exchange Between a Trump Judicial Pick and a GOP Senator, Annotated," *The Washington Post*, December 15, 2017, https://www.washingtonpost.com/news/the-fix/wp/2017/12/15/that-painful-exchange-between-a-trump-judicial-pick-and-a-gop-senator-annotated/.

73. De Vogue and Biskupic, "How the Trump White House."

74. Seung Min Kim, "Trump's Judge Picks: 'Not Qualified,' Prolific Bloggers," *Politico,* October 17, 2017, https://www.politico.com/story/2017/10/17/trump-judges-nominees-court-picks-243834; Harsh Voruganti, "Judge Charles Barnes Goodwin—Nominee

to the U.S. District Court for the Western District of Oklahoma," Vetting Room, December 12, 2017, https://vettingroom.org/2017/12/12/judge-charles-goodwin/; Bendery, "Donald Trump Renominates."

75. Kim, "Trump's Judge Picks"; Bendery, "Donald Trump Renominates."

76. Zoe Tillman, "One of Trump's Judicial Nominees Once Wrote That Diversity Is 'Code for Relaxed Standards,'" BuzzFeed, February 15, 2018, https://www.buzzfeed .com/zoetillman/one-of-trumps-judicial-nominees-once-wrote-that-diversity.

77. Bendery, "Donald Trump Renominates."

78. Jennifer Bendery, "Senate Advances Judicial Nominee Who Can't Say if Racial Bias Exists in the Justice System," *Huff Post,* February 15, 2018, https://www.huffingtonpost .com/entry/michael-brennan-trump-judicial-nominee_us_5a85dc8ae4b00bc49f4212ad.

79. Jordain Carney, "Senate Confirms Trump Judicial Pick Over Objections of Home-State Senator," *The Hill,* May 10, 2018, http://thehill.com/homenews/senate/387129 -senate-confirms-trump-judicial-pick-over-objections-of-home-state-senator; David Dayen, "Trump's Judicial Picks Are Keeping Republicans Happy—and Quiet," *New Republic,* June 9, 2017, https://newrepublic.com/article/143227/trumps -judicial-picks-keeping-republicans-happyand-quiet.

80. Bruce Bartlett, "First, Republicans Want Tax Cuts. Next, They'll Try Gutting Medicare and Social Security," *The Washington Post,* November 16, 2017, https://www .washingtonpost.com/news/posteverything/wp/2017/11/16/first-republicans-want -tax-cuts-next-theyll-try-gutting-medicare-and-social-security; Julian Zelizer, "Blowing Up the Deficit Is Part of the Plan," *The Atlantic,* December 19, 2017, https://www .theatlantic.com/politics/archive/2017/12/blowing-up-the-deficit-is-part-of-the-plan /548720/.

81. Zelizer, "Blowing Up the Deficit."

82. Richard Cowan and Susan Cornwall, "House Speaker Ryan to Quit, Shaking Republicans as Elections Near," Reuters, April 11, 2018, https://www.reuters.com/article/us -usa-congress-ryan/house-speaker-ryan-to-quit-shaking-republicans-as-elections -near-idUSKBN1HI1TE.

83. Jonathan O'Connell, David A. Fahrenthold, and Jack Gillum, "As the 'King of Debt,' Trump Borrowed to Build His Empire. Then He Began Spending Hundreds of Millions in Cash," *The Washington Post,* May 5, 2018, https://www.washingtonpost .com/politics/as-the-king-of-debt-trump-borrowed-to-build-his-empire-then-he -began-spending-hundreds-of-millions-in-cash/2018/05/05/28fe54b4-44c4-11e8 -8569-26fda6b404c7_story.html; Linda Qui, "Yep, Donald Trump's Companies Have Declared Bankruptcy . . . More Than Four Times," PolitiFact, June 21, 2016,

http://www.politifact.com/truth-o-meter/statements/2016/jun/21/hillary-clinton /yep-donald-trumps-companies-have-declared-bankrupt/; Aaron Blake, "Trump Won't Even Try to Balance the Budget Anymore—Thereby Breaking Oodles of Campaign Promises," *The Washington Post,* February 12, 2018, https://www .washingtonpost.com/news/the-fix/wp/2018/02/12/trump-wont-even-try-to-balance -the-budget-anymore-thereby-breaking-oodles-of-campaign-promises/.

84. Blake, "Trump Won't Even Try."

85. Ibid.

86. Stephanie Kelton, "How We Think About the Deficit Is Mostly Wrong," *The New York Times,* October 5, 2017, https://www.nytimes.com/2017/10/05/opinion/deficit-tax-cuts -trump.html; Lisa Mascaro, "'Deficit' No Longer a Dirty Word for the GOP: Trump's Tax Plan Adds More Than $2 Trillion in Red Ink," *Los Angeles Times,* October 5, 2017, http://www.latimes.com/politics/la-na-pol-gop-taxplan-20171005-story.html.

87. Jordain Carney, "CBO: Senate Tax Plan Increases Deficit by $1.4 Trillion," *The Hill,* December 2, 2017, http://thehill.com/blogs/floor-action/senate/362905-cbo -senate-tax-bill-increases-deficit-by-14-trillion.

88. Richard Cowan and Amanda Becker, "U.S. Senate Leaders Reach $300 Billion Federal Spending Deal," Reuters, February 7, 2018, https://www.reuters.com/article /legal-us-usa-congress-shutdown/u-s-senate-leaders-reach-300-billion-federal -spending-deal-idUSKBN1FS0AY.

89. Yuval Rosenberg, "The Trump Budget's $7.1 Trillion Hole," *Fiscal Times,* February 12, 2018, http://www.thefiscaltimes.com/2018/02/12/Trump-Budgets-71-Trillion-Hole; Brooks Jackson, "Trump's 'Deficit Reduction,'" FactCheck, February 14, 2018, https://www.factcheck.org/2018/02/trumps-deficit-reduction/.

90. Louis Nelson, "Trump: 'I'm the King of Debt,'" *Politico,* June 22, 2016, https:// www.politico.com/story/2016/06/trump-king-of-debt-224642.

91. Zoë Carpenter, "Obama: Inequality Is 'the Defining Challenge of Our Time,'" *The Nation,* December 4, 2013, https://www.thenation.com/article/obama-inequality -defining-challenge-our-time/; Pope Francis (@Pontifex), Twitter, April 28, 2014, 4:28 a.m., https://twitter.com/pontifex/status/460697074585980928; Larry Elliott and Graeme Warden, "Justin Trudeau Tells Davos: Tackle Inequality or Risk Failure," *The Guardian,* January 23, 2018, https://www.theguardian.com/business/2018/jan /23/justin-trudeau-tells-davos-tackle-inequality-or-risk-failure; Dylan Scott, "The Republican Tax Bill Is a Disaster for Income Inequality," Vox, December 20, 2017, https://www.vox.com/policy-and-politics/2017/12/20/16790606/gop-tax-vote-2017 -income-inequality.

92. Scott, "The Republican Tax Bill."

93. Ibid.; Damian Paletta, "Trump Could Personally Benefit from Last-Minute Change to Senate Tax Bill," *The Washington Post,* November 27, 2017, https://www.washingtonpost.com/news/business/wp/2017/11/27/trump-could-personally-benefit-from-last-minute-change-to-senate-tax-bill.

94. Scott, "The Republican Tax Bill."

95. Ibid.

96. John Cassidy, "The Final G.O.P. Tax Bill Is a Recipe for Even More Inequality," *The New Yorker,* December 14, 2017, https://www.newyorker.com/news/our-columnists/the-final-gop-tax-bill-is-a-recipe-for-even-more-inequality.

97. Ibid.

98. Charles Ballard, "Many of Trump's Policies Will Further Intensify Income Inequality," *The Hill,* February 10, 2017, http://thehill.com/blogs/pundits-blog/economy-budget/318941-many-of-trumps-policies-will-further-intensify-income.

99. Ibid.

100. David Graham, "'As I Have Always Said': Trump's Ever-Changing Positions on Health Care," *The Atlantic,* July 28, 2017, https://www.theatlantic.com/politics/archive/2017/07/as-i-have-always-said-trumps-ever-changing-position-on-health-care/535293/.

101. Matthew Nussbaum, "Agitated Trump Lashes Out at McConnell, Ryan, Obama, Clapper, Media," *Politico,* August 24, 2017, https://www.politico.com/story/2017/08/24/trump-twitter-storm-attacks-241983.

102. Rachel Roubein, "TIMELINE: The GOP's Failed Effort to Repeal ObamaCare," *The Hill,* September 26, 2017, http://thehill.com/policy/healthcare/other/352587-timeline-the-gop-effort-to-repeal-and-replace-obamacare.

103. Ibid.

104. Ibid.

105. Ibid.; Asawin Suebsaeng, Gideon Resnick, and Sam Stein, "A 'Suicide' Mission: White House and GOP Leadership Fear New Obamacare Repeal Push," *The Daily Beast,* June 5, 2018, https://www.thedailybeast.com/a-suicide-mission-white-house-and-gop-leadership-fear-new-obamacare-repeal-push.

106. Sarah Kliff, "Trump Is Slashing Obamacare's Advertising Budget by 90%," Vox, August 31, 2017, https://www.vox.com/2017/8/31/16236280/trump-obamacare-outreach-ads; Paul Demko and Rachada Pramkan, "Trump's War of Attrition Against Obamacare," *Politico,* July 21, 2017, https://www.politico.com/story/2017/07/21/trumps-war-of-attrition-against-obamacare-240777.

107. Larry Levitt, "The Trump Administration's Hidden Attacks on the Affordable Care Act," *the Washington Post,* January 5, 2018, https://www.washingtonpost.com/opinions /the-trump-administrations-hidden-attacks-on-the-affordable-care-act/2018/01/05 /bd7002da-f237-11e7-97bf-bba379b809ab_story.html; Catherine Rampell, "Trump's Obamacare Order Could Destroy the Health Care System," *The Washington Post,* October 12, 2017, https://www.washingtonpost.com/opinions/trumps-obamacare -order-could-destroy-the-health-care-system/2017/10/12/9660da88-af8a-11e7-be94 -fabb0f1e9ffb_story.html; Carolyn Johnson, "Trump Scrapped a Key Obamacare Payment. Here's What Comes Next," *The Washington Post,* October 13, 2017, https:// www.washingtonpost.com/news/wonk/wp/2017/10/13/how-trumps-big-health -care-decision-could-play-out/?utm_term=.dad8f45d6c6e.

108. Paige Winfield Cunningham, "The Health 202: A Eulogy for the Individual Man- date," *The Washington Post,* December 21, 2017, https://www.washingtonpost.com /news/powerpost/paloma/the-health-202/2017/12/21/the-health-202-a-eulogy-for -the-individual-mandate/5a3a94d430fb0469e883fd24/.

109. Ibid.

110. Dan Mangan, "3 Obamacare Taxes, Including One on Higher-Value Plans, Are Suspended in Deal to End Shutdown," CNBC, January 23, 2018, https://www.cnbc .com/2018/01/23/obamacare-taxes-were-suspended-in-deal-to-end-government -shutdown.html.

111. Matt Novak, "Trump Regime Says Obamacare Shouldn't Protect People with Pre- Existing Medical Conditions," Gizmodo, June 8, 2018, https://gizmodo.com/trump -regime-says-obamacare-shouldnt-protect-people-wit-1826662463.

112. Levitt, "The Trump Administration's Hidden Attacks"; Ezra Klein, "Poll: Re- publicans Hate 'Obamacare,' but Like Most of What It Does," *The Washington Post,* June 26, 2012, https://www.washingtonpost.com/news/wonk/wp/2012/06/26 /poll-republicans-hate-obamacare-but-like-most-of-what-it-does/.

113. Dylan Scott, "Children's Health Insurance Has Become a Political Hostage," Vox, January 19, 2018, https://www.vox.com/policy-and-politics/2018/1/18/16901526/congress -chip-crisis.

114. Ibid.

115. Natalie Schreyer, "The Trump Files: When Donald Took Revenge by Cutting Off Health Coverage for a Sick Infant," *Mother Jones,* August 25, 2016, https://www .motherjones.com/politics/2016/08/trump-files-donald-sick-infant-medical-care/.

116. Donald Trump (@realDonaldTrump), Twitter, May 15, 2015, 8:38 a.m., https:// twitter.com/realDonaldTrump/status/596338364187602944.

117. Ryan Koronowski, "Trump's Budget Cuts Medicare, Medicaid, and Social Security, Breaking Core Campaign Promise," ThinkProgress, February 12, 2018, https://thinkprogress.org/trump-promises-cuts-medicare-medicaid-social-security -36a0e8a57ae0/.

118. Ibid.; Margarida Jorge and Ethan Rome, "Seniors Will Pay the Price for Trump's Medicare Cuts," Marketwatch, February 18, 2018, https://www.marketwatch.com /story/seniors-will-pay-the-price-for-trumps-medicare-cuts-2018-02-14.

119. Koronowski, "Trump's Budget Cuts Medicare."

120. Ibid.

121. David Dayen, "The Biggest Trojan Horse in the Republican Tax Plan," *The New Republic,* November 7, 2017, https://newrepublic.com/article/145688/biggest-trojan -horse-republican-tax-plan; Sean Williams, "The 1 GOP Tax Provision Social Security Recipients Must Be Aware Of," Motley Fool, December 18, 2017, https://www.fool .com/retirement/2017/12/18/the-1-gop-tax-provision-social-security-recipients.aspx.

122. Dylan Scott, "The Trump Administration's Plan for Medicaid Work Requirements, Explained," Vox, January 12, 2018, https://www.vox.com/policy-and-politics/2018/1 /11/16877916/medicaid-work-requirements-trump-guidance.

123. Ibid.

124. Ibid.; Adam K. Raymond, "Michigan's Proposed Medicaid Work Requirement Comes with a Racist Twist," *New York,* May 3, 2018, http://nymag.com/daily /intelligencer/2018/05/michigans-medicaid-work-requirement-comes-with-racist -twist.html.

125. Addy Baird, "Trump Administration to Allow Lifetime Limits on Medicaid, Coverage for Thousands at Risk," ThinkProgress, February 6, 2018, https://thinkprogress .org/trump-medicaid-lifetime-coverage-70965a6cab92/.

126. Phil Galewitz, "Trump Officials Say No to Lifetime Limits on Medicaid," CNN, May 5, 2018, http://money.cnn.com/2018/05/08/news/economy/lifetime-limits -medicaid/index.html.

127. David Emery, "Read His Lips," Snopes, December 10, 2016, https://www.snopes.com /fact-check/trump-social-security/.

128. Glenn Thrush, "Trump's 'Harvest Box' Isn't Viable in SNAP Overhaul, Officials Say," *The New York Times,* February 13, 2018, https://www.nytimes.com/2018/02/13 /us/harvest-box-snap-food-stamps.html; Ryan Teague Beckwith, "Donald Trump Railed About a 'Food Stamp Crime Wave' in 2011. Now He Wants to Cut SNAP," *Time,* February 13, 2018, http://time.com/5155778/donald-trump-food-stamps -cuts/; "93 Percent of Federal SNAP Spending Is for Food," Center for Budget and

Policy Priorities, https://www.cbpp.org/93-percent-of-federal-snap-spending-is-for-food-0.

129. Sasha Abramsky, "'America's Harvest Box' Captures the Trumpian Attitude Toward Poverty," *The New Yorker,* February 14, 2018, https://www.newyorker.com/business/currency/americas-harvest-box-captures-the-trumpian-attitude-toward-poverty.

130. Beckwith, "Donald Trump Railed."

131. Ibid.

132. Ibid.; Thrush, "Trump's 'Harvest Box.'" Abramsky, "'America's Harvest Box.'"

133. Sharon Parrott, Aviva Aron-Dine, Dottie Rosenbaum, Douglas Rice, Ife Floyd, and Kathleen Romig, "Trump Budget Deeply Cuts Health, Housing, Other Assistance for Low- and Moderate-Income Families," Center on Budget and Policy Priorities February 14, 2018, https://www.cbpp.org/research/federal-budget/trump-budget-deeply-cuts-health-housing-other-assistance-for-low-and.

134. Terry M. Neal and Juliet Eiperin, "Bush Faults House GOP Spending Plan," *The Washington Post,* October 1, 1999, https://www.washingtonpost.com/wp-srv/politics/campaigns/wh2000/stories/congress100199.htm.

135. Maggie Haberman, "Donald Trump's More Accepting Views Set Him Apart in G.O.P," April 23, 2016, https://www.nytimes.com/2016/04/23/us/politics/donald-trump-gay-rights.html; "Timeline: Key Dates in President Trump's Relationship with the LGBT Community," *The Boston Globe,* January 16, 2018.

136. "Timeline: Key Dates in President Trump's Relationship."

137. Ibid.

138. Ibid.

139. Ibid.; German Lopez, "Military to Trump: We Won't Ban Transgender Service Members Just Because You Tweeted About It," Vox, July 27, 2017, https://www.vox.com/identities/2017/7/27/16050286/trump-transgender-military-ban.

140. Aaron Blake, "'It Will Be Fun to Watch [Democrats] Have to Defend This': Why Trump's Transgender Military Ban Should Frighten GOP," *The Washington Post,* July 26, 2017, https://www.washingtonpost.com/news/the-fix/wp/2017/07/26/why-trumps-decision-to-ban-transgender-people-from-the-military-should-frighten-republicans/.

141. Zack Ford, "Pence Secretly Drafted Trump's Latest Transgender Military Ban," ThinkProgress, March 25, 2018, https://thinkprogress.org/pence-responsible-for-trump-transgender-military-ban-f4d3b67bde47/; Martha Bebinger, "Trump Swaps Complete Ban for 'Qualified Ban' on Transgender Military Service," NPR, March 24, 2018, https://www.npr.org/2018/03/24/596656712/trump-swaps-complete-ban-for-qualified-ban-on-transgender-military-service.

142. Ryan J. Reilly, "Judge: Transgender People a Protected Class, and the Military Can't Enact Trump Ban," *HuffPost,* April 13, 2018, https://www.huffingtonpost.com/entry/transgender-ban-trump-military_us_5ad1572ee4b0edca2cb9eea1; Samantha Allen, "How Trump's Trans Military Ban Backfired. Spectacularly," *The Daily Beast,* April 22, 2018, https://www.thedailybeast.com/how-trumps-trans-military-ban-backfired-spectacularly.

143. "Timeline: Key Dates in President Trump's Relationship"; Scott A. Schoettes, "Trump Doesn't Care About HIV. We're Outta Here," *Newsweek,* June 16, 2017, http://www.newsweek.com/trump-doesnt-care-about-hiv-were-outta-here-626285.

144. "Timeline: Key Dates in President Trump's Relationship."

145. Ibid.

146. Editorial Board, "Where, Oh Where, Are All Trump's Political Appointees?," *The Washington Post,* August 23, 2017, https://www.washingtonpost.com/opinions/where-oh-where-are-all-trumps-political-appointees/2017/08/25/0217d2c4-7c62-11e7-9d08-b79f191668ed_story.html.

147. Brian Naylor, "Trump Administration Has More Than 250 Unfilled Jobs," NPR, November 22, 2017, https://www.npr.org/2017/11/22/566098660/trump-administration-has-more-than-250-unfilled-jobs.

148. Editorial Board, "Where, Oh Where?"

149. Tamara Keith, "Trump Leaves Top Administration Positions Unfilled, Says Hollow Government by Design," NPR, October 12, 2017, https://www.npr.org/2017/10/12/557122200/trump-leaves-top-administration-positions-unfilled-says-hollow-government-by-des.

150. John W. Schoen, "After 500 Days, Hundreds of White House Jobs Remain Unfilled by Trump Administration," CNBC, June 4, 2018, https://www.cnbc.com/2018/06/04/after-500-days-dozens-of-white-house-jobs-remain-unfilled.html.

151. Elaine Kamarck, "Federal Vacancies Have Left Trump's Government Home Alone," Brookings, December 14, 2017, https://www.brookings.edu/blog/fixgov/2017/12/14/trumps-government-home-alone/.

152. Ibid.

153. Christopher Ingraham and Tauhid Chappell, "Vermont Just Became the 9th State to Legalize Marijuana. Here's What Makes It Different," *The Washington Post,* January 22, 2018, https://www.washingtonpost.com/news/wonk/wp/2018/01/22/vermont-just-became-the-9th-state-to-legalize-marijuana-heres-what-makes-them-different; Aaron Smith, "Colorado Passes a Milestone for Pot Revenue," CNN, July 2017, http://money.cnn.com/2017/07/19/news/colorado-marijuana-tax-revenue/index.html; Abigail Geiger, "About Six-in-Ten Americans Support Marijuana

Legalization," Pew Research Center, January 5, 2018, http://www.pewresearch.org
/fact-tank/2018/01/05/americans-support-marijuana-legalization/; Katie Zezima,
"Study: Legal Marijuana Could Generate More Than $132 billion in Federal Tax
Revenue and 1 Million Jobs," *The Washington Post,* January 10, 2018, https://www
.washingtonpost.com/national/2018/01/10/study-legal-marijuana-could-generate
-more-than-132-billion-in-federal-tax-revenue-and-1-million-jobs/.

154. German Lopez, "The Trump Administration's New War on Marijuana, Explained,"
Vox, January 5, 2018, https://www.vox.com/policy-and-politics/2018/1/4/16849866
/marijuana-legalization-trump-sessions-cole-memo.

155. Ibid.

156. Ibid.

157. Ibid.

158. Ibid.

159. Ibid.; Alan Feuer, "Lawsuit Takes Aim at Trump Administration Marijuana Policy," *The New York Times,* February 13, 2008, https://www.nytimes.com/2018/02
/13/nyregion/marijuana-lawsuit-trump-sessions.html.

160. Willa Frej, "Trump Named the World's No. 1 Oppressor of Press Freedom," *Huff-
Post,* January 9, 2018, https://www.huffingtonpost.com/entry/trump-oppressor-press
-freedom_us_5a54bc75e4b003133ecc3439.

161. Ibid.

162. Seth Stevenson, "A Week on the Trail with the 'Disgusting Reporters' Covering
Donald Trump," *Slate,* March 20, 2016, http://www.slate.com/articles/news_and_poli
tics/cover_story/2016/03/on_the_trail_with_donald_trump_s_disgusting_press
_corps.html.

163. Chris Wallace, "The Media Is Giving Up Its Place in Our Democracy," *Washington Post,*
November 17, 2017, https://www.washingtonpost.com/opinions/trump-is-assaulting-our
-free-press-but-he-also-has-a-point/2017/11/17/b3b8ec24-c8b2-11e7-b0cf-7689a9f2d84e
_story.html.

164. Jeff Nesbit, "History Repeats: Propaganda and the Destruction of the Free Press,"
US News & World Report, October 26, 2017, https://www.usnews.com/news/at-the
-edge/articles/2017-10-26/trump-propaganda-and-the-destruction-of-the-free-press.

165. Wallace, "The Media Is Giving Up."

166. Ken Bredemeier, "Two Republican Senators Assail Trump for Media Attacks,"
Voice of America News, January 18, 2018, https://www.voanews.com/a/republican-sena
tors-assail-trump-media-attacks/4211911.html.

167. Daniel Politi, "Trump Calls NBC's Chuck Todd a 'Sleeping Son of a Bitch,'" *Slate,*

March 11, 2018, https://slate.com/news-and-politics/2018/03/donald-trump-calls-nbcs
-chuck-todd-a-sleeping-son-of-a-bitch.html.

168. Natasha Bach, "Trump Continues 'Fake News Media' Attacks After Calling for *The Washington Post* Reporter to be Fired," *Fortune,* December 11, 2017, http://www
.fortune.com/2017/12/11/donald-trump-fake-news-washington-post-weigel/; "Trump
Declares Unprecedented War on Media," Axios, November 29, 2017, https://www
.axios.com/trump-declares-unprecedented-war-on-media-1513307240-f6e837e9
-54bb-4d4b-8ed0-91db897ee609.html.

169. Noah Bierman and Jim Puzzanghera, "President Trump Threatens NBC's Broadcast Licenses Following Critical Stories," *Los Angeles Times,* October 11, 2017, http://
www.latimes.com/politics/washington/la-na-pol-essential-washington-updates
-president-trump-goes-after-nbc-s-1507732128-htmlstory.html.

170. Michael M. Grynbaum, "Trump Renews Pledge to 'Take a Strong Look' at Libel
Laws," *The New York Times,* January 10, 2018, https://www.nytimes.com/2018/01/10
/business/media/trump-libel-laws.html.

171. Matt Flegenheimer and Michael M. Grynbaum, "Trump Hands Out 'Fake News
Awards,' Sans the Red Carpet," *The New York Times,* January 17, 2018, https://www
.nytimes.com/2018/01/17/business/media/fake-news-awards.html.

172. Wallace, "The Media Is Giving Up."

173. Ibid.

174. Bredemeier, "Two Republican Senators."

175. "Extract from Thomas Jefferson to Edward Carrington," Monticello, January 16,
1787, http://tjrs.monticello.org/letter/1289.

176. Brandon Carter, "Trump Watches Up to Eight Hours of TV per Day: Report," *The Hill,* December 9, 2017, http://thehill.com/homenews/administration/364094-trump
-watches-at-least-four-hours-of-tv-per-day-report; Mallory Shelbourne, "Trump
Attacks NYT Report That He Watches Up to 8 Hours of TV a Day," *Hill,* December 11, 2018, http://thehill.com/homenews/administration/364237-trump-attacks
-nyt-report-that-he-watches-up-to-8-hours-of-tv-a-day.

177. Ibid.

178. Dave Itzkoff, "Trump Slings Twitter Insults with Alec Baldwin, His 'S.N.L.' Im-
personator," *The New York Times,* March 2, 2018, https://www.nytimes.com/2018
/03/02/arts/television/trump-alec-baldwin-snl.html; Mark Osborne, "Donald Trump
Attacks 'Alex' Baldwin on Twitter Over Impersonation," ABC News, March 2,
2018, http://abcnews.go.com/Politics/donald-trump-attacks-alex-baldwin-twitter
-impersonation/story?id=53459224.

179. Itzkoff, "Trump Slings Twitter Insults."

180. Zack Beauchamp, "Netanyahu Went on Fox & Friends to Lobby Trump on the Iran Deal," Vox, May 1, 2018, https://www.vox.com/world/2018/5/1/17306726/netanyahu-fox-and-friends-trump-iran-deal.

181. Will Oremus, "Fox News Is Losing Its Grip," *Slate,* May 25, 2017, http://www.slate.com/articles/news_and_politics/politics/2017/05/fox_news_refusal_to_cover_trump_s_scandals_makes_for_bad_ratings_and_boring.html.

182. Christopher Rosen, "All the Times Donald Trump Has Called the Media 'Fake News' on Twitter," *EW,* June 27, 2017, http://ew.com/tv/2017/06/27/donald-trump-fake-news-twitter/.

183. Program for Public Consultation, "Overwhelming Bipartisan Majority Opposes Repealing Net Neutrality, Survey Finds," PR Newswire, December 12, 2017, https://www.prnewswire.com/news-releases/overwhelming-bipartisan-majority-opposes-repealing-net-neutrality-survey-finds-300569665.html.

184. Gerry Smith, "Why Trump Wants to Toss Obama's Net Neutrality Rules: Quick-Take," *Bloomberg,* December 14, 2017, https://www.washingtonpost.com/business/why-trump-wants-to-toss-obamas-net-neutrality-rules-quicktake/2017/12/14/b0ae190c-e0ca-11e7-b2e9-8c636f076c76_story.html.

185. John Nichols, "Gutting Net Neutrality Is the Trump Administration's Most Brutal Blow to Democracy Yet," *The Nation,* December 14, 2017, https://www.thenation.com/article/gutting-net-neutrality-is-the-trump-administrations-most-brutal-blow-to-democracy-yet/.

186. Ibid.

187. Aja Romano, "Net Neutrality Is Now Officially on Life Support. Here's What Happens Next," Vox, December 14, 2017, https://www.vox.com/2017/12/14/16774148/net-neutrality-repeal-explained; Ro Khanna (@RoKhanna), Twitter, March 3, 2018, 7:57 p.m., https://twitter.com/RoKhanna/status/970146062802432001.

188. "Nearly Two Dozen Attorneys General Sue to Block FCC's Repeal of Net Neutrality Rules," *USA Today,* January 16, 2018, https://www.usatoday.com/story/tech/news/2018/01/16/nearly-two-dozen-attorneys-general-sue-block-fccs-repeal-net-neutrality-rules/1038532001/.

189. Cecilia Kang, "Washington Governor Signs First State Net Neutrality Bill," *The New York Times,* March 6, 2018, https://www.nytimes.com/2018/03/05/business/net-neutrality-washington-state.html; Eric Brackett, "Vermont Becomes Fifth State to Sign Order Supporting Net Neutrality," Digital Trends, February 17, 2018, https://www.digitaltrends.com/web/vermont-supports-net-neutrality/; Eric Fung, "Washington

State's Net Neutrality Law Is the Beginning of a Big Headache for Internet Providers," *The Washington Post,* March 6, 2018, https://www.washingtonpost.com/news/the -switch/wp/2018/03/06/washington-states-net-neutrality-law-is-the-beginning-of-a -big-headache-for-internet-providers/.

190. "Nearly Two Dozen Attorneys General Sue"; Cecilia Kang, "Senate Democrats Win Vote on Net Neutrality, a Centerpiece of 2018 Strategy," *The New York Times,* May 16, 2018, https://www.nytimes.com/2018/05/16/technology/net-neutrality-senate .html.

191. Jordan Fabian, "Trump Says Puerto Rico Relief Hampered by 'Big Water, Ocean Water,'" *The Hill,* September 29, 2017, http://thehill.com/homenews/administration /353094-trump-says-puerto-rico-relief-hampered-by-big-water-ocean-water.

192. Daniella Diaz, "Trump: We Cannot Aid Puerto Rico 'Forever,'" CNN, October 12, 2017, https://www.cnn.com/2017/10/12/politics/donald-trump-puerto-rico-tweets /index.html.

193. "Donald Trump Blames Puerto Ricans for Not Being Able 'to Get Their Workers to Help' After Hurricane Maria," *Fortune,* September 30, 2017, http://fortune.com /2017/09/30/donald-trump-blames-puerto-rico-hurricane-maria/.

194. Dana Milbank, "The Cameras Go Off, and Then Comes the Collapse," *The Washington Post,* December 22, 2017, https://www.washingtonpost.com/opinions/the -cameras-go-off-and-then-comes-the-collapse/2017/12/22/1c200bb2-e721-11e7-ab50 -621fe0588340_story.html; Sheri Fink, "Puerto Rico's Hurricane Maria Death Toll Could Exceed 4,000, New Study Estimates," *The New York Times,* May 29, 2018, https://www.nytimes.com/2018/05/29/us/puerto-rico-deaths-hurricane.html.

195. Ibid.; Daniella Silva, "Trump Defends Throwing Paper Towels to Hurricane Survivors in Puerto Rico," NBC News, October 8, 2017, https://www.nbcnews.com /politics/politics-news/trump-defends-throwing-paper-towels-hurricane-survivors -puerto-rico-n808861.

196. Patricia Mazzei and Agustin Armendariz, "FEMA Contract Called for 30 Million Meals for Puerto Ricans. 50,000 Were Delivered," *The New York Times,* February 6, 2018, https://www.nytimes.com/2018/02/06/us/fema-contract-puerto-rico.html.

197. Tami Abdollah, "AP EXCLUSIVE: Big Contracts, No Storm Tarps for Puerto Rico," Associated Press, November 28, 2017, https://www.apnews.com/cbeff1a93932 4610b7a02b88f30eafbb.

198. Steven Mufson, Jack Gillum, Aaron C. Davis, and Arelis R. Hernández, "Small Montana Firm Lands Puerto Rico's Biggest Contract to Get the Power Back On," *The Washington Post,* October 23, 2017, https://www.washingtonpost.com/national

/small-montana-firm-lands-puerto-ricos-biggest-contract-to-get-the-power-back-on
/2017/10/23/31cccc3e-b4d6-11e7-9e58-e6288544af98_story.html.

199. David Leonhardt, "Remember Puerto Rico," *The New York Times,* February 14, 2018, https://www.nytimes.com/2018/02/14/opinion/remember-puerto-rico.html.

200. German Lopez, "Trump's Pathetic Response to the Opioid Epidemic," Vox, January 23, 2018, https://www.vox.com/policy-and-politics/2018/1/23/16909984/trump -opioid-epidemic-2017; Lori Robertson, "Trump Misleads on Opioid Epidemic Fight," FactCheck, June 5, 2018, https://www.factcheck.org/2018/06/trump-misleads -on-opioid-epidemic-fight/.

201. Ibid.

202. Ibid.

203. Jesse Mechanic, "After Months of Inaction on the Opioid Crisis, Trump Sets the Stage for a Harmful Response," Truthout, February 15, 2018, http://www.truth-out .org/news/item/43548-after-months-of-inaction-on-the-opioid-crisis-trump-sets-the -stage-for-a-harmful-response; Sari Horwitz, "Sessions Assigns Dozens More Federal Agents to Combat Illicit Opioid Sales Online," *The Washington Post,* January 29, 2018, https://www.washingtonpost.com/world/national-security/sessions-assigns-dozens -more-federal-agents-to-combat-illicit-opioid-sales-online/2018/01/29/910eae46 -0522-11e8-94e8-e8b8600ade23_story.html.

204. Dan Diamond, "Exclusive: Trump Finalizing Opioid Plan That Includes Death Penalty for Dealers," *Politico,* March 15, 2018, https://www.politico.com/story/2018/03 /15/exclusive-trump-finalizing-opioid-plan-death-penalty-418488; Seung Min Kim, Jenna Johnson, and Philip Rucker, "At Pennsylvania Rally, Trump Again Calls for the Death Penalty for Drug Dealers," *The Washington Post,* March 10, 2018, https:// www.washingtonpost.com/politics/trump-to-rally-in-pennsylvania-ahead-of -special-house-election/2018/03/10/3eed9dc0-23f4-11e8-86f6-54bfff693d2b_story .html; German Lopez, "Trump's Opioid Crisis Plan: More Death Penalty, Fewer Prescriptions, More Treatment," Vox, March 19, 2018, https://www.vox.com/policy -and-politics/2018/3/19/17137852/trump-opioid-epidemic-plan-death-penalty.

205. Robertson, "Trump Misleads."

206. Ibid.

207. Paul Rosenberg, "This Is How the GOP Rigged Congress: The Secret Plan That Handcuffed Obama's Presidency, but Backfired in Donald Trump," *Salon,* June 13, 2016, https://www.salon.com/2016/06/13/this_is_how_the_gop_rigged_congress_the _secret_plan_that_handcuffed_obamas_presidency_but_backfired_in_donald _trump/; Tim Dickinson, "How Republicans Rig the Game," *Rolling Stone,* No-

vember 11, 2013, https://www.rollingstone.com/politics/news/how-republicans-rig-the-game-20131111.

208. David Daley, "Gerrymandering Did This: How the GOP's Redistricting Master Plan Brought Us Trumpcare—Even Though Most People Hate It," *Salon,* May 6, 2017, https://www.salon.com/2017/05/06/gerrymandering-did-this-how-the-gops-redistricting-master-plan-brought-us-trumpcare-even-though-most-people-hate-it/.

209. David Graham, "Has the Tide Turned Against Partisan Gerrymandering?," *The Atlantic,* January 23, 2018, https://www.theatlantic.com/politics/archive/2018/01/pennsylvania-partisan-gerrymandering-north-carolina-wisconsin-scotus/551177/; Ari Berman, "Trump's Pick to Run 2020 Census Has Defended Racial Gerrymandering and Voter Suppression Laws," *Mother Jones,* January 2, 2018, https://www.motherjones.com/politics/2018/01/trumps-pick-to-run-2020-census-has-defended-racial-gerrymandering-and-voter-suppression-laws/.

210. Berman, "Trump's Pick to Run 2020 Census"; Ari Berman, "Trump's Controversial Pick to Run the 2020 Census Withdraws," *Mother Jones,* February 12, 2018, https://www.motherjones.com/politics/2018/02/trumps-controversial-pick-to-run-the-2020-census-withdraws/.

211. Kevin Modesti, "Census 'Citizenship' Question Sets Off New California vs. Trump Immigration Argument," *LA Daily News,* February 16, 2018, https://www.dailynews.com/2018/02/16/census-citizenship-question-sets-off-new-california-vs-trump-immigration-argument/; Emily Baumgaertner, "Despite Concerns, Census Will Ask Respondents if They Are U.S. Citizens," *The New York Times,* March 26, 2018, https://www.nytimes.com/2018/03/26/us/politics/census-citizenship-question-trump.html; "Trump-Pence Sued Over Citizenship Question on 2020 Census," *Wisconsin Gazette,* June 6, 2018, http://www.wisconsingazette.com/news/trump-pence-sued-over-citizenship-question-on-census/article_8b719df0-6994-11e8-bb15-6b59b7e924a1.html.

212. "Trump's Infrastructure Plan Isn't a Plan. It's a Fantasy," *Los Angeles Times,* February 13, 2018, http://www.latimes.com/opinion/editorials/la-ed-trump-infrastructure-20180213-story.html.

213. Igor Bobic, "Trump's 'Infrastructure Week' Crumbles Again," *HuffPost,* February 15, 2018, https://www.huffingtonpost.com/entry/trump-infrastructure-week_us_5a8593fde4b0058d5566a668.

214. Bobic, "Trump's 'Infrastructure Week'"; "Trump's Infrastructure Plan."

215. Michelle Chen, "Trump's Infrastructure Plan Is Great, Unless You Want Actually Functioning Infrastructure," *The Nation,* February 16, 2018, https://www.thenation

.com/article/trumps-infrastructure-plan-is-great-unless-you-want-actually-functioning -infrastructure/; Igor Bobic, "Do You Like Paying Tolls? You're Gonna Love Trump's Infrastructure Plan," *HuffPost,* February 12, 2018, https://www.huffingtonpost.com /entry/trump-tolls-infrastructure_us_5a81b8bbe4b08dfc930673bb.

216. "Trump's Infrastructure Plan."

3: TRUMP'S WAR ON THE ENVIRONMENT

1. Robinson Meyer, "Could Scott Pruitt Have Fixed Oklahoma's Earthquake Epidemic?," *The Atlantic,* January 18, 2017, https://www.theatlantic.com/science/archive /2017/01/scott-pruitt-and-oklahomas-manmade-earthquakes/513437/; Nadja Popovich, Livia Albeck-Ripka, and Kendra Pierre-Louis, "67 Environmental Rules on the Way Out Under Trump," *The New York Times*, October 5, 2017, https://www .nytimes.com/interactive/2017/10/05/climate/trump-environment-rules-reversed .html; "Pruitt v. EPA: 14 Challenges of EPA Rules by the Oklahoma Attorney General," *New York Times,* January 14, 2017, https://www.nytimes.com/interactive/2017 /01/14/us/politics/document-Pruitt-v-EPA-a-Compilation-of-Oklahoma-14.html.

2. Daniel Setiawan, "Trump Made It a Lot Easier for Oil Companies to Drill in National Parks," *Mother Jones,* August 12, 2017, https://www.motherjones.com /environment/2017/04/national-parks-oil-gas-drilling/; Timothy Cama, "Interior Secretary Repeals Ban on Lead Bullets," *The Hill,* March 2, 2017, http://thehill.com/policy /energy-environment/322058-interior-secretary-repeals-ban-on-lead-ammunition; "National Environmental Scorecard: Ryan Zinke," League of Conservation Voters, http://scorecard.lcv.org/moc/ryan-zinke.

3. "Obama on Executive Actions: 'I've Got a Pen And I've Got a Phone,'" CBS D.C., January 14, 2014, http://washington.cbslocal.com/2014/01/14/obama-on-executive -actions-ive-got-a-pen-and-ive-got-a-phone/.

4. Popovich, Albeck-Ripka, and Pierre-Louis, "67 Environmental Rules."

5. Ibid.

6. "The EPA Rips Up the Clean Power Plan," *The Washington Post,* October 11, 2017, https://www.washingtonpost.com/opinions/the-epa-rips-up-the-clean-power-plan /2017/10/11/3e08f38e-adf5-11e7-be94-fabb0f1e9ffb_story.html.

7. Juliet Eilperin and Brady Dennis, "EPA to Roll Back Car Emissions Standards, Handing Automakers a Big Win," *The Washington Post,* April 2, 2018, https:// www.washingtonpost.com/national/health-science/epa-to-roll-back-car-emissions -standards/2018/04/02/b720f0b6-36a6-11e8-acd5-35eac230e514_story.html.

8. Popovich, Albeck-Ripka, and Pierre-Louis, "67 Environmental Rules."

9. Ibid.; "Trump Administration Denies Endangered Species Protection for 25 Species," Center for Biological Diversity, October 4, 2017, https://www.biologicaldiversity .org/news/press_releases/2017/25-species-10-04-2017.php; "Trump Administration Plans to Prematurely Remove Endangered Species Protections for Canada Lynx," Center for Biological Diversity, January 11, 2018, https://www.biologicaldiversity.org/news/press _releases/2018/canada-lynx-01-11-2018.php; Gregory Wallace, "WH Reviewing Proposal That Would Roll Back Protections for Threatened Species," CNN, April 5, 2018, https://www.cnn.com/2018/04/05/politics/endangered-species-act-blanket-rule /index.html; Miranda Green, "Trump's Pick to Oversee Wildlife Policy Has History of Opposing Endangered Species Act," *The Hill,* April 4, 2018, http://thehill.com /policy/energy-environment/381618-trump-appointee-to-oversee-wildlife-policy-has -history-of.

10. Jeremy Schulman, "Every Insane Thing Donald Trump Has Said About Global Warming," *Mother Jones*, December 5, 2016, https://www.motherjones.com/environment /2016/12/trump-climate-timeline/.

11. Ibid.

12. Ibid.

13. Ibid.

14. Justin Gillis and Nadja Popovich, "The U.S. Is the Biggest Carbon Polluter in History. It Just Walked Away from the Paris Climate Deal," *New York Times,* June 1, 2017, https://www.nytimes.com/interactive/2017/06/01/climate/us-biggest-carbon-polluter -in-history-will-it-walk-away-from-the-paris-climate-deal.html.

15. Michael Shear, "Trump Will Withdraw U.S. from Paris Climate Agreement," *New York Times*, June 1, 2017, https://www.nytimes.com/2017/06/01/climate/trump -paris-climate-agreement.html.

16. Ibid.

17. Ibid.

18. Zahra Hirji, "Every Country in the World Has Now Agreed to the Paris Climate Accord—Except the US," BuzzFeed, November 7, 2017, https://www.buzzfeed .com/zahrahirji/syria-has-joined-the-paris-climate-agreement.

19. Umair Irfan, "'Climate Change' and 'Global Warming' Are Disappearing from Government Websites," Vox, November 9, 2017, https://www.vox.com/energy-and -environment/2017/11/9/16619120/trump-administration-removing-climate-change -epa-online-website.

20. Ibid.

21. Ibid.; Julia Manchester, "Pruitt Personally Monitored Removal of Climate Change

Info from EPA Sites: Report," *The Hill,* February 2, 2018, http://thehill.com/home news/administration/371955-pruitt-personally-monitored-removal-of-climate -change-info-from-epa.

22. Ibid.

23. Irfan, "'Climate Change.'"

24. Ibid.

25. Ibid.

26. Ibid.

27. Ibid.

28. Sarah Fecht, "Arctic National Wildlife Refuge: How Drilling for Oil Could Impact Wildlife," Columbia Earth Institute, December 6, 2017, http://blogs.ei.columbia.edu /2017/12/06/arctic-national-wildlife-refuge-drilling-oil-impact-wildlife/.

29. Ibid.; Sydney Pereira, "Trump Calls Alaska's Wildlife Refuge, Where Hundreds of Spectacular Animals Live, 'One of the Great Oil Sites,'" *Newsweek*, January 10, 2018, http://www.newsweek.com/trump-alaska-wildlife-refuge-hundreds-animals-live -great-oil-site-777521.

30. Pereira, "Trump Calls Alaska's Wildlife Refuge."

31. Fecht, "Arctic National Wildlife Refuge."

32. Alex Nussbaum, "Arctic Refuge Just the Start of Trump's Move to Unlock Alaska Oil," *Bloomberg*, December 20, 2017, https://www.bloomberg.com/news/articles/2017 -12-20/arctic-refuge-just-the-start-as-trump-moves-to-unlock-alaska-oil.

33. Lisa Friedman, "Trump Moves to Open Nearly All Offshore Waters to Drilling," *New York Times*, January 4, 2018, https://www.nytimes.com/2018/01/04/climate/trump -offshore-drilling.html; Lauren Katz, "Ryan Zinke Spent His First Year in Office Selling Off Rights to Our Public Lands," Vox, March 5, 2018, https://www.vox.com /policy-and-politics/2018/3/5/16853432/ryan-zinke-interior-department-secretary.

34. Friedman, "Trump Moves to Open."

35. Ben Lefebvre and Anthony Adragna, "Trump Energy Team Draws Blowback on Florida Drilling Exemption," *Politico,* January 10, 2018, https://www.politico.com /story/2018/01/10/zinke-drilling-exemption-florida-276446; Gregory Wallace, "Zinke on Offshore Drilling Flip: Florida's 'Coastal Currents' Are Different," CNN, January 23, 2018, https://www.cnn.com/2018/01/23/politics/zinke-florida-tides/index.html.

36. Lefebvre and Adragna, "Trump Energy Team Draws Blowback"; Brett Samuels, "Trump Unhappy Over Zinke's Florida Drilling Exemption: Report," *The Hill,* January 21, 2018, http://thehill.com/policy/energy-environment/370032-trump-unhappy -over-zinkes-florida-offshore-drilling-exemption.

37. Dan Merica, "Nearly Every Governor with Ocean Coastline Opposes Trump's Drilling Proposal," CNN, January 12, 2018, https://www.cnn.com/2018/01/11/politics/governors-ocean-coastline-offshore-drilling-trump/index.html; Cameron Easley, "America's Most and Least Popular Governors," Morning Consult, October 31, 2017, https://morningconsult.com/2017/10/31/americas-most-least-popular-governors-october-2017/.

38. David Roberts, "Once and for All: Obama Didn't Crush US Coal, and Trump Can't Save It," Vox, January 30, 2018, https://www.vox.com/energy-and-environment/2017/4/28/15465348/obama-trump-regulations-coal.

39. Ibid.; Michael Grunwald, "Trump's Love Affair with Coal," *Politico,* October 5, 2017, https://www.politico.com/magazine/story/2017/10/15/trumps-love-affair-with-coal-215710.

40. Jonathan Thompson, "Trump Is King Coal's Last Gasp," *The New Republic,* September 21, 2017, https://newrepublic.com/article/144955/trump-big-coals-last-gasp.

41. Ibid.; Grunwald, "Trump's Love Affair."

42. Grunwald, "Trump's Love Affair."

43. Ibid.

44. Meghan Keneally, "What Trump Has Said About 'Clean Coal' and What It Is," *The Hill,* August 23, 2017, http://abcnews.go.com/US/trump-clean-coal/story?id=49376237.

45. Ibid.

46. Ibid.

47. Sam Schwarz, "Donald Trump Has Only Delivered 1,200 Coal-Mining Jobs, Despite Claiming to Have Created 45,000," *Newsweek,* December 19, 2017, http://www.newsweek.com/donald-trump-has-only-delivered-1200-coal-mining-jobs-despite-claiming-have-751885.

48. Ibid.

49. Gary Scott, "The Presidents and the National Parks," White House Historical Association, https://www.whitehousehistory.org/the-presidents-and-the-national-parks; David Mikkelson, "If You've Seen One Tree . . . ," Snopes, May 20, 2008, https://www.snopes.com/fact-check/if-youve-seen-one-tree/.

50. Scott, "The Presidents"; "Bush Creates World's Largest Ocean Preserve," NBC News, June 16, 2006, http://www.nbcnews.com/id/13300363/ns/us_news-environment/t/bush-creates-worlds-biggest-ocean-preserve/; Eric Lipton and Lisa Friedman, "Oil Was Central in Decision to Shrink Bears Ears Monument, Emails Show," *The New York Times,* March 2, 2018, https://www.nytimes.com/2018/03/02/climate/bears-ears-national-monument.html.

51. Lipton and Friedman, "Oil Was Central"; Katz, "Ryan Zinke Spent His First Year."

52. Katz, "Ryan Zinke Spent His First Year."

53. Ibid.; Lipton and Friedman, "Oil Was Central."

54. Lipton and Friedman, "Oil Was Central"; Kate Wheeling, "What Native Americans Stand to Lose if Trump Opens Up Public Lands for Business," *Pacific Standard,* December 7, 2017, https://psmag.com/environment/what-native-americans-stand-to-lose-if-trump-opens-up-public-lands-for-business.

55. Katz, "Ryan Zinke Spent His First Year"; Julie St. Louis, "Environmentalists Sue to Block Alaska Oil Leases," Courthouse News, February 2, 2018, https://www.courthousenews.com/environmentalists-sue-to-block-alaska-oil-leases/.

56. Katz, "Ryan Zinke Spent His First Year."

57. Ibid.

58. Katia Hetter, "America's Most Popular National Parks Are . . . ," CNN, March 1, 2018, https://www.cnn.com/travel/article/most-popular-national-park-service-sites-2017/index.html.

59. "Theodore Roosevelt and Conservation," National Park Service, https://www.nps.gov/thro/learn/historyculture/theodore-roosevelt-and-conservation.htm.

4: TRUMP FANS THE FLAMES OF RACISM

1. Rosalind S. Helderman and Jon Cohen, "As Republican Convention Emphasizes Diversity, Racial Incidents Intrude," *Washington Post,* August 29, 2012, https://www.washingtonpost.com/politics/2012/08/29/b9023a52-f1ec-11e1-892d-bc92fee603a7_story.html.

2. Robert Farley, "Was McCain Born in the USA?," PolitiFact, May 12, 2008, http://www.politifact.com/truth-o-meter/article/2008/may/12/born-usa/.

3. Liza Mundy, "Orly Taitz's Crusade to Challenge President Obama's Legitimacy," *Washington Post,* October 6, 2009, http://www.washingtonpost.com/wp-dyn/content/article/2009/10/05/AR2009100503819.html; Andrew Prokop, "Trump Fanned a Conspiracy About Obama's Birthplace for Years. Now He Pretends Clinton Started It," Vox, September 16, 2016, https://www.vox.com/2016/9/16/12938066/donald-trump-obama-birth-certificate-birther.

4. Prokop, "Trump Fanned a Conspiracy."

5. Ibid.

6. Ibid.; Chris Megerian, "What Donald Trump Has Said Through the Years About Where President Obama Was Born," *Los Angeles Times,* September 16, 2016, http://www.latimes.com/politics/la-na-pol-trump-birther-timeline-20160916-snap-htmlstory.html.

7. Prokop, "Trump Fanned a Conspiracy."

8. Ibid.

9. Megerian, "What Donald Trump Has Said."

10. Ibid.; Prokop, "Trump Fanned a Conspiracy."

11. Philip Bump, "2017: The Year That There Was Always a Trump Tweet," *Washington Post,* December 29, 2017, https://www.washingtonpost.com/news/politics/wp/2017/12/29/2017-the-year-that-there-was-always-a-trump-tweet/.

12. Chris Morris, "Donald Trump's Nearly Four-Decade War with the NFL: A Timeline," *Fortune,* September 25, 2017, http://fortune.com/2017/09/25/donald-trump-attack-nfl/.

13. Justin Tinsley, "Trump Versus the Wide World of Sports, A Timeline," Undefeated, November 20, 2017, https://theundefeated.com/features/trump-vs-the-wide-world-of-sports-a-timeline/.

14. Morris, "Donald Trump's Nearly Four-Decade War."

15. Ibid.

16. Ibid.

17. Antonio Moore, "Football's War on the Minds of Black Men," VICE, December 24, 2015, https://sports.vice.com/en_ca/article/eze4gj/footballs-war-on-the-minds-of-black-men; Wesley Lowery, "Aren't More White People Than Black People Killed by Police? Yes, but No," *The Washington Post,* July 11, 2016, https://www.washingtonpost.com/news/post-nation/wp/2016/07/11/arent-more-white-people-than-black-people-killed-by-police-yes-but-no.

18. Morris, "Donald Trump's Nearly Four-Decade War"; Joe Avella, "Trump Once Won a Lawsuit Against the NFL—but the Result Was an Embarrassment," *Business Insider,* September 25, 2017, http://www.businessinsider.com/donald-trump-nfl-league-usfl-sued-tweet-three-dollars-2017-9.

19. "Eagles' Visit to White House Canceled Over National Anthem Dispute," ESPN, June 5, 2018, http://www.espn.com/nfl/story/_/id/23698240/philadelphia-eagles-not-attend-white-house-ceremony-president-donald-trump; Candace Norwood and Louis Nelson, "NFL Players Rip into Trump After He Disinvited Eagles from the White House," *Politico,* June 5, 2018, https://www.politico.com/story/2018/06/05/trump-nfl-eagles-national-anthem-624179.

20. Norwood and Nelson, "NFL Players Rip into Trump"; Lorenzo Tanos, "Eagles 'Fans' Brought in for Trump's Celebration Couldn't Name Team's Starting Quarterback, Reporter Claims," Inquisitr, June 6, 2018, https://www.inquisitr.com/4929715/eagles-fans-brought-in-for-trumps-celebration-couldnt-name-teams-starting-quarterback-reporter-claims/; Tom Schad, "Two Men Take Knee During National Anthem at

Trump's White House Ceremony," *USA Today,* June 5, 2018, https://www.usato day.com/story/sports/nfl/2018/06/05/man-kneels-national-anthem-donald-trump -white-house-nfl/674505002/.

21. Jonathan Chait, "Trump Unable to Remember Words to 'God Bless America' at Fake Fan Rally," *New York,* June 5, 2018, http://nymag.com/daily/intelligencer/2018 /06/trump-forgets-words-to-god-bless-america-at-fake-fan-rally.html; "Does Donald Trump Really Not Know the Words to the National Anthem?," *Vanity Fair,* January 10, 2018, https://www.vanityfair.com/hollywood/2018/01/donald-trump-national -anthem-late-night.

22. Ibid.

23. Ric Bucher, "Is Stephen Curry the Best Shooter Ever? Yes, Say Many of NBA's All-Time Marksmen," Bleacher Report, http://bleacherreport.com/articles/2482473-is -stephen-curry-the-best-shooter-ever-yes-say-many-of-nbas-all-time-marksmen; Tinsley, "Trump Versus the Wide World."

24. Ibid.

25. Ibid.

26. Ibid.

27. Ibid.

28. Tim Bontemps, "LeBron James, Kevin Durant and Steph Curry Agree: We Don't Want White House Invite," *The Washington Post,* June 5, 2018, https://www.washing tonpost.com/sports/lebron-james-kevin-durant-and-steph-curry-agree-teams-dont -want-white-house-invite/2018/06/05/c7ddfd8c-68dc-11e8-9e38-24e693b38637_story .html.

29. Andrew Joseph, "The LaVar Ball–Donald Trump Feud Was the Dumbest Sports Controversy of 2017," *USA Today,* December 19, 2017, http://ftw.usatoday.com /2017/12/lavar-ball-donald-trump-year-in-review-feud-big-baller-brand-controversy -twitter-ucla-2017.

30. Ibid.; Arash Markazi, "Inside the International Incident That Rocked UCLA's Season," ESPN, March 2, 2018, http://www.espn.com/mens-college-basketball/story /_/id/22614341/liangelo-lavar-ball-donald-trump-shoplifting-scandal-rocked-ucla -ncaa-basketball-season.

31. Joseph, "The LaVar Ball–Donald Trump Feud."

32. "Trump Demands Apology from ESPN," *Los Angeles Times,* September 15, 2017, http://www.latimes.com/politics/la-pol-updates-trump-tweets-espn-apologize -htmlstory.html.

33. Ibid.; David Nakamura, "White House: ESPN's Jemele Hill Should Be Fired for

Calling Trump a 'White Supremacist,'" *The Washington Post,* September 13, 2017, https://www.washingtonpost.com/news/post-politics/wp/2017/09/13/white-house -espns-jemele-hill-should-be-fired-for-calling-trump-a-white-supremacist.

34. Deena Zaru, "9 Celebrity Feuds of 2017, Starring Donald Trump," CNN, December 30, 2017, https://www.cnn.com/2017/12/30/politics/trump-celebrity-twitter-feuds -2017/index.html.

35. Ibid.

36. Zaru, "9 Celebrity Feuds."

37. David Duke (@DrDavidDuke), Twitter, August 15, 2017, 5:45 p.m., https://twitter .com/DrDavidDuke/status/897559892164304896.

38. Yair Rosenberg, "'Jews Will Not Replace Us': Why White Supremacists Go After Jews," *The Washington Post,* August 14, 2017, https://www.washingtonpost.com/news /acts-of-faith/wp/2017/08/14/jews-will-not-replace-us-why-white-supremacists-go -after-jews.

39. Eve Peyser, "A Timeline of Trump's Post-Charlottesville Fuckups," VICE, August 17, 2017, https://www.vice.com/en_us/article/vbbbg8/a-timeline-of-trumps-post -charlottesville-fuckups.

40. Amy B. Wang, "One Group Loved Trump's Remarks About Charlottesville: White Supremacists," *The Washington Post,* August 13, 2017, https://www.washingtonpost .com/news/post-nation/wp/2017/08/13/one-group-loved-trumps-remarks-about -charlottesville-white-supremacists.

41. Peyser, "A Timeline of Trump's Post-Charlottesville Fuckups."

42. Ibid.

43. Ibid.

44. Ibid.

45. Mark Abadi, "Trump Had an Unusual Reaction to 9/11 Just Hours After the Attacks," *Business Insider,* September 11, 2017, http://www.businessinsider.com/trump-september -11-interview-tallest-building-manhattan-2017-9.

46. Sarah Posner and David Neiwert, "How Trump Took Hate-Groups Mainstream," *Mother Jones,* October 14, 2016, https://www.motherjones.com/politics/2016/10/donald -trump-hate-groups-neo-nazi-white-supremacist-racism/.

47. Ibid.

48. Elise Foley and Jesselyn Cook, "Trump Slams Protections for Immigrants from 'Shithole' Countries," *HuffPost,* January 12, 2018, https://www.huffingtonpost.com /entry/trump-immigrants-shithole-countries_us_5a57db94e4b04df054f757a0.

49. Chris Cillizza, "Here's Exactly How Dick Durbin Destroyed Kirstjen Nielsen's

'Shithole' Explanation," CNN, January 16, 2018, https://www.cnn.com/2018/01/16 /politics/durbin-nielsen-analysis/index.html.

50. Foley and Cook, "Trump Slams Protections."

51. Ibid.

52. Amy Davidson Sorkin, "Tom Cotton, David Perdue, and the Trap of Lying for Donald Trump," *The New Yorker,* January 16, 2018, https://www.newyorker.com /news/daily-comment/tom-cotton-david-perdue-and-the-trap-of-lying-for-donald -trump.

53. Shawn Boburg, "Donald Trump's Long History of Clashes with Native Americans," *The Washington Post,* July 25, 2016, https://www.washingtonpost.com/national /donald-trumps-long-history-of-clashes-with-native-americans/2016/07/25/80ea 91ca-3d77-11e6-80bc-d06711fd2125_story.html.

54. Ibid.

55. Ibid.

56. Simon Moya-Smith, "Trump's Disrespect for Native Americans Is Nothing New," CNN, November 29, 2017, https://www.cnn.com/2017/11/29/opinions/trump-native -americans-moya-smith-opinion/index.html.

57. Graham Lee Brewer, "Trump Takes a Hard Line on Tribal Health Care," High Country News, April 27, 2018, https://www.hcn.org/articles/indian-country-news -trump-takes-a-hard-line-on-tribal-health-care; Rebecca Pilar Buckwalter Poza, "The Trump Administration Is Going After Native Americans Now, Too," Daily Kos, May 2, 2018, https://www.dailykos.com/stories/2018/5/2/1761447/-The-Trump -administration-is-going-after-Native-Americans-now-too

58. Ibid.

59. Ibid.; Brian Resnick, "Trump Slashed Utah National Monuments by 2 Million Acres. Now Comes the Legal Battle," Vox, December 5, 2017, https://www.vox.com /energy-and-environment/2017/12/4/16733798/utah-national-monument-trump -bears-ears-staircase-escalante.

60. Resnick, "Trump Slashed Utah"; Kate Wheeling, "What Native Americans Stand to Lose If Trump Opens Up Public Lands for Business," *Pacific Standard,* December 7, 2017, https://psmag.com/environment/what-native-americans-stand-to-lose -if-trump-opens-up-public-lands-for-business.

61. Ibid.

62. Moya-Smith, "Trump's Disrespect for Native Americans."

63. Ibid.

64. Ibid.

5: TRUMP'S CABINET OF THIEVES

1. Louis Nelson, "Trump: My Cabinet Has 'Highest IQ of Any Cabinet Ever Assembled,'" *Politico,* January 19, 2017, https://www.politico.com/story/2017/01/trump-cabinet-highest-iq-233853.

2. Pema Levy, "The Harsh, Petty, and Highly Political Law of Jeff Sessions," *Mother Jones,* May/June 2017, https://www.motherjones.com/politics/2017/04/jeff-sessions-alabama-trump-voting/.

3. Peter Baker, Michael Schmidt, and Maggie Haberman, "Citing Recusal, Trump Says He Wouldn't Have Hired Sessions," *The New York Times,* July 19, 2017, https://www.nytimes.com/2017/07/19/us/politics/trump-interview-sessions-russia.html; Margaret Hartmann, "The Complete History of President Trump's Feud with Jeff Sessions," *New York,* March 1, 2018, http://nymag.com/daily/intelligencer/2018/03/history-trump-jeff-sessions-feud.html.

4. Hartmann, "The Complete History."

5. Ibid.

6. Ibid.

7. Peter Baker, "Why Is Trump Mad at Sessions? A Tweet Provides the Answer," *The New York Times,* June 5, 2018, https://www.nytimes.com/2018/06/05/us/politics/trump-sessions-tweet-russia.html.

8. Max Greenwood, "Rosenstein, Sessions Spotted Dining Together Hours After Trump Criticism," *The Hill,* February 28, 2018, http://thehill.com/blogs/blog-briefing-room/news/376171-rosenstein-sessions-spotted-dining-together-hours-after-trump; Sarah Ferris, "Trump Gets First Senate Endorsement," *The Hill,* February 28, 2016, http://thehill.com/blogs/ballot-box/presidential-races/271109-gop-senator-expected-to-endorse-trump; David Cole, "Attorney General Jeff Sessions Is More Dangerous Than Trump," ACLU, May 24, 2017, https://www.aclu.org/blog/criminal-law-reform/attorney-general-jeff-sessions-more-dangerous-trump.

9. Cole, "Attorney General Jeff Sessions."

10. Ibid.

11. Ibid.; Levy, "The Harsh, Petty."

12. Cole, "Attorney General Jeff Sessions"; Jelani Cobb, "Will Jeff Sessions Police the Police," *The New Yorker,* April 24, 2017, https://www.newyorker.com/magazine/2017/04/24/will-jeff-sessions-police-the-police.

13. Monique Judge, "Jeff Sessions Believes Increase in Violent Crime Is Result of Lack

of Respect for Police Officers," The Root, February 28, 2017, https://www.theroot .com/jeff-sessions-believes-increase-in-violent-crime-is-the-1792841093.

14. Ibid.; Nicole Lewis, "Attorney General Jeff Sessions's Claim That a Violent Crime Wave Is Sweeping the Nation," *The Washington Post,* September 1, 2017, https:// www.washingtonpost.com/news/fact-checker/wp/2017/09/01/attorney-general-jeff -sessions-claim-that-a-violent-crime-wave-is-sweeping-the-nation/.

15. Cole, "Attorney General Jeff Sessions."

16. Ibid.

17. Ibid.; Ari Berman, "Jeff Sessions Has Spent His Whole Career Opposing Voting Rights," *The Nation,* January 10, 2017, https://www.thenation.com/article/jeff-sessions -has-spent-his-whole-career-opposing-voting-rights/.

18. Emily Stewart, "Jeff Sessions Cited a Bible Passage Used by American Slaveholders to Defend Trump's Family Separation Policy," Vox, June 15, 2018, https://www.vox .com/policy-and-politics/2018/6/15/17467772/jeff-sessions-bible-passage-slavery -romans-13.

19. Benjamin Goggin, Pete Williams, and Julia Ainsley, "A Timeline of Jeff Sessions' Alleged Perjury," Digg, November 2, 2017, http://digg.com/2017/jeff-sessions-russia -perjury; Ken Dilanian, Pete Williams, and Julia Ainsley, "McCabe Authorized Per- jury Investigation into Sessions," NBC News, March 21, 2018, https://www.nbcnews .com/politics/politics-news/mccabe-authorized-perjury-investigation-sessions -n858891.

20. Gregory Korte, "Why Secretary of State Rex Tillerson Was Fired Now and What It Means for North Korea Talks," *USA Today,* March 13, 2018, https://www.usatoday .com/story/news/politics/2018/03/13/why-secretary-state-rex-tillerson-fired-now -and-what-analysis-why-now-and-what-means-going-ahead-kor/417732002 /; Susan Glasser, "The Foreign Capital Rex Tillerson Never Understood: Trump's Washington," *Politico,* March 13, 2018, https://www.politico.com/magazine/story /2018/03/13/rex-tillerson-exit-washington-dc-donald-trump-217356.

21. Dexter Filkins, "Rex Tillerson at the Breaking Point," *The New Yorker,* October 16, 2017, https://www.newyorker.com/magazine/2017/10/16/rex-tillerson-at-the-breaking -point.

22. Ibid.

23. Ibid.; Zack Beauchamp, "Rex Tillerson Has Been Fired. Experts Say He Did Dam- age That Could Last 'a Generation,'" Vox, March 13, 2018, https://www.vox.com /world/2018/3/13/16029526/rex-tillerson-fired-state-department.

24. Dexter Filkins, "How Rex Tillerson Wrecked the State Department," *The New*

Yorker, November 30, 2017, https://www.newyorker.com/news/news-desk/how
-rex-tillerson-wrecked-the-state-department.

25. Dan Drollette Jr., "8 of the 9 Top Jobs at the State Department Will Sit Empty," *The Bulletin,* March 13, 2018, https://thebulletin.org/8-9-top-jobs-state-department -will-sit-empty11605; Laura Koran, Aaron Kessler, and Joyce Tseng, "Map: Trump Continues to Leave Key State Department Posts Empty," CNN, December 8, 2017, https://www.cnn.com/2017/12/07/politics/trump-ambassador-vacancies/index.html.

26. Michal Kranz, "America Might Be Losing Its Place on the World Stage—and Diplomats Worry That 'Things Will Start to Fall Apart,'" *Business Insider,* October 13, 2017, http://www.businessinsider.com/state-department-trump-tillerson-2017 -10; John W. Schoen, "After 500 Days, Hundreds of White House Jobs Remain Unfilled by Trump Administration," CNBC, June 4, 2018, https://www.cnbc.com /2018/06/04/after-500-days-dozens-of-white-house-jobs-remain-unfilled.html; "Tracker: Current U.S. Ambassadors," American Foreign Service Association, http://www.afsa.org/list-ambassadorial-appointments.

27. Beauchamp, "Rex Tillerson Has Been Fired."

28. Zachary Cohen, "Trump Proposes $54 billion Defense Spending Hike," CNN, March 16, 2017, https://www.cnn.com/2017/03/16/politics/donald-trump-defense-budget -blueprint/index.html; Jeffrey Goldberg, "A Senior White House Official Defines the Trump Doctrine: 'We're America, Bitch,'" *The Atlantic,* June 11, 2018, https://www .theatlantic.com/politics/archive/2018/06/a-senior-white-house-official-defines-the -trump-doctrine-were-america-bitch/562511/.

29. Filkins, "Rex Tillerson at the Breaking Point"; Beauchamp, "Rex Tillerson Has Been Fired."

30. Dan Mangan, "Rex Tillerson Found Out He Was Fired as Secretary of State from President Donald Trump's Tweet," CNBC, March 13, 2018, https://www.cnbc.com /2018/03/13/tillerson-learned-he-was-fired-from-trumps-tweet.html.

31. Ibid.; Lachlan Markay and Asawin Suebsaeng, "John Kelly: Rex Tillerson Was on the Toilet When I Told Him He'd Be Getting Fired," *The Daily Beast,* March 16, 2018, https://www.thedailybeast.com/john-kelly-rex-tillerson-was-on-the-toilet-when -i-told-him-hed-be-getting-fired.

32. Beauchamp, "Rex Tillerson Has Been Fired"; Jeet Heer, "You'll Miss Him When He's Gone," *The New Republic,* March 13, 2018, https://newrepublic.com/article /147447/youll-miss-hes-gone-tillerson-versus-pompeo.

33. Heer, "You'll Miss Him."

34. Alex Ward, "Mike Pompeo, Your Likely New—and Trump-Friendly—Secretary Of

State," Vox, March 13, 2018, https://www.vox.com/world/2017/11/30/16719690/mike -pompeo-tillerson-fired-haspel-cia-state-department; Shane Harris, Carol D. Leon-nig, Greg Jaffe, and David Nakamura, "CIA Director Pompeo Met with North Ko-rean Leader Kim Jong Un Over Easter Weekend," *The Washington Post,* April 18, 2018, https://www.washingtonpost.com/politics/us-china-trade-dispute-looms-over -trump-summit-with-japans-abe/2018/04/17/2c94cb02-424f-11e8-bba2-0976a82b05a2 _story.html.

35. Ward, "Mike Pompeo."

36. Heer, "You'll Miss Him."

37. Zack Beauchamp, "Watch Cory Booker Confront Mike Pompeo on His Ties to Islamophobes," Vox, April 12, 2018, https://www.vox.com/world/2018/4/12/17230078 /mike-pompeo-secretary-of-state-confirmation-cory-booker; Tara Isabella Burton, "Mike Pompeo, Trump's Pick for Secretary of State, Talks About Politics as a Battle of Good and Evil," Vox, March 15, 2018, https://www.vox.com/identities/2018/3/15 /17117298/mike-pompeo-trump-secretary-of-state-politics-battle-evangelical-holy -war-christian; Eugene Scott, "Cory Booker Grills Mike Pompeo on Whether He Believes Being Gay Is a 'Perversion,'" *The Washington Post,* April 12, 2018, https:// www.washingtonpost.com/news/the-fix/wp/2018/04/12/cory-booker-grills-mike -pompeo-on-whether-he-believes-being-gay-is-a-perversion/.

38. Ken Klippenstein, "Pompeo Discussed Rapture at CIA," *The Young Turks,* April 23, 2018, https://tytnetwork.com/2018/04/23/pompeo-discussed-rapture-at-cia/; Michelle Goldberg, "This Evil Is All Around Us," *Slate,* January 12, 2017, http://www.slate.com /articles/news_and_politics/politics/2017/01/mike_pompeo_trump_s_pick_for_the _cia_wants_a_holy_war.html.

39. Zack Stanton, "How Betsy DeVos Used God and Amway to Take Over Michigan Politics," *Politico,* January 15, 2017, https://www.politico.com/magazine/story/2017 /01/betsy-dick-devos-family-amway-michigan-politics-religion-214631; Catherine Brown and Ulrich Boser, "The DeVos Dynasty: A Family of Extremists," Center for American Progress, January 23, 2017, https://www.americanprogress.org/issues /default/news/2017/01/23/296947/the-devos-dynasty-a-family-of-extremists/.

40. Stanton, "How Betsy DeVos Used God"; Brown and Boser, "The DeVos Dynasty."

41. Stanton, "How Betsy DeVos Used God."

42. Ibid.

43. Katie Reilly, "The Biggest Controversies from Betsy DeVos's First Year," *Time,* December 14, 2017, http://time.com/5053007/betsy-devos-education-secretary-2017 -controversies/.

44. Alia Wong, "DeVos Digs Herself Deeper," *The Atlantic,* March 4, 2018, https://www
    .theatlantic.com/education/archive/2018/03/betsy-devos-60-minutes/555566/.

45. Reilly, "The Biggest Controversies"; Moriah Balingit and Danielle Douglas-Gabriel,
    "Congress Rejects Much of Betsy DeVos's Agenda in Spending Bill," *The Washington
    Post,* March 22, 2018, https://www.washingtonpost.com/news/education/wp/2018
    /03/21/congress-rejects-much-of-betsy-devoss-agenda-in-spending-bill.

46. Reilly, "The Biggest Controversies."

47. Jennifer Abel, "Erik Prince: Five Fast Facts You Need to Know," Heavy.com,
    April 4, 2017, https://heavy.com/news/2017/04/erik-prince-blackwater-seychelles
    -trump/.

48. Ibid.; James Risen, "Blackwater Founder Moves to Abu Dhabi, Records Say," *The
    New York Times,* August 17, 2010, https://www.nytimes.com/2010/08/18/world/18
    blackwater.html.

49. Abel, "Erik Prince: Five Fast Facts"; Jesse Berney, "Who Cares What Erik Prince
    Thinks?," *Rolling Stone,* August 31, 2017, https://www.rollingstone.com/politics
    /features/who-cares-what-erik-prince-thinks-about-war-in-afghanistan-w500603.

50. Abel, "Erik Prince: Five Fast Facts"; Karoun Demirjian, "Schiff Wants to Ask
    Trump Supporter Erik Prince if He Lied About Meeting with Russian," *The
    Washington Post,* March 8, 2018, https://www.washingtonpost.com/powerpost/top
    -intel-committee-democrat-wants-to-re-interview-a-trump-supporter-to-see-if-he
    -lied-about-a-meeting-with-a-russian/2018/03/08/6147588e-22eb-11e8-badd-7c9
    f29a55815_story.html.

51. Demirjian, "Schiff Wants to Ask"; Sari Horowitz and Devlin Barrett, "Mueller
    Gathers Evidence That 2017 Seychelles Meeting Was Effort to Establish Back Chan-
    nel to Kremlin," *The Washington Post,* March 7, 2018, https://www.washingtonpost
    .com/world/national-security/mueller-gathers-evidence-that-2016-seychelles
    -meeting-was-effort-to-establish-back-channel-to-kremlin/2018/03/07/b6a5fb8c
    -224b-11e8-94da-ebf9d112159c_story.html.

52. Mark Mazzetti, Ronen Bergman, and David D. Kirkpatrick, "Trump Jr. and
    Other Aides Met with Gulf Emissary Offering Help to Win Election," *The New
    York Times,* May 19, 2018, https://www.nytimes.com/2018/05/19/us/politics/trump-jr
    -saudi-uae-nader-prince-zamel.html.

53. Rebecca Leber, "Making America Toxic Again," *Mother Jones,* March/April 2018,
    https://www.motherjones.com/politics/2018/02/scott-pruitt-profile-epa-trump/.

54. Ibid.

55. Ibid.; Dan Mangan, "EPA Chief Scott Pruitt Took First-Class, Military, Charter

Flights That Cost Taxpayers More Than $163,000 in First Year Alone: Report," CNBC, March 21, 2018, https://www.cnbc.com/2018/03/21/epa-chief-scott-pruitt-took -flights-costing-taxpayers-163000.html; Jennifer A. Dlouhy and Jennifer Jacobs, "EPA Chief's $50-a-Night Rental Raises White House Angst," *Bloomberg,* March 30, 2018, https://www.bloomberg.com/news/articles/2018-03-30/epa-chief-s -50-a-night-rental-said-to-raise-white-house-angst; Ellen Knickmeyer and Michael Biesecker, "EPA Director Laughs Off Chick-Fil-A Controversy as Senior Aide Quits," *Time,* June 6, 2018, http://time.com/5303918/epa-scott-pruitt-chick-fil-a-aide -quits/; Emily Tilly, "Former Gov. Chris Christie on Pruitt Controversy: 'I Don't Know How You Survive This One,'" CBS News, April 2, 2018, https://www .cbsnews.com/news/chris-christie-scott-pruitt-controversy-i-dont-know-how-you -survive-this-one/.

56. Leber, "Making America Toxic Again."

57. Ibid.; Amy Thompson and Rebecca Leber, "It's Been One Year of Amazing Scott Pruitt Accomplishments, All of Them Horrible," *Mother Jones,* March/April 2018, https://www.motherjones.com/environment/2018/02/its-been-one-year-of-amazing -scott-pruitt-accomplishments-all-of-them-horrible/.

58. Leber, "Making America Toxic Again."

59. Ibid.; Thompson and Leber, "It's Been One Year."

60. Leber, "Making America Toxic Again."

61. Zeke Miller, "Scandal-plogued EPA Administrator Pruitt Resigns," Associated Press, July 5, 2018, http://apnous.com/ab1f1723fbfc4685bf29cb195570d3500/Scandal- plogued-EPA-Administrator-Pruitt-resigns.

62. Timothy Egan, "The Mad King Flies His Flag," *The New York Times,* January 19, 2018, https://www.nytimes.com/2018/01/19/opinion/public-lands-trump-zinke.html; Cristina Alesci, Sara Ganim, Rene Marsh, and Gregory Wallace, "Interior Secretary Ryan Zinke's NRA Visit Among Several Trips Being Questioned," CNN, Febru- ary 27, 2018, https://www.cnn.com/2018/02/27/politics/ryan-zinke-nra/index.html; Anthony Adragna, "Interior Spent $139K on Zinke Office Doors," *Politico,* March 8, 2018, https://www.politico.com/story/2018/03/08/ryan-zinke-office-doors-in terior-448425.

63. Egan, "The Mad King"; Elizabeth Kolbert, "The Damage Done by Trump's Department of the Interior," *The New Yorker,* January 22, 2018, https://www .newyorker.com/magazine/2018/01/22/the-damage-done-by-trumps-department-of -the-interior; Alesci, Ganim, Marsh, and Wallace, "Interior Secretary Ryan Zinke's NRA Visit."

64. Lauren Katz, "Ryan Zinke Spent His First Year in Office Selling Off Rights to Our

Public Lands," Vox, March 5, 2018, https://www.vox.com/policy-and-politics/2018/3
/5/16853432/ryan-zinke-interior-department-secretary.

65. Ibid.

66. Darryl Fears, "It's Been a Rough Year for Interior Secretary Ryan Zinke—and It's
Still January," *The Washington Post,* January 29, 2018, https://www.washingtonpost
.com/news/energy-environment/wp/2018/01/29/its-been-a-rough-year-for-interior
-secretary-ryan-zinke-and-its-still-january; Darryl Fears and Dino Grandoni, "The
Trump Administration Has Officially Clipped the Wings of the Migratory Bird
Treaty Act," *The Washington Post,* April 13, 2018, https://www.washingtonpost.com
/news/energy-environment/wp/2018/04/13/the-trump-administration-officially
-clipped-the-wings-of-the-migratory-bird-treaty-act/.

67. Richard Gonzales, Kirk Siegler, and Colin Dwyer, "Trump Orders Largest National Monument Reduction In U.S. History," NPR, December 4, 2017, https://
www.npr.org/sections/thetwo-way/2017/12/04/567803476/trump-dramatically
-shrinks-2-utah-national-monuments.

68. Julie Turkiwitz, "New Interior Secretary Ryan Zinke Words, Actions Differ on Environment," *The New York Times,* March 1, 2017, https://www.seattletimes.com/nation
-world/new-interior-secretary-ryan-zinke-words-actions-differ-on-environment/.

69. Juliet Eilperin, Amy Goldstein, and John Wagner, "HHS Secretary Tom Price Resigns Amid Criticism for Taking Charter Flights at Taxpayer Expense," *The Washington Post,* September 29, 2017, https://www.washingtonpost.com/news/post-politics
/wp/2017/09/29/trump-to-decide-friday-night-whether-to-fire-hhs-secretary-price/.

70. Adam Cancryn, Jennifer Haberkorn, and Rachana Pradhan, "Tom Price's Radically
Conservative Vision for American Health Care," *Politico,* November 29, 2016,
https://www.politico.com/story/2016/11/tom-price-radically-conservative-healthcare
-vision-231965.

71. Eilperin, Goldstein, and Wagner, "HHS Secretary Tom Price Resigns."

72. Ibid.

73. Ibid.

74. Dina Maron, "What You Need to Know About Alex Azar, Trump's HHS Nominee," *Scientific American,* November 28, 2017, https://www.scientificamerican.com
/article/what-you-need-to-know-about-alex-azar-trumps-hhs-nominee/.

75. Ibid.

76. Ibid.; James Elliott, "Alex Azar, Trump's HHS Pick, Has Already Been a Disaster
for People with Diabetes," *The Nation,* November 21, 2017, https://www.thenation
.com/article/alex-azar-trumps-hhs-pick-has-already-been-a-disaster-for-people
-with-diabetes/.

77. Alec MacGillis, "Is Anybody Home at HUD?," *New York,* August 22, 2017, http://nymag.com/daily/intelligencer/2017/08/ben-carson-hud-secretary.html.

78. Ibid.; Philip Bump, "Ben Carson Did Not Grow Up Living in Public Housing," *Washington Post,* December 6, 2016, https://www.washingtonpost.com/news/the-fix/wp/2016/12/06/ben-carson-didnt-grow-up-living-in-public-housing/.

79. Ben Terris, "Ben Carson, or the Tale of the Disappearing Cabinet Secretary," *The Washington Post,* February 6, 2018, https://www.washingtonpost.com/lifestyle/style/ben-carson-or-the-tale-of-the-disappearing-cabinet-secretary/2018/02/05/74c46de8-04ff-11e8-b48c-b07fea957bd5_story.html; MacGillis, "Is Anybody Home at HUD?"

80. MacGillis, "Is Anybody Home at HUD?"

81. Ibid.

82. Ibid.

83. Leila Atassi, "HUD Secretary Ben Carson Wants to Triple Rent for Some Low-Income Families, Encourage 'Self-Sufficiency,'" Cleveland.com, April 25, 2018, http://www.cleveland.com/metro/index.ssf/2018/04/hud_secretary_ben_carson_wants_1.html.

84. MacGillis, "Is Anybody Home at HUD?"

85. Jon Swaine, "Michael Cohen Case Shines Light on Sean Hannity's Property Empire," *The Guardian,* April 23, 2018, https://www.theguardian.com/media/2018/apr/22/michael-cohen-sean-hannity-property-real-estate-ben-carson-hud.

86. Ibid.; Jon Swaine, "Sean Hannity: 400% Rise in Eviction Orders Since Host Bought Georgia Apartment Complex," *The Guardian,* April 27, 2018, https://www.theguardian.com/us-news/2018/apr/27/sean-hannity-eviction-orders-georgia-apartment-complex.

87. Glenn Thrush, "'I Take Responsibility,' Carson Says of $31,000 Furniture Purchase," *The New York Times,* March 22, 2018, https://www.nytimes.com/2018/03/22/us/politics/ben-carson-hud-dining-set.html.

88. Glenn Thrush, "Ben Carson of HUD on His Vexing Reign: Brain Surgery Was Easier Than This," *The New York Times,* March 5, 2018, https://www.nytimes.com/2018/03/05/us/ben-carson-hud.html.

89. George Dvorsky, "Why Rick Perry Would Be a Disaster as Energy Secretary," Gizmodo, December 13, 2016, https://gizmodo.com/why-rick-perry-will-be-a-disaster-as-energy-secretary-1790062509; Chris Cillizza, "The 48 Seconds That Define Rick Perry's Political Career," *Washington Post,* September 12, 2015, https://www.washingtonpost.com/news/the-fix/wp/2015/09/12/the-48-seconds-that-defined-rick-perrys-political-life/.

90. Mallory Shelbourne, "Rick Perry Misunderstood Energy Secretary Job: Report," *The*

Hill, January 27, 2017, http://thehill.com/policy/energy-environment/315005-rick -perry-misunderstood-energy-secretary-job-report.

91. Tom di Christopher, "Energy Secretary Rick Perry Promotes 'New Energy Realism': Fewer Regulations and More Innovation," CNBC, March 7, 2018, https:// www.cnbc.com/2018/03/07/energy-sec-rick-perry-promotes-a-new-era-of-us-energy -innovation.html.

92. Dartunorro Clark, "Energy Secretary Rick Perry Says Fossil Fuels Can Prevent Sexual Assault," NBC News, November 2, 2017, https://www.nbcnews.com/politics /white-house/rick-perry-says-fossil-fuels-can-prevent-sexual-assault-n816896.

93. Dvorsky, "Why Rick Perry Would Be a Disaster"; Chuck McCutcheon, "Trump Energy Pick Perry Pushed to Store Nuclear Waste in His Own State," *Scientific American,* December 15, 2016, https://www.scientificamerican.com/article/trump -energy-pick-perry-pushed-to-store-nuclear-waste-in-his-own-state/.

94. Brad Plumer, "Rick Perry's Plan to Rescue Struggling Coal and Nuclear Plans Is Rejected," *The New York Times,* January 8, 2018, https://www.nytimes.com/2018/01 /08/climate/trump-coal-nuclear.html.

95. Ibid.

96. Simon Edelman, "Why I Blew the Whistle on the Rick Perry Meeting," CNN, March 29, 2018, https://www.cnn.com/2018/03/29/opinions/rick-perry-meeting -opinion-edelman/index.html; Carolyn Kormann, "A Whistle-Blower Alleges Corruption in Rick Perry's Department of Energy," *The New Yorker,* April 5, 2018, https://www .newyorker.com/science/elements/a-whistle-blower-alleges-corruption-in-rick-perrys -department-of-energy.

97. Edelman, "Why I Blew the Whistle"; Plumer, "Rick Perry's Plan"; Kormann, "A Whistle-Blower Alleges Corruption."

98. Jon Hecht, "7 Times Donald Trump & His Cronies Ripped Goldman Sachs— Before Bringing Its Employees into the White House," Bustle, December 1, 2016, https://www.bustle.com/articles/197882-7-times-donald-trump-his-cronies-ripped -goldman-sachs-before-bringing-its-employees-into.

99. William D. Cohan, "The Untold Story of How Gary Cohn Fell for Donald Trump," *Vanity Fair,* June 24, 2017, https://www.vanityfair.com/news/2017/06/the-untold-story -of-how-gary-cohn-donald-trump-goldman-sachs-alumni.

100. Ibid.

101. Peter Dreier, "The Worst of Wall Street: Meet Donald Trump's Finance Chairman," *The Nation,* May 10, 2016, https://www.thenation.com/article/the-worst-of -wall-street-meet-donald-trumps-finance-chairman/.

102. Ibid.

103. Ibid.

104. Alex Horton and Damian Paletta, "Mnuchin Pushes Back Against Reports That He Requested Government Jet for his European Honeymoon," *The Washington Post,* September 14, 2017, https://www.washingtonpost.com/news/wonk/wp/2017 /09/14/mnuchin-eclipses-past-travel-backlash-with-pricey-request-european -honeymoon-by-military-jet/; Victoria Guida, "Mnuchin's Plane Travel Cost Taxpayers $1 Million, Documents Show," *Politico,* March 15, 2018, https://www .politico.com/story/2018/03/15/steven-mnuchin-plane-travel-cost-421176.

105. Justin Fox, "Steve Mnuchin Says the Darnedest Things," *Bloomberg,* November 22, 2017, https://www.bloomberg.com/view/articles/2017-11-22/steve-mnuchin-says-the -darnedest-things; Jordan Weissman, "Judging by This *New York Times* Story, Steve Mnuchin Is a Liar," *Slate,* November 30, 2017, https://slate.com/business/2017 /11/steve-mnuchin-has-been-lying-about-the-tax-plan.html.

106. Fox, "Steve Mnuchin Says"; Weissman, "Steve Mnuchin Is a Liar."

107. Weissman, "Steve Mnuchin Is a Liar."

108. Alexander Kaufman, "Donald Trump Taps Billionaire Who Owned Deadly Coal Mine for Commerce Secretary," *HuffPost,* November 17, 2016, https://www.huffing tonpost.com/entry/trump-wilbur-ross_us_582b4c04e4b01d8a014abacb.

109. Ibid.

110. Jon Swaine and Luke Harding, "Trump Commerce Secretary's Business Links with Putin Family Laid Out in Leaked Files," *The Guardian,* November 5, 2017, https://www.theguardian.com/news/2017/nov/05/trump-commerce-secretary-wilbur -ross-business-links-putin-family-paradise-papers.

111. Kaufman, "Donald Trump Taps Billionaire."

112. Ibid.

113. Cohan, "The Untold Story."

114. Ibid.

115. Jay Willis, "Gary Cohn, Who Was Fine with Charlottesville, Courageously Quits Over Donald Trump's Dumb Tariffs," *GQ,* March 6, 2018, https://www.gq.com /story/gary-cohn-resigns-white-house.

116. Ibid.

117. Dylan Matthews, "Larry Kudlow, Trump's New Top Economic Adviser, Explained," Vox, March 15, 2018, https://www.politico.com/story/2018/03/15/steven -mnuchin-plane-travel-cost-421176.

118. Ibid.

119. Ibid.

120. Ibid.

121. Renae Merle, "Mulvaney Discloses 'Hierarchy' for Meeting Lobbyists, Saying Some Would Be Seen Only if They Paid," *Washington Post,* April 25, 2018, https://www .washingtonpost.com/news/business/wp/2018/04/25/mick-mulvaney-faces-backlash -after-telling-bankers-if-you-were-a-lobbyist-who-never-gave-us-money-i-didnt-talk -to-you/.

122. Michael Grunwald, "Mick the Knife," *Politico,* September 1, 2017, https://www .politico.com/magazine/story/2017/09/01/mick-mulvaney-omb-trump-budget -profile-feature-215546.

123. Ibid.

124. Ibid.

125. Bess Levin, "Trump's Entire Budget Is Based on a $2 Trillion Accounting Trick," *Vanity Fair,* May 23, 2017, https://www.vanityfair.com/news/2017/05/trumps-entire -budget-is-based-on-a-2-trillion-accounting-trick; Stan Collender, "This Is Why OMB Director Mulvaney Should But Won't Be Fired," *Forbes,* June 4, 2017, https:// www.forbes.com/sites/stancollender/2017/06/04/this-is-why-omb-director -mulvaney-should-but-wont-be-fired/.

126. Levin, "Trump's Entire Budget"; Collender, "Mulvaney Should But Won't Be Fired."

127. Justin Miller, "Mick Mulvaney Leads the Race for Worst Cabinet Official," *American Prospect,* January 24, 2018, http://prospect.org/blog/tapped/mick-mulvaney -leads-race-worst-cabinet-official; Catherine Rampell, "How Mick Mulvaney Is Dismantling a Federal Agency," *The Washington Post,* January 25, 2018, https://www .washingtonpost.com/opinions/mick-mulvaney-cant-legally-kill-the-cfpb-so-hes -starving-it-instead/2018/01/25/4481d2ce-0216-11e8-8acf-ad2991367d9d_story.html.

128. Miller, "Mick Mulvaney Leads the Race"; Rampell, "Dismantling a Federal Agency."

129. Chris Arnold, "Trump Official Wants to Put Tight Leash on Consumer Watchdog Agency," NPR, April 2, 2018, https://www.npr.org/sections/thetwo-way/2018/04/02 /598820472/trump-official-wants-to-put-tight-leash-on-consumer-watchdog -agency.

6: TRUMP'S WHITE HOUSE STAFF

1. Chris Weigant, "RNC PR BS," *Huff Post,* March 20, 2013, https://www.huffingtonpost .com/chris-weigant/rnc-pr-bs_b_2919334.html.

2. Molly Ball, "The Final Humiliation of Reince Priebus," *The Atlantic,* July 30, 2017, https://www.theatlantic.com/politics/archive/2017/07/the-final-humiliation-of -reince-priebus/535368/.

3. Ibid.

4. Andrew Prokop, "Reince Priebus's Ouster as Chief of Staff, Explained," Vox, July 28, 2017, https://www.vox.com/2017/7/28/15724206/reince-priebus-fired-trump.

5. Ashley Parker, Josh Dawsey, and Philip Rucker, "'When You Lose That Power': How John Kelly Faded as White House Disciplinarian," *The Washington Post,* April 7, 2018, https://www.washingtonpost.com/politics/when-you-lose-that-power-how-john -kelly-faded-as-white-house-disciplinarian/2018/04/07/5e5b8b42-39be-11e8-acd5 -35eac230e514_story.html; Tina Nguyen, "As His Presidency Staggers, Trump Fixates on the Fate of Reince Priebus," *Vanity Fair,* May 31, 2017, https://www .vanityfair.com/news/2017/05/reince-priebus-greek-ambassador-trump.

6. Ball, "The Final Humiliation."

7. Ibid.

8. Alicia Cohen, "Reince Priebus Parted Ways with White House on Airport Tarmac," *The Hill,* July 28, 2017, http://thehill.com/blogs/blog-briefing-room/news/344404 -reince-preibus-parted-ways-with-white-house-on-airport-tarmac.

9. Glenn Thrush, Michael D. Shear, and Eileen Sullivan, "John Kelly Quickly Moves to Impose Military Discipline on White House," *The New York Times,* August 3, 2017, https://www.nytimes.com/2017/08/03/us/politics/john-kelly-chief-of -staff-trump.html.

10. Ibid.

11. Ibid.

12. Maggie Haberman, Glenn Thrush, and Peter Baker, "Inside Trump's Hour-by-Hour Battle for Self-Preservation," *The New York Times,* December 9, 2017, https:// www.nytimes.com/2017/12/09/us/politics/donald-trump-president.html.

13. Gabriel Sherman, "'I've Got Another Nut Job Here Who Thinks He's Running Things': Are Trump and Kelly Heading for Divorce?," *Vanity Fair,* January 22, 2018, https://www.vanityfair.com/news/2018/01/are-trump-and-kelly-heading-for -divorce.

14. Eric Levitz, "John Kelly Told Trump He's Willing to Resign: Report," *New York,* February 9, 2018, http://nymag.com/daily/intelligencer/2018/02/john-kelly-told-trump -hes-willing-to-resign-report.html; John Bowden, "Trump Called Priebus to Complain About Kelly: Report," *The Hill,* February 8, 2018, http://thehill.com/homenews /administration/373080-trump-called-priebus-to-complain-about-kelly-report.

15. Peter Baker, "Pitched as Calming Force, John Kelly Instead Mirrors Boss's Priorities," *The New York Times,* October 25, 2017, https://www.nytimes.com/2017/10/25/us /politics/trump-kelly.html.

16. Ibid.; Levitz, "John Kelly Told Trump"; Parker, Dawsey, and Rucker, "'When You Lose That Power.'"

17. Parker, Dawsey, and Rucker, "'When You Lose That Power.'"

18. Tina Nguyen, "The Agony of Sean Spicer," *Vanity Fair,* February 9, 2017, https://www.vanityfair.com/news/2017/02/sean-spicer-press-secretary-donald-trump.

19. Ryan Lizza, "Sean Spicer Will Be Remembered for His Lies," *The New Yorker,* July 21, 2017, https://www.newyorker.com/news/ryan-lizza/sean-spicer-will-be-remembered -for-his-lies.

20. Ibid.

21. Nguyen, "The Agony of Sean Spicer."

22. Callum Borchers, "Sean Spicer Basically Admitted That He Was Willing to Lie for Trump," *The Washington Post,* September 14, 2017, https://www.washingtonpost .com/news/the-fix/wp/2017/09/14/sean-spicer-basically-admitted-that-he-was -willing-to-lie-for-trump.

23. Ibid.

24. Greg Price, "Sarah Huckabee Sanders Is a 'Liar' Who Spews 'Horseshit' for Trump, GOP Strategist Says," *Newsweek,* November 28, 2017, http://www.newsweek.com /sanders-likes-horeshit-trump-724412.

25. Ibid.

26. Gabriel Schoenfeld, "Sarah Huckabee Sanders and the Lying Liars in the Trump White House: Have We Ever Seen a Spokesperson This Loose with the Truth?," *New York Daily News,* February 6, 2018, http://www.nydailynews.com/opinion/sarah -huckabee-sanders-lying-liars-white-house-article-1.3802422.

27. Margaret Sullivan, "Sarah Huckabee Sanders Is at Her Worst When Talking About Respect for Women," *The Washington Post,* February 13, 2018, http://www .chicagotribune.com/news/opinion/commentary/ct-sarah-huckabee-sanders-trump -women-20180213-story.html.

28. Tina Kelley, "Ron Ziegler, Press Secretary to Nixon, Is Dead at 63," *The New York Times,* February 11, 2003, https://www.nytimes.com/2003/02/11/us/ron-ziegler-press -secretary-to-nixon-is-dead-at-63.html.

29. "Donald Trump's File," PolitiFact, http://www.politifact.com/personalities/donald -trump/; "Sarah Huckabee Sanders' File," PolitiFact, http://www.politifact.com /personalities/sarah-huckabee-sanders/.

30. Jennifer Hansler, "Former Clinton Press Secretary: Sanders Should Quit if Trump Lies Again," CNN, May 5, 2018, https://www.cnn.com/2018/05/05/politics/joe-lockhart -sarah-sanders-cnntv/index.html.

31. Fraser Nelson, "The Mind of Donald Trump, as Explained by Anthony Scaramucci," *Spectator,* April 14, 2018, https://www.spectator.co.uk/2018/04/the-mind-of-donald-trump-as-explained-by-anthony-scaramucci/.

32. Russell Berman, "Who Is Anthony Scaramucci?," *The Atlantic,* July 21, 2017, https://www.theatlantic.com/politics/archive/2017/07/who-is-anthony-scaramucci/534543/.

33. Ibid.

34. Tessa Stuart, "Anthony Scaramucci's 10 Days in the White House, Ranked," *Rolling Stone,* July 31, 2017, https://www.rollingstone.com/politics/news/scaramuccis-10-days-at-the-white-house-ranked-w495122.

35. Ibid.; Andrew Prokop, "Anthony Scaramucci Is Out Just 10 Days After Being Named White House Communications Director," Vox, July 31, 2017, https://www.vox.com/2017/7/31/16071196/anthony-scaramucci-communications-director-fired-trump.

36. Prokop, "Anthony Scaramucci Is Out."

37. Joshua Green, "This Man Is the Most Dangerous Political Operative in America," *Bloomberg,* October 8, 2015, https://www.bloomberg.com/politics/graphics/2015-steve-bannon/; David Graham, "Why Trump Turned on Steve Bannon," *The Atlantic,* January 3, 2018, https://www.theatlantic.com/politics/archive/2018/01/the-president-vs-steve-bannon/549617/.

38. Graham, "Why Trump Turned."

39. Andrew Prokop, "President Bannon, Explained," Vox, February 8, 2017, https://www.vox.com/policy-and-politics/2017/2/8/14525228/president-bannon-steve; Ashley Parker, "Bannon Declares War with Republican Leadership in Congress," *The Washington Post,* September 10, 2017, https://www.washingtonpost.com/politics/bannon-declares-war-with-republican-leadership-in-congress/2017/09/10/57c08fa2-9668-11e7-87fc-c3f7ee4035c9_story.html.

40. Prokop, "President Bannon."

41. Ibid.

42. Gabriel Sherman, "'I Have Power': Is Steve Bannon Running for President?," *Vanity Fair,* December 12, 2017, https://www.vanityfair.com/news/2017/12/bannon-for-president-trump-kushner-ivanka; Graham, "Why Trump Turned."

43. Sherman, "'I Have Power.'"

44. Rick Noack, "Comey Said Working with Trump Reminded Him of the Mob—Let's Break That Comment Down," *The Washington Post,* April 13, 2018, https://www.washingtonpost.com/news/worldviews/wp/2018/04/13/comey-said-working-with-trump-reminded-him-of-the-mob-lets-break-that-comment-down/.

45. Daniel Golden, "The Story Behind Jared Kushner's Curious Acceptance into

Harvard," ProPublica, November 28, 2016, https://www.propublica.org/article/the
-story-behind-jared-kushners-curious-acceptance-into-harvard.

46. Judd Legum, "7 Jobs Jared Kushner Is Now Doing for the United States of America,"
ThinkProgress, March 31, 2017, https://thinkprogress.org/7-jobs-jared-kushner
-is-now-doing-for-the-united-states-of-america-6f0a799462ed/.

47. David Freedlander, "Meet the Real Jared Kushner," *Politico,* May 25, 2017, https://
www.politico.com/magazine/story/2017/05/25/jared-kushner-russia-fbi-donald
-trump-215191.

48. Andrew Prokop, "Jared Kushner's Many, Many Scandals, Explained," Vox, March 2,
2018, https://www.vox.com/policy-and-politics/2018/3/1/17053398/jared-kushner
-scandals-russia-clearance-loans; Shane Harris, Carol D. Leonnig, Greg Jaffe, and
Josh Dawsey, "Kushner's Overseas Contacts Raise Concerns as Foreign Officials Seek
Leverage," *The Washington Post,* February 27, 2018, https://www.washingtonpost
.com/world/national-security/kushners-overseas-contacts-raise-concerns-as-foreign
-officials-seek-leverage/2018/02/27/16bbc052-18c3-11e8-942d-16a950029788_story
.html.

49. Prokop, "Jared Kushner's Many, Many Scandals"; Sarah Ellison, "Exiles on Pennsylvania Avenue: How Jared and Ivanka Were Repelled by Washington's Elite," *Vanity
Fair,* August 27, 2017, https://www.vanityfair.com/news/2017/08/jared-kushner-ivanka
-trump-repelled-by-washington-elite.

50. Prokop, "Jared Kushner's Many, Many Scandals."

51. Cristiano Lima, "Kushner Gets Permanent Security Clearance, Lawyer Says," *Politico,* May 23, 2018, https://www.politico.com/story/2018/05/23/jared-kushner-security
-clearance-permanent-605352; Amber Phillips, "Jared Kushner Has Gotten Away
with More Security Clearance Omissions Than Most Federal Employees," *The
Washington Post,* February 23, 2018, https://www.washingtonpost.com/news/the
-fix/wp/2018/02/28/jared-kushner-has-gotten-away-with-security-clearance
-omissions-that-typically-fell-less-influential-federal-employees/.

52. Ibid.

53. Sherman, "'I Have Power'"; Ellison, "Exiles on Pennsylvania Ave."

54. Ibid.

55. Ibid.

56. Annie Karni, "After Climate Loss, Ivanka Moves On," *Politico,* June 1, 2017,
https://www.politico.com/story/2017/06/01/ivanka-trump-climate-deal-239041;   Jess
Bolluyt, "The Many Scandals of Ivanka Trump," Cheatsheet, March 30, 2018,
https://www.cheatsheet.com/culture/the-many-scandals-of-ivanka-trump.html/.

57. Virginia Heffernan, "Ivanka Trump: Born to Legitimize Corruption and Make the

Shoddy Look Cute," *Los Angeles Times,* March 3, 2018, http://www.latimes.com /opinion/op-ed/la-oe-heffernan-ivanka-legitimizing-20180303-story.html.

58. Ibid.

59. Rebekah Entralgo, "Ivanka Trump's Clothing Company Will Be Spared from Tariffs, Thanks to Her Dad," ThinkProgress, April 6, 2018, https://thinkprogress .org/ivanka-trump-clothing-tariffs-437840f07b83/; Sui-Lee Wee, "Ivanka Trump Wins China Trademarks, Then Her Father Vows to Save ZTE," *The New York Times,* May 28, 2018, https://www.nytimes.com/2018/05/28/business/ivanka-trump -china-trademarks.html.

60. Kristine Phillips, "'Go Buy Ivanka's Stuff,' Kellyanne Conway Said. Then the First Daughter's Fashion Sales Exploded," *The Washington Post,* March 10, 2017, https:// www.washingtonpost.com/news/business/wp/2017/03/10/go-buy-ivankas-stuff -kellyanne-conway-said-then-the-first-daughters-fashion-sales-exploded.

61. Callum Borchers, "Cindy McCain Sounds Off on Trump: 'We Don't Need More Bullying, and I'm Tired of It,'" *The Washington Post,* February 28, 2018, https://www .washingtonpost.com/news/the-fix/wp/2018/02/28/cindy-mccain-sounds-off-on -trump-we-dont-need-more-bullying-and-im-tired-of-it/.

62. Ellison, "Exiles on Pennsylvania Ave."

63. Ibid.; Devan Cole, "New Book Alleges Kellyanne Conway Is the 'Number One Leaker' in Trump White House," CNN, April 1, 2018, https://www.cnn.com/2018 /04/01/politics/ronald-kessler-jake-tapper-interview/index.html.

64. Molly Ball, "Kellyanne's Alternative Universe," *The Atlantic,* April 2017, https:// www.theatlantic.com/magazine/archive/2017/04/kellyannes-alternative-universe /517821/.

65. Ibid.; Callum Borchers, "'Morning Joe' Has Blacklisted Kellyanne Conway. And That's Not All," *The Washington Post,* February 15, 2017, https://www.washingtonpost .com/news/the-fix/wp/2017/02/15/morning-joe-has-blacklisted-kellyanne-conway -and-thats-not-all/.

66. "Kellyanne Conway's PolitiFact File," PolitiFact, http://www.politifact.com/personalities /kellyanne-conway/.

67. Michelle Ye He Lee, "White House Adviser Kellyanne Conway Violated Hatch Act, Federal Investigator Says," *The Washington Post,* March 6, 2018, https://www .washingtonpost.com/politics/white-house-adviser-kellyanne-conway-violated -hatch-act-federal-investigator-says/2018/03/06/28995c06-2162-11e8-94da -ebf9d112159c_story.html.

68. Dan Merica, "Kellyanne Conway's Husband Is Still Trolling the White House,"

CNN, March 29, 2018, https://www.cnn.com/2018/03/28/politics/kellyanne-conway -husband-trolling-white-house/index.html; Veronica Stracqualursi, "Kellyanne Conway's Husband Appears to Defend FBI Raid of Michael Cohen," CNN, April 10, 2018, https://www.cnn.com/2018/04/10/politics/george-conway-trump-tweets/index .html.

69. Merica, "Kellyanne Conway's Husband Is Still Trolling."

70. Julia Ioffe, "The Believer: How Stephen Miller Went from Obscure Capitol Hill Staffer to Donald Trump's Warm-Up Act—and Resident Ideologue," *Politico,* June 27, 2016, https://www.politico.com/magazine/story/2016/06/stephen-miller-donald-trump -2016-policy-adviser-jeff-sessions-213992; Ashley Parker and Josh Dawsey, "Stephen Miller: Immigration Agitator and White House Survivor," *The Washington Post,* January 21, 2018, https://www.washingtonpost.com/politics/stephen-miller-immigration -agitator-and-white-house-survivor/2018/01/21/7a1f7778-fcae-11e7-b832-8c26844b74fb _story.html.

71. Parker and Dawsey, "Stephen Miller."

72. Baker, "Pitched as Calming Force."

73. Matt Flegenheimer, "Stephen Miller, the Powerful Survivor on the President's Right Flank," *The New York Times,* October 9, 2017, https://www.nytimes.com/2017/10/09 /us/politics/stephen-miller-trump-white-house.html.

74. Ioffe, "The Believer."

75. Chris Cillizza, "The 24 Most Grotesque Lines from Jake Tapper's Stephen Miller Interview," CNN, January 7, 2018, https://www.cnn.com/2018/01/07/politics/jake -tapper-stephen-miller/index.html.

76. Ibid.; Javier E. David, "Stephen Miller Backs Trump as 'Genius,' and Gets Kicked Off CNN," CNBC, January 7, 2018, https://www.cnbc.com/2018/01/07/stephen -miller-backs-trump-as-genius-and-gets-kicked-off-cnn.html.

77. Nicole LaFond, "Bolton Didn't Expect Job Announcement: 'I Think I'm Still a Fox News Contributor,'" *Talking Points Memo,* March 23, 2018, https://talkingpointsmemo .com/livewire/bolton-think-still-fox-news-contributor; Zack Beauchamp, "John Bolton, Trump's Ultra-Hawkish New National Security Adviser, Explained," Vox, March 22, 2018, https://www.vox.com/world/2018/3/22/17153338/john-bolton-national -security-advisor-trump-hr-mcmaster.

78. Beauchamp, "John Bolton."

79. Mitchell Plitnik, "John Bolton: The Essential Profile," RightWeb, March 23, 2018, https://www.commondreams.org/views/2018/03/23/john-bolton-essential-profile; Fred Kaplan, "It's Time to Panic Now," *Slate,* March 22, 2018, https://slate.com/news

-and-politics/2018/03/john-bolton-named-national-security-advisor-its-time-to
-panic-now.html.

80. Beauchamp, "John Bolton."

81. Ibid.

82. Kaplan, "It's Time to Panic Now."

83. Beauchamp, "John Bolton."

84. Julie Hirschfeld Davis, "Trump on Kim Jong-un: Once a 'Madman,' Now a 'Very Honorable' Leader," *The New York Times,* May 10, 2018, https://www.nytimes.com /2018/05/10/us/politics/trump-kim-jong-un-language.html; Rick Noack, "Trump Just Contradicted Bolton on North Korea. What's the 'Libya Model' They Disagree On?," *Washington Post,* May 17, https://www.washingtonpost.com/news/world/wp /2018/05/16/whats-this-libya-model-north-korea-is-so-angry-about/.

85. Eric Levitz, "Trump Sidelines Bolton to Keep Peace with North Korea," *New York,* June 5, 2018, http://nymag.com/daily/intelligencer/2018/06/trump-sidelines -bolton-to-keep-peace-pompeo-with-north-korea-summit.html.

86. Tara Golshan, "The Mess Surrounding Trump's Campaign Manager Corey Lewandowski and Reporter Michelle Fields, Explained," Vox, April 14, 2016, https://www.vox.com/2016/3/29/11325328/michelle-fields-donald-trump-corey -lewandowski-assault-explained; Kerry Sanders and Jon Schuppe, "Authorities Drop Battery Charges Against Trump Campaign Manager Corey Lewandowski," NBC News, April 2016, https://www.nbcnews.com/news/us-news/authorities-drop -battery-charges-against-trump-campaign-manager-corey-lewandowski-n556051.

87. Golshan, "The Mess Surrounding Trump's Campaign Manager Corey Lewandowski."

88. Ibid.

89. Paola Chavez, "Corey Lewandowski Responds to Sexual Assault Allegation: 'I'm Going to Let the Process Play Forward,'" ABC News, December 28, 2017, http:// abcnews.go.com/Politics/corey-lewandowski-responds-sexual-assault-allegation-im -process/story?id=52024142.

90. Jane Coaston, "The White House's Story on Rob Porter Is Falling Apart," Vox, February 15, 2018, https://www.vox.com/policy-and-politics/2018/2/13/17007892/rob -porter-white-house-story-what-we-know; Bruce Golding, "Love Triangle Reportedly Led to Leak of Porter's Wife-Beating Accusations," *New York Post,* March 18, 2018, https://nypost.com/2018/03/18/love-triangle-reportedly-led-to-leak-of-porters-wife -beating-accusations/.

91. Coaston, "The White House's Story."

92. Ibid.

93. Jeremy Diamond, "Trump on Rob Porter: 'We Wish Him Well . . . He Did a Good Job,'" CNN, February 9, 2018, https://www.cnn.com/2018/02/09/politics/trump-rob-porter/index.html; Maggie Haberman, "Trump Talks of Bringing Back Rob Porter, Aide Accused of Spousal Abuse," *The New York Times,* March 26, 2018, https://www.nytimes.com/2018/03/26/us/politics/trump-rob-porter.html.

94. Golding, "Love Triangle."

95. Ibid.

96. Elise Viebeck, "Second White House Official Departs Amid Abuse Allegations, Which He Denies," *The Washington Post,* February 9, 2018, https://www.washingtonpost.com/politics/second-white-house-official-departs-amids-abuse-allegations-which-he-denies/2018/02/09/72ba47e6-0d0d-11e8-8b0d-891602206fb7_story.html.

97. Ibid.

7: TRUMP'S "AMERICA FIRST!" MEANS "AMERICA LAST"

1. Carlos Ballesteros, "The U.S. Is Now the Only Country Not in the Paris Climate Agreement," *Newsweek,* November 7, 2017, http://www.newsweek.com/trump-paris-climate-agreement-syria-703765.

2. John Kruzel, "What You Need to Know Ahead of Donald Trump's Iran Deal Deadline," PolitiFact, May 3, 2018, http://www.politifact.com/truth-o-meter/article/2018/may/03/what-you-need-know-ahead-donald-trumps-iran-deal-d/; Anne Gearan and Karen DeYoung, "Trump Announces Plans to Pull Out of Iran Nuclear Deal Despite Pleas from European Leaders," *The Washington Post,* May 8, 2018, https://www.washingtonpost.com/politics/trump-will-announce-plans-to-pull-out-of-iran-nuclear-deal-despite-pleas-from-european-leaders/2018/05/08/4c148252-52ca-11e8-9c91-7dab596e8252_story.html.

3. Kruzel, "What You Need to Know."

4. Susan E. Rice, "Trump's Most Foolish Decision Yet," *The New York Times,* May 8, 2018, https://www.nytimes.com/2018/05/08/opinion/trump-iran-deal-foolish.html; Zack Beauchamp, "It's Nearly Unanimous: Foreign Policy Experts Think Trump Made the Wrong Choice on Iran," Vox, May 9, 2018, https://www.vox.com/world/2018/5/9/17335456/iran-nuclear-deal-trump-scholars.

5. Max Boot, "Trump Should Strengthen the Iran Nuclear Deal, Not Blow It Up," *The Washington Post,* May 1, 2018, https://www.washingtonpost.com/news/global-opinions/wp/2018/05/01/trump-should-strengthen-the-iran-nuclear-deal-not

-blow-it-up/; Adam Shaw, "Mike Pompeo, Trump's Pick for Secretary of State, Promises to 'Push Back' Against Russian Aggression," Fox News, April 12, 2018, http://www.foxnews.com/politics/2018/04/12/mike-pompeo-trumps-pick-for -secretary-state-promises-to-push-back-against-russian-aggression.html.

6. Steven Nelson, "Trump Says Other Countries 'All Very Happy' with Iran Deal Decision," *Washington Examiner,* May 9, 2018, https://www.washingtonexaminer.com /news/white-house/trump-says-other-countries-all-very-happy-with-iran-deal -decision; Willa Frej and Nina Golgowski, "World Leaders Condemn Trump for Withdrawing from Iran Nuclear Deal," *HuffPost,* May 8, 2018, https://www .huffingtonpost.com/entry/world-leaders-react-trump-iran-nuclear-deal_us_5af 1550be4b0ab5c3d6936fb.

7. Katrina Manson, "Trump Suggests He Could Be Persuaded to Stay in Iran Deal," *Financial Times,* April 25, 2018, https://www.ft.com/content/be81212a-47cf-11e8 -8ee8-cae73aab7ccb.

8. Alex Ward, "Why Killing the Iran Deal Makes Trump's North Korea Talks Much, Much Harder," Vox, May 8, 2018, https://www.vox.com/2018/3/26/17147604/iran -deal-trump-deadline-explained-north-korea.

9. Saba Hamedy and Joyce Tseng, "All the Times President Trump Has Insulted North Korea," CNN, March 9, 2018, https://www.pbs.org/wgbh/frontline/article/the -u-s-and-north-korea-on-the-brink-a-timeline/; Quint Forgey, "Trump Praises Kim Jong Un as 'Very Honorable,'" *Politico,* April 24, 2018, https://www.politico .com/story/2018/04/24/trump-praise-kim-jong-un-547610; "Donald Trump: N Korea's Kim Jong-un a 'Smart Cookie,'" BBC News, April 30, 2018, http://www .bbc.com/news/world-asia-39764834.

10. Hamedy and Tseng, "Insulted North Korea"; Priyanka Boghani, "The U.S. and North Korea on the Brink: A Timeline," *Frontline,* April 18, 2018, https://www.pbs .org/wgbh/frontline/article/the-u-s-and-north-korea-on-the-brink-a-timeline/.

11. Mythili Sampathkumar, "Donald Trump Deserves 'Little Credit' for North and South Korean Peace Agreement, Experts Say," *Independent,* April 27, 2018, https:// www.independent.co.uk/news/world/americas/us-politics/north-korea-south -korea-donald-trump-korean-war-nuclear-weapons-a8326321.html.

12. David E. Sanger, Choe Sang-Hun, and William J. Broad, "North Korea Tests a Ballistic Missile That Experts Say Could Hit California," *The New York Times,* July 8, 2017, https://www.nytimes.com/2017/07/28/world/asia/north-korea-ballistic -missile.html; David E. Sanger and Choe Sang-Hun, "North Korean Nuclear Test Draws U.S. Warning of 'Massive Military Response,'" *The New York Times,* Septem-

ber 3, 2017, https://www.nytimes.com/2017/09/03/world/asia/north-korea-tremor
-possible-6th-nuclear-test.html.

13. Mythili Sampathkumar, "US-North Korea Summit: A Timeline of the Tumultu-
ous Relations Between the Two Nations," *Independent,* May 24, 2018, https://www
.independent.co.uk/news/world/asia/trump-us-north-korea-summit-kim-jong-un
-timeline-history-relationship-a8367651.html; Shannon Vavra, "Behind Kim Jong-
un's Slew of Meetings with World Leaders," Axios, April 1, 2018, https://www.axios
.com/why-kim-jong-un-is-suddenly-meeting-with-a-slew-of-world-leaders-1e4
bc98e-3b06-4d24-894e-57d9aaefa555.html.

14. Amber Phillips, "The Letter Trump Sent to Kim Jong Un Canceling the Summit,
Annotated," *The Washington Post,* May 24, 2018, https://www.washingtonpost.com
/news/the-fix/wp/2018/05/24/the-letter-trump-sent-to-kim-jong-un-canceling-the
-summit-annotated/.

15. "Trump Kim Summit: Six Odd Moments from the Day," BBC News, June 12, 2018,
https://www.bbc.com/news/world-asia-44453334.

16. Alex Pappas, "Trump Praises Kim Jong Un as 'Strong,' 'Funny,' 'Smart' and a
'Great Negotiator' in Hannity Interview," Fox News, June 13, 2018, http://www
.foxnews.com/politics/2018/06/12/trump-praises-kim-jong-un-as-strong-funny
-smart-and-great-negotiator-in-hannity-interview.html; Philip Rucker, "Trump
Praises Kim's Authoritarian Rule, Says 'I Want My People to Do the Same'," *The
Washington Post,* June 15, 2018, https://www.washingtonpost.com/politics/trump
-praises-kims-authoritarian-rule-says-i-want-my-people-to-do-the-same/2018/06/15/cea
20aa2-70a5-11e8-bf86-a2351b5ece99_story.html.

17. "Trump and Kim's Joint Statement," Reuters, June 12, 2018, https://www.nytimes
.com/reuters/2018/06/12/world/asia/12reuters-northkorea-usa-agreement-text.html.

18. Boghani, "The U.S. and North Korea." Emily Stewart, "North Korea Is Reportedly
Making More Nuclear Weapon Fuel," *Vox,* June 30, 2018, https://www.vox.com
/world/2018/6/30/17520638/north-korea-increased-activity-nuclear-trump.

19. Louis Jacobson, "Tracking Donald Trump's Evolving Positions on Afghanistan,"
PolitiFact, August 22, 2017, http://www.politifact.com/truth-o-meter/article/2017
/aug/22/tracking-donald-trump-evolving-position-Afghanista/; Gregory Krieg,
"The Trump Era Has Been Very Good to Iraq War Hawks," CNN, March 26, 2018,
https://www.cnn.com/2018/03/23/politics/trump-bush-iraq-war-john-bolton/index
.html.

20. Kevin Baron, "The War in Iraq Isn't Done. Commanders Explain Why and
What's Next," *Defense One,* March 22, 2018, https://www.defenseone.com/threats

/2018/03/war-iraq-isnt-done-commanders-explain-why-and-whats-next/146889/; David Nakamura and Abby Philip, "Trump Announces New Strategy for Afghanistan That Calls for a Troop Increase," *Washington Post,* August 21, 2017, https://www.washingtonpost.com/politics/trump-expected-to-announce-small -troop-increase-in-afghanistan-in-prime-time-address/2017/08/21/eb3a513e-868a -11e7-a94f-3139abce39f5_story.html; Wesley Morgan and Brian Bender, "America's Shadow War in Africa," *Politico,* October 12, 2017, https://www.politico.com /story/2017/10/12/niger-shadow-war-africa-243695.

21. Margaret Sullivan, "Middle East Civilian Deaths Have Soared Under Trump. And the Media Mostly Shrug," *Washington Post,* March 18, 2018, https://www.washing tonpost.com/lifestyle/style/middle-east-civilian-deaths-have-soared-under-trump -and-the-media-mostly-shrug/2018/03/16/fc344968-2932-11e8-874b-d517e912f125 _story.html.

22. Ibid.

23. Ibid.; Murtaza Hussein, "Dozens of Civilians Killed When U.S. Bombed a School and a Market in Syria," *The Intercept,* September 25, 2017, https://theintercept.com /2017/09/25/syria-us-airstrike-civilian-death-hrw-tabqa/.

24. Margaret Hartmann, "Trump Questioned Why CIA Avoided Killing Terrorist's Family: Report," *New York,* April 6, 2018, http://nymag.com/daily/intelligencer/2018 /04/trump-asked-why-cia-drone-avoided-terrorists-family-report.html.

25. Krishnadev Calamur, "Syria's War Is Fueling Three More Conflicts," *Atlantic,* February 13, 2018, https://www.theatlantic.com/international/archive/2018/02/syria -conflict/553154/; John Ismay, "U.S. Says 2,000 Troops Are in Syria, a Fourfold Increase," *The New York Times,* December 6, 2017, https://www.nytimes.com/2017/12/06 /world/middleeast/us-troops-syria.html; Helene Cooper, Thomas Gibbons-Neff, and Ben Hubbard, "U.S., Britain and France Strike Syria Over Suspected Chemical Weapons Attack," *The New York Times,* April 13, 2018, https://www.nytimes.com /2018/04/13/world/middleeast/trump-strikes-syria-attack.html.

26. Nakamura and Philip, "Trump Announces New Strategy."

27. Courtney Kube, "The Taliban Is Gaining Strength and Territory in Afghanistan," NBC News, January 30, 2018, https://www.nbcnews.com/news/world/numbers-afgha nistan-are-not-good-n842651.

28. "Operation Enduring Freedom: Coalition Military Fatalities by Year," iCasualties .org, http://icasualties.org/oef/; Neta Crawford, "US Budgetary Costs of Post-9/11 Wars Through FY2018: $5.6 Trillion," Costs of War, http://watson.brown.edu /costsofwar/papers.

29. "Body Count: Casualty Figures after 10 Years of the War on Terror," Physicians for Social Responsibility, March 2015, https://www.psr.org/wp-content/uploads/2018/05/body-count.pdf.

30. Nakamura and Philip, "Trump Announces New Strategy"; Jack Moore, "Trump's Afghanistan Troop Surge Is Complete, Raising Total Number of U.S. Servicemen to 14,000," *Newsweek,* November 17, 2017, http://www.newsweek.com/trumps-afghanistan-troop-surge-complete-raising-total-number-us-servicemen-714588; Dan Lamothe, "In a New Wave of the Afghanistan Air War, the U.S. Strikes a Little-Known Militant Group," *The Washington Post,* February 6, 2018, https://www.reuters.com/article/us-afghanistan-blast-trump/trump-rejects-peace-talks-with-taliban-in-departure-from-afghan-strategy-idUSKBN1FI2BU.

31. Richard Allen Greene and Mona Basu, "Muted Ceremony Marks End of Iraq War," CNN, December 15, 2011, https://www.cnn.com/2011/12/15/world/meast/iraq-us-ceremony/index.html.

32. "Chart: US Troop Levels in Iraq," CNN, October 21, 2011, https://www.cnn.com/2011/10/21/world/meast/chart-us-troops-iraq/index.html.

33. Maher Chmaytelli and Ahmed Aboulenein, "Iraq Declares Final Victory Over Islamic State," Reuters, December 9, 2017, https://www.reuters.com/article/us-mideast-crisis-iraq-islamicstate/iraq-declares-final-victory-over-islamic-state-idUSKBN1E30B9.

34. Crawford, "US Budgetary Costs"; Bob Davis, "Bush Economic Aide Says the Cost of Iraq War May Top $100 Billion," *The Wall Street Journal,* September 16, 2002, https://www.wsj.com/articles/SB1032128134218066355; Lawrence Lindsey, "What the Iraq War Will Cost the U.S.," *Forbes,* January 10, 2008, http://archive.fortune.com/2008/01/10/news/economy/costofwar.fortune/index.htm; Martin Wolk, "Cost of Iraq War Could Surpass $1 Trillion," NBC News, March 17, 2006, http://www.nbcnews.com/id/11880954/print/1/displaymode/1098/.

35. Crawford, "US Budgetary Costs."

36. Ismay, "U.S. Says 2,000 Troops Are in Syria."

37. Morgan and Bender, "America's Shadow War."

38. Ibid.; Philip Carter and Andrew Swick, "Why Were US Soldiers Even in Niger? America's Shadow Wars in Africa, Explained," Vox, October 26, 2017, https://www.vox.com/world/2017/10/26/16547528/us-soldiers-niger-johnson-widow-africa-trump.

39. Carter and Swick, "Why Were US Soldiers Even in Niger?"

40. Ibid.; Morgan and Bender, "America's Shadow War."

41. Morgan and Bender, "America's Shadow War"; Carter and Swick, "Why Were US Soldiers Even in Niger?"

42. Micah Zenko, "How Donald Trump Learned to Love War in 2017," *Foreign Policy,* December 29, 2017, http://foreignpolicy.com/2017/12/29/how-donald-trump-learned-to-love-war-in-2017/.

43. Ibid.

44. Jennifer Wilson and Miah Zenko, "Donald Trump Is Dropping Bombs at Unprecedented Levels," *Foreign Policy*, August 09, 2017, https://foreignpolicy.com/2017/08/09/donaldtrump-is-dropping-bombs-at-unprecedented-levels; Cynthia McFadden, William M. Arkin, and Tim Uehlinger, "How the Trump Team's First Military Raid in Yemen Went Wrong," CBS News, October 2, 2017, https://www.nbcnews.com/news/us-news/how-trump-team-s-first-military-raid-went-wrong-n806246; Barbara Starr and Ryan Brown, "First on CNN: US Drops Largest Non-Nuclear Bomb in Afghanistan," CNN, April 14, 2017, https://www.cnn.com/2017/04/13/politics/afghanistan-isis-moab-bomb/index.html.

45. Ibid.

46. Joshua Goodman, "Trump Pressed Aides on Venezuela Invasion, US Official Says," *Associated Press,* July 5, 2018, https://www.apnews.com/a3309c4990ac4581834d4a654f7746ef.

47. Froma Harrop, "Canada and Mexico Just Aren't That into Us Anymore," *The Seattle Times,* March 2, 2018, https://www.seattletimes.com/opinion/canada-and-mexico-just-arent-that-into-us-anymore/.

48. Jon Lee Anderson, "How Mexico Deals with Trump," *The New Yorker,* October 9, 2017, https://www.newyorker.com/magazine/2017/10/09/mexico-in-the-age-of-trump.

49. Jacqueline Thomsen, "Trump: Mexico Will Pay for the Wall 'in the End,'" *The Hill,* May 29, 2018, http://thehill.com/homenews/administration/389814-trump-mexico-will-pay-for-the-wall-in-the-end; Richard Wike, Bruce Stokes, Jacob Poushter, and Janell Fetterolf, "U.S. Image Suffers as Publics Around World Question Trump's Leadership," Pew Research Center, June 16, 2017, http://www.pewglobal.org/2017/06/26/u-s-image-suffers-as-publics-around-world-question-trumps-leadership/; Robert Valencia, "Mexicans Hate America More Under President Trump: Poll," *Newsweek,* September 14, 2017, http://www.newsweek.com/trump-mexico-pew-research-poll-border-wall-us-mexico-border-disapproval-665078.

50. Anderson, "How Mexico Deals with Trump"; Ryan Lizza, "Donald Trump Blows Up the U.S.-Mexico Relationship," *The New Yorker,* January 27, 2017, https://www.newyorker.com/news/ryan-lizza/donald-trump-blows-up-the-u-s-mexico-relationship.

51. Ibid.

52. Louis Nelson, "Trump Attacks Canada and Mexico Over Trade," *Politico,* March 5, 2018, https://www.politico.com/story/2018/03/05/trump-canada-mexico-nafta-trade-435820; Zeeshan Aleem, "Trump Still Wants Mexico to Pay for the Wall. He Also Wants Tariffs. He Can't Have Both," Vox, March 13, 2018, https://www.vox.com/world/2018/3/12/17109282/trump-border-wall-mexico-tariffs; Thomsen, "Trump: Mexico Will Pay."

53. Anderson, "How Mexico Deals with Trump."

54. Evan Annett, "Canada in the Year of Trump: A Guide to What Happened," *The Globe and Mail,* January 20, 2018, https://www.theglobeandmail.com/news/world/us-politics/canada-donald-trump-justin-trudeau-first-year-guide/article32788087/.

55. Wike, Stokes, Poushter, and Fetterolf, "U.S. Image Suffers."

56. Annett, "Canada in the Year of Trump."

57. Ibid.; Nelson, "Trump Attacks."

58. Jim Zarroli, "Trump Policies Put a Strain on U.S. Relations with Canada," NPR, March 6, 2018, https://www.npr.org/2018/03/06/591085351/trump-policies-put-a-strain-on-u-s-relations-with-canada.

59. Robert Fife, "Trudeau, Macron Lay Down Hard Line on U.S. Tariffs Ahead of G7," *The Globe and Mail,* June 7, 2018, https://www.theglobeandmail.com/world/article-trudeau-macron-lay-down-hard-line-on-us-tariffs-ahead-of-g7/; Chris Cillizza, "The Absolute Chaos of Donald Trump's G7 Meeting (and What It Means Moving Forward)," CNN, June 11, 2018, https://www.cnn.com/2018/06/11/politics/donald-trump-g7-chaos/index.html.

60. Harrop, "Canada and Mexico."

61. Kathy Kay, "Europe Hates Trump. Does It Matter?," BBC, March 4, 2016, http://www.bbc.com/news/magazine-35702584; "The World Is Crumbling in Front of Our Eyes,'" *Der Spiegel,* November 9, 2016, http://www.spiegel.de/international/europe/european-leaders-and-politicians-react-to-trump-victory-a-1120478.html; Markus Becker, "Trump's Election Triggers Deep Concern in Europe," *Der Spiegel,* November 10, 2016, http://www.spiegel.de/international/europe/european-union-worried-about-trump-presidency-a-1120672.html.

62. "The World Is Crumbling."

63. Ibid.

64. Becker, "Trump's Election."

65. Leonid Bershidsky, "Trump May Go Too Far in Alienating Europe," *Bloomberg,* May 1, 2018, https://www.bloomberg.com/view/articles/2018-05-01/trump-risks

-going-too-far-in-alienating-u-s-s-european-allies; Ken Thomas and Paul Wiseman, "President Trump's Tariffs Draw Threats of Retaliation from EU, Mexico and Canada," AP, June 1, 2018, http://time.com/5297073/donald-trump-steel-aluminum-tariffs-eu-canada-mexico/.

66. Steven Castle, "Trump's Tweets Manage a Rare Feat: Uniting Britain, in Outrage," *The New York Times,* November 30, 2017, https://www.nytimes.com/2017/11/30/world/europe/trump-tweets-uk-visit.html; Yasmeen Serhan, "The U.K. State Visit That Never Was," *The Atlantic,* January 12, 2018, https://www.theatlantic.com/international/archive/2018/01/trump-uk-state-visit/550385/.

67. James Masters, "Donald Trump Attacks the UK's Health Service, and Britain Hits Back," CNN, February 5, 2018, https://www.cnn.com/2018/02/05/politics/trump-nhs-healthcare-tweet/index.html.

68. Ibid.

69. Jack Webb and Jon Sharman, "Watch Trump and Macron Awkwardly Touch Each Other in a Series of Excruciating Exchanges During US Visit," *Independent,* April 25, 2018, https://www.independent.co.uk/news/world/americas/trump-macron-handshakes-video-us-state-visit-france-white-house-a8321481.html.

70. David A. Andalman, "Trump Torches Macron, His Last Friend in the G-7," CNN, June 5, 2018, https://www.cnn.com/2018/06/04/opinions/trump-macron-merkel-shifting-alliances-andelman/index.html; Michelle Kosinski and Maegan Vasquez, "Trump's Phone Call with Macron Described as 'Terrible,'" CNN, June 4, 2018, https://www.cnn.com/2018/06/04/politics/donald-trump-emmanuel-macron-call-terrible/index.html; Fife, "Trudeau, Macron."

71. Cillizza, "Absolute Chaos."

72. Wike, Stokes, Poushter, and Fetterolf, "U.S. Image Suffers."

73. D'Angelo Gore, "What's Trump's Position on NATO?," Factcheck, May 11, 2016, https://www.factcheck.org/2016/05/whats-trumps-position-on-nato/; Frank Langfitt, "Trump's Relationship with NATO, 1 Year into His Presidency," NPR, December 28, 2017, https://www.npr.org/2017/12/28/574314910/trumps-relationship-with-nato-1-year-into-his-presidency.

74. Susan Glasser, "Trump National Security Team Blindsided by NATO Speech," *Politico,* June 5, 2017, https://www.politico.com/magazine/story/2017/06/05/trump-nato-speech-national-security-team-215227; Alex Ward, "Trump Just Committed to NATO's Article 5. Finally," Vox, June 9, 2017, https://www.politico.com/magazine/story/2017/06/05/trump-nato-speech-national-security-team-215227.

75. Ward, "Trump Just Committed"; "Trump Shoves Fellow NATO Leader Aside on

His First Summit," Reuters, May 25, 2017, https://www.reuters.com/article/us-usa
-trump-europe-montenegro/trump-shoves-fellow-nato-leader-aside-on-his-first
-summit-idUSKBN18L2FK.

76. Langfitt, "Trump's Relationship with NATO."

77. Dan De Luce, Robbie Gramer, and Emily Tamkin, "Trump's Shadow Hangs Over
NATO," *Foreign Policy,* January 29, 2018, http://foreignpolicy.com/2018/01/29
/trumps-shadow-hangs-over-nato-transatlantic-alliance-europe-defense-deterrence
-europe-mattis-jens-stoltenberg/.

78. Langfitt, "Trump's Relationship with NATO."

79. Domenico Montanaro, "6 Strongmen Trump Has Praised—and the Conflicts It
Presents," NPR, May 2, 2017, https://www.npr.org/2017/05/02/526520042/6-strongmen
-trumps-praised-and-the-conflicts-it-presents.

80. Ibid.

81. Ibid.

82. Ibid.

83. Ibid.

84. Ibid.; Kareem Fahim, "Turkey Condemns U.S. Over 'Aggressive' Acts Against
Erdogan's Guards During D.C. Visit," *The Washington Post,* May 22, 2017, https://
www.washingtonpost.com/world/turkey-condemns-us-over-aggressive-acts-against
-its-bodyguards-in-dc-during-president-erdogans-visit-in-washington/2017/05/22
/05133db6-3ef4-11e7-b29f-f40ffced2ddb_story.html.

85. Montanaro, "6 Strongmen."

86. Ibid.

87. Ibid.

88. Krishnadev Calamur, "Nine Notorious Dictators, Nine Shout-Outs from Donald
Trump," *The Atlantic,* March 4, 2018, https://www.theatlantic.com/international
/archive/2018/03/trump-xi-jinping-dictators/554810/.

89. Ibid.

90. Ibid.; "Donald Trump's Ex-Wife Once Said Trump Kept a Book of Hitler's Speeches
by His Bed," *Business Insider,* September 1, 2015, http://www.businessinsider.com
/donald-trumps-ex-wife-once-said-he-kept-a-book-of-hitlers-speeches-by-his-bed
-2015-8.

91. Calamur, "Nine Notorious Dictators."

92. Gregg Carlstrom, "Why Israel Loves Trump," *Politico,* March 21, 2016, https://
www.politico.com/magazine/story/2018/03/01/benjamin-netanyahu-washington
-trip-217216.

93. Ibid.; Aaron David Miller, "How Netanyahu Will Use Trump to Save His Hide," *Politico,* March 1, 2018, https://www.politico.com/magazine/story/2018/03/01/benjamin -netanyahu-washington-trip-217216.

94. Mehdi Hasan, "Trump's Transition Team Colluded with Israel. Why Isn't That News?," *The Intercept,* December 5, 2017, https://theintercept.com/2017/12/05/michael -flynn-jared-kushner-israel-settlements-trump/.

95. Ibid.

96. Miller, "How Netanyahu Will Use Trump"; Jack Mirkinson, "The White House Silence on Gaza Speaks Volumes," Splinter, April 3, 2018, https://splinternews.com/the -white-house-silence-on-gaza-speaks-volumes-1824294631; Zack Beauchamp, "Ne-tanyahu's Allegedly Huge Iran Revelation, Explained," Vox, April 30, 2018, https:// www.vox.com/world/2018/4/30/17303576/netanyahu-iran-deal-speech-amad.

97. Jennifer Williams and Sarah Wildman, "Trump's Recognition of Jerusalem as Israel's Capital, Explained," Vox, December 6, 2017, https://www.vox.com/world /2017/12/6/16741528/trump-jerusalem-speech-israel-tel-aviv.

98. Ibid.; "State, Defense, and CIA Chiefs All Opposed Jerusalem Declaration, CNN Says," *Times of Israel,* December 7, 2017, https://www.timesofisrael.com/state -defense-and-cia-chiefs-all-opposed-jerusalem-declaration-cnn-says/.

99. Williams and Wildman, "Trump's Recognition of Jerusalem"; David M. Halbfin-ger, Isabel Kershner, and Declan Walsh, "Israel Kills Dozens at Gaza Border as U.S. Embassy Opens in Jerusalem," *The New York Times,* May 14, 2018, https://www .nytimes.com/2018/05/14/world/middleeast/gaza-protests-palestinians-us-embassy .html.

100. Williams and Wildman, "Trump's Recognition of Jerusalem"; Stephen Collinson, "Trump's Jerusalem Decision Promises Upheaval," CNN, December 6, 2017, https://www.vox.com/world/2017/12/6/16741528/trump-jerusalem-speech-israel-tel -aviv; Alexia Underwood, "GOP Megadonor Sheldon Adelson Could Help Pay for the US Embassy in Jerusalem," Vox, February 23, 2018, https://www.vox.com /world/2018/2/23/17044284/adelson-gop-trump-jerusalem-embassy-israel -palestinians.

101. Zack Beauchamp, "Netanyahu's Allegedly Huge Iran Revelation, Explained," Vox, April 30, 2018, https://www.vox.com/world/2018/4/30/17303576/netanyahu-iran -deal-speech-amad; Zack Beauchamp, "Netanyahu Went on Fox & Friends to Lobby Trump on the Iran Deal," Vox, May 1, 2018, https://www.vox.com/world/2018/5/1 /17306726/netanyahu-fox-and-friends-trump-iran-deal.

102. Beauchamp, "Iran Revelation."

103. Zack Beauchamp, "The Hilarious Trump Orb Photo Is a Nearly Perfect Metaphor for His Foreign Policy," Vox, May 22, 2017, https://www.vox.com/world/2017/5/22/15674782/trump-orb-what.

104. Ibid.; Aaron David Miller and Richard Sokolsky, "Donald Trump Has Unleashed the Saudi Arabia We Always Wanted—and Feared," Foreign Policy, November 10, 2017, http://foreignpolicy.com/2017/11/10/donald-trump-has-unleashed-the-saudi-arabia-we-always-wanted-and-feared/.

105. Robin Wright, "The Saudi Royal Purge—with Trump's Consent," The New Yorker, November 6, 2017, https://www.newyorker.com/news/news-desk/the-saudi-royal-purge-with-trumps-consent.

106. Krishnadev Calamur, "Did Russian Hackers Target Qatar?," The Atlantic, June 6, 2017, https://www.theatlantic.com/news/archive/2017/06/qatar-russian-hacker-fake-news/529359/; Adam Segal, "The Hacking Wars Are Going to Get Much Worse," New York Times, July 31, 2017, https://www.nytimes.com/2017/07/31/opinion/hacking-qatar-emirates.html; Zeeshan Aleem, "Saudi Arabia's Diplomatic War with Qatar, Explained," Vox, June 6, 2017, https://www.vox.com/world/2017/6/6/15739606/saudi-arabia-ties-qatar-trump.

107. Aleem, "Saudi Arabia's Diplomatic War."

108. Nawal Al-Maghafi, "The Catastrophe of Saudi Arabia's Trump-Backed Intervention in Yemen," The New Yorker, November 17, 2017, https://www.newyorker.com/news/news-desk/the-catastrophe-of-saudi-arabias-trump-backed-intervention-in-yemen.

109. Alex Ward, "Lawmakers Just Tried—and Failed—to End US Support for the Saudi War in Yemen," Vox, March 20, 2018, https://www.vox.com/world/2018/3/20/17144332/senate-yemen-saudi-arabia-sanders-lee-murphy.

110. Missy Ryan and Josh Dawsey, "Why Trump Lashed Out at Saudi Arabia About Its Role in Yemen's War," The Washington Post, December 29, 2017, https://www.washingtonpost.com/world/national-security/why-trump-lashed-out-at-saudi-arabia-about-its-role-in-yemens-war/2017/12/29/7df59788-e750-11e7-ab50-621fe0588340_story.html; Zack Beauchamp, "America Is Fawning Over Saudi Arabia's Repressive Dictator," Vox, April 6, 2018, https://www.vox.com/2018/4/6/17202562/mohammed-bin-salman-america-visit; Karen DeYoung and Steven Mufson, "Trump Meets with Saudi Crown Prince, and Talks About Money," The Washington Post, March 20, 2018, https://www.washingtonpost.com/world/national-security/trump-meets-with-saudi-crown-prince-and-talks-about-money/2018/03/20/5bb4048e-2c74-11e8-8688-e053ba58f1e4_story.html.

111. Tamara Keith, "Trump Leaves Top Administration Positions Unfilled, Says Hollow Government by Design," NPR, October 12, 2017, https://www.npr.org/2017/10/12/557122200/trump-leaves-top-administration-positions-unfilled-says-hollow-government-by-des.

112. Dexter Filkins, "How Rex Tillerson Wrecked the State Department," *The New Yorker,* November 30, 2017, https://www.newyorker.com/news/news-desk/how-rex-tillerson-wrecked-the-state-department.

113. Dan Drollette Jr., "8 of the 9 Top Jobs at the State Department Will Sit Empty," *The Bulletin,* March 13, 2018, https://thebulletin.org/8-9-top-jobs-state-department-will-sit-empty11605.

114. Erica Pandey, "38 U.S. Ambassadorships Remain Vacant," Axios, April 30, 2018, https://www.axios.com/countries-missing-us-ambassadors-south-korea-eu-31d03e54-4a5d-49c9-bc6a-9877ada1bef0.html.

115. Zack Beauchamp, "The State Department's Collapse, as Explained by Rex Tillerson," Vox, April 19, 2018, https://www.vox.com/world/2018/4/19/17257158/trump-state-department-tillerson-new-yorker; Evan Osnos, "Trump vs. the Deep State," *The New Yorker,* May 21, 2018, https://www.newyorker.com/magazine/2018/05/21/trump-vs-the-deep-state.

116. Ibid.

8: TRUMP'S RUSSIAN CONNECTIONS

1. Martin Matishak and Kyle Cheney, "Senate Intelligence Leaders: Russians Schemed to Help Trump," *Politico,* May 16, 2018, https://www.politico.com/story/2018/05/16/russians-schemed-to-help-trump-senate-intel-591882.

2. "Trump's Russia Cover-Up by the Numbers—75+ Contacts with Russia-Linked Operatives," Moscow Project, May 8, 2018, https://themoscowproject.org/explainers/trumps-russia-cover-up-by-the-numbers-70-contacts-with-russia-linked-operatives/.

3. Andrew Prokop, "All of Robert Mueller's Indictments and Plea Deals in the Russia Investigation So Far," Vox, May 23, 2018, https://www.vox.com/policy-and-politics/2018/2/20/17031772/mueller-indictments-grand-jury.

4. Caleb Melby and Keri Geiger, "Behind Trump's Russia Romance, There's a Tower Full of Oligarchs," *Bloomberg,* March 16, 2017, https://www.bloomberg.com/news/articles/2017-03-16/behind-trump-s-russia-romance-there-s-a-tower-full-of-oligarchs; David Ignatius, "A History of Donald Trump's Business Dealings in Russia," *The Washington Post,* November 2, 2017, https://www.washingtonpost.com/opinions

/a-history-of-donald-trumps-business-dealings-in-russia/2017/11/02/fb8eed22-ba9e
-11e7-be94-fabb0f1e9ffb_story.html.

5. Max Bergmann and James Lamond, "Trump's Attitude Toward Russia Sanctions Makes a Mockery of the United States," *Foreign Policy,* March 1, 2018, http:// foreignpolicy.com/2018/03/01/trumps-attitude-toward-russia-sanctions-makes-a -mockery-of-the-united-states/.

6. Jennifer Earl, "The Internet Can't Get Over Donald Trump's Response to Being Called a 'Puppet,'" CBS News, October 19, 2016, https://www.cbsnews.com/news /the-internet-cant-get-over-donald-trumps-response-to-being-called-a-puppet/.

7. Andrew Kaczynski, Chris Massie, and Nathan McDermott, "80 Times Trump Talked About Putin," CNN, March 2017, http://www.cnn.com/interactive/2017/03 /politics/trump-putin-russia-timeline/.

8. David Remnick, "Trump and Putin: A Love Story," *The New Yorker,* August 3, 2016, https://www.newyorker.com/news/news-desk/trump-and-putin-a-love-story.

9. Kaczynski, Massie, and McDermott, "80 Times Trump Talked."

10. Ibid.

11. Franklin Foer, "Putin's Puppet," *Slate,* July 4, 2016, http://www.slate.com/articles/news _and_politics/cover_story/2016/07/vladimir_putin_has_a_plan_for_destroying_the _west_and_it_looks_a_lot_like.html.

12. Ibid.; Jonathan O'Connell, David A. Fahrenthold, and Jack Gillum, "As the 'King of Debt,' Trump Borrowed to Build His Empire. Then He Began Spending Hundreds of Millions in Cash," *The Washington Post,* May 5, 2018, https://www.wash ingtonpost.com/politics/as-the-king-of-debt-trump-borrowed-to-build-his-empire -then-he-began-spending-hundreds-of-millions-in-cash/2018/05/05/28fe54b4-44c4 -11e8-8569-26fda6b404c7_story.html; Anita Kumar, "Buyers Tied to Russia, Former Soviet Republics, Paid $109 Million Cash for Trump Properties," *McClatchy,* June 19, 2018, http://www.mcclatchydc.com/news/politics-government/white-house/article210 477439.html.

13. Foer, "Putin's Puppet."

14. Remnick, "Trump and Putin."

15. Rachel Wolfe, "Trump's Advisers Told Him 'DO NOT CONGRATULATE' Putin—and He Did Anyway," Vox, March 21, 2018, https://www.vox.com/policy-and -politics/2018/3/21/17147684/do-not-congratulate-trump-putin; Chris Cillizza, "The absolute Chaos of Donald Trump's G7 Meeting (and What It Means Moving Forward)," CNN, June 11, 2018, https://www.cnn.com/2018/06/11/politics/donald -trump-g7-chaos/index.html; Kevin Liptak, "Trump Casts Doubt on Russian Election

Meddling Ahead of Putin Summit," CNN, June 28, 2018, https://www.cnn.com /2018/06/28/politics/donald-trump-russia-putin-summit/index.html.

16. Dan De Luce, Robbie Gramer, and Emily Tamkin, "Trump's Shadow Hangs Over NATO," *Foreign Policy,* January 29, 2018, http://foreignpolicy.com/2018/01/29 /trumps-shadow-hangs-over-nato-transatlantic-alliance-europe-defense-deterrence -europe-mattis-jens-stoltenberg/; Bergmann and Lamond, "Trump's Attitude"; Patricia Zengerle and Doina Chiacu, "U.S. Elections 'Under Attack' by Russia: U.S. Intelligence Chief," Reuters, February 13, 2018, https://www.reuters.com /article/us-usa-security-russia-elections/u-s-2018-elections-under-attack-by-russia -u-s-intelligence-chief-idUSKCN1FX1Z8.

17. Jonathan Swan, "Inside the Room: White House Flare-Up Over McCain Leak," Axios, May 12, 2018, https://www.axios.com/white-house-sarah-sanders-john-mc cain-kelly-sadler-8a4e33f7-c2bd-4cc6-aebd-57594d7ab4f4.html.

18. Callum Borchers, "The Amazing Story of Donald Trump's Old Spokesman, John Barron—Who Was Actually Donald Trump Himself," *The Washington Post,* May 13, 2016, https://www.washingtonpost.com/news/the-fix/wp/2016/03/21/the-amaz ing-story-of-donald-trumps-old-spokesman-john-barron-who-was-actually-donald -trump-himself.

19. Matt Apuzzo, Maggie Haberman, and Matthew Rosenberg, "Trump Told Russians That Firing 'Nut Job' Comey Eased Pressure from Investigation," *The New York Times,* November 22, 2017, https://www.nytimes.com/2017/05/19/us/politics/trump -russia-comey.html; Howard Blum, "Exclusive: What Trump Really Told Kislyak After Comey Was Canned," *Vanity Fair,* November 22, 2017, https://www.vanityfair .com/news/2017/11/trump-intel-slip.

20. Apuzzo, Haberman, and Rosenberg, "Trump Told Russians"; Blum, "Exclusive: What Trump Really Told Kisylak."

21. Apuzzo, Haberman, and Rosenberg, "Trump Told Russians."

22. Blum, "Exclusive: What Trump Really Told Kisylak."

23. Ibid.; Yonah Jeremy Bob and Michael Willner, "Did Obama's Team Warn Israel That Trump Would Share Intel with Russia?," *The Jerusalem Post,* February 14, 2018, https://www.jpost.com/Israel-News/PM-indirectly-confirms-Israel-was-source-of -Trump-intel-leak-to-Russia-533423.

24. Sharon LaFraniere, Mark Mazzetti, and Matt Apuzzo, "How the Russia Inquiry Began: A Campaign Aide, Drinks and Talk of Political Dirt," *New York Times,* December 30, 2017, https://www.nytimes.com/2017/12/30/us/politics/how-fbi-russia -investigation-began-george-papadopoulos.html.

25. Eileen Sullivan and Glenn Thrush, "George Papadopoulos, First to Plead Guilty in Russia Inquiry," *The New York Times,* October 30, 2017, https://www.nytimes.com /2017/10/30/us/politics/george-papadopoulos-russia-trump.html; Linda Qiu, "Trump Falsely Claims Russia Investigation Started Because of Steele Dossier," *The New York Times,* May 21, 2018, https://www.nytimes.com/2018/05/21/us/politics/fact-check-trump -russia-investigation-steele-dossier.html.

26. LaFraniere, Mazzetti, and Apuzzo, "How the Russia Inquiry Began."

27. Ibid.

28. Ibid.

29. Ibid.

30. Ibid.; Sullivan and Thrush, "George Papadopoulos."

31. Marshall Cohen, "Papadopoulos' Wife Asks Trump for a Pardon," CNN, June 7, 2018, https://www.cnn.com/2018/06/06/politics/george-papadopoulos-wife-pardon/index .html.

32. Andrew Prokop, "The Trump Tower Meeting at the Center of the Russia Investigation, Explained," Vox, February 26, 2018, https://www.vox.com/2018/2/26/16964328 /trump-tower-meeting-mueller-russia.

33. Ibid.; Rosalind Helderman and Karoun Demirjian, "Thousands of Pages of Congressional Testimony Shed Light on 2016 Trump Tower Meeting," *The Washington Post,* May 16, 2018, https://www.washingtonpost.com/politics/thousands-of-pages -of-congressional-testimony-shed-light-on-2016-trump-tower-meeting/2018/05/16/316 192fc-58b4-11e8-8836-a4a123c359ab_story.html.

34. Helderman and Demirjian, "Thousands of Pages"; Aaron Blake, "7 Big Things We Just Learned from the Trump Tower Meeting Transcripts," *The Washington Post,* May 16, 2018, https://www.washingtonpost.com/news/the-fix/wp/2018/05/16/5-things -we-just-learned-from-the-trump-tower-meeting-transcripts/.

35. Prokop, "The Trump Tower Meeting."

36. Ibid.

37. Ibid.

38. Ibid.; Adam Rawnsley, "'Infuriated' Jared Kushner Lost His Cool When Russians Didn't Deliver Hillary Dirt," *The Daily Beast,* May 16, 2018, https://www.thedailybeast .com/infuriated-jared-kushner-lost-his-cool-when-russians-didnt-deliver-hillary -dirt.

39. Blake, "7 Big Things."

40. Prokop, "The Trump Tower Meeting."

41. Ibid.; Jo Becker, Mark Mazzetti, Matt Apuzzo, and Maggie Haberman, "Mueller

Zeros In on Story Put Together About Trump Tower Meeting," January 31, 2018, https://www.nytimes.com/2018/01/31/us/politics/trump-russia-hope-hicks-mueller .html.

42. Prokop, "The Trump Tower Meeting."

43. Michael S. Schmidt, Maggie Haberman, Charlie Savage, and Matt Apuzzo, "Trump's Lawyers, in Confidential Memo, Argue to Head Off a Historic Subpoena," *The New York Times,* June 2, 2018, https://www.nytimes.com/2018/06/02/us/politics/trump -lawyers-memo-mueller-subpoena.html.

44. "Trump's Russia Cover-Up By the Numbers."

45. Andrew Prokop, "Jeff Sessions's Russia Testimony Problem Keeps Getting Worse," Vox, November 14, 2017, https://www.vox.com/policy-and-politics/2017/11/3/16599426 /jeff-sessions-russia-testimony; Marshall Cohen, "Jeff Sessions' Many Denials on Russia, Explained," CNN, November 14, 2017, https://www.cnn.com/2017/11/14 /politics/jeff-sessions-denials-on-russia/index.html.

46. Prokop, "Jeff Sessions's Russia Testimony Problem."

47. Ibid.

48. Zeeshan Aleem, "All the Times Jared Kushner Has Failed to Tell Congress Something Important," Vox, November 20, 2017, https://www.vox.com/policy-and -politics/2017/11/20/16670484/jared-kushner-russia-scandal-wikileaks.

49. Ibid.

50. Ibid.; Jeremy Herb and Evan Perez, "Kushner Testified He Did Not Recall Any Campaign WikiLeaks Contact," CNN, November 18, 2017, https://www.cnn.com /2017/11/17/politics/jared-kushner-july-testimony-did-not-recall-campaign-wikil eaks-contact/index.html.

51. Ibid.

52. Ibid.

53. Chuck Todd, Mark Murray, and Carrie Dann, "Explaining the Michael Flynn Controversy—a Timeline," NBC News, December 4, 2017, https://www.nbcnews .com/politics/first-read/explaining-michael-flynn-controversy-timeline-n826216; Zack Beauchamp, "The 3 Trump-Russia Scandals, Explained," Vox, March 2, 2017, https://www.vox.com/world/2017/2/15/14620560/trump-flynn-russia-campaign.

54. Dana Priest, "The Disruptive Career of Michael Flynn, Trump's National-Security Adviser," *The New Yorker,* November 23, 2016, https://www.newyorker.com/news /news-desk/the-disruptive-career-of-trumps-national-security-adviser.

55. Ibid.

56. Beauchamp, "The 3 Trump-Russia Scandals, Explained."

57. Ibid.

58. Ibid.

59. Ibid.

60. Todd, Murray, and Dann, "Explaining the Michael Flynn Controversy"; Ruth Marcus, "Trump Made Pence and Sessions Leave Before He Talked to Comey. What Was He Hiding?," *The Washington Post,* May 16, 2017, https://www.washingtonpost.com/blogs/post-partisan/wp/2017/05/16/is-this-criminal-obstruction-of-justice.

61. Andrew Prokop, Zack Beauchamp, and Alex Ward, "Michael Flynn Has Signed a Plea Deal with Robert Mueller. Trump Should Be Very Worried," Vox, December 1, 2017, https://www.vox.com/2017/12/1/16706534/michael-flynn-fbi-charged-deal; Andrew Prokop, "What Michael Flynn Has Actually Admitted to So Far, Explained," Vox, December 1, 2017, https://www.vox.com/policy-and-politics/2017/12/1/16724232/flynn-testify-against-trump.

62. Jason Abbruzzese, "Yes, Donald Trump's Tweet About Michael Flynn Is a Legal Liability," Mashable, December 4, 2017, https://mashable.com/2017/12/04/donald-trump-flynn-tweet-obstruction-legal-analysis/.

63. Mark Jacob and Stephan Benzkofer, "10 Things You Might Not Know About Robert Mueller," *Chicago Tribune,* March 23, 2018, http://www.chicagotribune.com/news/opinion/commentary/ct-perspec-thingsmueller-0325-story.html; Andrew Prokop, "Paul Manafort's Central Role in the Trump-Russia Investigation, Explained," Vox, October 30, 2017, https://www.vox.com/policy-and-politics/2017/8/31/16125776/paul-manafort-russia-trump-mueller.

64. Ibid.

65. Abigail Tracy, "Rick Gates Could Be More Dangerous Than Trump's Allies Thought," *Vanity Fair,* March 30, 2018, https://www.vanityfair.com/news/2018/03/rick-gates-donald-trump-robert-mueller-russia; Darren Samuelsohn, "How Much Is Rick Gates Telling Mueller About Trump?," *Politico,* March 26, 2018, https://www.politico.com/story/2018/03/26/rick-gates-mueller-trump-484739.

66. Franklin Foer, "Paul Manafort, American Hustler," *The Atlantic,* March 2018, https://www.theatlantic.com/magazine/archive/2018/03/paul-manafort-american-hustler/550925/.

67. Ibid.

68. Ryan Teague Beckwith and Alana Abramson, "Who Is Carter Page? Meet the Donald Trump Advisor at the Center of the GOP Memo," *Time,* February 2, 2018, http://time.com/5128614/carter-page-gop-memo-fisa-warrant/; Jason Zengerle, "What (If Anything) Does Carter Page Know?," *The New York Times,* December 18,

2017, https://www.nytimes.com/2017/12/18/magazine/what-if-anything-does-carter-page-know.html.

69. Ibid.

70. Ibid.

71. Brent D. Griffiths, "Carter Page: I May Have Discussed Russia in Emails with Papadopoulos," *Politico,* October 30, 2017, https://www.politico.com/story/2017/10/30/page-papadopoulos-russia-probe-244349; Luke Harding, "Why Carter Page Was Worth Watching," *Politico,* February 3, 2018, https://www.politico.com/magazine/story/2018/02/03/carter-page-nunes-memo-216934.

72. Steven Perlberg, "Carter Page Is Trying to Shop a Book Around," BuzzFeed, July 17, 2017, https://www.buzzfeed.com/stevenperlberg/carter-page-is-trying-to-shop-a-book-around.

73. Tina Nguyen, "Donald Trump Is Obsessed with the Pee Tape," *Vanity Fair,* April 20, 2018, https://www.vanityfair.com/news/2018/04/comey-memos-pee-tape-trump; Naomi Fry, "When We Think About the Pee Tape," *New Yorker,* April 18, 2018, https://www.newyorker.com/culture/culture-desk/when-we-think-about-the-pee-tape.

74. Nguyen, "Donald Trump Is Obsessed."

75. Andrew Prokop, "The 'Pee Tape' Claim, Explained," Vox, April 23, 2018, https://www.vox.com/2018/4/15/17233994/comey-interview-trump-pee-tape-russia.

76. Beauchamp, "The 3 Trump-Russia Scandals, Explained."

77. David Corn, "A Veteran Spy Has Given the FBI Information Alleging a Russian Operation to Cultivate Donald Trump," *Mother Jones,* October 30, 2016, https://www.motherjones.com/politics/2016/10/veteran-spy-gave-fbi-info-alleging-russian-operation-cultivate-donald-trump/; Matthew Yglesias and Andrew Prokop, "The Steele Dossier, Explained," Vox, February 2, 2018, https://www.vox.com/2018/1/5/16845704/steele-dossier-russia-trump; Jane Mayer, "Christopher Steele, the Man Behind the Trump Dossier," *The New Yorker,* March 12, 2018, https://www.newyorker.com/magazine/2018/03/12/christopher-steele-the-man-behind-the-trump-dossier.

78. Mayer, "Christopher Steele."

9: TRUMP'S IMPEACHABLE OFFENSES

1. Kenneth C. Davis, "The History of American Impeachment," *Smithsonian,* June 12, 2017, https://www.smithsonianmag.com/history/what-you-need-know-about-impeachment-180963645/.

2. David A. Fahrenthold and Jonathan O'Connell, "What Is the 'Emoluments Clause'?

Does It Apply to President Trump?," *The Washington Post,* January 23, 2017, https://www.washingtonpost.com/politics/what-is-the-emoluments-clause-does-it-apply-to-president-trump/2017/01/23/12aa7808-e185-11e6-a547-5fb9411d332c_story.html; Jeff Stein and Libby Nelson, "Donald Trump and the Emoluments Clause, Explained," Vox, January 24, 2017, https://www.vox.com/policy-and-politics/2016/11/23/13715150/donald-trump-emoluments-clause-constitution.

3. Stein and Nelson, "Donald Trump."

4. Steve Reilly and Nick Penzenstadler, "Trump's Company Earned $40M from Washington Hotel in 2017, Disclosure Shows," *USA Today,* May 16, 2018, https://www.usatoday.com/story/news/2018/05/16/trumps-dc-hotel-earns-his-company-40-m-during-first-year-office/616833002/; Christina Wilkie, "RNC Spent $424,000 at Trump-Owned Properties in the First Two Months of 2018," CNBC, March 21, 2018, https://www.cnbc.com/2018/03/21/rnc-spent-424000-at-trump-owned-properties-in-the-first-two-months-of-2018.html.

5. Maya Oppenheim, "Melania Trump 'Earned More than $100,000 from Photo Deal for Positive Stories'," *Independent*, July 3, 2018: https://www.independent.co.uk/news/world/americas/melania-trump-photo-deal-cost-earnings-first-lady-getty-images-a8428911.html.

6. Brad Heath, Fredreka Schouten, Steve Reilly, Nick Penzenstadler, and Aamer Madhani, "Trump Gets Millions from Golf Members. CEOs and Lobbyists Get Access to President," *USA Today,* September 8, 2017, https://www.usatoday.com/story/news/2017/09/06/trump-gets-millions-golf-members-ceos-and-lobbyists-get-access-president/632505001/.

7. Erwin Chemerinsky, Zephyr Teachout, and Laurence Tribe, "We're the Lawyers Suing President Trump: His Business Dealings Violate the Constitution," Vox, January 31, 2017, https://www.vox.com/the-big-idea/2017/1/31/14446106/trump-business-corruption-emoluments; Ben Mathis-Lilley, "It's Amazing How Many Countries Appear to Be Trying to Bribe Our President Right Now," *Slate,* May 16, 2018, https://slate.com/news-and-politics/2018/05/trump-and-foreign-bribery-a-rundown-of-possibilities.html.

8. Stein and Nelson, "Donald Trump."

9. Ibid.

10. Mathis-Lilley, "It's Amazing."

11. Matthew Yglesias, "Trump Helps Sanctioned Chinese Phone Maker After China Delivers a Big Loan to a Trump Project," Vox, May 15, 2018, https://www.vox.com/policy-and-politics/2018/5/15/17355202/trump-zte-indonesia-lido-city; Sui Lee-Wee,

"Ivanka Trump Wins China Trademarks, Then Her Father Vows to Save ZTE," *The New York Times,* May 28, 2018, https://www.nytimes.com/2018/05/28/business /ivanka-trump-china-trademarks.html.

12. Zack Beauchamp, "Mueller's Obstruction of Justice Case Against Trump Looks Damning," Vox, January 24, 2018, https://www.vox.com/world/2018/1/10/16855518 /trump-mueller-obstruction-case-strong; Nancy LeTourneau, "Mueller's Four Findings on Trump's Obstruction of Justice," *Washington Monthly,* April 13, 2018, https:// washingtonmonthly.com/2018/04/13/muellers-four-findings-on-trumps-obstruction -of-justice/.

13. Beauchamp, "Mueller's Obstruction of Justice Case"; LeTourneau, "Mueller's Four Findings."

14. LeTourneau, "Mueller's Four Findings."

15. Ibid.

16. Ibid.; Michael Schmidt and Julie Hirschfeld Davis, "Trump Asked Sessions to Retain Control of Russia Inquiry After His Recusal," *The New York Times,* May 29, 2018, https://www.nytimes.com/2018/05/29/us/politics/trump-sessions-obstruction.html.

17. Beauchamp, "Mueller's Obstruction of Justice Case."

18. LeTourneau, "Mueller's Four Findings."

19. Aaron Rumar, "Trump Admits to Obstruction of Justice on Twitter, Says He Only Did It to 'Fight Back,'" ThinkProgress, April 11, 2018, https://thinkprogress.org /trump-admits-obstruction-of-justice-twitter-cohen-afe2ca0f6983/.

20. Zack Beauchamp, "'Spygate,' the False Allegation That the FBI Had a Spy in the Trump Campaign, Explained," Vox, May 25, 2018, https://www.vox.com/2018/5/25 /17380212/spygate-trump-russia-spy-stefan-halper-fbi-explained.

21. LeTourneau, "Mueller's Four Findings."

22. Peter Baker, "Trump Pardons Scooter Libby in a Case That Mirrors His Own," *The New York Times,* April 13, 2018, https://www.nytimes.com/2018/04/13/us/politics /trump-pardon-scooter-libby.html.

23. Beauchamp, "Mueller's Obstruction of Justice Case."

24. Jason Abbruzzese, "Yes, Donald Trump's Tweet About Michael Flynn Is a Legal Liability," Mashable, December 4, 2017, https://mashable.com/2017/12/04/donald -trump-flynn-tweet-obstruction-legal-analysis/.

25. LeTourneau, "Mueller's Four Findings"; Steve Benen, "So Much for 'Law and Order': Trump Finds New Ways to Abuse His Pardon Power," MSNBC, May 31, 2018, http://www.msnbc.com/rachel-maddow-show/so-much-law-and-order-trump -finds-new-ways-abuse-his-pardon-power.

26. Sean Illing, "I Asked 11 Legal Experts if Trump's Lawyer Obstructed Justice," Vox, March 29, 2018, https://www.vox.com/2018/3/29/17174042/trump-pardons-manafort -flynn-mueller-probe.

27. Seung Min Kim, "'A Tremendous Abuse': Senate Republicans Warn Trump Not to Pardon Himself," *The Washington Post,* June 4, 2018, https://www.washingtonpost .com/politics/a-tremendous-abuse-senate-republicans-warn-trump-not-to-pardon -himself/2018/06/04/85cc9170-684f-11e8-bbc5-dc9f3634fa0a_story.html.

28. Beauchamp, "'Spygate.'"

29. Ibid.

30. Ibid.

31. Dylan Matthews, "The Definitive Guide to the Stormy Daniels Scandal," Vox, April 6, 2018, https://www.vox.com/2018/3/24/17151786/stormy-daniels-explained; Michael Finnegan, "Tracing the Twists, Turns and Falsehoods of Trump's Stormy Daniels Scandal," *Los Angeles Times,* May 4, 2018, http://www.latimes.com/politics/la -na-pol-trump-stormy-timeline-20180503-story.html.

32. Ibid.

33. Ibid.

34. Ibid.

35. Finnegan, "Tracing the Twists."

36. Matthews, "The Definitive Guide."

37. Andrew Prokop, "Michael Cohen: Trump's Fix-It Guy and FBI Raid Subject, Explained," Vox, April 11, 2018, https://www.vox.com/policy-and-politics/2018/4/11 /17218010/michael-cohen-raid-fbi-trump-mueller-explained.

38. Ibid.

39. Matthews, "The Definitive Guide."

40. Ryan J. Reilly, Nick Visser, and Nick Baumann, "What Did AT&T and Novartis Get for the Money They Paid Trump's Lawyer?," *HuffPost,* May 11, 2018, https://www .huffingtonpost.com/entry/michael-cohen-trump-stormy-daniels-payments_us _5af24625e4b00a3224ee318e.

41. Emily Stewart, "AT&T's and Novartis's Payments to Michael Cohen Are Definitely Sketchy but Maybe Not Illegal," Vox, May 11, 2018, https://www.vox.com/policy-and -politics/2018/5/9/17336856/michael-cohen-novartis-att-shell-company.

42. Ryan Bort, "And Now the World Waits for Michael Cohen to Flip on Trump," *Rolling Stone,* June 15, 2018, https://www.rollingstone.com/politics/news/will-michael -cohen-flip-on-trump-w521578. George Stephanopoulos, "Exclusive: Michael Cohen Says Family and Country, Not President Trump, Is His 'First Loyalty'," *ABC*

News, July 2, 2018, https://abcnews.go.com/Politics/michael-cohen-family-country
-president-trump-loyalty/story?id=56304585.

43. Adam Davidson, "Michael Cohen and the End Stage of the Trump Presidency," *The New Yorker,* April 14, 2018, https://www.newyorker.com/news/news-desk/michael
-cohen-and-the-end-stage-of-the-trump-presidency.

10: CLOSING ARGUMENTS

1. Jason Kurtz, "Jake Tapper: Donald Trump Just 'Can't Quit' Hillary Clinton," CNN, January 10, 2018, https://www.cnn.com/2018/01/10/politics/donald-trump-hil
lary-clinton-jake-tapper-the-lead-he-cant-quit-her-cnntv/index.html.

2. Robert Farley, "Fact Check: Trump Claims Massive Voter Fraud; Here's the Truth," *USA Today,* January 26, 2017, https://www.usatoday.com/story/news/poli
tics/2017/01/26/fact-check-trumps-bogus-voter-fraud-claims-revisited/97080242/; Cathleen Decker, "Trump Says He Won the Electoral College in a Landslide, but He Ranked Near the All-Time Bottom," *Los Angeles Times,* November 28, 2016, http://
www.latimes.com/nation/politics/trailguide/la-na-trailguide-updates-landslide-trump
-not-so-according-to-a-1480376870-htmlstory.html.

3. Gregory Krieg, "It's Official: Clinton Swamps Trump in Popular Vote," CNN, December 22, 2016, https://www.cnn.com/2016/12/21/politics/donald-trump-hillary
-clinton-popular-vote-final-count/index.html; Benjamin Kentish, "Donald Trump Has Lost Popular Vote by Greater Margin Than Any US President," *Independent,* December 12, 2016, https://www.independent.co.uk/news/world/americas/us-elections
/donald-trump-lost-popular-vote-hillary-clinton-us-election-president-history-a7470116
.html; Mona Chalabi, "Who Are the Three-Quarters of Adult Americans Who Didn't Vote for Trump?," *The Guardian,* January 18, 2017, https://www.theguardian
.com/us-news/2017/jan/18/american-non-voters-election-donald-trump.

4. Decker, "Trump Says He Won."

5. Krieg, "It's Official."

6. Kentish, "Donald Trump Has Lost."

7. Farley, "Fact Check."

8. Ibid.

9. German Lopez, "Trump's Voter Fraud Commission, Explained," Vox, January 3, 2018, https://www.vox.com/policy-and-politics/2017/6/30/15900478/trump-voter-fraud-sup
pression-commission.

10. Rachelle Hampton, "The Most Underplayed Story of the 2016 Election Is Voter Suppression," *New Republic,* November 2017, https://newrepublic.com/minutes

/145387/underplayed-story-2016-election-voter-suppression; Ari Berman, "Rigged: How Voter Suppression Threw Wisconsin to Trump," *Mother Jones,* November /December 2017, https://www.motherjones.com/politics/2017/10/voter-suppression -wisconsin-election-2016/.

11. Hampton, "The Most Underplayed Story"; Berman, "Rigged"; Ari Berman, "Top Republican Official Says Trump Won Wisconsin Because of Voter ID Law," *Mother Jones,* April 16, 2018, https://www.motherjones.com/politics/2018/04/top-republican -official-says-trump-won-wisconsin-because-of-voter-id-law/.

12. Berman, "Rigged"; Berman, "Top Republican Official."

13. Hampton, "The Most Underplayed Story."

14. Berman, "Rigged."

15. Peter Baker, "Trump Wields Pardon Pen to Confront Justice System," *The New York Times,* May 31, 2018, https://www.nytimes.com/2018/05/31/us/politics/dsouza-par don.html.

16. Jackie Calmes, "Trump Pardons Former Arizona Sheriff Joe Arpaio, Convicted of Contempt of Court for Violating Latinos' Rights," *Los Angeles Times,* August 25, 2017, http://www.latimes.com/politics/la-na-pol-trump-arpaio-pardon-2017-story .html; Dahlia Lithwick, "Was Trump's Pardon of Joe Arpaio Unconstitutional?," *Slate,* September 15, 2017, http://www.slate.com/articles/news_and_politics/juris prudence/2017/09/was_trump_s_pardon_of_joe_arpaio_unconstitutional.html; Valeria Fernandez, "Arizona's 'Concentration Camp': Why Was Tent City Kept Open for 24 Years?," *The Guardian,* August 21, 2017, https://www.theguardian.com /cities/2017/aug/21/arizona-phoenix-concentration-camp-tent-city-jail-joe-arpaio-immi gration.

17. Phillip Smith, "Joe Arpaio Has Been a World-Class Jerk for Longer Than You Ever Knew," Alternet, September 3, 2017, https://www.alternet.org/drugs/joe-arpaio -world-class-jerk-lot-longer-you-ever-knew; Lithwick, "Was Trump's Pardon of Joe Arpaio Unconstitutional?"

18. Brandon Carter, "Arpaio on Trump: 'I Can Read His Mind Without Even Talk- ing to Him,'" *The Hill,* February 28, 2018, http://thehill.com/blogs/blog-briefing -room/news/376141-arpaio-on-trump-i-can-read-his-mind-without-even-talking -to-him.

19. Andrew Restuccia and Josh Gerstein, "Trump Issues Pardon for Lewis 'Scooter' Libby," *Politico,* April 13, 2018, https://www.politico.com/story/2018/04/13/trump-par don-scooter-libby-522055.

20. Ibid.

21. Ibid.

22. Alex Nichols, "Dinesh D'Souza Is the Perfect Propagandist for Trump's America," Outline, October 3, 2017, https://theoutline.com/post/2364/dinesh-dsouza-trump -propaganda; Eugene Scott, "Here's a Reminder of Some of Dinesh D'Souza's Inflammatory Comments," *The Washington Post,* May 31, 2018, https://www.washing tonpost.com/news/the-fix/wp/2018/05/31/heres-a-reminder-of-some-of-dinesh-dsou zas-inflammatory-comments/.

23. Baker, "Trump Wields Pardon Pen"; Christiano Lima, "Trump Says He'll Pardon Conservative Filmmaker Dinesh D'Souza," *Politico,* May 31, 2018, https://www.poli tico.com/story/2018/05/31/trump-says-hell-pardon-conservative-filmmaker-dinesh -dsouza-615326.

24. "5 Fast Facts About Dinesh D'Souza and Trump's Presidential Pardon," CBS News, May 31, 2018, http://cbslocal.com/2018/05/31/dinesh-dsouza-pardon/; Louis Nelson, "D'Souza on Pardon: Trump Said I Had 'Been Screwed,'" *Politico,* June 1, 2018, https://www.politico.com/story/2018/06/01/dinesh-dsouza-trump-pardon-reaction -616317.

25. Jeremy Diamond, "Trump Floats Martha Stewart Pardon, Rod Blagojevich Com- mutation," CNN, May 31, 2018, https://www.cnn.com/2018/05/31/politics/martha -stewart-rod-blagojevich-trump-pardons/index.html.

26. Laura Vozzella and Fenit Nirappil, "Virginia Republican's Ad Ties Opponent to MS-13. Democrats Compare It to 'Willie Horton,'" *The Washington Post,* Sep- tember 22, 2017, https://www.washingtonpost.com/local/virginia-politics/virginia -republicans-ad-ties-opponent-to-ms-13-democrats-compare-it-to-willie-horton /2017/09/20/28d673bc-9e49-11e7-8ea1-ed975285475e_story.html; Daniel Drezner, "Donald Trump Cannot Stop Endorsing Losers," *The Washington Post,* Decem- ber 13, 2017, https://www.washingtonpost.com/news/posteverything/wp/2017/12/13 /donald-trump-cannot-stop-endorsing-losers/.

27. Ben Kamisar, "Trump Blasts Gillespie Over Va. Loss: He 'Did Not Embrace Me or What I Stand For,'" *The Hill,* November 7, 2017, http://thehill.com/homenews /campaign/359279-trump-blasts-gillespie-over-va-loss-he-did-not-embrace-me-or-what -i-stand.

28. Drezner, "Donald Trump Cannot Stop"; Charles Bethea, "Locals Were Troubled by Roy Moore's Interactions with Teen Girls at the Gadsden Mall," *The New Yorker,* November, 13, 2017, https://www.newyorker.com/news/news-desk/locals -were-troubled-by-roy-moores-interactions-with-teen-girls-at-the-gadsden-mall; Scott Detrow and Jessica Taylor, "RNC Restores Financial Support for Roy Moore as

Trump Gives Full Endorsement," NPR, December 4, 2017, https://www.npr.org
/2017/12/04/568274917/removing-any-qualifications-trump-endorses-roy-moore.

29. Drezner, "Donald Trump Cannot Stop"; Amy Davidson Sorkin, "Donald Trump,
Roy Moore, and the Degradation of the G.O.P.," *The New Yorker,* December 18, 2017,
https://www.newyorker.com/magazine/2017/12/18/donald-trump-roy-moore-and
-the-degradation-of-the-gop.

30. Harry Enten, "Pennsylvania's Special Election Isn't an Isolated Incident. The GOP
Is in Trouble," CNN, March 14, 2018, https://www.cnn.com/2018/03/14/politics
/pennsylvania-special-election-not-isolated/index.html.

31. Ibid.

32. Frank Rich, "The Original Donald Trump," *New York,* April 29, 2018, http://
nymag.com/daily/intelligencer/2018/04/frank-rich-roy-cohn-the-original-donald
-trump.html.

33. Ibid.; Marie Brenner, "How Donald Trump and Roy Cohn's Ruthless Symbiosis
Changed America," *Vanity Fair*, August 2017, https://www.vanityfair.com/news
/2017/06/donald-trump-roy-cohn-relationship.

34. Brenner, "Ruthless Symbiosis."

35. Ibid.

36. Ibid.

37. Rich, "The Original Donald Trump."

38. Ibid.; Brenner, "Ruthless Symbiosis."

39. Brenner, "Ruthless Symbiosis."

40. Ibid.; Franklin Foer, "Paul Manafort, American Hustler," *The Atlantic,* March 2018,
https://www.theatlantic.com/magazine/archive/2018/03/paul-manafort-american
-hustler/550925/.

41. Brenner, "Ruthless Symbiosis."

42. Ibid.

43. Ibid.

44. Philip Bump, "The Confusing Timeline on Roger Stone's Communications with
WikiLeaks," *The Washington Post,* March 13, 2018, https://www.washingtonpost
.com/news/politics/wp/2018/03/13/the-confusing-timeline-on-roger-stones-commu
nications-with-wikileaks/; Ali Dukakis, "Mueller's Grand Jury Questions Roger
Stone's Social Media Adviser," ABC News, June 1, 2018, https://abcnews.go.com
/Politics/muellers-grand-jury-questions-roger-stones-social-media/story?id=5559
1772.

45. Brenner, "Ruthless Symbiosis."

46. Eric Hananoki and Timothy Johnston, "Here Are 13 Other Repugnant Comments Ted Nugent Should Apologize For," Media Matters, February 21, 2014, https://www.mediamatters.org/blog/2014/02/21/here-are-13-other-repugnant-comments-ted-nugent/198174.

47. Deena Zaru, "Amid Griffin Outrage, the Left Asks: What About Ted Nugent?," CNN, June 1, 2017, https://www.cnn.com/2017/06/01/politics/kathy-griffin-ted-nugent-donald-trump/index.html.

48. Lisa De Moraes, "Samantha Bee Apologizes Defiantly for Last Week's First-Daughter Slur on 'Full Frontal,'" *Variety,* June 6, 2018, https://deadline.com/2018/06/samantha-bee-ivanka-trump-apology-feckless-donald-trump-immigration-full-frontal-tbs-video-1202404885/.

49. Hananoki and Johnston, "Here Are 13 Other Repugnant Comments."

50. Ibid.

51. Ibid.

52. Ibid.

53. Melina Delkic, "Why Does President Donald Trump Hate Dogs?," *Newsweek,* October 25, 2017, http://www.newsweek.com/does-donald-trump-hate-dogs-why-would-he-do-692092; Kyle Fitzpatrick, "Donald Trump Doesn't Even Have a Dog—and That Says a Lot About Him," Yahoo, January 24, 2018, https://www.yahoo.com/lifestyle/donald-trump-doesn-apos-t-143500914.html.

54. Kristen Bellstrom, "Donald Trump Says Men Who Take Care of Their Kids Are Acting 'Like the Wife,'" *Fortune,* April 24, 2016, http://fortune.com/2016/04/24/trump-act-like-wife/.

55. Delkic, "Why Does President Donald Trump Hate Dogs?"

56. Ibid.

EPILOGUE: AND ONE REASON TRUMP MUST STAY

1. George Will, "Trump's Moore Endorsement Sunk the Presidency to Unplumbed Depths," *Washington Post,* December 13, 2017, https://www.washingtonpost.com/opinions/trumps-moore-endorsement-sunk-the-presidency-to-unplumbed-depths/2017/12/13/3c245482-e036-11e7-bbd0-9dfb2e37492a_story.html.

2. Jane Mayer, "The Danger of President Pence," *The New Yorker,* October 23, 2017, https://www.newyorker.com/magazine/2017/10/23/the-danger-of-president-pence.

3. Ibid.

4. Ibid.

5. Ibid.

6. Ibid.; McKay Coppins, "God's Plan for Mike Pence," *The Atlantic,* January/February 2018, https://www.theatlantic.com/magazine/archive/2018/01/gods-plan-for-mike-pence /546569/.

7. Coppins, "God's Plan."

8. Sarah Posner, "Pence May Deny It. But He's Preparing for a Post-Trump Landscape," *The Washington Post,* August 9, 2017, https://www.washingtonpost.com/blogs/plum-line /wp/2017/08/09/pence-may-deny-it-but-hes-preparing-for-a-post-trump-land scape/; Mayer, "The Danger of President Pence."

9. Mayer, "The Danger of President Pence."

10. Ibid.

11. Ibid.; Coppins, "God's Plan"; Erin Schumaker, "Mike Pence's Defining Moment as Governor? Enabling an HIV Outbreak," *Huff Post,* October 6, 2016, https://www .huffingtonpost.com/entry/mike-pence-indiana-hiv_us_57f53b9be4b002a7312022ef.

12. Coppins, "God's Plan"; Mayer, "The Danger of President Pence."

13. George Will, "Trump Is No Longer the Worst Person in Government," The *Washington Post,* May 9, 2018, https://www.washingtonpost.com/opinions/trump-is -no-longer-the-worst-person-in-government/2018/05/09/10e59eba-52f1-11e8-a551 -5b648abe29ef_story.html.

14. Abigail Tracy, "Omarosa Is Right: Why President Pence Could Be More Terrifying than Trump," *Vanity Fair,* February 13, 2018, https://www.vanityfair.com/news/2018 /02/omarosa-is-right-why-president-pence-could-be-more-terrifying-than-trump.